HANDBOOK ON CHILD

About the Author

Smt. Pramila Pandit Barooah (*b*. 1922) received her Masters degree from the Home Economics College (with Major in child development and minor in Nutrition and Extension) at the Oregan State University, U.S.A., and has had an opportunity to visit other countries round the globe to see for herself the work pertaining to the child. She has toured extensively in the country and has been working with and for the children, wherever she happened to be since 1943. She has worked in villages, tribal areas and in towns, in Maharashtra (then Central Province and Berar), Naini, Allahabad (U.P.). In Assam she worked in villages starting schools and working with the village folks, where nobody dared to go. She was able to help the Assam Agriculture University in starting the Home Science College and was its Hony. Dean of the College. She also worked in Meghalaya.

She worked with Indian Council for Child Welfare as an Office Bearer for 18 years, in Swami Shivananda Memorial Institute for 10 years, as Treasurer in Bharat Grameen Mahila Sangh and later as President in Country Women's Association of India.

Giving up organisation work, she started doing writing work and has so far written 13 books mainly to enlighten children and which will give their knowledge them and enlighten them about the country.

This particular book is mainly for organisations, Universities, Colleges and those interested in child study and research.

Concepts in Communication
Informatics & Librarianship (CICIL)-79

General Editor: **S.P. Agrawal**

HANDBOOK ON CHILD

(With Historical Background)

Revised and Enlarged Edition

PRAMILA PANDIT BAROOAH
Former Secretary General
Indian Council of Child Welfare

CONCEPT PUBLISHING COMPANY, NEW DELHI-110059

ISBN 81-7022-735-6

First Published 1992

Second Revised and Enlarged Edition 1999

Published and Printed by
Ashok Kumar Mittal
Concept Publishing Company
A/15-16, Commercial Block, Mohan Garden
NEW DELHI-110059 (India)

Phones : 5648039, 5649024
Fax : 091-11-5648053

GENERAL EDITOR'S INTRODUCTION

Will all the pious platitudes mouthed, charters adopted, resolutions passed and policies proclaimed enable us to usher in ideal circumstances in which the nation's children will grow up with healthy minds in healthy bodies? Going by the ground realities, not in the foreseeable future, certainly not by AD 2000.

Yet this is not to say that there is no need or scope to take or improve legal measures. While the general scene may be bleack, it is good to see the silver linings in what has been attempted in the matter of child welfare so far. This is what the author has done in this publication.

The importance of statistical information can never be over-emphasised. It highlights the different aspects of any area of development and is crucial for evaluating the effectiveness of the measures taken. In this revised edition a chapter on 'Statistics on Children in India' has been added to make it more useful. A need was felt that the workers and the planners should be made aware of the important legislative measures about the children, particularly about the adoption. The present publication attempts to fulfil this need by adding a new chapter on 'Child Legislation' which also includes the latest Superme Court ruling on the subject.

Besides above the author has also added a very useful chapter on 'Indigenous Medicines' for the benefit of the rural people who lack proper medical facilities and for the poor in urban areas.

In every area of development our Five-Year Plans play a pivotal role. They give a comprehensive view of the progress made in the major sectors and suggest measures to be taken for further progress. Moreover, they are authentic documents brought out by the Central Government. In view of the importance of these Plans the revised edition of the present publication has also included the Eighth Five-Year Plan (1992-97) and the Approach Paper to the Ninth Plan (1997-2000).

S. P. Agrawal

ACKNOWLEDGEMENTS

A word about the book . . . .

The pages contain material which has been taken and compiled from various sources. I felt compelled to do it after working 'with and for child' for more than 40 years.

I realised that Organisations, Institutions, Plans, Programmes, Celebrations for Children were being taken for granted. Very few knew the historical background, or how they came to be, in 'tit-bits' only.

With birth of every new generation, new values and visions crop up, 'Old is Gold' doesn't exist, old system and methods are forgotten and along with that are forgotten 'those' who laid the foundation of different aspects related to and concerning child. Seeing things done in routine manner without much depth or understanding it urged me to collect facts and material by writing to other States, visiting libraries and institutions. Digging into years old files, magazines, bulletins and annual reports before they find their way into the "Kabadi Sack".

Since the First Edition was out of stock, I was requested by the publisher for the second edition. For this purpose I had to bring it up with up-to-date information.

Thanks to my husband Dr. S.R. Barooah, who continuously encouraged me and helped me to go round and collect the latest information. My special thanks go to Miss Lira Goswami, Advocate, Partner Associated Law Advisor, for going through the chapter of Legislation and helping with the latest addition on Adoption. My thanks also go to Mr. Madan Bezbarua, Principal, Advisor Planning Commission, who helped me Five Year Plans and specially the Eighth Five Year Plan and the Ninth Five Year Plan Approach Paper. Also the new two chapters that I wanted to add on 'Indigenous Medicines' and 'Statistics on Children of India', I was given help by NIPPCED for the latter.

It will serve as a reference and hope it helps all Child Welfare Organisations and Institutions and Child Welfare Workers at various levels. It will be more beneficial if it can be translated by States in their local languages.

PRAMILA PANDIT BAROOAH

INTRODUCTION TO THE REVISED EDITION

Why this revised edition?

It was not a small wonder but a great surprise when I had received communication from University in U.S.A. that my book "Handbook on Child, with Historical Background has been put on the shelf of the University Library. They requested me to send a few copies more. Again I got request from some foreign embassies here for the book and other individuals in the country.

Unfortunately I could not oblige any one, as the book was out of stock. At this juncture it was planned to prepare a revised edition. Much thought and hard work went into it.

It was decided and declared that children should be given the highest priority in National Development Planning. By endorsing 27 survival and development goals for the year 2000 laid by the World Summit, India firmly reaffirmed its commitment to advance the cause of children in India. The Department of Women and Child Development under the Ministry of Human Resource Development in pursuance of this formulated the *National Plan of Action of Children in 1992.*

The National Plan of Action of Children (NPAC) has been worked out keeping in mind the needs, rights and aspirations of 300 million children in the country and sets out quantifiable time dimensions to *India's Charter of Action for Children* by 2000 A.D. The Central Government urged all the *States/Union Territory Governments* to prepare *Plan of Action for Children* for their State/Union Territories, taking into account the regional disparities. The Government of India also ratified the *Convention on the Rights of Child* on 2nd December 1992.

India's population has nearly trebled from 361 million in 1951 to 900 million in 1994; an addition of 539 million people over 45 years period. By the year 2001, population projection indicate that India will have more than a billion inhabitants.

Therefore, a detail chapter on "Statistics on Children in India" is added in this revised edition. A strong data base is critical for any meaningful planning for development. It is also important to have the data to understand the impact of specific measures as also the general process of development of any group of people in any area of development. It helps in relation with various aspects relating to children. The information and data is important, collected from different sources and compiling them in a comprehensive manner so as to get a picture of the child in India, from different aspects, for the users and planners.

Chapter on Child Legislation had an extra addition on Adoption after the latest Supreme Court Judgement and action taken, rules and regulations formed regarding Adoption, specially for Inter-country adoption.

The Five Year Plans are important. The Eighth Five Year Plan of India (1992-97) is added, which recognised "Human Development" as the core of all development efforts. The priority sector of the plan that contribute towards realisation of the goal are health, nutrition, education, literacy and basic needs. In the last decade of this century, dramatic technological development particularly in health, nutrition and related spheres have opened up new vistas of opportunities for redeeming our age-old pledges to the cause of children. It also includes the "Approach Paper to the Ninth Five Year Plan (1997-2002)".

To help the parents and families in rural and poor urban areas, a chapter on "Indigenous Medicines" is added. This helps to give medicines within one house for immediate relief before approaching or waiting for medical aid.

Latest addition and up-to-date information is added on topics, various in numbers like Child Prostitution, Child Labour, Health, Nutrition, Immunization, Education, Adolescent Girl, Girl Child, Disabled Children, Juveniles etc. etc.

As per 1991 Census 150 million children, constituting 17.5 per cent of India's population, who are below the age of 6 years. A majority of them live in economic and social environment which could impede the child's physical and mental development. *Integrated Child Development Services (ICDS)* is India's response to the challenge of meeting the holistic needs of the child. Today it is one of the world's largest and most unique programme for early childhood care and development of children under 6 years of age. ICDS seeks to translate the national commitment to promoting the young child's right to survival and development into reality—in nearly 70 per cent of India's Community Development blocks and 260 urban (slum) low income group pockets.

India's commitment to the cause of children is as old as its civilisation. It has been a time honoured belief in our culture that the child is the gift of God. A gift that must be nurtured with care and affection, within the family and society.

Unfortunately over the years in the pre-independence period, due to socio-economic and cultural changes, the code of child centredness got replaced by neglect, abuse and deprivation, particularly in the poverty afflicted sections of the society. From being advantaged children plummeted into disadvantaged group.

Such a scenario made it imperative to intervene for providing car and protection to children, setting up extra government and voluntary sectors became inevitable.

In India, independence ushered in a new era in the field of child welfare and child development.

This revised edition will help every individual working with and for child. Also research scholars, universities, NGOs, various Children Institutions and Organisations.

PRAMILA PANDIT BAROOAH

CONTENTS

LIST OF TABLES

1

EVOLUTION OF CHILD CARE AND WELFARE SERVICES IN INDIA

Man on Earth

Man's earliest true ancestor appeared on earth more than 2 million years ago, but it was not until 10,000 to 15,000 years ago, that his descendents had peopled almost not until he had mastered fire and learnt to protect himself from the elements did he venture north into colder latitudes.

For most of human life the Biblical lifespan of three score years and ten has been far beyond realistic expectation. Only one person in the ten survived the age of 40 and it would be rare to meet a person of 50. Almost all women would be potential child bearers, and the majority would be pregnant or nursing at any one time.

A high proportion of each group would be children, many dying before adulthood, infanticide was normal practice, since some infants, who were weak, or difficult to feed or to carry would have been simply redundant. Hunting accidents besides disease and starvation would have been a frequent cause of death.

Land and the People

India is one of the oldest civilization with a kaleidoscopic variety and rich cultural heritage. It is the 7th largest country in the world. Indian subcontinent covers an area of 32,87,263 sq. kms. and is bound in the North by the snow covered Himalayas towering over the gangetic plain, in the South by the Deccan Plateau, in the East by the Bay of Bengal and in the West by the Arabian Sea. The countries having a common border with India are Afghanistan and Pakistan to North West, China, Bhutan and Nepal to North, Myanmar to East and Bangladesh to East of Bengal. Sri Lanka is separated by a narrow channel of sea formed by the Palk Strait and Gulf of Manor. With its 26 States and 6 Union Territories, it reflects not only geographical but also a rich cultural diversity. It is a land of 844 million people (1991 Census). Of which 684.7 million live in rural India.

Religion is an important dimension of the Indian culture. Varied religious groups have thrived together from time immemorial in this secular state. The principal religions are Hindu, Muslim, Christian, Sikh, Buddhist and Jain; Hindus being 82 per cent.

The civilization of India is one of the most ancient in the world. Some aspects of this civilization stretch back for more than 4,000 years: eventhough few countries have experienced so many invasions, endured so many periods of apparent anarchy, or seen so many great empires rise and fall.

Ancient History

Since ancient times "The Family" has been the most important child care Institute in India. A satisfactory rearing of the child was ensured by an effective social organisation through the Institution of "Joint Family," and close knit community. These stressed co-operative responsibility and provided care and protection to children.

The traditional cultural attitude towards the child in India, shows not only longing for children but a faith and belief that satisfaction of marriage really does not take place until children are born in the family.

Each development phase in the life of the child was marked by elaborate ceremonies which symbolised the importance attached to the proper and systematic upbringing of the child. Ancient texts provide detail instructions about child care at-home. The *Kalpa Sutras*, written between the 7th and the 2nd century B.C., only 16 of the *Griha Sutras* are available today for reference, as the remaining are lost. One finds in them prescribed *Sanskaras*, each meant help in 'Living' the vedic knowledge and to cultivate a 'value' in life. Together they determine qualitative development and endow maturity, involving both body and mind.

Few *Sanskaras* concerning childhood and adolescent are mentioned below which are practiced today also.

1. *Namkaran Sanskar* (Naming of the Child)

This centre around naming the baby and is done on the 10th or 12th day of child birth. It is establishing the specific identity of the new born as a member of the family.

2. *Nikrashan Sanskar*

After 40 days or during the 4th month after child birth, the mother and the infant for the first time cross the threshold of their home, where they were in a secluded, protected, clean and hygienic environment. They first visit the temple to have "Devdarshan" and "Suryadarshan." It is from now accepted that the mother and infant are coming out to establish contact outside the home, and to invite "Active Immunity" to consequent exposure to communicable stresses and strains of life.

3. *Annaprasan or Ushtavan*

When the infant is 6 months old it is considered to be time for weaning to start. It involves adding of other food to the infants dietary, but to continue with the breast-feeding, and this has been recognised since centuries in India.

4. *Chooda Karma or Chowla Karma or Vapan Vidhi*

This *sanskar* is known by either of these names. This is the first hair cut of the child. This is done after the completion of first year of life. The entire scalp is shaved.

5. *Upanayan Ceremony*

This *sanskara* is held as the second birth of the child. This is done when the child completes his fifth or seventh year of age. With this *sanskara*, the parents and the family who bore the entire responsibility of the child's upbringing, part with it in favour of a preceptor who is an expert, a professional in the art and craft, and science and education. Normally for 12 years, during which the child lives away from home admitted to the homestead of an *acharya* and is now in company with member of other similarly accepted children for training.

After the *Upanayan* ceremony they are given a nine rounds thread made together to wear, this to remind them of the nine virtues they must follow in life, such as honesty, good habits, good thinking, education, respect to the elders, meditation, charity, humility etc. and to cultivate within them these in their every day life from an early age. (Formerly this ceremony was done by all with out any caste or sex distinction. But today it is not so, it is the prerogative of Brahmin boys only and is done more as a symbol and has become a ritual). As times are changing many perform the *Upanayan* ceremony, when the boys are much older. Some do it first before performing marriage, a ritual act.

Human life has been intimately connected with customs and conventions from earliest times, and have been part of the glorious Indian heritage, whether they are followed or not. Customs has its own significance which ensures continuance, and are also affected by the location of the community. This is also very true of the Muslims, who came to India, and the Moghal Empire lasted from 1526 to 1707, i.e., nearly 181 years. Though all the Muslims have same faith, the Indian Muslims have different customs compared to the Muslims of other countries, as there has been an influence of Hindu culture on them. Strangely enough, even in India they have regional variations (like Hindus and other religions) as is seen in their daily life the impact of different regions.

The Muslims who made India their home, adopted many of the local customs and adapted others to suit their religious genius. One cannot deny the effects of environment on an individual, thus Muslims also bear the stamp of Indianness.

The Muslims also like Hindus have childhood customs as follows:

Muslims

1. *Azan*

When a child is born in the Muslim house, it is given a bath at first instance. A pious member recites, *Azan* in the right ear and *Iqamat* in the left ear of the child. The *Azan* is given in Arabic and means to inform and call for *Namaz. Iqamat* literary means "stand up for prayer". This customs was started by Prophet Mohammed.

2. *Chhati* (the sixth day)

Both the mother and child are given bath.

3. *Aqiqa*

Literary means hair on the head of the body. This is the seventh day, when the baby is given a name, and its announced on at the *Aqiqa* ceremony, i.e., when the child's hair are removed. The sacrificial meat is distributed, but generally both sides grand-parents and the parents do not take *Aqiqa* meat. In case of birth of a male child 2 goats or 2 sheep are sacrificed. The hair are weighed and its equal in gold and/or silver is donated. In case of girl, only one goat or one sheep is sacrificed and the hair consigned to the river.

4. *Chilla*

The mother takes a big bath and the mother and child are freed from confinement.

5. *Muranda*

When the child is five months old and able to clinch his fists, balls of *motichoor* to resemble the fists are sent by the maternal grand mother and distributed amongst family members.

6. *Khatna* (Circumcision)

The removal of the fore-skin of the penis is called *Khatna*, and is also known as *Sunnat* and thus becoming a Muslim which was practiced by Prophet Mohammed. It is a must from the religious point of view. It is done at the age of seven upto the age of 12 years old. However, it may be done when the child is one week old. The fore-skin is tied in a cloth and tied to the left foot to ward of evil. When the wound heals up, the skin is thrown away and *Ghori charana* (mounting the mare) ceremony was celebrated earlier.

7. *Bismillah*

Among Muslims *Bismillah* means initiation into religious education. A child is sent to school when he is 4 years, 4 months and 4 days old. This schooling ceremony is called *Bismillah*, and in certain areas this ceremony is known as *Maktab*. When the child is able to learn and understand, he is initiated into Arabic primer called *Qaida* (before he begins to study the *Quran*), after which the child starts taking religious education.

8. *Hadiya or Amin*

After the *Bismillah*, the child begins to study the *Quran*. *Hadiya* or *Amin* ceremony is observed when he completes the study of *Quran*, and on completion the teacher asks the children to stand and start reciting *Amin*, which literally means "O God so be it." This custom is important from both religious and social point of view. Religious, in the sense that the child completes the study of scriptures, and socially the child get an opportunity to mix with other children and thus learns social behaviour.

9. *Roza* (fasting)

A child is expected to observe the *Roza* when he is 7 to 11 years old. The child is kept diverted throughout the day by all possible means. Special arrangements are made for *Aftari*, i.e., completing the *Roza*. First *Roza* of the child is observed with great enthusiasm. The girls do the same learning etc. as boys but within the house.

Sikh

After the child is born on the 13th day the *Garanthi* comes from the Gurudwara gives *Amrit* to mother and child, they are taken to the kitchen, to make everything touchable and eatable. This is done in the case of boy, girl in the same way, no difference is made.

After 40 days the mother and child go to the Gurudwara, and the child is given the name.

Dastar Bandhi is a function held in the house when the child is about 4-5 years old approximately, and the *Ardas* of *Granthsaheb* is done. The *Garanthi* and others are fed.

Anytime after the age of 5 years old the boy is given the *Pagdi* and the importance of *5 K's* is explained.

5 *K's* stand for *Kes, Kripan, Kangi, Kada* and *Kacha* which they have to start using it. The reading of scriptures and prayers are learnt from the parents.

Christians

The Christians have two important ceremonies. Which might slightly differ from state to state.

When the child is about 8-10 days old, the parents select the God-mother and God-father, for the child.

The parents select a name and the God-mother and the God-father takes the child to the church for the Baptism. The parent may go if wanted.

The name is given and the child is blessed by the priest with holy water. When the child is 6-7 years old, the child starts learning the catechism generally the father teaches him/her, and the child starts attending the Sunday school regularly.

When the child has finished learning the catechism and knows all the prayers, he is taken for his first Holy Communion to the church and it is the Bishop who give his blessings and performs the ceremony for the group of children present. It is only after the first Communion that the child is taken into the fold of Christianity. This is very important for the Roman Catholics and a 'must', it is only after this he is declared a Catholic. Generally the definite day and date is declared in the church, hence those children who have to take their first Holy Communion, come on that day and the Bishop also comes and does the ceremony. It is same for both girls and boys.

Parsees

First important event in a Zoroastrian's life is the initiation or *Navjote* ceremony, which takes place between the ages of 7-12 years in the presence of parents, relatives and friends.

Religion of Parsees is Zoroaster, followers of Prophet Zarathushtra. The Prophet believed and put great emphasis on the fact that a child born of Zoroastrian parents is not held to be a Zoroastrian till he chooses the faith at the *Navjote* ceremony when he is invested with the *Sudra* and the *Kusti*, the two great symbols of religion.

Before the *Navjote*, every child is taught the *Kusti* prayer and also how to tie *Kusti* on the *Sudra*.

Kusti was first introduced by *Yima* (Jamshed)—according to Iranians traditions. Zoroastrians accepted the custom but felt it should be tied over a sacred shirt, the *Sudra* known to Pahlavi as "Vohu Manik Vastra" the garment of Vahu Mana the good mind. It was also ordered that a prayer (Dinik Nirangha) to be recited when the *Kusti* ritual was performed.

The *Kusti* which symbolises the tenets of the faith is woven of 72 threads of fine lambs wool as there are 72 chapters of *Yasna* the book of worship. Only members of priestly families may weave a *Kusti,* for it is sanctified by special prayer at every stage of weaving.

The *Sudra* is made of white muslin cloth, with a V shaped neck, at the bottom of which is a square one inch pocket with a slit. This pocket is known as the 'Kisseh-i-Kerfeh' pocket of good deeds. This symbolises purity, to remind that in comparison with God's goodness, whatever man may do is just one square inch.

Ceremony of *Navjote* is performed early morning or evening, facing the east. After a bath child is given leaf of pomergranate and a little drink of Haoma juice. Pomergranate symbolises wisdom and the juice immortality. The priest brings the child on the stage and burns a sandlewood fire in an *Afarghan* (fire censer). Child wears a white *pyjama* called *Ijar* and a *shawl* is wrapped on the upper part. The priest invests the child with *Sudra* then holding the *Kusti*, chants prayers ending with FRAVARANE, taking the faith.

The *Kusti* is wound thrice round the waist—signifying that person must dedicate every thought, word and deed to the service of Ahura Mazda. The first knot of *Kusti* is tied on the word "Shyaothenenam" meaning action and the prayer "Ahuna Vairya" recited twice. Today *Kusti* ritual is performed in the morning, after bath and before retiring to bed.

This is the most important and educational ceremony in Parsees, performed for both girls and boys in the same manner, at a young age.

Condition of Children in India

India's commitment to the cause of children is as old as its civilization. It has been a time honoured belief in our culture that the child is a gift of God. A gift that must be nurtured with care and affection, within the family and the society. Unfortunately, over the years in the pre-independence period, due to socio-economic and cultural changes, the code of child centredness got replaced by neglect, abuse and deprivation, particularly in the poverty afflicted sections of the society. From being advantaged children plummeted into disadvantaged group.

Though ancient texts provide details in upbringing of the children, concentrating on their religious training which they think will put them on the right path, yet it can be noticed and noted that within this general attitude of regarding children as desirable in themselves, an unmistakable preference for the 'Male Child' has been evident. The attitude of the family must be changed as it was not there earlier, neither it is today with children in general, specially with the 'Girl Child' who is unwanted and suffers, as in cases as such....

1. *Infanticide*

The period before coming of Islam, was known as "Dark Age." During this time, the Arabs who entered Sindh, also use to kill their newly born female child as their birth in the family was considered as an insult and humiliation to them. Here the father would kill the child by any method, or even burying her alive in the sand. This was stopped after the arrival of Prophet, who held women in great esteem, and due to him they got their status.

Infanticide was a normal practice in India even more than 5000 years back. May be for different reasons but it was normal, when the infants were found weak, starving and difficult to feed or to carry. This murderous tradition even in Independent India continue in certain parts of the country, especially in case of girls.

As traditionally demanded in some states of India, if a female child is born, the infant is killed before the child sees the light of the day. A bag full of sand is used to suffocate the child or a heavy dose of opium is administered, if the new born is tough enough to resist this, then she is simply strangulated. All this is done by the mother, while the women stand round and provoke her to get rid of the unwanted. Traditions are changing but rather very slowly. Section 302 of the Indian Penal Code calls it "Culpable Homicide amounting to murder." The Female Infanticide Act of 1870 was prevalent in some parts of the country, but this was repealed. Today there is no such Act to prohibit it, although there are several provisions in the Indian Penal Code 1860.

2. *Child Sacrifice*

Its unbelievable that people still believe and continue with 'Child Sacrifice' for getting certain desires fulfilled by such sacrifices, at the instance of fake *Sadhus* or such magicians who earn money through it. Very recently a case took place in a nearby State, where the disappeared child was found strangled with hair and tongue cut.

The distruction of any child living or unborn is a reprehensible practice. Even the abortions been made legal, and performed in pursuance of the so-called family planning is most abhorrent. Sometimes they may be necessary in exceptional circumstances, otherwise it should be considered as murder most foul, as deliberate destruction of unborn children, cold blooded abortions is uncivilised in the extreme. If Infanticide is a crime, so too is abortions, foeticide, embryocide and very little difference can be seen.

Sex determination clinics are increasing. Laws have been passed against it in Mumbai, but there are other places where they are flourishing. The sex of the foetus can be determined from cells in the amniotic fluid. If the unborn child is female it can be aborted and in a sample study in 1988, it showed that out of 8000 foetuses aborted, 7,999 were females. The test is known as amniocentesis, this is actually for detecting congenital defects but is misused in this country.

The values propagated in these enlightened times are strange indeed. Children have a right to be born, male or female children, it is their birth right, to be born and to share in the joys and sorrows of this life. It is their right of entry into this many splendoured and many hued world with its thousands of miseries too. It is selfish in the extreme to snuff out a life in the womb, very selfish to think that another being has no right to exist.

Because of the prevalence of female foeticide, the Central Government has passed the Prenatal Diagnostic Techniques Act (Regulation and Prevention of Misuse) which will have precedence over the existing legislation on sex determination tests in Maharashtra, Rajasthan and Punjab and the proposed legislation in Haryana. The new legislation states categorically that those conducting the diagnostic procedures should not communicate to the women or her relatives the sex of the foetus. Misuse of the diagnostic procedure could result in imprisonment of three years and a fine of Rs. 10,000. The registration of Doctors, who are convicted for abuse of the new technology, could be suspended.

3. *Child Marriage*

Social and cultural milieu of India has long favoured universality of marriage and early marriage for girls—even before the legal age of 18 years. According to the National Sample Survey (43rd round), in rural India, 44 per cent of girls in the age group of 15 to 19 years and 5 per cent in the age group of 10 to 14 years were married in 1987-88. The corresponding Urban proportions were 21 per cent, 1.4 per cent respectively. The mean age of girls during the decade has increased from 15.5 in 1981 to 19.5 in 1991. Child marriages are still culturally prevalent in some parts of rural India, mainly in Rajasthan, Uttar Pradesh, Bihar and Madhya Pradesh.

Child marriage was and is still a serious problem in the country. They are performed and against the law, punishable by fines and even imprisonment. But rarely is the law enforced and the marriages are rarely reported or anyone prosecuted.

The Child Marriage Restrain Act of 1929, also known as the Sarda Act, was amended in 1978 to raise the minimum marriage age of girls to 18 years and for boys to 21 years. Under the new Act, Police officers are competent to investigate offences as if they are cognizable but would not be able to arrest any person without a warrant or an order of a magistrate. However, the Act does not invalidate child marriage as it would adversely affect the status of girls.

The Act prescribed penalties for its violation of Section 50 of the Act, imposed penalties on the priests who performed the ceremony. The marriage if performed then the validity of the child has to be considered according to the personal laws of the parties, which differ among the different communities. According to the Hindu Marriage Act 1955, such marriage is neither void or voidable. Under the Muslim Law it is voidable at the option of the girl. Under the Parsi and Christian Laws unless the consent of the guardian is sought, it is considered invalid.

More and more people are aware that the child marriages are illegal, hence their performance is very secretive and known only to the relatives and villagers are quiet about it. Yet child marriages which are banned by Government are still taking place throughout India. This practice is still prevalent in some states and marriages take place in groups on the festival of *Akha Teej*. In rural Rajasthan this tradition which is 100 years old, is very strong, hence Child Marriages occur like 'Doll's Marriages' in tens of thousands each year. Most of the time the girl is sent to the husband's place months after she reaches puberty. The ceremony is called *Goana*.

4. *Widow Marriage*

In some States the widow marriages are still banned, and rarely a young widower will be ready to marry a widow as she is considered "In-auspicious." In some States the heads of the widows are shaved off and they are made to look ugly. The Hindu Widow Marriage Act 1856 was an enabling measure permitting and legalising the marriage and offspring of the marriage of an Hindu widow remarrying. But this Act was repealed in 1983. In the general law of maintenance, Section 125 of the Criminal Procedure Code applies to all but this section does not provide for maintenance of widow daughter or daughter-in-law, minor or otherwise. In Rajasthan if a child becomes a widow before even going to her husband's place or reaching puberty, she is not allowed to marry. This is the case in many rural areas or orthodox homes in other States also. In the Patel community of Rajasthan the widow is not married, but is given to an older man as his common wife. Slowly this practice is changing among the urban and educated masses and remarriage has started taking place, at times against the wishes of the elders.

5. *Purdah*

Some of the practices which became a part of the social system were a handicap to the development of the girl child. They were confined to the seclusion of the house which left them in total ignorance. Even the young brides were not allowed to come before the elders without covering their heads or faces. In some places even the feet are not supposed to be seen.

This custom is slowly on the decline; as more and more women are taking jobs outside their homes. But in rural areas though they move about freely, they have to cover their heads and faces before the men. This is more prevalent in the North.

6. *Devadasi*

Young girls dedicated to the temple was a challenge to social conscience of the people. The type of *Devadasi* mentioned in the *Artha Vastra* were not enslaved to the temples or objects of worship. She was not a temple dancer or a courtisan, but was more like a nun. Post Vedic period was the period of *Puranas*. During this period the priest came to occupy the top position. They preached gifting of girls to the service of God or temple. Thus the *Padma Purana* in its *Srishtikanda* recommends the purchase of pretty girls (virgins) by the people for gifting them to temples. The *Bhavishya Purana* laid down that the only way to centure entry to Suryalok or Heaven was to offer a band of beautiful girls. These *Puranas* are ascribed to the 3rd century A.D., when due to poverty and want of money the families sold their girls to the temple. By the 7th century A.D. temple activity was very exclusive in South due to Royal interests. Beyond 10th century the total number of *Devadasis* in any temple was in direct proportion to wealth and prestige of the temple.

With the invasion by the Muslims marked the beginning of the decline of *Devadasi* system and institution. When the British came, they took steps to abolish it during 1906-1907. The Indian Penal Code was amended and Sections 372-373 declared the practice to be illegal. But in the South this system continued and by the 20th century it turned into an Institution of Prostitution and completely commercialised. Since Independence some change has taken place. But even today this system is still flourishing and is unchecked. In Karnataka—thousands of minor girls are initiated into the cult of Goddess Yallamma every year during *Magh Purnima*. During the period 1989, in one Belgaon District 390 minor girls were inducted into Devadasi system. Though Law prohibits the action, the government takes no action and on the contrary traffic and crowds are managed by the police.

Actually no definite estimates are available about the number of child *Devadasis* and *Jogins*, though this system has been in existence traditionally in some societies as a socially sanctioned form of exploitation of women particularly those from lower socio-economic groups, specially in the states of Karnataka, Maharashtra and Andhra Pradesh.

Devadasis—little girls of just 12 or 13 form 80 per cent of the brothel population. Interestingly, the "Signs" used to identify the "chosen" child (who is then dedicated to the Goddess Yallamma) are those of ill health—white patches of eczema, leprosy, even mentally retardation. In prostitution, this was one way of making lucrative way of making use of otherwise "worthless" children.

The tribes who, in the past lived on the earnings of their prostitute women are now part of a systematic lucrative urban traffic in child prostitution. The best organised are *Bedias* of Central India who send their daughters traditionally famous for their erotic, singing and dancing to large Indian cities.

The Dormara Tribe of Telangana, first marries at puberty the eldest girl of every family to the village deity. Then she is raped for a week by elders and priests within the temple. Her family and the villagers feast outside. Scores of such children die of injuries and shock. Those who survive become *Venkatasanto* prostitutes for the village males. Their income is the family's main livelihood. Entire village of *Venkatasanis* live together in the Warangal and Nizamabad district of Andhra Pradesh.

The National Crime Records Bureau reported 100 per cent increase in kidnapping in last 2 years, 60 per cent are forcibly married and then hidden by the brothel until they reach profitable age of 9-13 years. (*Times of India*, dated April 16, 1997, Article 'Child Prostitution' by Shahnaz Anklesariya Aiyar).

7. *Jogins*

In Andhra Pradesh, there are *Jogins* who are condemned to this trade of prostitution at an early age of six. In actual ceremony, the drinking and revery, the girls are dressed as brides and the priest ties the *Mangalsutra*. As soon as they reach puberty, they are deflowered by some rich merchant or businessman, and they pass on from one to another.

8. *Prostitution*

However, the business in the Child Prostitution is growing in India. Prostitution in India has manifested itself in various forms with varying degrees of social sanction. There is now increasing concern about children being inducted for commercial purposes into the trade and becoming subjects of shocking sexual abuse and sexual diseases. All nations in the UN are committed to suppress and prevent trafficking in persons for exploitation and for immoral purposes. There are no reliable statistics available about the number of prostitutes—least of all about Child Prostitutes. According to newspaper reports, there are 0.4 million child prostitutes. Some studies on prostitutes and child prostitution point out there are some castes and communities in various pockets of the country in which family based prostitution is traditionally practiced.

The Supreme Court of India in a 'Public Interest Litigation' in 1990 on the subject of Child Prostitution has passed an order stating that that Central and State Governments should set up Advisory Committees to suggest measures to be taken in eradicating child prostitution.

Government of India constituted a Central Advisory Committee which included representative from some ministries and voluntary organisations. A sub-committee was constituted to frame recommendations/plan of action for legal and non-legal approaches for the rescue and rehabilitation of child prostitutes. The plan of action was finalised and accepted and the implementation machinery was set up.

All methods are used to get young girls for this trade. They are lured under false promise of marriage, at times kidnapped even at the age of 6 years old. The condition of young prostitutes is miserable and they suffer from psychosomatic pains in the abdomen, get headaches, diarrhoea, loss of appetite, insomnia and hallucinations. Their future is dim as the children of prostitutes follow the steps of their mothers and the boys become pimps.

According to the Country Report prepared for the "Convention on the Rights of the Child" (December 1994), Prostitution in India has manifested itself in various forms with varying degrees of social sanction. Actually child sex is rapidly growing business, where children are prostituted before they are 15 years old. Ironically, the scare of the killer AIDS virus has translated into a rise in demand from prostitute users for supposedly uninfected children. There is increasing concern about children being inducted for commercial purpose into the trade and becoming subjects of shocking sexual abuse and sexual diseases. Many children are thrust into prostitution by their families. It is family members of girls—acting independently who execute a sizeable percentage of the total trafficking operation. Most of the children belong to schedule castes. Almost all are poor. A sizeable number are tribals. Most come from the Southern States of Andhra Pradesh, Karnataka, Tamil Nadu, Maharashtra and West Bengal.

Legal Provisions: The Government of India enacted the Suppression of Immoral Traffic in Women and Girls Act, 1956. In 1986 this Act was amended and provided enhanced penalties for offences involving children and minors. It continued to prohibit prostitution in its commercialised form without rendering prostitutions. The Indian Penal Code includes sexual offences—procuration of minor girls (Section 366A), importation of minor girls from foreign country (Section 366B), Selling minor for purposes of prostitution (Section 372) and makes them punishable by law. The Juvenile Justice Act, 1986 has elaborated provisions for the care, protection, treatment, education, vocational training, development and rehabilitation of children rescued from those procuring, inducing and taking persons for the sake of prostitutions.

Despite stringent laws, very little is done for these innocents. The few that try to and manage to escape, have to fight their way through social stigma and are usually caught and ultimately come back to the same place again. "It is a self-defeating exercise, and a child prostitute is nobody's baby."

The British earlier took steps to abolish prostitutions during 1906-1907. In 1924 the Indian Panel Code was amended and Sections 372-373 declared the practice as illegal, and those who did it under the age of 18 were prosecuted. There was Immoral Traffic in Women and Girls Act 1956, which has been amended and now called "the Suppression of Immoral Traffic in Women and Girls (Amendment) Act 1986." It got President's assent on 8th September 1988.

9. *Sati*

Burning of the widow on the pyre of her husband was a common practice and a characteristic which existed among the Aryan tribes also. During the Muslim period Akbar attempted reforms and forbade the practice of *Sati*. Also Raja Ram Mohan Roy's name is closely associated with the abolition of *Sati*. Actually Regulation No. 17 passed on 8-12-1829 by the foremost social reformer Lord William Bentick outlawed widow burning.

In spite of the provision in the Law for the prevention of suicide, the continuance of *Sati* and its glorification has been on increase. Therefore, the Act called 'the Commission of Sati (Prevention) Act 1987 was passed and received the consent of the President on 3-1-1988. Accordingly there are heavy punishments for offences relating to *Sati*.

10. *Child Export*

Many families because of economic hardship have been selling their children, they come mainly from backward areas with low literacy rates. This selling racket is found in Rajasthan, Hyderabad, Mumbai and Delhi and other places. It mainly deals with minor boys under 10 years of age for camel racing and using them for this barbaric sport. The children or their parents are aware of the purpose they actually are taken for. The parents are told they will be trained to take care of the camels.

The Desert Paradise as it is known by in Abu Dhabi has camel races four times a year, when all the Sheiks, King and Sultan from the area come to witness this race. Actually the whole Saudi Arabia gather together for this festival held in great pomp and show with glaring music going on. Here takes place the 5 km. camel race. The children are given drugs and an electric shock before they go in for the race. One child is strapped to one camel's back. As the race starts the child jokey starts crying and shouting, mainly due to fright and discomfort. The more children wail the faster the camels pick up speed and moves faster and the crowds roar with excitement. On completion of the race, the children are immediately taken to an enclosure, from where they watch the winners taking their prizes. Later they are removed to hospitals for the treatment of their hurts and shocks. Young minor boys are taken as they are light in weight, they are lured not only from India but from other countries belonging to the third world.

12. *Eunuchs*

Desperation takes many into the fold of eunuchs. If one peers deep into how the numbers of eunuchs which are much over 11 lakhs in India is swelling, one can find out the darker ways of functioning behind it. By castrating, eunuchs manage to increase their tribe, as this seems the only way.

The word Eunuch is derived from the Greek word 'Eunoukhos' which literally means bed chamber attendant.

In Mughal periods, eunuchs for obvious reasons were put in charge of the *harems*. The eunuchs were generally strong men who were subjected to castration, then they were put in charge of the *harem* as outside guards. This was the practice with kings of that time because they wanted someone who could defend the *harem* and in no way harm the women. This custom was prevalent during the Greek and Roman empires also.

In the total population of eunuchs in India, 75 per cent are castrated males. The world of Eunuchs is highly organised. They have their community with clans, with one *Guru* heading it. Each *Guru* has his own *Sthan* (area) within which he operates. In Delhi alone there are over 10,000 eunuchs with 40 *Gurus*. He hangs over his group of eunuchs like the sword of Domocles.

The eunuchs get hold of the parents who have abnormal children born and they take them into their fold. In India there are Doctors and Quakes who in collision with the organised gangs indulge in castrating male children into eunuchs, male children are lured or kidnapped for the purpose. There is lot of money in this business for both Doctors trained in this craft and the eunuchs.

12. *Child Beggars*

There are more than 150,000 child beggars in the country (aged up to 14 years). Begging has never been discouraged in India. Mandicants have been venerated by Hindus, Muslims, Christians, Buddhists—all alike. All major religions recommend alms giving as an easy way out for the penitent.

West Bengal has largest number of beggars numbering approximately 4,83,030 or more. They came to this state from Bihar, Orissa and U.P. The British banned beggary in Calcutta in 1852. There was an uproar against it, but 40 years later Law was amended and begging banned in South Calcutta. Unfortunately sporadic drives or legislations are no solution to this problem. Neither police have enough legal or other means to combat the begging menace.

Kinds of Beggars

There are different kinds of beggars—

1. *Religious Beggars*

Begging in the name of religion, popularly posing as *Sanyasi, Yogi, Sadhu, Vairagi, Fakir, Kabir Panthi, Darvesh*, etc. with saffron coloured clothes wood bead necklaces, a bowl in hand, reciting holy verses, correctly or incorrectly (eat and drink well and live well). This class constitutes 20 per cent.

2. *Invalid Beggars*

Beg by exploiting the sympathy of the people through exhibition of their physical disability. They are about 15 per cent.

3. *Diseased Beggars*

Exhibiting bodily ailments, wounds, soars and scars and majority suffer from infectious diseases, their living conditions are very unhygienic and are permanent dwellers. They constitute 11 per cent.

4. *Professional Beggars*

They constitute 40 per cent or more. They are able bodied and live in dirty lanes and houses and avoid work professionally :

(a) They indulge in decoity, theft, unlicensed prostitution.
(b) Buying or purchasing young babies for exclusive purpose of training them for begging.
(c) They also go and purchase orphans or illegitimate children, or even kidnap them for employment in begging.
(d) The children acquired are deliberately maimed or disfigured.
(e) These disfigured children are sold or mortgaged. They fetch a good high price for more pathetic and disfigured child.

5. *Casual Beggars*

They are over 15 per cent. This class works during day time and are involved in robbery in the night. The boys in the family are taught the art of pick-pocket and thefts. Girls are used for prostitution hiring, to supplement their income. In a family of beggars—children are the biggest source of incomes. More than half of their income comes from and through children—which is by unfair and unlawful means.

Therefore, children and infants are deliberately maimed by parents or owners, as they are better source of income. They are exploited and made objects of pity and used for begging in public places and the children are kept under strict vigilance and made to obey.

Begging is carried on and mainly done with the assistance of women and children. They come from situation of economic deprivation, distribution and neglect. It is a multifaced problem. Education is important but due to migratory nature of most of the beggars there is a hindrance in the schooling of the children besides this they consider educating their children and spending on them money for education as an economic wastage.

Solution

Begging is a serious social problem in India. This problem is acting like poison and becoming a menace to the society. Neither law, punishment, fine or imprisonment can solve the problem. It can be corrected and solved by:

(a) Creating public opinion against begging,
(b) People should be made conscious of the number of idlers and parents who are party to this anti-social activity like begging,
(c) Public must be made aware that they are parasites and burden on society,
(d) Alms giving whether out of piety or other concerns should be stopped or banned, because it amounts to abetting the profession,
(e) Beggars Asylums to provide vocational guidance and training in different occupations and handicrafts, and
(f) Separate homes for diseased beggars, and separate settlement for lepers or send these particular class of beggars to an already established Leper Home. Even Indira Gandhi once said that kidnapping children and maiming them for the purpose of beggary was a "heinous crime." Begging by children must stop and completely banned.

In this one decade it is noted that 12 to 15 children are missing daily, and not even 3 are traced. In Bihar there was an organised child running racket, but no action to taken. In Delhi child missing cases rose from 5007 to 7879 within one year. Calcutta police recorded in one year 3431 children lost, but no effort made for the search. These are the "blossoms in dust, who do not know what is childhood.

13. *Street Children*

Children driven by circumstances to make street their home are indeed the worst neglected among the entire population of the country.

Children of the Street

They abandoned me, now what will become of me? What will be?
How good it is to be prepared for the pitfalls of life.

I am the future. Nothing will happen, nothing will change.
I am a child of the street.
From the centres, from the corners.
The days pass and I am here, where everything is seen.

Where the struggle for survival is constant. And for a piece of bread, they robbed my love. They robbed me and left without an affection. They left me marginalised for you. What fault have, I, a child, a kid with nothing in life. Do you understand?

Delivered to the life of streets. I, a being without love.
I cry for affection, for the maternal breast, I cry.

Even though they can criticise me—why don't they do something to help us?

I need affection. I need closeness and guidance.
It is not my fault that I'm a street child, that I am an abandoned child.
Do you know what I want? I only want the right to be a person, to be able to dream like every one of having liberty.
Have you ever imagined the life of an abandoned child? Without any help?
Abused by life?

Meeting face to face with brute liberty? I don't want to be given up like a freak to life. Let me be a person, at least to be happy, to be a child, to believe in fairy tales, to believe that Santa Claus exists, to feel human warmth.

Let me live my childhood
Is it much to ask? (Gaura Rosa da Silva, Brazil)

The most vulnerable group of children in physical, psychological and organisational terms are surely the 'Street Children' who live, work, sleep and sometimes die uncared for an unprotected. Reliable statistics about their numbers are difficult, while some place a national figure over one lakh is stated, while it is indicated that this figure exists in Mumbai streets alone.

Most of these children are destitutes or abandoned, who spend their time mostly on the streets and also sleep on the streets and in public places.

Majority of the children on the streets are working children who are thoroughly exploited and oppressed. These children are not even counted or considered part of any statistics. Therefore, they are not of any concern to any legislation or subjects of any policies or there are any programmes or benefits for them.

Life of Street children violates all the survival, protection and development rights of the child. Environmental degradation, migration and displacement of families have led to exodus to cities and expansion of slums and pavement dwellings. Child care and development are seriously hampered in these families. Women in the single-parent families and female headed households are worst affected as they have the main responsibility for the children but they are neither trained or experienced. The children most often spend their time on the street. Large number of street children suffer destitution neglect, abuse and exploitation. They are subjected to harassment and eviction by the municipal authorities because of their unauthorised occupation of city roads and vacant places.

It is estimated that 500,000 children live on streets in seven cities: Bangalore, Mumbai, Calcutta, Delhi, Hyderabad, Kanpur and Chennai. The majority of these children are over eight years of age, have never attended schools and have parents who have low paid unskilled jobs.

Neither the Juvenile Justice Act of 1986 or the National Policy for Children recognises the needs of street children or mentions them in the Policy. The National Plan of Action includes them in the category of children in specially difficult circumstances. Only recently schemes have been launched with a view to support and strengthen voluntary organisations engaged in the welfare and development of the street children, to enable them to reach out to a large number of such children.

The first aim of the scheme is to provide integrated community-based non-institutional basic services for the care, protection and development of the street children, facing destitution.

The second aim is programme intervention for reduction of exploitation and abuse and withdrawal of children in hazardous work. The scheme has focussing on the preventive and rehabilitative aspects.

Categories of Street Children

There are three categories of street children:

1. Working children who have family contact on more or less regular contacts on regular basis. They return home at the end of the day. This class is 75 per cent of the street children.

2. These are about 20 per cent or more who see and look at street as their home and seek a sense of belonging among companions. Family ties exist but are remote and home visits are rare.
3. Abandoned children are about 5 per cent of all the street children and are those who have no family at all. They are on their own for material and psychological survival.

They are alienated socially plus the psychological depression and deprivation acts as permanent blockade to their personality development. While it is obvious that food, clothing, shelter, education and recreation are almost nil.

The most noticeable psychological trait of the street child is a fierce assertion of his independence. Having run away from all that was secure, the urge is irresistible to keep going. Their perception of the police is one of fear and distrust and this further exposes them to exploitation. Group survival is the norm and in-group feelings are as positive as the out-group is negative. Hence except for the group of 'gang' member, others—outsiders—on the street are feared and distrusted.

Schemes

There are many schemes taken up to have homes which enable to shelter the street children—from shanty towns, railway stations, and destitute family situation. It is the most urgent need, more than the funds, the need is for dedicated and enthusiastic volunteers. The children mostly belong to the age group of 11 to 18 years old. Some projects take care of 55-60 children daily in an open setting, where they may spend the night if they wish, and some go out to work.

Generally railway stations are full of children who earn in the mornings and spend the night on the platform where their all needs are met. But when there is a shelter, they prefer to come to it, as they can sleep in peace without being chased by the police or assaulted by drug addicts and abused by homosexuals. Here each child has to be given individual attention and the needs of each child are different.

Institutions

Will a child turn to a government institution or government type institution? If it does, will the child stay there?

The workload on the staff does not encourage quality, motivation or commitment. They find unequal to the task assigned to them and hence take refuge in indifference and over a period of time become desensitised. The limitations of such institutions are serious and correcting them will require substantial funds and a different kind of effort.

Solutions to the problem of street children have to be in voluntary sector. Government is best suited to lending indirect support through allotment of funds.

Organisations

Few organisations are trying and experimenting 'half way approach'. These experiments fall in two categories.

1. It is an open house, when children come on certain days for few hours for a wash, snack or a game and then again disperse to the streets. In this categories are projects like the Nirmala Niketan and Social Work Project *Vatsalya* run by Jain Mahila Samaj at Chowpatty. Vatsalya have been given identity cards. The aim of the project is to motivate children to organise their own world, have their own leaders and decide what they want to do and authorities help them to take up activities of their choice—Vocational training or some hobby.

Another project is run by Don Bosco called 'Shelter' project, at Dadar—Mumbai.

2. The second approach is closely related to the first, except it gives more importance to taking services right up to the point where children congregate or live.

Yuva goes rights on the pavement along with the pavement schools, teaching reading writing and arithmetic.

"Referral Centre" runs from a church compound at VT Mumbai itself. Again hear the 3 R's are taught and also vocational training is been given. *Sneha Sadan* runs 13 homes in different parts of the city, with 20 children who have food, roof, and lots of love, an atmosphere of complete freedom, and a sense of belonging, that gives them back their self-respect and a place in society.

14. *The Girl Child*

It was in 1986 at the SAARC meeting that government leaders of 7 South Asian countries decided to make the 'Child' a priority for planning.

A major recommendation at that meeting was for planners, administrators, social workers and governments of SAARC region to come together and deliberate on the 'Girl Child'. Hence a workshop on the 'Girl Child' was organised at Delhi 1988.

The deliberations shed light on the unfortunate conditions of the Indian girl child. How she is under attack before her birth and regarded as unlucky and liability when she is born. She is not only neglected but deprived on necessary daily needs.

The Indian girl child is often uneducated, underfed, undernourished and her health needs are neglected. She is considered and treated like a second class individual and this traditional culture of discrimination which runs through all sections of society.

Ignorance and lack of information and education can be blamed for much of the sufferings and conditions of the Indian girl child—and she is always at a risk. Sex discrimination is a major factor contributing to the poor health of girls in societies where sons are preferred to daughters. Health implications of sex discrimination in childhood finds over-whelming evidence of differential feeding leading to differential nutritional status between boys and girls. Also during sickness, girls are cared less than the boys. This daughter neglect results in "excess" female mortality in childhood. Among the long term health effects of daughter neglect are short maternal height and small pelvis that can lead to low birth-weight low birth-weight babies and damage to reproductive system.

The National Policy for Children formulated in 1974 does not mention the girl child. However, India has adopted a separate "National Plan of Action" for children in 1992 which includes the objective of removing the gender bias and improving the status of the child in the society so as to provide her with equal opportunities for her survival and development to her full potential. India adopted a separate National Plan of action for SAARC Decade of the girl child for 1991-2000 A.D. In pursuance of which the various Departments of Government, i.e., Department of Women and Child Development, Department of Family Welfare and Department of Education giving special emphasis on gender-specific interventions and programmes with the support of NGOs.

A scheme for adolescent girls was started to meet the needs of adolescent girls in the age group of 11 to 18 years, for health, nutrition, non-formal education and literacy, and social and recreational needs, recognising their potential role as effective social animators at the village level. The girl child has become the focus of universalisation of primary education in an effort to achieve "Education for All by 2000 A.D." Special emphasis is being given to the enrolment and retention of the girl child under various programmes of the Department of Education.

On the whole the enrolment of girls in schools has increased eight-fold from 5.4 million in 1950-51 to 44.9 million in 1992-93. In 1992-93, the school enrolment at primary stage was above 100 in many states.

The girls child's life always seems to be at a disadvantage and risk. If she survives the first year of life, she finds herself married and then abandoned by her husband and in-laws, or sold to a brothel or to become a *devadasi*. She may become a domestic servant for which one needs no qualification except pair of strong arms and hands and good physique.

Article 2 the rights of the child should be protection against all forms of discrimination on the basis of the child's sex. However, gender bias is entrenched deeply in the cultural heritage of the Indian society. Traditionally, India, a society that idolises sons, an obsession that cuts across all differences of caste, class and religion. Sons were and are still considered ritually and economically desirable.

Girl child especially in rural areas remain deprived of adequate access to basic health care, nutrition and education. Inevitable, more girls than boys suffer from malnutrition and succumb to diseases. There were an estimated 7.8 million fewer female-to-male ratio of 0.949. The adverse female to male ratio among children is attributable to the systematic deprivation and unequal treatment of girls vis-a-vis boys reported and documented in several parts of the country. To add to this are the incidences of female infanticide and selective abortion of female foetus in some areas.

The Girl child has become the focus of universalisation of primary education in an effort to achieve "Education for All by 2000 A.D." Special attention and emphasis is being given to the enrolment and retention of the girl child under various programmes of the Department of Education.

All these efforts have resulted in reversing the trends to reduce gender inequality. As per 1991 data out of the total female population, about 36 per cent girls were in the age group 0-14. There is a decline in female mortality rates, especially in the age group 0-4 years and 5-14 years indicating improvements in the survival of the girl child. In the age group 0-4 years, the mortality rate declined from 43.3 in1981 to 27.5 in 1991, while in the age group of 5-14 years the decline was from 3.1 in 1981 to 2.2 in 1991.

The sex differentials in literacy are still very pronounced, though there has been a marked improvement in the female literacy rate from

29.75 per cent in 1981 to 39.29 per cent in 1991. On the whole enrolment of girls in schools has increased eight-fold from 5.4 million in 1950-51 to 44.9 million in 1992-93. In 1992-93, the school enrolment at primary stage was above 100 in many states.

The Eighth Five Year Plan strategy, stated that social discrimination against the girl child will be effectively countered, through a massive campaign, to ensure equal treatment and equal opportunity for their growth and development. A holistic approach has increasingly been emphasised including appropriate intervention, gender sensitization, advocacy, social mobilization and using media for changing attitudes.

Though 1990 was declared as the year of the child, her status is unlikely to improve. She will still remain at the lowest rung of the ladder, unwanted by her family, abused, not bothered about or concern shown by employees, unless some concrete measures are taken to help her sincerely and genuinely.

15. *Adolescent Girls*

Adolescence is the state or process of growing up; the period of life from puberty to maturity, terminating legally in the age of maturity. Since it is time of major physical, congnitive and psychological growth and change, it offers great opportunity for directing youthful energy and preparing them to become productive confident adults. A number of adolescents in India, particularly girls from low socio-economic groups, live under suboptimal conditions marked by poor nutritional status, high level of morbidity and mortality. Quite few of them are unable to achieve proper growth. They have limited access to education and training. Despite the Child Marriage Restraint Act, early marriage is still prevalent causing teenage pregnancies. For most of them who passes through or crossed impoverished childhood, adolescence offers the second chance for catch-up growth. The adolescent girls' own health and nutritional status and that of the next generation would largely be determined by their own knowledge, skill and competence.

Government of India in 1990 introduced a scheme for adolescent girls, recognising that girls in the age-group of 11-18 years are in need of appropriate initiation into adulthood as they are not covered by any programme in terms of their crucial needs. This is operative in about 507 ICDS blocks in all the States and UTs and about 0.45 million girls are being covered by this scheme. There are 5 broad objectives—The girls receive training in areas of health and nutrition, child care, literacy and numerous skills through the non-formal system of education, to stimulate a desire for more social exposure and knowledge and to help them improve their decision-making capabilities; train and equip the girls to improve and upgrade home-based skills.

The scheme envisages setting up of Balika Mandals. In these Balika Mandals girls meet in groups, discuss their problems receive some non-formal education and get a chance for recreation and interaction with other adolescent girls. They also get training in vocational skills.

In order to better address concerns for women and the girl child, it was necessary to design interventions for adolescent girls. This is arrived at breaking the inter generational life cycle of nutritional disadvantage, and providing a supportive environment for self-development.

For the first time in India, a special intervention has been devised for Adolescent Girls. This intervention focuses more on school drop-outs, girls in the age group of 11-18 years, to meet their needs of self-development.

This scheme attempts to mobilise and enhance the potential of adolescent girls as social animators. It also seeks to improve their capabilities in addressing nutrition and health issues—through centre-based instructions, training camps, and learning as well as sharing of experiences.

16. *Birth Registration*

Article 7 of the CRC (Convention on the Rights of Child) makes it parents' responsibility to register the child and birth of the child.

In our country, there is a regular system for registration of birth, deaths and names. The office of the Registrar General of India, under the Ministry of Home Affairs handles the subject of registering the birth and name of the newborns as it is governed by the provisions of the Registration of Births and Deaths Act, 1969 (RBD). Rules have been framed under this Act by various State Governments between 1970 and 1982. Under this Act, registration of all births occurring in the country has been made compulsory and free of charge, if reported within the prescribed time-limit. At present, the period prescribed for the registration of birth varies from 14 to 21 days in various parts of the country. Section 13 of the Act also has provision for delayed registration for events which could not be registered within the normal reporting period. Under Section 12 of this Act, the first copy of the extracts of registration, which is also known as birth certificate is given free of charge. The necessary reporting form prescribed for the birth registration of a newborn contains an item on name of the child. Concerted efforts are being made to create awareness for improved timely registration of newborns as it is vital for ascertaining correct age of the child and availing rights.

In practice, many parents do not register child birth due to low awareness, home-based deliveries and illiteracy. The report of vital statistics in India (1987) shows that the coverage of births by the registration system is 100 per cent only in 6 states and three of the Union Territories. In order to increase the rate of birth registration an element of compulsion for obtaining birth certificates has been introduced in certain urban areas. This includes compulsory production of birth certificate at the first school admission and for obtaining ration cards. This has improved the rate of registration of births. Media has been effectively used for promoting awareness of benefits arising out of universal birth registration.

Pre-Independence

During the early years, the country and the public generally showed very little concern for the child. Even the citizens renowned for their public spirit and philanthropy did not realise how the indigent children of the country were neglected and exploited. During the pre-independence period social welfare were sporadic, *ad-hoc* and for the most part, uncoordinated as they were structured to meet purely local needs. Many National and Statewise organisations were established in the first part of the 19th Century, which were mainly concerned with the children such as orphans, destitute, vagrancy and handicap etc.

Besides the Social Welfare Organisations, the first effort to start pre-school education can be traced back to 1885 when the missionary organisations pioneered the efforts for providing pre-school education by opening kindergartens. In the early 20th Century, theosophists and other private agencies organised and tried to popularise pre-school education. The influence of Annie Besant and Ravindranath Tagore contributed towards spreading the movement, and between 1920-1930 the ten years witnessed a mushroom growth of many nursery schools throughout the country, particularly in South India. With arrival of Maria Montessorie in India and her association with Mahatma Gandhi gave further impetus to the movement. Her basic philosophy was in the belief that both the body and mind of a child must be nourished simultaneously.

During the early years of the century, the country and the public generally showed little concern for the dependent child. Even Mumbai, the first and foremost in the sphere of local self-government had not a single institution charged with duty, armed with legal authority and endowed with financial resources, to reclaim children from slums and streets, and haunts of vice and shame. It was backward in the domain of child welfare.

A conscious move in this direction came when in 1914 the apathy of the public regarding welfare of the juvenile offenders sent to reformatory in Mumbai was deplored in the report of the I.G. Police. Shri R.P. Masani raised larger issues in the columns of *Times of India* and asked "why not deal with the cause of child dependency and delinquency and reduce the number of children passing through the courts of reformation?" Having read this article on "Child protection" in papers, Sir John Wardla then a prominent figure in public life personally approached him to start immediately reclaiming children from the streets and told him "if you can find worker, I will find money." Thus was established in January 1917, Society for the Protection of Children in Western India. The Society managed to achieve two main objectives:

1. To prevent the wastage of children of the city.
2. To cleanse society setting right the grievous wrong of its children.

It was this society which submitted to the government specific provisions for a comprehensive enactment on the subject for having special legislation. It took 6 years for the Children Act to be passed and put it into statute book, and three years more to put it into operation. Since special agency for assisting in the work was needed, therefore, in 1927 the Children's Aid Society was set up to act as a non-official auxiliary body for assisting government in implementing the provisions of the Act. Mumbai was specially grateful to Dr. Clifford Manshadt for his pioneering work in establishing institutions for the best of the children. The Children's Aid Society assisted government and cooperated with the existing organisations engaged in work of protection and welfare of the children and took vagrant children into residential care.

In 1920 a children's organisation called Balkan-ji-Bari was formed with children as their members.

In 1924 Guild of Service started its child welfare services in Chennai and South India. In 1945 Kasturba Gandhi National Memorial Trust was created for the welfare of women and children. Its main work was in rural areas and gave grants in-aid to the rural organisations or their units for balwadis and creches. It has always been the non-government organisations and Institutions that have created 'Systems' with their own enterprise and vision to work for and coach the weaker sections and did social work for the poor, needy, handicap and orphans. There have been also movements like Shriniketan and Gandhiji's *Antodaya* systems and Nai Talim, programmes by Ramakrishna Mission, Arya Samaj Mandals and Gurukula that were created.

Post-Independence

Shri Jawaharlal Nehru with reference to social welfare in India said:

> "Social Welfare is not a new activity in India. It is as old as India itself. There are many subjects that are of interest to one. If I may be allowed to lay greater stress on some, then they would be the Welfare of Children and the status of women, and the tribal and hill people in the country. Children I think, all over India should have the first claim on us, because they represent the India of tomorrow."

Scheme for Integrated Child Development Services (ICDS), was implemented, ICDS aimed to provide a package of services consisting of supplementary nutrition, Immunisation, health check ups, referral services, health and nutrition education to the pregnant and nursing mothers in rural, tribal and urban areas, and non-formal education to the children in the age groups of 0-6 years. The ICDS scheme was launched on 2nd October, 1975. Training centres were started to give training to girls from local areas for three months to make them able to run the *Anganwadis*. In this Plan period Day Care centres and creches were organised on a larger scale. Programmes for handicap and children in need were expanded.

During the Sixth Plan (1979-1984), Early Childhood Education Scheme was introduced, the aim of which was to retain children in schools and reduce 'Drop-outs' Also high priority was given to Primary, i.e., Elementary education.

Other Activities for Children

Since Independence, there have been many programmes and activities for children in various parts of the country, both government and privately sponsored. Among these are:

1. *Children's Film Society*

The children's film movement in India first took of in 1951, with the Film Enquiry Committee recommending the production of special films for children. The movement got a fillip when 3 films festivals were held in Delhi between 1952 to 1954. Festivals were arranged in 1953 at Mumbai, Mussorie, Mysore, Nainital and Hyderabad among others.

Due importance was accorded to children's entertainment by the authorities, when they first established the first children's cinema at Delhi in December 1954. The following year Government of India announced its intention to set up a body called "Children's Film Society, India."

A Children's Film Society of India (CFSI) was established in April 1955 and formerly registered. It primary objective was for providing children with clean and healthy entertainment through films, specially produced, distributed and exhibited for their benefit and also with a view to withdrawing them from the undesirable effect of commercial films. The Children's Film Society functions as an autonomous body under the administrative control of the financial support from the Ministry of Information and Broadcasting, Government of India.

A landmark in the history of the children's film movement was the production of its first film *Jaldeep* by the society in 1956. In the same year Chennai established a special theatre for children and called it *Balar Aranga* which in 1981 became the venue of the 2nd International Neo Youth Competitive Film Festival. Between 1960-1973, the Indian Institute of Childrens Films, based at Calcutta organised both national and international film festivals. CFSI has been instrumental in organising several successful film festivals—domestic, international and competitive—between 1973-1985, encouraging the growth of general children's film movement in the country. These festivals and seminars have helped in identifying and recognising the needs and desires of the children in India. In 1981, Dr. V. Shantaram, Chairman of CFSI then, was presented the CIFEJ Jury award for his outstanding contribution to the Children's Film movement in the country.

The Society engages itself in the production of 16 and 35 mm feature films, featurettes and short films in all the major Indian languages. The outdoor shooting of the film is undertaken at locales in various parts of the country. Children are able to enjoy picturesque and natural surroundings. It also helps them to learn, see and get familiarised with rich Indian culture and heritage. Film produced in one language are dubbed in other languages so that children coming from one language zone enjoy them equally. CFSI also makes puppets and animations films, mostly in colour. In addition encourages co-production with foreign and Indian film makers.

Besides this the society generally tries to import award winning films from other countries, and are dubbed in Hindi and other languages, so that children get an idea about children in other countries.

The Society has approximately 243 films in stock which include foreign films, and also 101 feature films and 142 short films, cartoons puppet films and 114 from abroad. The CFSI's mobile van takes films to rural areas and has covered nearly 2 crore children in the country. The children of both urban and rural areas see the best of children's films through the week-long and mini film festivals organised at various places throughout the year. In addition the CFSI films are telecasted on Doordarshan network, hence there is a greater coverage. It also supplies films from 16 mm library to schools, community centres and welfare organisations. It also launched a pilot project of taking mobile film unit into the Adivasi areas of Maharashtra.

The Children's Film Society organises international Children's Film Competitions every two years, generally in November commencing on 14th which is Universal Children's Day and also Pt. Jawaharlal Nehru's birthday, thus encouraging Children's Film movement. This International Children's Film Festival was first held in Mumbai in 1979, second at Chennai in 1981, and the third at Calcutta in 1983 and the fourth in Bangalore.

It has started exporting films to various countries since 1981, which has brought to the country a good foreign exchange to its credit.

It is a Pandora's box of treasure for children, a treasure which would make the children today better and brighter citizens of tomorrow.

2. *Bal Bhavan and National Children's Museum*

Bal Bhavan was established in June, 1956 at a temporary site near Ramlila Grounds. It moved to this present 12.5 acres of centrally located site under the low slung roof of a sprawling building, unique in its architecture on the 15th of October, 1960. About the same time, i.e., during 1956 the idea of Children's Museum, initiated by the Prime Minister began taking place.

To avoid duplication and foster close working of activities of the two institutions, i.e., Bal Bhavan and National Children's Museum, a

Joint Board, namely Bal Bhavan Board was appointed early in 1956 as an autonomous Society under the Ministry of Education, Government of India to govern the affairs of these two institutions.

The memorandum of Association of the Bal Bhavan maintains a theoretical distinction of the purposes of two institutions, namely—

Bal Bhavan established to—"afford opportunities to children for education through recreation and physical activities, and to promote social contacts among children of all classes and communities."

National Children's Museum established to—"operate a suitable programme of training and research in order to promote education of children through visual aid, to provide them with opportunity for expression of creative talents.

However, it was soon seen that this sort of categorical separation of purposes was not right as their inter-relatedness must be considered and both the institutions were located at the same sight and governed by the same board. Therefore, the two institutions were integrated as one institution as of 15th November 1962 under the Directorship of Dr. Prabha Sahasrabudhe. It was resolved that the integrated institution be known as Bal Bhavan and National Children's Museum.

This Institution is essentially a recreational-education centre for children. It is an institution planned and organised:

(i) to provide Delhi children with experience and activities otherwise not available to them,

(ii) to offer certain educational services to the local schools in order to enrich their curricula and extra-curricula activities,

(iii) to provide leadership and guidance to teachers towards fostering a creative approach in teaching of art and science,

(iv) to provide training facilities for recreational workers and children's museum personnel, and

(v) to offer the Nation a prototype comprehensive Children's Institution, i.e., establish an ideal Bal Bhavan.

This is an Institution whose foremost loyalty should and will be for child. It is a purposefully planned environment where the child will be offered experiences (through his participation in institution programmes and activities) to reinforce his knowledge and reason, to cultivate his imagination and sensitivities, to enlarge his capacity for wonder and love, to intensify his comprehension and his feeling of compassion, to support his aspiration and ambition, and to help him in his effort towards establishing his individuality.

Creative and recreational programming for out of school hours, i.e., education to complement what happens in schools must also be responsible for demonstrating what should happen in schools. Such institutions must become active educational centres activating, reactivating, demonstrating, and initiating programmes in different aspects of education. Institutions of this nature must have programmes not only for children but also for teachers, schools, parents involved in their activities as well.

Organisation

Towards this purpose the Institution has been organised in seven departmental sections, each with a well qualified and experienced Incharge Assistant Director at its head. The sections, the activities and the programmes are as follows :

Physical Education: Field games, Athletics, Swimming, Gymnasium, Indoor-Games, Health Education, Physical fitness programme, Camping, Field trips, Excursions.

Art Section: Art Studios—Juniors 6-12, Painting, Claying Collages, Constructive sewing, Creative stichery, Art Aid services for schools, Morning school visit programme, Art exhibition, Field trips.

Craft Section: Art Studios—(13-16 seniors), Crafts: Ceramics, Painting, Oil Painting, Designing, 3 dimensional design and Sculpture, Pottery, Wood work, Leather work, Metal work, Paper Machine. Gallery: Visits and Field trips.

Science Section: Science clubs, Weather club, Plant club, Animal club, Star gazers, Bird watchers, Chemists, Mechanical hobbies—Radio, Auto Mechanics, Electrical trades, Science services to schools, Science exhibitions and exhibits.

Music, Drama, Dance Sections: Dance workshop, Music studios, Drama festivals, Children's theatre, Concerts, Puppet theatre, Costume making, Cultural and National events.

Library-School Section: Children's Library, Reference Library, Story hour, Debating, Recitation, Museum and Bal Bhavan Publicity, Publications, Schools liaison work, Special service for teachers.

National Children's Museum: Collection of material and objects of educational value for children, Museum exhibits on curricula and extra curricular topics, preparation and circulation for exhibits, Display material, Study kits, Field trip portfolios, Science albums, Demonstrations, Recorded songs, etc., etc.

Bal Bhavan Railway: Joy rides for adults and children.

Membership

Membership programmes are open to all the children, between 5 to 16 years age. It can accommodate 500 children in the membership programme in the Institution on daily basis. To prompt contacts among children from different economic strata of society, registration of members is limited in each income group. There is also School membership programme and School Visit plans.

Bal Bhavan

The Bal Bhavan Society in 1994, has a membership of about 25,000 children in Delhi alone, and about 2000 in regional centres. It has introduced and initiated a number of creative and innovative programmes.

Children Theatre

As early as 2000 B.C. Chinese use to have dramatic religious festivals. The art of shadow play had reached a high degree of perfection by 1000 B.C. In Java nobody knows how far back the shadow puppets go, they are thought to be of great antiquity. Formerly it was performed in the family and later shadow plays became professional entertainment.

Japan had dolls theatre for entertainment, string instruments were used and dramas wee enacted by puppets and story chanted by minstrel.

Children's theatre first came from France. In this year 1984 children presented a play in the beautiful theatre set in the midst of a garden in a country estate near Paris. This performance was in the first known theatre for children. Madam de Geules—a musician and actress wrote a whole series of plays for children and these were along with many others, published in 1779-80 in 4 volumes entitled *Le Theatre D'Education.*

Many other authors wrote plays for children in France and England. In 1800 Arnand Berquin published 4 volumes of short plays for "Domestic Recreation and Amusement." In England Maria Edgeworth published a series of little volumes called The *Parents Assistant* in 1800. In U.S.A. in 1921, Clara Tree Major put up plays for boys and girls every Saturday morning also presented series of classics for schools. For the first time school work was formerly correlated with theatre production. In 1938 she toured from coast to coast and had 6 companies. Her plays mainly dominated children's classics.

In India, open air festivals connected with religious worship and these have been cultivated by Hindus for several thousands of years.

Though dancing, music and poetry predominated on such occasions, they were more than often dramatic in character, especially when they celebrated the lives of deities.

According to some authorities India was the birthplace of the puppets. A very old Indian tale gives an account of basketful of wooden dolls presented by the daughter of celebrated machanician to a princess. "One of these could be made to fly through air by pressing a wooden peg, another to dance, another to talk." It is said that large talking puppets were even used on the stage with human actors.

The 20th Century finds children's theatre still to develop in most part of India. The Mumbai Government through its visual education department, has for the past few years been sponsoring a children's theatre when children give variety of programmes and enact small plays specially written for them.

Play competitions are held in Calcutta, Delhi, Chennai and other cities. Schools are slowly becoming aware of the need for this activity in their curricula and are offering opportunities for children plays, rhythms and mimics.

There is evidence that in near future, before the turn of this century, India will be taking steps to train leaders in both children's theatre and creative drama Plans for research in children's plays and stories in the Indian languages and in the folklore of European and Asian countries are being made in order to build up a body of material which can be adapted for both formal and informal drama.

The National School of Drama established its "Theatre-in-Education (TIE) Company" in October 1989 with the belief that it could provide a unique and valuable service for the children of schools in their pursuit of knowledge and development.

Drama is primarily a living experience. *Drama* is doing and 'Educational Drama' is learning by doing. By Drama, what people understand means 'Theatre'. It is essentially an adult activity. While 'Educational Drama' is concerned with child and his/her growth towards a balanced and matured adulthood. Theatre has its own place within Educational Drama to be introduced at the appropriate time and mental maturity.

Main purpose of introducing drama in schools must be educational. It is a way for the education of the heart "which Gandhiji spoke about, for it is a means of stimulating, controlling and expressing the emotions.

As in the infancy of civilisation we find Theatre, so also in the infancy of each person's life we find it. To infuse life and character into many role plays, like *Rama* and *Sita*, are theatrical devices we have instinctively used during childhood. It is nature's in-built method of learning and a meaningful dealing with life, its joys and sorrows.

Therefore, in Theatre-in-Education they are reunited and provide a powerful and a very effective learning medium for all categories of children.

Manuscripts/Writers

Children's Book Trust Initially, there was a lot of difficulty in getting good manuscripts. So, Children's Book Trust (CBT) started a workshop for writers which lasted for more than 3 years, with 60 odd participants (Delhi-based) meeting once a month to assess their writings, engage in writing exercises, and listening to experts in the field. The workshop yielded fairly good manuscripts.

In 1978, the CBT organised its first competition for writers. Over 300 manuscripts were received from all over India. CBT thus became aware of writing talents and was benefited by the best of writing for children. The competition has since been continued as an annual feature, yielding some 10-12 prize winning manuscripts (not only fiction and picture books but non-fiction, biographies, information books, etc.) and revealing greater and increasing interest in children's literature. In 20-22 years CBT has built up a cadre of writers for children.

Similarly, CBT also organised 3 workshops for illustrators, taking into consideration the importance of drawings and designing of children's books. As a result the CBT could establish a full-fledged Art Department and encourage freelance artists by giving them book assignments.

Magazine

In 1968 CBT launched *Children's World* an illustrated magazine for children. Main purpose was to encourage creative talents in children by publishing their contribution (drawings and writings). The magazine in its 20th years of publication has in these 20 years moulded a large number of writers. Nearly 50 per cent of space in devoted to contribution from children. The magazine is published only in English. Special numbers are brought out in April (Annual), August (Independence day), November (Diwali), and January (Republic day).

(Besides the magazine *Children's World* in English, there are today 78 magazines being published for children in India. They are published in 17 languages. There are 22 which are published in Bengali,

19 published in Hindi and 13 in English. Some are only in one language and others in two or more languages. *Champak* magazine is the only one which is printed in 9 languages, while the *Indrajal* comics in 6 languages. These are weekly, fortnightly and monthly).

Other Activities

1. Shankar's International Children's Competition (originally organised by Shankar's Weekly in 1949) was taken over by the CBT in 1962. This competition is now in its 40th year. On an average 150,000 entries are received from nearly 100 countries from children up to 16 years. More than 800 prizes are awarded every year (100 of them for written work). The prize winning entries are published in *Shankar's Children's Art Number* (an annual publication). The prize winners receive complementary copies; and the participants can purchase them at half price.

2. An on-the-spot painting competition is generally conducted in Delhi in February every year. Some 15,000 children participate, and prepare 30,000 entries under the 3 age groups (5-8, 9-12 and 13-16). Some 200 prizes are awarded.

Theatre-in Education (TIE) Company, welcomes physical and vocal participation of the children. They invite children to take on roles, direct action, make decision and solve problems. Main point is that whatever form the plays or workshop take, whether they be for children or by children, they provide to raise questions, to involve and to instruct.

The TIE Company places the children and their development needs at the heart of its work. All concerns are focused on the children and their awareness and understanding of themselves and world around them. It educates a child as a whole person and engages the children physically, mentally, emotionally and even spiritually at times.

Theatre is fun where children are involved and concerned. It motivates children in positive ways, and liberates the children from desk-bound routine into something more exciting, creative, related and relevant to their needs.

Mr. Narry John, Director of TIE, says that the Chinese proverb should become their motto.

I hear : I forget,
I see : I remember,
I do : I understand.

4. *Shankar's Contribution.* Children's Book Trust (CBT) was founded by Mr. K. Shankar Pillai (Shankar), and established as registered body in 1957.

Initial Activity

Through advertisements in the national dailies, the CBT invited manuscripts. A majority of them were found unsuitable for children. Therefore, Mr. Shankar started writing himself, and his first book *The King's Choice* 4 colour book was published in 1961. Pandit Jawaharlal Nehru suggested to him that books should be produced in large numbers, so as to reach several children and should be inexpensive.

Hence, effort were made and chanellised towards putting up a building for the Trust and installing a modern printing press. "Nehru House" and "Indraprastha Press" were formerly opened in 1965 by President Radhakrishnan.

2. *Publications*

Dr. Radhakrishnan also released the 5 books printed at Indraprastha Press. Between 1965 and 1987, CBT brought out 200 original titles in English. Simultaneously some 180 titles in Hindi (including translations from English and a few original titles have also been published. Another 100 books (all of them translations from English) have also come out in Bengali, Urdu, Punjabi, Gujarati, Kannada, Tamil and Malayalam. More than 50 titles have foreign editions as well as versions in foreign languages, like Dutch, German, Russian, Austrian, Japanese, Indonesian, African, Czech, etc., etc.

CBT has a full-fledged Hindi Department to bring out books in Hindi. A panel of translators help the CBT in other languages. The printing is done at Indraprastha Press and the books are distributed by the State Governments.

3. *Dolls Museum*

"Shankar's International Dolls Museum" (inaugurated in 1965 with 1000 dolls from Shankar's personal collection) has more than 6000 costume dolls from about 85 countries. It is the largest collection in the world. The 5000 dolls collected between 1965 and now have mostly come as gifts from various countries, especially at the time of the visit of dignitaries.

To give Indian dolls in exchange, a Doll's workshop attached to the museum was started with 10 artists who make dolls (Indian) in authentic details. The groups attempted are—Man and woman (from each state), Brides of India, Tribes of India, Dances of India etc. Some 150/160 characters (Indian) have by now been fashioned. These have also found their way to several museums all over the world, and have participated in the festivals of India.

4. *Library*

CBT's library for children received an endowment from Dr. B.C. Roy Memorial Trust earmarked for a Library. It is, therefore, called after Dr. B.C. Roy. It has over 30,000 books and periodicals, and has nearly 2000 members who can take books home for a fortnight. The reading room is open on all days. The books are in English, Hindi and all other regional languages. The library has a colour TV to enable members to watch special programmes. A movie projector and a slide projector. 16 mm films are shown on every second Saturday. The library has a play corner for the tiny tots and an aquarium.

5. *Children's Day*

Children's day is celebrated all over the country on the 14th November every year. There are special programmes focussing on children and functions involving dignitaries concerned in different states and Delhi. Special stamp with the first day cover is brought and released.

(Special chapter in details with history is given separately on 'Universal Children's Day).

6. *Changing Concept of 'Child Welfare' in the Government*

Child Welfare as distinct from other aspect of social welfare is an integral part of the Economic Plan. There is a difference in the concept of Social Welfare as applied to Child Welfare on one hand, and applied to adult on the other. Social Welfare for an adult is a part of the expenditure, and for the child it is a part of investment.

Since independence in all the Five Year Plans, unfortunately there was not a single group or body existing or working in a co-ordinated way for the different services of Child Welfare. The services were split up among the various Central Government Ministries, several ministries were dealing with some identical programmes which were operated through the State Governments. Co-ordination was important and necessary and hence a new body called "Co-ordination Committee on Child Welfare" was formulated under a resolution.

Programmes relating to Child Welfare were scattered among Ministries of Community Development and Co-operation, Health, Education and Home Affairs. Therefore, Ministry of Education which was concerned with child welfare programmes was given the administrative responsibility for child welfare and also co-ordination of the activities of other ministries and organisations in connection with child welfare.

Under the umbrella of social welfare, child welfare has gone from ministry to ministry like a ping pong ball till the International Year of Child, when at last a separate Ministry of Social Welfare came into existence, which unfortunately was again split in 1985.

From 1958-1960,	the social welfare was under Ministry of Education.
From 1960-1961,	child welfare was looked after by department of social security which was under the Ministry of Law and Social Security.
From 1961-1964,	child welfare was under the Ministry of Education and was known as the Ministry of Education, Social Welfare and Culture.
From 1964-1966,	it was again handled by the Ministry of Law and Social Security.
From 1966-1969,	it was under the Ministry of Planning and handled by the Department of Social Welfare.
From 1969-1979,	it was handled by the Department of Social Welfare under the Ministry of Education.

In 1979, the Ministry of Social Welfare was established as an independence Ministry composing different units for women, children, handicap, research etc.

In 1985 beginning it was renamed Ministry for Human Resource and Development under a Cabinet Minister. Under this umbrella one State Minister looked after Women, Welfare and Sports, Youth Affairs and Child Development. Under another State Minister was Department of Education and Culture. Then there was Ministry of Welfare under a State Minister who looked after children totally and also the handicap, scheduled caste, scheduled tribe, backward class and welfare of the children.

Today child welfare and child development has gained importance and the government as well as public in general have become conscious and aware of its need and priority in planning for the future of our country.

In 1989—The Ministry of Human Resource and Development was under a Cabinet Minister with State Minister which looked after (i) Youth and Sports, (ii) Culture and Art, (iii) Education. Ministry of Welfare was made independent under a Cabinet Minister with State Minister looking after totally "Women and Children" in every aspect.

Training of Professionals in Social Welfare

There are superb examples of social workers, who have given much to the mankind than they received. But the number of social workers did not keep up with the pace with the growing consciousness of the social problems, India got its independence on the 15th of August, 1947. Constitution was adopted in 1950 and beginning of 1951. Independence ushered a new era in the field of Child Welfare. The Constitution in its Directive Principles of State Policy, made several provisions for Social Welfare and Development of children.

There were no major programmes for children at the Central level during the first few years of Independence in 1947, except those undertaken by some ministries.

The Ministry of Railways provided scholarships to the children of its employees for technical education and vocational training. Assistance to the children of Mica Labour Fund Act 1917, and the Factories Act 1948 provided for setting up 'Creches' for the children of mothers who worked.

With the advent of the era of planning in the country and the establishment of Planning Commission in 1951, child welfare started receiving great attention and the Five Year Plans were formulated. Successive Plans gave special attention to the needs of the children, but unfortunately no child as a whole. There was in those Plans an element of adhocism, hence the impact of the government programme was marginal due to coverage of limited child population. Even though considerable grant-in-aid were given to voluntary organisations, which resulted in expansion of child welfare activities, but they were not evenly distributed all over the country. While child welfare formed a part of the social welfare in the Five Year Plans, programmes having a direct bearing on the total development of the child was cut across sectors of National Development of Education, Health, and Nutrition.

Thus in 1952 Indian Council for Child Welfare (ICCW) was formed. It was the first National Organisation to mobilise voluntary activities in every State in favour of all aspects of children's needs.

In 1953, the Central Social Welfare Board was established. They gave grants to non-government agencies and voluntary organisations all over the country and also directly launched important programmes, for improving lives of children and women.

It was only during the Fifth Five Year Plan (1974-1979) that Child Welfare was given a major thrust in terms of allocations and introduction of new schemes and mere sympathy with the suffering is not enough. Human nature and human problems demand a deep and sympathetic understanding of the needs of the child and grown up individuals, and of social conditions, which produce criminals, prostitutes, slums, epidemics, broken homes, orphans and destitutes and frustrated lives.

The practice of careful preparation of individuals for a life of social services was there from early ancient times, but the form this preparation took was one of apprentices. But the formal education in social work consisting of a course of lectures and opportunities for supervised work, began in India in the form of short courses for training, organised by Social Service League in Mumbai in 1920s. The courses were for young men and women who wanted to offer their voluntary services for social work. There was no training for the paid workers or for the professionals.

Growth of Professional Training

For eleven years between 1936-1947, the Tata Institute was the only school importing professional education in social work. In 1947-1948, the second school was established in Delhi under the auspices of the National Y.W.C.A. of India, Burma and Ceylon with a substantial grant from Foreign Division of Ys of United States and again the founder Director was an American. After nearly two years of experimentation the school in 1949 entered upon a regular 2 years programme imparting training in social work and was affiliated as a graduate school to the University of Delhi for the Master of Arts Degree. It was then merged with the University and became one of its departments under the faculty of Sciences. Following within two years a third school was founded as a part of the University of Baroda and became an independent faculty. Since then more schools at graduate level have come up. There are 179 Universities all over India and they belong to different disciplines. But only 14 Universities offer degree in Master of Social Work (MSW).

Besides professional schools a large number of *ad hoc* institutions and centres have come up recently under the auspices of Government and Voluntary agencies. These institutions offer short term courses in such fields as community development, rural welfare, tribal welfare, social education, Bal Sevika Training Centres, Anganwadi Training, Nursery school training, creches training etc. The growth of such training institutions has been fairly rapid partly because of the increased need of welfare personnel, upon the introduction of Extension Welfare programmes under the Five Year Plans. The multiplicity of training institutions with divergent approaches, with different standards and with varying duration of training.

Problems of social welfare and development have become an integral concern of the process of planning and development at the National, State and Local level, as well as International level. There are 65 Government Organisations, 103 National Voluntary Organisations and 13 International Voluntary Organisations and 27 United Nations Agencies of which 6 are more important from children's point of view.

2

CHILD LEGISLATION

Laws for the Welfare of Nation's Children

Historical Introduction

The early part of the 19th century saw no substantial body of law relating to the liabilities, treatment of welfare of children. Under the common law principle of equality before the law, everyone was liable to ordinary proceedings in the ordinary courts and hence no special provision was made for the children. The principle of criminal liability was expressed in terms of the knowledge of right and wrong. This was applied to children on the basis that a child under the age of 7 could not commit an offence.

The common law principles needed radical change in the light of the social conditions following the Industrial Revolution. There was an increase in young offenders and children going wayward who needed to be dealt with institutions distinct and separate from ordinary courts.

In India the apprentice act passed in 1850 sought to provide for better treatment of children between 10 to 18 years of age. Then came the Reformatory Schools Act 1876 and modified in 1897, which provided special courts which could order 3-7 years detention and training instead of punishment.

The first move to enact a Children's Act came from the Indian Jails Committee (1919-1920) which recommended special treatment for young offenders to reform and rehabilitate them. The Children's Act in various states in the 20's were a sequel to the committees recommendations. These acts were enacted to provide for:

1. Custody, trial, maintenance, welfare, education and punishment of young offenders.
2. For protection of children and young persons who are neglected destitutes or moral danger or in need of protection.

First came the Children's Act of Madras in 1920, then in Bengal in 1922, followed by Bombay in 1924. Legislation was passed in other States to provide for separate procedure and institutions for the trial, custody, correction and rehabilitation of delinquent children. The trend continued and although there were some variations in the legislation enacted by different states, they were basically welfare oriented and recognised the importance of understanding the situation of the child. Each subsequent amendment attempted to provide a more effective set of procedures and institutions to help in the rehabilitation of the child.

Study of the statutes in the country would reveal that only a few laws relating to children were enacted before independence. Moreover, Indian Legislation before independence was largely based on the Legislative practices and trends in U.K. The Government of India's commitment to welfare, it enacted in the Post-Independence period, many social legislation unprecedented in its long history. These laws derive their legitimacy and strength from the Indian Constitution, the International Labour Organisation (ILO) conventions and recommendations, also from the Declaration of the Rights of Child adopted by the General Assembly of United Nations, and the resolution adopted by Government of India on National Policy for Children.

The Indian Parliament and State Legislature have been very generous in enacting social legislations. It began with the enactment of the Hindu Adoption and Maintenance Act 1956. In 1960 Government of India enacted the Children's Act which though applicable to Union Territories, has been conceived as a model piece of Legislation. The provision of Central Children's Act 1960 as amended in 1978 should be incorporated in the Children's Acts.

According to the Act the competent Authority will be:

(1) Children's Homes,
(2) Special Schools,
(3) Observation Homes, and
(4) After Care Organisations. He has authority to establish more than one, as the need may be, in different areas.

The Juvenile Justice Act 1986

The Act provides for the care, protection, treatment, development and rehabilitation of neglected or delinquent juveniles and for the adjudication of certain matters relating to, and disposition of delinquent juveniles.

According to the Act the State Government:

1. May Constitute one or more Juvenile Welfare Board.
2. May constitute one or more Juvenile Court.
3. May establish Juvenile Homes.
4. May establish and maintain Special Homes.
5. May establish Observation Homes.
6. May establish After Care Organisations.
7. State Government may create a Fund for the welfare and rehabilitation of the Juveniles.
8. May constitute an Advisory Board.
9. May appoint Probation officers for inspection of Homes.

The date on which this act comes into force in any state, and if there is any Act corresponding to this Act, that law stands repealed. Except that repeal will not effect any investigation, legal proceedings or remedy may be instituted, continued or enforced and any such penalty, or punishment may be imposed, as if this Act has not been passed.

Adoption

Article 44 of the Constitution of India provides that the State shall endeavour to secure for its citizens a *uniform code* throughout the country. Yet there is no Uniform Civil Law on adoption, to help thousands of children who are orphaned, destitute or born out of wed-lock to have a home or family, so that it will have a home, name, rights, and a feeling of belonging.

The Guardianship and Wards Act 1890 is out dated and yet the communities in India and Adoptive parents (excepting Hindus) have to depend on it. It does not bestow on the child the right and status of son/ daughter, legal or natural.

A Nation have reached the importance and necessity of full development of children in recent years. Programmes and services have been organised for children in India as in other countries which have strengthened the welfare of children and improved their status. But the objectives cannot be fully achieved without appropriate and effective legislative framework. Therefore, laws are equally important and necessary for children's development and welfare along with children's programmes and services.

The Constitution of India, realising the requirement, embodied many provisions having a bearing on the welfare of nations children. According to the Constitutional provisions, there are about 250 Central and State enactments pertaining to children on the statute books. These enactments cover diverse facets of a child's life, such as legitimacy, guardianship, maintenance, welfare, reformation social defence, education and health etc.

Besides this the Government of India also adopted a national policy for children in 1974, which consider nation's children as a supremely important asset and their nature and solicitude nations prime responsibility.

In spite of this the community by and large is not fully aware of the existing legislative and their implications. The laws are neither taken seriously nor enforced or implemented by the State machinery. They are violated and circumscribed by the concerned people with implicity. Besides these have many structural loopholes and other important areas not covered adequately.

Child development and welfare is an important social objective and it refers to taking care of all aspects related to child care. Law is one of the important means to achieve this goal. Unfortunately at present, there is no uniformity of laws regulating and controlling different facets related to child. In some cases it is the personal law that governs in others it is the secular law. There diversity and interaction raises problems which hamper achievement of this objective.

A uniform policy covering all spheres of child development is required. Religious laws should be replaced by a uniform legislation on children. Laws related to children should aim at giving every child on an environment which is most conducive to their welfare and balanced development.

The responsibilities of the State towards children are ensured in our Constitution. Only a few laws relating to children were enacted before Independence. Consonant with its commitment to welfare, the Government of India enacted in the Post-Independence period, a plethora of social legislation unprecedented in its long history. These laws derive their legitimacy and strength from the Indian Constitution, the International Labour Organisation (ILO) convictions and recommendations as also from the declaration of the Rights of the Child adopted by the Central Assembly of United Nations and the Resolution adopted by Government of India on National Policy for Children.

While many legislations have been enacted to protect, promote and safeguard the interests of children, their implementation leaves much to be done.

SPECIFIC LEGISLATION

1. Child Marriage Restraint Act 1929

This Act is popularly known as the Sharda Act. The Act is applicable to all communities and all persons living in India except the State of Jammu and Kashmir. The Act, only restrains the people from performing child marriage and to make the restraint effective. It imposes some penalties on persons bringing about such marriages as a "Child" as defined in the Sharda Act is a boy below age 18 and a girl below the age of 15 years. The Sharda Act was drastically amended in March 1978 and the changes came out with force on 2nd October, 1978. Thus the Age of Male was raised to 21 and that of a Female to 18 years.

Definitions

In this Act—

(a) "Child" means a person, who, if a male has not completed 21 years of age, and if a female, has not completed 18 years of age;
(b) "Child marriage" means a marriage to which either of the contracting parties is a child;
(c) "Contracting party to a marriage" means either of the parties whose marriage is thereby solemnised; and
(d) "Minor" means a person of either sex who is under 18 years of age.

Punishment

(a) There is punishment for male adult below 21 years of age marrying with simple imprisonment which may extend to 15 days, or fine which may extend to one thousand rupees or both;
(b) Punishment for male adult above 21 years of age, marrying a child, shall be punishable with simple imprisonment which may extend to 3 months and shall be liable to fine;
(c) Punishment for whoever performs, conducts or directs any child marriage shall be punishable with simple imprisonment which may extend to 3 months and shall also be liable to fine unless he proves that he had reasons to believe that the marriage was not child marriage; and

(d) Punishment for Parents or Guardian concerned or connected with a child marriage where a minor contracts child marriage any person haviny charge of the minor whether parents or guardian or in any capacity lawful or unlawful and fails to prove it will be punished with imprisonment, fine. Provided no woman shall be punishable with imprisonment.

2. Legitimacy of Children of Void and Voidable Marriages

Law of Legitimacy

The Indian Evidence Act, 1872, is the general law in this respect. Section 112 of the Evidence Act provides a presumption of legitimacy of a child born during continuation of a valid marriage between its parents or within 280 days after its dissolution.

The mother remaining unmarried, unless it can be proved that the husband had no access to the wife at any time when the child would have been conceived. For application of the Evidence Act it is necessary that the child was born during marriage or within 280 days of its dissolution and the mother remaining unmarried.

Such marriages must be valid marriage.

This does not apply to child born of an invalid marriage. Moreover, it does not deal with the children of invalid or void marriage, it is to be determined by reference to its personal law.

(i) Any child born or conceived before the degree of nullifying is granted under Section 11 or Section 12 of the Marriage and Divorce Act, would be considered to be a legitimate child, of the parents as if the marriage has been dissolved. But such a child can inherit the property of parents only;

(ii) Children born of void marriages are illegitimate. The Hindu Marriage Act, and the Special Marriage Act are exceptions and declare children born of void or voidable marriage to be legitimate though giving limited inheritance rights to children who would have been illegitimate but for the passing of the Act;

(iii) Illegitimate child do not have inheritance rights but are entitled to be maintained; and

(iv) No law provides for legitimation, i.e., confirms restrospective legitimation to a child born prior to the marriage of its parents.

3. The Hindu Widow's Remarriage Act 1956

The Hindu Widow's Remarriage Act 1956 is hereby repealed, enacted by the Parliament in the 34th year of the Republic of India. This Act was repealed and may be called as the Hindu Widow's Remarriage (Repeal) Act, 1983. This Act protects her rights and removes obstacles.

Effects of Repeal of the Act

(i) Right of matter of guardianship of the Child by first marriage is not lost because of remarriage;
(ii) Where a mother is appointed a guardian under the Guardian and Wards Act, there is nothing in Hindu Law, to remove mother from guardianship of her infant child merely because she is remarried;
(iii) Widow Remarriage under Customary Law, Right of Guardianship of her children is not forfeited;
(iv) A Hindu widow after remarriage cannot claim to have right to give her son by first marriage in adoption;
(v) Her rights which she had from before are not taken away under this or any other Act;
(vi) If the widow remarrying is a minor, whose marriage has not been consummated, she shall not marry without the consent of her father or next paternal male relations; and
(vii) If the widow is of full age or whose marriage has been consummated, her own consent shall be sufficient consent to constitute her remarriage lawful and valid.

4. Posthumus Child

Under the Hindu Succession Act 1956, the right to the property arises from the date of conception and when the child who is in the womb of the mother at the time of death of her husband and is born alive, shall have the right to inherit, as if she/he had been actually born.

Law of Adoption

Article 521 and 35 refers to Adoption of Children

Adoption and informal foster-care are part of age-old, tradition in India. From ancient times the practice of Adoption of a child by childless

Hindu couples has been carried out with rituals and ceremonies whereby the entire community is made aware of the irrevocable legal status of the child. Like in all patriarchal societies the emphasis was on adoption of a male child to continue the family lineage and do the religious duties, but adoption of girls was also prevalent. However, adoption was parent-centred to fulfil the needs of the parent rather than child-centred.

Adoption played a very different role in Ancient civilisations as in Babylon, China and Romans. There its primary function was to censure the continuity of the family. The concept of the welfare of the child is a new phenomenon.

Adoption was not unknown in Ancient India. The traditional law was laid down by the "Smritikaras" as modified by customs and usage and as interpreted and applied by judicial decisions. However, the law was varied and uncertain according to the different schools exercising their influence in different parts of the country.

The Traditional Law

1. Authorised a Hindu father without a son to adopt a male child.
2. It did not permit a widow to adopt a son unless authorised by the deceased husband.
3. Adoptee must belong to the same caste as the adoptive father.
4. An orphan (unless custom permitted) an illegitimate boy or a deaf could not be adopted.
5. The natural father could give his son in adoption without his wife's consent.
6. There was no uniformity regarding age and the Bombay school permitted adoption even of a married man by a younger man.

To remove these uncertainties and to resolve the conflicting judicial dicta that the Hindu Adoption and Maintenance was passed in 1956.

Hindu Adoption and Maintenance Act 1956

This Act not only sought to codify the laws relating to its subject matter but also altered the existing law to a great extent. This Act applies only to "Hindu" as defined under the Act, thus embracing only the Buddhists, Jains, Sikhs and other reformist sects.

This Act has given a uniform code on this subject of adoption for the whole of India. The Act came into operation with effect from December 21, 1956.

Essential Clauses:

1. Only the parents or gaurdians can give a child in adoption.
2. The person adopting must have the right to take and be lawfully capable of taking a son or daughter in adoption.
3. Adoption by a person of unsound mind is no adoption at all.
4. It must be done with the consent of his wife, unless she is dead or is no more a Hindu.
5. A female Hindu can adopt, in her own rights provided that she is not married, or a widow, or a divorcee, or her husband has ceased to be a Hindu.
6. In case of abondoned children or where parentage is not known, the guardian can give the child with the permission of the court.
7. The person adopted must be lawfully capable of taken in adoption. A minor who is a Hindu and has not completed age of 15 years may be adopted.
8. The condition relating to adoption include actual giving and taking of child with the intention of transferring the child to the family of its adoption must be complied with.
9. If the adoption is of a son, then the adoptive father or mother must not have a Hindu son, grand-son, or great grandson living at the time of adoption.
   (a) If the adoption is of a daughter, the adoptive father or mother must not have a Hindu daughter or a son's daughter at the time of adoption;
   (b) If the adoption is to be made by a Hindu of a minor female then the adoptive should be atleast 21 years older than the minor female child;
   (c) If the adoption is to be made by a female Hindu of a minor male child, then the adoptive mother should be atleast 21 years older than the person to be adopted;
   (d) The child cannot be adopted simultaneously by 2 or more persons; and
   (e) The child must be taken and given in adoption.

The effect of adoption is that an adopted child shall be deemed to be the child of his or her adoptive father or mother for all purposes with effect from the date of adoption, and all the ties of the child of natural parents or guardian shall be deemed to have been severed and replaced by those created by the adoption in the adoptive family. An adoption does not deprive the adoptive parents of the power to dispose of his or her property by transfer or by will.

Muslim: Adoption is regulated by custom, there is no Koranic law to that effect. In fact, the *Holy Koran* decrees service of the orphans to be the best service. Adoption is certainly not an anthema in Islam. However, a *tobanni* (Arabic equivalent to Adoption) cannot under the Islamic law suppressed or abrogate the claims of kith and kin as prescribed by *Holy Koran*, i.e., an adopted child cannot legally have share in the ancestral property and inheritance of his adoptive parents. Though he may be given under a valid deed a gift or will, out of one's personal earnings, but there it is evident that Islam does not prohibit adoption. Only implication is that an adoptive child cannot be recognised as the biological child. The adopted child is entitled to love, affection, home, security and every consideration within the ambit of Shariat.

Among the Muslim countries there was a system of Adoption known as *Motabanna*. The adopted child who is a *Motabanna* of the adopted was treated as a son and brought up as a son and might even be left a will of 1/3 or even 1/2 of the property in the life time of his parents. He did not inherit through his adoptive parents, but through his natural parents. Hence did not say there can be no adoption. There are no fundamental laws regarding adoption in Islam. Though the Islamic rules very clearly allow adoption, even on oral commitments made before two respectable persons and does not require a written will. But such child may not be accepted by Muslim society after the death of parents. Islamic rules do not permit an unwanted or abandoned child in the society.

Parsees: They do not recognise Adoption. However, a widow of a Parsee dying issueless can adopt a *Palak* on the 4th day of her husband's death, for the *ad hoc* purpose of performing certain religious rites for the deceased soul. This being a temporary adoption, it does not confer any proprietary rights on the *Palak*. The Parsees believe that a person not born a Parsee can never become a Parsee.

Christians: They do not have any adoption laws of their own. When a child is taken, he has to be converted into a Christian. Personal Law in cases of intestacy the wife gets 1/2 portion of man's estate and the remaining was equally divided among children, except in cases of Travancore and Cochin districts, as they followed Church Law known as Common Law. In short, the church looked on adoption as a natural phenomenon and the prevailing Christian Personal laws of inheritance and intestacy had no religious basis.

When India gained Independence in 1947, it was decided that all matters pertaining to family life would continue to be governed by the personal laws of each religion. The customary practice among Hindus was codified and incorporated into the Hindu Maintenance and Adoption Act in 1956. All others who wished to take a child into their family could do so only on guardianship under the *Guardian and Wards Act 1890.*

The Guardian and Wards Act, 1890

In oldern times the property of minor was protected by the State. The ancient text of Hindu Law did not provide for the management of the property of the minor beyond stating that Guardianship was vested in the Kings. Before this Act came into force, the laws on this subject were not uniform and there were those passed mostly by the Bombay, Madras, and Bengal Presidencies. In the 19th Century, four such legislations were passed, both with passage of time, it was found necessary to consolidate and amend them. Thus the *Guardianship and the Wards Act 1890* came into being receiving assent of the Governor General on 21st March, 1890. This Act mentions two kinds of Guardians—(1) Guardianship of the Minor, (2) Guardianship of the property of the minor. The Act mainly deals with the appointment of the Guardians of the both the purposes, and secondly their rights, duties and liabilities. It is applicable to all members of all religions, castes and communities. This Act does not take away the rights of a person belonging to other religions as long as the personal laws or statutory law governing those religions provide what has been stated in the Act. If any laws personal or statutory are silent on any issue, the Guardian and Wards Act will be applicable to them. Section 7, gives the court the power to appoint or declare a person as the guardian or the person and/or property of the minor for his welfare.

The adoptive parents and other communities (except Hindus) have to depend on it, in the absence of Adoption Law in the country. Unfortunately, it does not bestow on the child the right of son/daughter, or gives it any status legal or natural.

As mentioned above the Guardians Act provides that a person may be appointed Guardian in relation to a minor for its welfare. In doing so the court has to consider matters like age, religion, sex of the child, capacity and character of the proposed guardian, nearness in relation, relationship between the two, deceased parents' wishes if any, and child's own preferences, if capable of forming any.

1. A Guardian cannot be appointed for a minor married girl, whose husband is fit and capable of being her guardian.
2. A minor whose father is alive and is fit to be the guardian in the opinion of the court. Mother gets preference over the father in case of illegitimate children.
3. A minor whose property is under the superintendence of the Court of Wards is competent to appoint a guardian.
4. Guardian did vested with the custody of their wards, though personal laws of Hindus and Muslims vest primarily with the mother with a custody of infant.

Guardianship ceases on:

1. Death, discharge or removal of Guardian;
2. Attainment of majority of the minor;
3. Marriage in case of minor girls;
4. Assumption of superintendence over the ward by Court of Wards. Under the Guardians Act, question of custody of the child is directly linked with guardianship. It is necessary to be the Guardian in order to secure custody of the minor child.

Guardian of the property has to look after it carefully as a prudent man would deal with it. He cannot sell or mortgage it or transfer minor's property without the permission of the court. The court will give permission either due to necessity or evident advantage to the ward.

The Guardians Act has another advantage. If any person except Hindus wants to provide care to children other than one's own one has to take resort to the Guardian and Wards Act, as there is no other Adoption law available to persons belonging to other communities other than Hindus.

In 1967, 1972, 1978, 1980 attempts have been made to introduce a Uniform Adoption Bill in Parliament, which would enable persons of all religious backgrounds to take a child in Adoption. The Bills have failed due to the opposition from certain minority religious sections who claim adoption is not permitted in their religion.

The late 50's and the 60's saw the advent of intercountry adoption in India. With less adopted children in the West and better communication through the international media bringing the needs of children in distress to their notice, individual and organisations started coming in search of Indian children. The '70s saw an increased number of Indian children being taken abroad. The Ministry of Welfare has been emphasising on promoting in-country adoptions so that as far as possible, the children can grow up in their own social, cultural and ethnic milieu. Inter-country adoptions are to be resorted to only when all avenues for in-country adoptions have been exhausted.

Inter-country adoption is regulated by the guidelines issued by the Ministry of Welfare in pursuance of the directions given by the Supreme Court. These guidelines lay down the conditions for recognition of voluntary organisations, role of Central and State Governments and the procedure to be followed. The Ministry of Welfare grants recognition to both Indian and foreign agencies which are engaged in sponsoring children for adoption abroad. There are at present (1994) 55 Indian Voluntary agencies and 273 foreign agencies which have been recognised. During 1993, 1,382 children were adopted in the country and 1,134 were sponsored for inter-country adoption.

Note on Supreme Court Judgement

The Supreme Court banned inter-country adoption by individuals and private agencies, and directed Government of India to authorise competent agencies in India and abroad to co-ordinate in the placement of Indian children abroad. It also identified scrutinising agencies to assist the court in adjudicating inter-country adoption cases and Voluntary Co-ordinating Agencies (VCA) to ensure that sufficient opportunity is given to every child to find a home within India. It also gave directions for formulation of a Central Adoption Resource Agency (CARA) to act as a National Co-ordinating Body for Inter-Country Adoption.

Note on Government of India Revised Guidelines

This imposes obligations on State Governments to issue special license to do in-country adoption.

Norms and Guidelines Presently to be followed while Placing an Indian Child within India or Outside India

Placement agencies are required to adhere to the following order of *priority* while considering the adoption of Indian children :

1. Indian families in India
2. Indian families abroad

3. One parent of Indian origin abroad
4. Foreign parents.

Recognised Indian Placement Agency

An agency which has initially received licence to do adoption may apply to Government of India and obtain a special recognition to do inter-country adoption. Such an agency must be a reputed one engaged in other child welfare activities apart from adoption work. It must have other sources of finances and not be solely dependent on income from adoption services for the survival.

Foreign Sponsoring Agency

These are foreign adoption agencies that have received recognition to co-ordinate adoption of Indian children in their respective countries. Their main function is to identify prospective adoptive parents in their country. The foreign sponsoring agency also acts as co-ordinator between foreign parents and the recognised Indian placement agency. It also gives an undertaking to the Indian court

— that law in their country would enable the parents to adopt a child.
— that they would do the adoption follow up and send periodic report to court.
— in the event of any disruption in the adoption, it will take charge of the minor, place the child with another suitable family or arrange for the safe return of the child to India.

Scrutinising Agency

Whenever a petition is filed in the court by a foreigner for adoption of an Indian Child the concerned court must send all the papers to the Scrutinising Agency for its report. It is the job of a Scrutinising Agency to verify that all the norms and guidelines laid down are adhered to and the child is legally free for adoption and the agencies involved are duly licensed to do the job. Based on the report they would pass an order placing foreign adopting parents as the legal guardians for the child with a direction, that parents must legally adopt the child within 2 years as per the laws of their country.

Central Adoption Resource Agency (CARA)

In pursuance of the Supreme Court directive CARA was set up on June 26, 1990 under the Ministry of Welfare, Government of India.

CARA maintains liaison with Indian Diplomatic Missions abroad to safeguard the interest of children of Indian origin adopted by and for foreign parents.

— Monitors the functions of all agencies in adoption
— Issues "No objection certificate" for every foreign placement after verification
— Acts as clearing house of information about children available for adoption.

Government of India issued certain guidelines vide Ministry of Welfare Resolution dated 4th July, 1989. In the light of experience gained in the implementation of the guidelines issued in 1989, it was felt necessary to revise guidelines previously issued. Accordingly a Task Force consisting of cross-section of representatives of agencies involved in adoption under the chairman was constituted on 12th August, 1992. The Task Force submitted its report on 28th August, 1993, Government of India examined the report of the Task Force in consultation with the Department of Legal Affairs.

One of the recommendations relates to change in the status of CARA from a wing of Ministry of Welfare to an 'Autonomous body' to be registered under the Registration of Societies Act.

There are 18 functions of CARA and there is a Procedure to be followed. At every end of quarter the placement agency should provide information on the number of children given in inter-country adoption and the number given in inter-country adoption and the number awaiting adoption to CARA. The decision of CARA is final.

Voluntary Co-ordinating Agency (VCA)

It is an association of all licensed agencies in a particular region and is recognised by the Government of India. Such agencies are created in pursuance of the Supreme Court decision. The main purpose of this agency is to ensure that Indian children get sufficient opportunity to find suitable placement within India.

It is mandatory for the Agency to register the child with VCA. If the VCA is unable to find a suitable Indian family within 60 days, it would issue a *clearance certificate* stating it is unable to find a suitable Indian family and such a certificate is essential for foreign placement of the child. There will be a VCA in every State or even in one city where there are many placement agencies. Every VCA has 9 functions and each VCA must be registered. After getting the information, it is forwarded to CARA by the placement agency and clearance from VCA. Then it is sent to the competent Court.

Anomalies and Inconsistencies in Adoption Laws

The need for a uniform Adoption Law applicable to all persons irrespective of their religious backgrounds under which every child who is permanently placed with a family will have the irrevocable legal status of a natural born child, is acutely felt by all concerned. The restriction that only one child of each sex is permitted needs to be removed, and to create awareness and social acceptance of adoption of unrelated children. Although there is an increase in number of parents desirous of taking a child in adoption in certain urban areas, there are still vast areas in the country where this awareness has yet to be created.

When India gained Independence in 1947 it was decided that all matters pertaining to family life would continue to be governed by the personal laws of each religion. The customary practice among Hindus was codified and incorporated into the Hindu maintenance and Adoption Act of 1956. All others who wished to take the child into their family could do so and others under the Guardian and Wards Act 1890.

Labour Laws

The United Nations Declaration says:

The child shall be protected against all forms of neglect, cruelty and exploitation.

He shall not be the subject of traffic, in any form. The child shall not be admitted to employment before an appropriate minimum age; he shall on no case be caused or permitted to engage in any occupation or employment which would prejudice his health or education or interfere with his physical, mental or moral development. There are number of ILO conventions and recommendations dealing with child labour. India is a party to a number of these conventions (though not all). Some of the conventions have special provisions for countries like India.

The Indian Constitution has laid down the special objective of protection of children from unsuitable employment and moral material abandonment, so that their tender age is not abused. A number of enactments regulate the employment of children between 12 to 18 years of age. Apart from prescribing the minimum age of employment in specified occupations, these Acts restrict the hours of work, stipulate rest periods and leave with wages, prohibit night employment require a certificate of physical fitness.

Child labour policies in India have undoubtedly been influenced by some of the conventions with respect to minimum age and night work adopted by the International Labour Organisation (ILO). It must be noted generally that the existing legal provisions still do not cover a large number of children engaged in unorganised sections and unregulated employment such as domestic service, public recreations, street hawking etc.

1. **The Children (Pledging of Labour) Act 1933**
   (Amended by Act No. 3 of 1951 and A.O. 1950)

Under this Act any person employing or making agreement with parents or organisation for child's labour will be punished. Parents or Guardians who give a pledge or make an agreement for children's services in return for payment or any benefit in return are liable for a fine of Rs. 50. The employer who makes the agreement with parents or guardians for child's labour will be fined Rs. 200.

2. **The Employment of Children Act 1938**

   (i) It prohibits employment of children under 15 years in occupations connected with transport of passengers, goods or mails by Railways; or connected with the Port authority within the limit of any port. This Act has no provision for maximum hours of work.

   (ii) Children below 14 years cannot be employed for—Cement manufacture including packing, Mica cutting, and splitting, soap and shellac manufacturing, wool cleaning, manufacturing of matches, explosives and firework, tanning, workshop connected with carpets, weaving and cloth printing, and dyeing.

The Child Labour Prohibition and Regulation Act 1986 regulated employment of children as per Constitutional provision.

3. The Minimum Wages Act 1948

It provides for the fixation of :

(a) A minimum time rate of wages;
(b) A minimum piece rate wages;
(c) A guaranteed time-rate wages, and
(d) An overtime wages, for the different occupations, localities, of classes of work for adults, adolescents, children and apprentices. They permit children above 12 years age for maximum 6 hours a day, and the minimum wage for an unskilled worker has been fixed at Rs. 300 per month.

4. The Factory's Act 1948

It prohibits the employment of children up to the age of 14 years. It extends and applicable to whole of India, and is applicable to establishments employing 10 or more workers with power or 20 or more workers without power. The Act prohibits the employment of child or an adolescent (those between ages 15 to 18) unless he is certified by an authorised surgeon as to his physical fitness for work. The fitness certificate is valid for a year only. Moreover children are not allowed to work for more than 4-1/2 hours on any day.

5. The Plantation Act 1951

It covers all tea, coffee, rubber, cinchona and cardamom plantations, and measuring 10.17 hectares or more in which 30 or more persons are employed. The minimum age of employment is 12 years. Adolescents between ages 15 to 18 are employed on the same basis as provided under the Factories Act 1948. The maximum hours of prescribed are 40 hours a week.

6. The Mines Act 1952

This is an all India Act. It covers all workers working in mines both underground and on surface. No person below the age of 15 is permitted to work on the surface, and a person must have completed age of 16 years and in addition a fitness certificate given by an authorised surgeon is essential. Even at this age the maximum hours of work allowed are 4-½ hours per day.

7. The Merchant Shipping Act 1958

Applies to ships registered in India and provides that the employment of children below the age of 15 years with certain exemptions is prohibited. Also persons below 18 years cannot be employed as trimmers and stokers.

8. Motor Transport Workers Act 1961

This applies to whole of India. It covers every motor transport undertaking employing 5 or more transport workers. The State Governments are, however, empowered to apply all or any of the provisions of this Act to any motor transport undertakings employing less than 5 workers. The Act prohibits the employment of children below 15 years of age in any capacity in the motor transport undertakings. Employment of those between 15 to 18 is regulated on the same lines as provided under the Factories Act 1948. The Maximum hours of work prescribed are six hours.

9. The Apprentice Act 1961

This Act says that no person under the age of 14 years would be given training unless he has such standard of education or physical fitness as may be prescribed.

10. Beedi and Cigar Workers—Conditions of Employment Act 1966

In this minimum age fixed for employment of children is 14 years for any work in any industrial premises.

11. Radiation Protection Rules 1971 framed under Atomic Energy Act 1972

This covers all workers, working at places where radiation takes place. All factories/mines producing atomic/other minerals or such other products, eminating radiation. Children below the age of 18 years are prohibited, except in circumstances when they are permitted by competent authority to work at places where mean radiation sources are utilised.

12. Bonded Labour

The Indian Parliament had enacted a Law by the name—The Bonded Labour System (Abolition) Act 1976, by banishing all kinds of bondage in the country. The highest number is Agricultural bonded labourers. 25 per cent of the bonded labourers belong to the group below 20 years old. This shows that child and youth bondage has taken roots in the Indian Rural Society.

13. The Shops and Establishment Acts (State Acts)

These Acts prohibit children under twelve in all states (exception Andhra Pradesh where the minimum age is 14 years) to work in shops and commercial establishments in various states, specially between 7 p.m. and 6 a.m. part of the day, and the maximum hours of work during the day varies from 5-7 hours.

14. Unorganised Sectors

Legal measures have proved inadequate to eliminate the evil of child labour particularly in the unorganised industries and rural vocations. Even though laws are enacted, implementation is difficult due to scattered nature of employment.

The Children (Amendment) Act, 1978 (No. 15 of 1978)

This was an Act to amend the Children Act, 1960. It was enacted by Parliament in the 29th Year of the Republic of India. In 1960, the Government of India enacted the Children Act 1960 (No. 60 of 1960) on 26th December 1960, enacted by Parliament in the 11th Year of the Republic of India. It was to provide for the care, protection, maintenance, welfare, training, education and rehabilitation of neglected or delinquent children and for the trial of delinquent children in the Union Territories. It was also intended as a model of legislation to be followed by other states.

This 1960 Children's Act was amended in 1978, to make it more effective and meet the requirements of delinquent and neglected children, allowed flexibility in the use of institutions for the neglect and delinquent children and made available. Aftercare services, when the children leave the Children Homes and Special schools.

Only 17 states have enacted Children Act, of which two states have still to enforce legislation. Bihar promulgated Children Act in 1979. Moreover the Children's Act has still to be enforced in 6 Union Territories. While Nagaland, Orissa, Sikkim and Tripura still do not have any legislation.

Suppression of Immoral Traffic in Women and Girls Act 1956

Young girls in danger of exploitation are protected under the Children's Act, as well as this Act. Some of the State Acts provide punishment for those who induce the children to lead an immoral life or who behave immorally with girls. This Act was amended in 1986 and called "The Suppression of Immoral Traffic in Women and Girls (Amendment) Act 1986."

Prevention of Vagrancy and Beggary Acts

A child who is found begging is defined as a neglected child. There are various State Acts to prevent the evil of vagrancy and beggary among persons, including children.

Children, Students and Youth (Rights and Welfare) Bill 1975

The Bill envisages the setting up of a Board called Youth Rights and Welfare Board by the Central Government. The duties of the Board are to safeguard the rights of the children, students and youth and to look after their welfare.

Education

All the States have Compulsory Primary Education Acts, except Manipur, Nagaland and Tripura. Among the Union Territories Andaman and Nicobar Islands, Chandigarh and Delhi have such legislations. Other 6 have still to enact legislation for compulsory education.

Young Persons (Harmful Publications) Act 1956

This is a Central Act, aimed to prevent the dissemination of certain publications considered harmful to young persons. A "harmful" publication relates to stories and publication of such material portraying the commission of offences or Acts of violence or cruelty or incidents of repulsive or horrible nature (which may incite or encourage the committing of offences or Acts of Violence or Cruelty). A "young" person means a person under 20 years of age, under this Act.

Health

Vaccination Act 1880: This was an act to give powers to prohibit inoculation and to make the vaccination of children compulsory in certain Municipalities and Cantonments. But this does not apply today as "Small Pox" has now been totally eradicated from the country, hence no compulsory vaccination.

Whooping Cough Bill 1976

The Bill was introduced in April 1976, to provide for the prevention and eradication of whooping cough for India. There is no central act on this subject, but the Bill never materialised into an Act.

Prevention of Smoking (Acts)

There exist legislative measures in various States to prevent children from smoking and also punish those who encourage others to smoke. (But not aware of definite state legislation preventing children from smoking).

Maintenance

All children in India are entitled to maintenance either under the Criminal Procedure Code or their Personal Laws. Section 125 of the Criminal Procedure Code provides, *inter alia*, that if any person having sufficient means, refuses or neglects to maintain his legitimate or illegitimate minor children, who are unable to maintain themselves, can be ordered to maintain them. The maximum amount payable is limited to Rs. 500 per month under it. Personal Statutory Laws relating to marriage and divorce provide for maintenance of legitimate children whose parents seek a matrimonial relief under the enactment. No illegitimate child can claim maintenance under Personal Laws of Parsees, Christians and Muslims, excepting obligation of mother of an illegitimate child under Hanafi School of Muslim Law. Hindus have an additional remedy, both for legitimate and illegitimate children in terms of the Hindu Adoption and Maintenance Act.

Constitutional Provisions

The State of India is committed to provide for the welfare of children. This commitment arises from certain Constitutional provisions.

India is a welfare state and the philosophy of the welfare state is very much reflected in the 'Directive Principles of State Policy of the Constitution' Accordingly, a few articles specifically provide for the protection and welfare of children.

Article 15(3), enables the state to make special provisions for women and children.

Article 24 provides: "No child below age of 14 years shall be employed to work in any factory or mine or employed in any hazardous employment."

Article 39—Clause (e) and (f) provides: "The health and strength of workers, men and women, and the tender age of children are not abused and that citizens are not forced by economic necessity to enter vacations unsuited to their age or strength" and that "children are given opportunities and facilities to develop in a healthy manner and in conditions of freedom and dignity and that childhood and youth are protected against exploitation and against moral and material abandonment."

The Indian Laws mainly deal with four matters:

1. Minimum age of children,
2. Medical examination of children,
3. Maximum hours of work,
4. Prohibition of night work of children.

Article 45 provides: "The state shall endeavour to provide within a period of 10 years from the commencement of the Constitution for free and compulsory education for all children until they complete the age of 14 years."

Article 44 relates to Uniform Civil Code throughout the territory of India. This directive has stood in the Constitution for years now without any success towards a Uniform Civil Code, though there is a great need of it.

Article 23 lays down that Traffic in human beings and beggars and other forms of forced labour are prohibited in any contravention of the provisions shall be an offence punishable in accordance with law. (This includes traffic in women and children for immoral or other purposes).

Article 47 : In it contains the directive that the State shall regard the raising of the level of nutrition and the standard of living of its people and improvement of public health among its primary duties.

Dr. Rajendra Prasad has very rightly said: "A Constitution is a lifeless thing. It acquires life because of men who control it and operate. If the people who are elected are capable and are men of character and integrity they would be able to make the best of even a defective Constitution or Law. If they are lacking in these qualities, no Constitution or Law can help the country."

The Indian Penal Code 1860

This deals for:

(a) Causing miscarriage, of injuries to unborn children, of the exposure of infants, of the concealment of births,
(b) Causing miscarriage without woman's consent,
(c) Death caused by act done with intent to cause miscarriage, of woman with a child, does any act which causes the death of such woman, shall be punished with imprisonment for a term which may extend to 10 years and liable to fine. If act done without woman's consent, then there is life imprisonment,
(d) Act done with intent to prevent child being born alive or to cause it to die after birth,
(e) Causing death of quick unborn child by act amounting to culpable homicide,
(f) Exposure and abandonment of child under 12 years, by parent or person having care of it, and
(g) Concealment of birth by secret disposal of dead body.

ACTS OF PARLIAMENT APPLYING DIRECTLY TO CHILDREN AND/OR THOSE IN WHICH THERE ARE PROVISIONS RELATING TO CHILDREN

Part I—Introductory

Constitution of India 1950

Part II—Laws Relating to Child Labour

Apprentices Act 1961
Beedi and Cigar Workers (Conditions of Employment) Act, 1966
Children (Pledging of Labour) Act, 1933
Constitution of India, 1950
Employment of Children Act, 1935
Factories Act, 1948
Indian Contract Act, 1872
Inland Steam-vessels Act, 1917
Merchant Shipping Act, 1958
Mines Act, 1952
Motor Transport Workers Act, 1951
Plantations Labour Act, 1951

Part III—Child Education

Andhra Pradesh Primary Education Act, 1961
Assam Elementary Education Act, 1962
Bihar and Orissa Primary Education Act, 1919
Bombay Primary Education Act, 1947
Child Education
Constitution of India, 1950
Delhi Primary Education Act, 1960
Gujarat Compulsory Primary Education Act, 1961
Himachal Pradesh Compulsory Primary Education Act, 1953
Karnataka Compulsory Primary Education Act, 1961
Kerala Education Act, 1959
Kerala Pradesh Primary Education Act, 1961
Orissa Education Act, 1969
Punjab Primary Education Act, 1960
Rajasthan Primary Education Act, 1964
Tamil Nadu Elementary Education Act, 1920
U.P. Basic Education Act, 1972
West Bengal (Rural) Primary Education (Temporary) Provisions Act, 1969
West Bengal Urban Primary Education Act, 1963

Child Health

Assam Students and Juvenile Smoking Act, 1923
Bengal Juvenile Smoking Act, 1919
Jammu & Kashmir Juvenile Smoking Act, 1986 F
Juvenile Smoking Act, K-1096 (Cochin 2 of 1906)
Karnataka Prevention of Juvenile Smoking Act, 1911
M.P. Vaccination Act, 1968
Maharashtra Vaccination Act, 1964
Punjab Juvenile Smoking Act, 1918
Punjab Vaccination Act, 1953
Rajasthan Prevention of Juvenile Smoking Act, 1950
Rajasthan Vaccination Act, 1957
Vaccination Act, 1880

Child Welfare

Andhra Pradesh (Andhra Areas) Children Act, 1920

Andhra Pradesh (Telangana Area) Children Act, 1951
Andhra Pradesh Prevention of Beggary Act 1977, No. XX of 1350 Fasli.
Assam Children Act, 1970
Assam Prevention of Bengal Act, 1964
Bengal Vagarancy Act, 1943
Bihar Children Act, 1970
Bihar Prevention of Beggary Act, 1951
Bombay Children Act, 1948
Bombay Prevention of Begging Act, 1959
Children Act, 1960 (Destitute and Delinquent Child)
Code of Criminal Procedure, 1973
Cochin Vagarancy Act, K-1120
East Punjab Children Act, 1949
Jammu & Kashmir Children Act, 1970
Karnataka Children Act, 1964
Kerala Children Act, 1972
Madhya Pradesh Bal Adhiniyam, 1970
Rajasthan Children Act, 1970
Reformatory Schools Act, 1897
Saurashtra Children Act, 1954
Suppression of Immoral Traffic in Women and Girls Act, 1956
Tamil Nadu Children Act, 1920
Tamil Nadu Prevention of Begging Act, 1945
Travancore Prevention of Begging Act, K-1120
U.P. Children Act, 1952
West Bengal Children Act, 1959

Part IV—Criminal Law

Bombay Children Act, 1948
Bombay Children Act, 1964
Child Marriage Restraint Act, 1929
Children Act, 1960
Code of Criminal Procedure, 1898
Code of Criminal Procedure, 1973
Constitution of India, 1950
Customs Act, 1962
Hyderabad Children Act, 1951
Indian Penal Code, 1890
Karnataka Children Act, 1964

Madras Children Act, 1920
Press and Regulation of Books Act, 1867
Probation of Offenders Act, 1958
Reformatory Schools Act, 1897
Saurashtra Children Act, 1956
Suppression of Immoral Traffic Act, 1956
Tamil Nadu Children Act, 1920
U.P. Children Act, 1951
West Bengal Children Act, 1959
Young Persons Harmful Publications Act, 1956

Part V—Family Law

Caste Disabilities Removal Act, 1850
Child Marriage Restraint Act, 1929
Child Marriage Restraint Act (Amendment Act XLI), 1949
Child Marriage Restraint (Amendment) Act, 1978
Christian Marriage Act, 1872
Civil Code, 1926 (Turkey)
Code of Criminal Procedure, 1898
Code of Criminal Procedure, 1973
Constitution of India, 1950
Dissolution of Muslim Marriages Act, 1939
Guardians and Wards Act, 1890
Hindu Adoptions and Maintenance Act, 1956
Hindu Marriage Act, 1955
Hindu Minority and Guardianship Act, 1956
Hindu Succession Act, 1956
Indian Divorce Act, 1869
Indian Evidence Act, 1872
Indian Majority Act, 1875
Indian Penal Code, 1860
Indian Succession Act, 1925
Marriage Laws (Amendment) Act, 1976
Muslim Personal Law (Shariat) Application Act, 1937
Parsi Marriage and Divorce Act, 1936
Special Marriage Act, 1954

Part VI—Contract and Torts

Apprentices Act, 1961

Fatal Accidents Acts, 1855
Guardians and Wards Act, 1890
Hindu Minority and Guardianship Act, 1956
Indian Contract Act, 1872
Indian Majority Act, 1875
Infants Relief Act, 1874
Occupiers' Liability Act, 1957
Partnership Act, 1932
Specific Relief Act, 1877
Specific Relief Act, 1963
Transfer of Property Act, 1882

TABLE OF ACTS RELATING TO CHILDREN

Central Acts

Guardian and Wards (Act VIII of 1890)
Guardian and Wards (Repealed in Parts) Acts, (IV) of 1908
Guardian and Wards Act, (IV of) 1926
Indian Succession Act, (XVIII of) 1927
Indian Succession Act, (XIV of) 1928
Indian Succession (Repealed by) Act, (XVIII of) 1928
Guardian and Wards Act, (XVII of) 1929
Child Marriage Restraint Act, (XIX of) 1929
Child Marriage Restraint Act, (VIII of) 1930
Children (Pleading of Labour) Act, (II of) 1933
Children (Pleading of Labour) Amendment Act, (III of) 1933
Guardian and Wards (Act, I of 1938)
Indian Succession (Repealed by) Act, (I of) 1938
Employment of Children Act, (XXVI of) 1938
Indian Succession (Act XXI of 1938)
Child Marriage Restraint Act, (VII of) 1938
Child Marriage Restraint Act, (XIX of) 1938
Employment of Children Act, (XV of) 1939
Child Marriage Restraint (Extended to Berar) Act, (IV of) 1941
Guardian and Wards (Extended to Berar) Act (IV of) 1941
Child Marriage Restraint Act, (XXV of) 1942
Employment of Children Act, (XXV of) 1942
Industrial Disputes Act, (XVI of) 1947
Employment of Children Act, (LXIII of) 1948

Industrial Disputes (Amended in Madras by Madras) Act, (XII of) 1949
Employment of Children Act, (XL of) 1949
Guardian and Wards Act, (XL of) 1949
Child Marriage Restraint Act, (XLI of) 1949
Industrial Disputes Act, (LIV of) 1949
Industrial Disputes Act, (XLVII of) 1950
Child Marriage Restraint Act, (III of) 1951
Employment of Children Act, (III of) 1951
Guardian and Wards Act, (III of) 1951
Industrial Disputes (Amended in Uttar Pradesh by Uttar Pradesh) Act, (XXV of) 1951
Industrial Disputes Act, (XL of) 1951
Employment of Children Act, (XLVII of) 1951
Industrial Disputes Act, (LXV of) 1951
Industrial Disputes Act, (XVIII of) 1952
Industrial Disputes Act, (XLII of) 1953
Hindu Succession Act, (XXX of) 1956
Guardian and Wards (Supplemented) Act, (XXXII of) 1956
Hindu Minority and Guardianship Act, (XXXII of) 1956
Hindu Adoption and Maintenance Act, (LXXVIII of) 1956
Hindu Succession (Repealed in parts) Act, (LXXVII of) 1956
Women's and Children's Institutions (Licensing) Act, (CV) 1956
Industrial Disputes Act, (XVIII of) 1957
Probation of Offenders Act, (XX of) 1958
Hindu Succession (Amended in Kerala by Kerala) Act, (XXVIII of) 1958
Industrial Disputes Act, (XIX of) 1959
Women's and Children's Institutions (Licensing Repealed) Act, (X of) 1960
Hindu Adoption and Maintenance (Repealed in Parts) Act, (LVIII of) 1960
Hindu Adoption and Maintenance (by) Act, (XXVI of) 1960
Hindu Succession (Amended in Kerala by Kerala) Act, (XVI of) 1961
Maternity Benefit Act, (LIII of) 1961
Hindu Adoption and Maintenance Act, (XLV of) 1962
Industrial Disputes Act, (X of) 1963
Industrial Disputes Act, (LII of) 1963
Industrial Disputes Act, (XVIII of) 1964

Industrial Disputes (Amended by) Act, (XXXVI of) 1964
Industrial Disputes Act, (XXXV of) 1965
Child Marriage Restraint (Extended to Pondicherry by Pondicherry) Act, (XXVI of) 1968
Guardian and Wards Act, (XXVI of) 1968
Hindu Adoption and Maintenance Act, (XXVI of) 1968
Hindu Minority and Guardianship Act, (XXVI of) 1968
Industrial Disputes Act, (V of) 1970
Children (Pledging of Labour) Act, (LI of) 1970
Employment of Children Act, (LI of) 1970
Industrial Dispute Act, (LI of) 1970
Maternity Benefit Act, (LI of) 1970
Industrial Disputes Act, (KLV of) 1971
Maternity Benefit Act, (XXI of) 1972
Maternity Benefit Act, (LII of) 1973
Hindu Succession (Repealed in Parts) Act, (LVI of) 1974
Industrial Disputes (Repealed by) Act, (LVI of) 1974
Hindu Adoption and Maintenance (Amended in U.P. by Uttar Pradesh) Act, (LVII of) 1976
Maternity Benefit Act, (LII of) 1976
Industrial Disputes Act, (XXI of) 1976
Industrial Disputes Act, (XXXII of) 1976
Child Marriage Restraint Act, (II of) 1978

3

INTERNATIONAL UNION FOR CHILD WELFARE (IUCW)

Rue de Varembe I. 1211 Geneva 20

On 20th September 1946, the International Union for Child Welfare (IUCW) came into existence as a result of the merger of the Save the Children International Union (SCIU) which was constituted in 1913-1946 and the International Association for the Promotion of Child Welfare (IAPCW) 1912-1946. SCIU devoted itself exclusively for relief work. IAPCW dealt chiefly with legal matters and medico social questions.

The prerogatives of the two separate organisations became those of the unique organisation which was composed of members organisations constituted as "National Sections" and individual members (themselves belonging to national sections).

Those who are associated with IUCW, and those who should know about IUCW should know about its founder, Englantyne Jebb, who was considered "more flame than woman" and whose influence reached out to the furthest corners of the wcrld. She fought with rare courage to rally international solidarity to the cause of the child victims of the First World War. She was endowed with an iron will, a devouring zeal and a beat for authority, she was clear-sighted in the face of any situation and had the gift of arousing other people's sense of responsibility and social awareness. In her opinion, the true level of a country was to be judged by the protection it accorded to its weakest members.

In order to bring relief to the children of the countries in need, she approached to all classes of the population in the more favoured countries. She appealed to the Churches, to the economic organisations, to youth, to the children at school. She emphasised that "Three things are required to save the children from misery: Money, knowledge and Good-will. Money is there but we spend it on other things. We have knowledge but we do not apply it. If we cultivate the good will, it will enable us resolutely to utilise our resources in money and knowledge for the Saving of the Children of the World and with their future of the race."

Charity was a duty in her eyes not a gift; during the audience granted to her by Pope Benedict XV on 27th December, 1919, he told her "Having put your hand to the plough, do not turn back." These words haunted her throughout. She pursued her work, as a pioneer in child protection and welfare following temporary relief action the importance of permanent preventive action on behalf of children and youth had come home to her. In order to establish the principles of this and with the help of her closest fellow-workers, she accordingly drafted the "Declaration of the Rights of the Child."

She felt that assistance to children is a world responsibility: "The whole world stands to lose if the children of any nation are allowed to grow up degenerated and demoralised through hunger, and the whole stands to gain if they grow up strong and healthy, able and willing to grow up strong and healthy, able and willing to work for the good of their fellow-men, for better or for worse, the world can be revolutionised in one generation according to how we deal with the children."

Her clear sighted vision gave her ideas their prophetic value. Later she felt the need to concentrate on those lands that are now known as developing countries. Few days before her death in 1928, she summoned her fellow workers to her bedside in order to tell about her plans she had set her heart on the feeling that we absolutely must concern ourselves, with Africa and Asia. This wish was fulfilled few years later by the members.

The IUCW is an International Non-Governmental umbrella organisation, a type of federation of member organisations, both National and International. These member organisations may be official, semi-official or voluntary, their specific characteristics varying greatly. The character of IUCW can be perceived from the unity that it succeeds in forging among its members, despite their diversity and with full respect for the forging genious of each.

The IUCW has done pioneer work, improving the methods of child care and studying often neglected problems. It continues to develop and extend its programme to many countries, devoting its attention and make efforts to co-operating in the development of the Third World. IUCW has been a neutral forum for the airing and exchange of views on child and youth welfare.

The world needs such a meeting point, far removed from all political or nationalistic passions, where men and women may gather in order to face their responsibilities and grapple with their creative ideas.

Its members are indeed very different, they may be Ministers, Ministerial directorates or services, voluntary or semi-voluntary agencies, organisations recognised as being of public utility, child welfare institutions etc. They work accordingly at local, national and international level, 111 members who belong to 52 countries of all continents, and their staff may consists of professional or volunteers. These member organisations are interested in technical co-operation, research, public relation and fund raising. Their activities cover all aspects of child welfare; nutrition, health, physical and mental hygiene etc.

This unity the members achieve among themselves through the frequent co-ordination of their efforts and by exchanging the results of their experience is all the more remarkable, in that it stimulates the creative imagination of each organisation thereby preserving vital forces which might be sapped if exercised in big organisation weighted down by red tape.

The IUCW's organs are:

The General Council (the sovereign body), representing the national sections and the countries where the national sections are represented.

When UNICEF was established it was wondered if in these circumstances, was the parallel existence of an International Non-Governmental Organisations like IUCW justified.

In 1954-56, in order to clarify this, an International Committee of Experts undertook a study for the purpose of specifying the aims, present position and role of the IUCW throughout the world.

The Committee came to an agreement that "Despite the greater prestige and superior financial resources of International Organisations, the services of an International Non-Governmental Organisations working for children throughout the world is needed as much today as at any previous time and is perhaps more than ever necessary." The reasons given by the Experts included:

— the great extent of the current needs of children which are far beyond the sum of present resources;
— the greater flexibility and freedom of private organisations, not being submitted to political pressures and influence in reaching decisions, which can be arrived at more promptly than in the case of official agencies;

- the freedom of access of an international private agency to provincial or local authorities, private agencies and citizen within countries, without the necessity of going through National Governments but with appropriate consultation with national Authorities; and
- the absence of any Inter-Governmental Organisation of world-wide scope with broad responsibility for all aspects of child welfare.

Hence an International Non-Governmental Organisation for child welfare is necessary.

Therefore, the International Union for Child Welfare should continue. The International Committee of Experts stated:

> "The Committee is convinced that the International Union for Child Welfare should be continued, its role clarified its membership strengthened and enlarged, its financial support broadened and increased, and its programmes expanded and enriched, as greater financial resources became available."

Original Programmes

1. *Sponsorship*

Mr. William Andrew Machenzie (Treasurer of SCIU in 1921) who conceived the idea of "Sponsorship School" during his visit to the countries receiving relief had been struck by how demoralised were the children who came to fetch their meals from the canteen or who queued up for clothes, and they left with only a number of name on the card. Mr. Machenzie took it upon himself to put the unfortunate of these children in contact directly with persons who would undertake to send them gifts or money with a personal message. On receipt of this card an individual or a group sponsors pledged themselves to pay a sum regularly for a specific child. The child in exchange would send the sponsor his news. This way the exchange of correspondence grew and lasting ties established. Anonymity disappeared this way and long term action established and encouraged.

2. *Circulating Cradles*

At the birth of a baby, the members were provided with a little bed or basket with a layette for the child. This service was rendered for a period of nine months, and this service was greatly appreciated in the countries where not a scrap of linen was found and the babies were wrapped in a newspaper.

3. *Children's Drawings*

First world competition for children's drawing was organised at the suggestions of SCIU to its 35 national committees, in order to illustrate the principles of the Declaration of Geneva, adopted in 1924 by the League of Nations, had to be made known to the masses and be an widely diffused as possible. Two thousand master pieces were selected at the Geneva Headquarters and exhibited in the classroom of schools. Many medals were awarded to the winners, and the youngest participants was a five years of age.

4. *Rights of Children*

In 1923, SCIU felt the need of establishing a charter of Rights of Child, thus laying the base of child welfare work. On 17th May 1923, the General Council Sovereign Authority of SCIU unanimously approved the draft with 5 articles called "Declaration of Geneva." On 26th September 1924, the 5th Assembly of the League of Nations unanimously adopted the Declaration of Geneva and asked the state members of the League to be guided by its principles in the work of child welfare.

This was again amended by IUCW in 1948 and revised it with additional clauses. In 1950, the United Nations' Economic and Social Council submitted a new project, but it was only in 1959 that the U.N. adopted the new 10-point Declaration of the 'Rights of Child'.

5. *World's Children's Day*

In 1952, IUCW proposed dedication of a day each year to the Children of the World.

> The 1953 as "World's Children's Day" over 40 countries and territories organised special ceremonies to strengthen the feeling of International Solidarity for the well-being of children. One year later, the General Assembly of the United Nations adopted a Resolution, proposed by India which recommended that "with effect from 1956 a Universal Children's Day shall be instituted by all countries."

Goals

The International Union of Child Welfare, an International Non-Governmental Organisation, aims to promote recognition throughout the world of the principles of the Declaration of the Rights of Child, to come to the assistance of the least privileged children and adolescents, to raise the standards of child welfare, and to contribute to the moral, physical and intellectual development of children and adolescents.

To this end, the IUCW studies the conditions and needs of children, proposes reforms, stimulates work at the national level, encourages the co-ordination of this work, and co-operates with other organisations having similar aims. Its member organisations and its secretariat raise funds which are used for carrying out programmes.

Child welfare, in the widest sense of the term, involves the child, the family and their environment. The IUCW's mandate is to work for the development of children and adolescents aged between 0 and approximately 20 years in such diverse fields as health and hygiene of mothers and children, nutrition, juvenile delinquency, adoption, physical and mental handicaps, vocational training for adolescent, training of staff and of those who train the staff and senior officials of child welfare services.

In this way, the General Secretary of the IUCW is at the service of its members and who is concerned by child welfare.

Important Dates

1920 : The Save the Children Fund International Union (SCFIU) founded at the initiative of Eglantyne Jebb (1876-1928) and under the auspices of the ICRC, after an appeal to all churches and trade unions.

1920/21 : Relief Programme for Child Victims of the First World War in Central Europe and the USSR.

1922/23 : Relief Programme for Greek children forced to leave Asia Minor.

1923 : Proclamation of the Declaration of the Rights of the Child (called the Declaration of Geneva), drawn up by the SCFIU and adopted the following year by the League of Nations.

1925 : First General Congress of the Child held in Geneva and attended by over 1,000 delegates from 53 countries.

1926 : International Child Welfare Review launched; documentation centre set up at the SCFIU.

1931 : First International Conference on African children (Geneva).

1935 : In October 1935, first Balkan Congress was organised in Athen by a Greek member organisation of SCIU aimed at enabling neighbouring countries to share similar problems, exchange their knowledge and pool their experience and method of work. In 1938 the representative of Balkan countries met again in Belgrade for 2nd Congress.

1946 : The Save the Children Fund International Union and the International Association for Child Welfare, founded in Brussels, merged to become the International Union for Child Welfare (IUCW). The international headquarters remained in Geneva.

1947 : The IUCW obtained consultative status with the Economic and Social Council of the UN, and later with the UNICEF, as well as with its specialised institutions (ILO, WHO and UNESCO).

1948 : Revision of the Declaration of Geneva, and first meeting of the IUCW General Council attended by 44 member organisations (39 full and 5 associate from 30 countries).

1949 : Creation of the IUCW advisory committee on delinquent and social maladjusted children, which in 1972 was to become the IUCW Advisory Group on the social problems of children and youth.

1952 : First Child Welfare Conference in Asia (Mumbai).

1953 : First Universal Children's Day, instituted by the IUCW and later organised in collaboration with UNICEF. Indian Council for Child Welfare (ICCW) was the first organisation in India to become a full member of the 'UCW.

1959 : The General Assembly of the United Nations adopted and proclaimed the Declaration of the Rights of the Child, the principles of which found their inspiration in the previous declaration of the IUCW.

1960 : The IUCW had 83 member organisation (52 full, 21 associated and 10 subscribers) in 44 countries.

1962 : First "IUCW" programme, of international co-operation in Africa.

1970 : After 50 years of activity, the IUCW commemorate its jubilee; at that time it had 112 members (64 full, 31 associate and 17 subscribers) in 51 countries.

1971 : The IUCW obtained consultative status with the Council of Europe.

1972 : Co-operation agreement signed between the IUCW and the Inter-American Children's Institute.

1973 : First experiment with a regional exchange programme for senior professionals in child welfare working in Africa.

1974 : The IUCW organised an international symposium in France on the problems of mental retardation caused by socio-cultural factors, with a view to setting up a standing advisory group in this field.

1975 : The IUCW has 164 members (79 full, 46 associates and 39 subscribers) in 61 countries and is working on the revision of its statutes.

1979 : The 'symposium of Arab and African experts responsible for child and youth Welfare' met in Tangiers in March 1979. It was organised under the auspices of the IUCW. This symposium marked an important step forward in the history of Child Welfare.

1983 : 54 development projects undertaken in 15 countries of the Third World. By their very diversity these Projects are aimed at creating an environment conducive to the full development of communities where children are usually in majority. Such projects as building day care centres, rural schools, health centres for handicapped children in general and deaf children in particular, digging wells, promoting integrated development at regional level and setting up multi-purpose child and family welfare centres in villages in rural areas are all projects which directly or indirectly affect lives of children.

It started a "Project Bank" and its other new projects were:

1. Building of a reception centre for socially maladjusted minors in Ouagadougou (Upper Volta).
2. Setting up of workshops and other facilities for the training and advancement of women in rural districts near the town of Cuenca (Ecuador).
3. Integrated development in Fernandez de al, are of the poor districts of Paiaguay.

4. Community Development in Leandro Oviedo (Paiaguay).
5. Integrated Child Family Welfare Project in (Sri Lanka)
6. Social Welfare Service for Children residing at home in the Southern Outskirts of Berut (Lebanon).
7. Setting up of a day care centre in the southern outskirts of Berut.

1984 : Assistance to children and young people in situations of danger and disaster has been a priority of the IUCW. Since its foundation national disasters (earthquakes and floods etc.) armed conflicts, famine and epidemics are some of the circumstances which cause the loss of countless lives among children and young people.

Due to insufficient means, IUCW cannot respond adequately or fully to the numerous requests for assistance which its secretariat receives. Moreover not only action is required when needs are made known but this action should be immediate. Therefore, the IUCW has requested its donors to set up a special emergency fund.

Two types of situations for which help of the IUCW is requested.

Children caught up in armed conflicts.

Child victims of drought and famine.

1985 : 1985 is a significant year, good reasons being that for the last decade in the history of IUCW a way is opened for the membership of national public and private bodies directly concerned with improving the conditions of children and young people. Also the aim to realise by preparing children and young people for taking up responsibilities of a world in which this inter-dependence will be increasingly present in the acts and relationships of daily life. IUCW invites its members to participate in different programmes which it carries out with a growing member of partners and by fostering the kind of solidarity that is based on not only national consideration but open to international relations. This involves working side by side with other bodies and on the ideological basis of active neutrality laid down by the Declaration of right of the child.

Its structure consisted of:

Member Organisations

195 members in 90 countries—

as full members
as associate members and correspondents,

Its General Council—

— meets every two years in a different country
— lays down general policies and programmes
— voting rights for full member organisations

Executive Board—

— meets twice a year in Geneva.
— responsible for management policy.
— made up of 33 members.
— sets up a number of standing committees.
— Programme Committee and Planning Bureau for Regional Meetings.
— Finance Committee.
— Committee of Membership, Dues and Statutory Questions.
— International Projects Committee.
— Committee on Publications and Documents.

The Executive Board may also set up "ad-hoc Committees" General Secretariat:

— manages and administrates the IUCW
— implements general policy decisions
— raises funds, employs staff
— suggests new methods, promotes experimental projects.

Further, the IUCW has set up an International Advisory Group on Social Problems of Children and Young People.

Role of the Member Organisations

During its 55 years of activity, the IUCW has grouped together 164 organisations run by professionals in 61 countries throughout the world.

About 45 per cent of the full members are public and governmental ·rganisations working at the national level, particularly specialised ervices of government ministries. The rest, made up of private or semi-rivate organisations together with child welfare institutions, work at he local national or international level.

The delegates to the General Council decide on the overall policy to e adopted by the IUCW.

The members work with the General Secretariat through:

— benefiting from the various services offered by the latter (information, studies, etc.).
— providing the General Secretariat with regular information about their activities.
— giving the secretariat financial support—besides the annual dues—in order to contribute to technical projects managed by the secretariat.

Member's work for child welfare may be carried out in their ·spective countries or in another country, through a bilateral or ultilateral agreement, and with or without assistance from the General ·cretariat of the IUCW.

ole of the General Secretary

* A technical body at the service of its members and all who are concerned with child welfare. It is made up of a small team of full time staff: project co-ordinators, study officers, organizers of international meetings, publication and documentation specialists, translators, secretaries etc.
* A centre for consultants and research workers under contract, who contribute to the IUCW's work through studies and specialised knowledge.
* A liaison service with organisations, professionals and officials in charge of child welfare and youth policy. The Secretariat puts forward experimental programmes to the decision-making bodies of the IUCW; these programmes are designed to meet the changing needs and priorities in various regions of the world. It invites contributions to finance these programmes, not only from its member organisations, but also from official bodies foundations and commercials firms, with reference to the principles of the Declaration of the Rights of the Child.

* A Documentation centre which draws up specialised bibliographies and provides documentation for professionals and research workers in the field of child welfare. The centre has more than 10,000 books and receives regularly some 450 periodicals.
* A centre for organising regional and international meetings on child welfare problems, offering the possibility for those concerned to exchange their experiences and thoughts and to make the results known on a wide scale.

  Thus it pools experiences and exchange of information either within the framework of its statutory meetings, or by means of advisory groups, regional meetings and specialised meetings.
* Assists in the on-going training of child welfare workers and support services in programme management and coordination.
* International comparative studies are carried out on pre-school education, children of migrant workers, child abuse, adoption etc.
* An information service which, since 1936, has published the International Child Welfare Review, the IUCW's periodical, to which several other international organisations directly concerned with children and adolescents also contribute. It is published in three languages (English, French and Spanish). Since 1975, the Review has been made available in micro-form.
* *Relations with International Organisations*

  A Non-Governmental Organisation the IUCW has an International calling which has led it to co-operate with the large international governmental organisations. Today it enjoys consultative status with the United Nations Economic and Social Council, UNICEF, the Council of Europe and the U.N. specialised agencies (FAO, ILO, UNESCO, WHO). The IUCW is moreover a member of several international non-governmental councils. Finally, it collaborates actively with about fifteen international non-governmental organisations concerned with children and adolescents, particularly with the International Association of Youth Magistrates, the International Council for Social Work, the International Federation for parent Education and the International Association of workers for maladjusted children.

IUCW's Contribution to the Country

IUCW has two types of programmes of assistance for and from member countries.

One is for its members to take up the programme directly, and second the financial contribution to IUCW to conduct the programme.

In 1952 for the first time in Asia, Child Welfare Conference was held in Mumbai. It was organised by IUCW with ICCW as host. The theme for the Conference was "Child Welfare in Asia, Social Service and the Improvement of Living Conditions." 700 delegates, mainly from Asia, set together, representing 26 countries. The official Opening Session, which was presided over by the Indian Minister of Health was honoured by the presence of Pandit Jawaharlal Nehru, the Governor of the State and the Mayor of Mumbai.

In 1955, Consultative Commission for Asian countries met at Delhi. This meeting followed up the resolution taken by the Mumbai Conference. It brought together representatives from Burma, the Chinese People's Republic, India, Indonesia, Japan and Pakistan and observers from the United Nations, UNICEF, WHO, UNESCO and the International Service Conferences.

In 1970, the International Children's Centre, Paris and ICCW with the support of Government of India and UNICEF organised the Seminar on the pre-school child in Chennai.

IUCW undertook emergency relief programme in rehabilitating the refugees and children from Bangladesh, with centres in Calcutta and Tripura.

The Canadian Save the Children Fund assisted the Tibetan refugees programme from 1964-1968.

Save the Children Fund England, is operating since 1965 sponsorship programme in Chennai and Calcutta and Delhi.

Save the Child Fund (SCF) also had a 'Nutrition on Wheels' project malnutrition in big cities in India. The cost of the project is £3980 per annum. Twelve nutrition vans were donated by SCF. The project was run by Mrs. Mary Clubwala Jadhav.

4. SCF maintained a home for the refugee children in Simla.
5. SCF also spent £423980 relief programme during the famine period in Bihar.
6. SCF organised two emergency hospitals during the Bangladesh refugees influx at Salt Lake and Kalyani and undertook Nutrition programmes to help children recover from malnutrition.

7. Radda Barnens Ricksforbund Sweden made contribution from 1964-1969, for various projects at Vellore, Delhi, Ellora Tirupattur, Karigiri, Calcutta.
8. SOS International provided the entire capital cost and running expenses for SOS Children's village at Salt Lake, Calcutta. The Save the Children's Federation of the United States offered self-service to the refugees worth 10 million dollars, and Red Barnet of Denmark sent relief services, to victims of the Orissa Cyclones SCF, England Medical Services. Danish Save the Children Organisation, took a leprosy control project in Andhra Pradesh and Orissa on the basis of an invitation from Late Prime Minister Jawaharlal Nehru. The Leprosy Control Project covered a total population of 2.6 million. A 50 bedded hospital, psychotherapy centres and laboratory were established under the project.
9. IUCW also conducted Bal Sevika Training programme for nutrition workers and also assisted ICCW in holding refresher courses and seminars.

ICCW has always been represented on IUCW Executive Board.

In conclusion, IUCW has consistently and effectively worked for the betterment of children's lives and accomplished a great deal in past, both at international and field level. When today's children look back on these years, they will be convinced that IUCW did the best they could for the welfare of the children.

Today we can refer to International Union for Child Welfare (IUCW) as 'Once upon a time' as unfortunately it has been wound up. All the same it is important to mention and remember it as it has played a very important role in 'Child Welfare' and deserves not to be forgotten.

4

UNITED NATIONS' CHILDREN'S FUND (UNICEF)

One of the first substantive decision of the UN General Assembly was to establish UNICEF. It was created on the 11th December 1946. The immediate purpose was to provide urgent relief to children in Europe who managed to survive the Second World War.

In its early years UNICEF resources were largely devoted to meeting the emergency needs of the children in post-war Europe and China for food, medicines and clothing.

The mandate of UNICEF, to help to protect children everywhere from adversity and to prepare them for life, derives from the aspirations of the UN Charter "to save succeeding generations from the scourge of war and to provide social progress and better standards of life in larger freedom."

UNICEF is a network of country and regional offices, serving 128 countries in the developing world, supported by partner National Committees and other voluntary organisations in the industrial world. UNICEF is an integral but semi-autonomous part of the United Nations with its own 41 member Executive Board, India is one of them, which usually meets once a year to establish policy, review programmes and approve budget. It works within the principles established by the Economic and Social Council (COSOC).

In December 1950, the General Assembly enlarged the organisation's mandate to address the problem of children in the developing world. In October 1953, the General Assembly decided that UNICEF should continue this work indefinitely and its name was changed to "United Nations Children Fund," which was earlier known as "United Nations Children's Emergency Fund," though changed the well known UNICEF acronym was retained. In 1965 UNICEF was awarded the Noble Peace Prize, linking work for children to world peace.

UNICEF is unique among UN organisations because quite an amount of its funds are received from public—practically one-fifth. Its actions were planned for and more at community level, where it benefited the children to start with. Thus it makes it possible for a link between children and families and a community support world-wide.

UNICEF funding is voluntary, whether public or government. In 1989, more than120 governments provided 76 per cent of UNICEF income. These included countries where it is assisting in developing work, also volunteer fund raising was initiated by National Committee for UNICEF.

The National Committee primarily organised in industrial countries, who are concerned with increasing financial and other support for UNICEF and concern for children. They do this either indirectly through public education or directly through selling greeting cards and other activities. Actually the Committee plays a very prominent and important role in generating a better public understanding of the needs of children in need countries and UNICEF's efforts to meet them and solve them.

Currently UNICEF co-operates in programmes in 128 countries. Of these 44 are in Africa, 34 in Asia, 35 in Latin America, 14 in Middle East and North Africa and one in Central and Eastern Europe.

In 1976, Economic and Social Council recommended that the General Assembly proclaim 1979 as the International Year of the Child (IYC). Thus 1979 observance of the IYC generated great interest and concern with the problems of children and much new activity along with a growing recognition among Governments of the need for a regular review of the situation of children and of the policies and programmes affecting them. The year began with "Music for UNICEF" a meet at the UN as continuing fund raising effort of music industry. At the end of the year the UN General Assembly designated UNICEF as the lead agency of the UN system responsible for co-ordinating the development aspects of the follow-up activities of the year.

"The year 1990 may not have borne the official designation—that belonged to 1979—but it can be called that REAL International Year of the Child, a year of unprecedented action and promise for the young. The World Summit for Children was its high point, one of the pivotal events that shape and accelerate qualitative change"—says the Executive Director of UNICEF—Mr. James P. Grant. It was according to him the high point of a four decades effort by UNICEF to place children's needs at the top of world's agenda and source of deep satisfaction to the entire UNICEF family. It was in 1990 that the critical factors fell into place, making it possible for civilisation to move collectively to ensure a significant better future for all children.

The Convention has already proven effective as a vehicle for mobilising on children's issues. For UNICEF the Convention has served as an important guideline for the global goals for children in the 1990s to ensure survival, protection and development of all children.

According to December 1990 statement, UNICEF work with 121 developing countries to help meet the essential and required needs of all children. Of its total annual budget, approximately 45 per cent is devoted to child health and nutrition programme, 17 per cent to water supply and sanitation, 9 per cent for education, 7 per cent for community based services and 8 per cent to emergency relief.

UNICEF came to India in 1949. It started in a small way with relief supplies to children in need, skim milk powder, drugs, vaccines etc. The early years of UNICEF in India bore the stamp of emergency campaigns like mass feeding programmes particularly during drought or floods and large scale drives against communicable diseases.

By the mid-1950 there was a shift and UNICEFs assistance was for long term social and human development needs. UNICEF encouraged a country-wide milk preservation scheme by supplying processing equipment for public sector dairies. Help was also extended for the initial manufacture of Penicillin and Pesticide DDT.

A phase programme was initiated for equipping thousands of primary and subsidiary health centres, the paediatric wards and district hospitals, urban family centres and training institutes for nurses, midwives and health volunteers. Over the next two decades virtually all of India's 5400 primary health centres and 38000 sub-centres received UNICEF's assistance.

In 1961 the UNICEF Regional Office for South Central Asia was established in New Delhi incorporating existing UNICEF India Office. Around this period Government welcomed UNICEF's assistance to a nation-wide village level nutrition programme. These programmes with practical bias were launched in Community Development Blocks across the country.

UNICEF assistance was extended through 1970 to low cost production for community use of appropriate weaning protein-rich and ready to eat foods. Around 1963 UNICEF along with UNESCO interested itself in the new Science Curriculum for primary schools and began to support science education at primary level. By 1978 over 4800 'science kits' were supplied and 75000 primary school teachers, numerous teacher educators, science supervisors and craft instructors were trained. Tools, books and equipment were supplied to over 8000 teachers and training schools. Nearly 10 million primary school children benefited.

The drought in 1967 briefly brought back the country and UNICEF to the emergency approach. Modern high speed drilling rigs were flown and they moved from village to village in U.P. and Bihar boring hundreds of drinking water wells before the rain started. This experience led by 1970 to a nation-wide village water supply programme with priority to arid, hard-rock areas. The programme continued in a more varied form as a first line defence against child malnutrition and water borne disease.

A pilot project was undertaken for pre-vocational training for the large out-of school population. About 40 training centres were supported by UNICEF in association with ILO and UNESCO.

The UNICEF approach to India's Fifth Five Year Plan shifted the focus of action on behalf of children of Early Childhood—from preparing motherhood to age six. UNICEF programme were increasingly suffused with the purpose and principles of the Basic Source Strategy, which was endorsed by UN General Assembly in 1976.

The Integrated Child Development Services (ICDS), a scheme in which UNICEF came closest of all in its assisted projects to the concept of the basic services strategy.

With the world-wide observance in 1979 of the International Year of the Child the focus fell more sharply on the unmet needs of the children. As a result new programme thrusts were developed by UNICEF around old but neglected problems. The International year of Disabled persons 1981, brought home the unsuspectibly large extent of childhood disability and the easily preventable cause of most of them. Hence emphasis was put on proper infant feeding practices, universal immunisation and other basic services needed for children's development. A concrete drive was also made on the on-going programmes, against Goitre (salt iodisation), anaemia (iron) fortified salt, blindness (Vit. A, especially through vegetable sources). Ensuring the supplies is one aspect and ensuring that learning leads to practice is another.

While UNICEF support to some sectoral programmes remains as part of a lingering tradition, there is increasing mutual reinforcement of UNICEF assistance in the fields of education, health, environmental sanitation and drinking water supply.

Social Change

As year rolled UNICEF became more interested in nurturing the seeds of social development in the minds of people rather than the linear expansion of institutional facilities. The annual allocation of Funds to India have gradually increased, actually doubled. The accent was more on capital intensity to the human contribution—to training, innovation, awareness building, changes in attitude and behaviour, value orientation, research, self-monitoring and open evaluation. There is a change in the nature of UNICEF co-operation, from centralised, vertically administered national programmes to the village, block, district, state, country and peoples level, with priority to pockets of poverty and backwardness. The development directions are specific to problems, areas and people. The emphasis is on prevention rather than treatment. The aim is to inform and empower people to care for their children within the means available to them, and actually it costs very little to mothers. Given the public responsibility to feed hungry families until they have the capacity to feed themselves, and the parental responsibility to limit the family, size, children presently at risk should get off to a hopeful start in life.

In short, the story of UNICEF in India may be summed up as "in the early days UNICEF meant skim milk powder primarily, then a mid-wife kit, a jeep, and a set of garden tools.... In due course UNICEF will be associated in peoples mind not so much with the material symbols as with children growing up better fed, healthy, and educated with a purpose to take their active place in building tomorrow's India."

50th Anniversary

1996 UNICEF celebrated its 50th Anniversary. It reflects the progress made so far on the major tasks that remain on the lessons that have been learnt so far.

The average life expectancy of a child has increased in just three decades from 37 to 67 years. As recently as 1960, fewer than 1/2 of the world's children had a primary education. Ten years later, fewer than 10 per cent were immunized against the main childhood diseases. By 1995 almost 80 per cent of children were in school and an equal percentage were protected by vaccines, child mortality rates were reduced by more than 1/2 between 1960 and 1995.

Yet too many children still become victims of war, exploitation and neglect. And country can yet claim to be able to offer girls and women equal opportunities with boys and men.

UNICEF has been able to negotiate in the modest of conflicts in order to bring relief to children caught in the cross fire. It is also evident in the near-universal ratification of the Convention on the Rights of the Child, which has revolutionalised our approach to human development.

Virtually all countries agree that the needs of children, including their survival, protection of good health, education and freedom of self-expression, are basic human rights that should be enjoyed equally by girls and boys, regardless of their national cultural, religious or ethnic heritage. It is the aim of UNICEF to ensure that it becomes a reality soon. (This is the just of the forward in the Annual Report of UNICEF 1996 by Boutros Boutros-Ghali, United Nations Secretary General).

UNICEF Finances

Governments contributed $645 million to UNICEF $1 billion budget in 1995. Among the top 20 donors, 11 increased their contribution over 1994. A contribution of $10 million from the European Union and $6 million from the European Agencies, brought the total from the governments and intergovernmental organisations to $661 million.

UNICEF has country programmes agreements with 145 countries. 118 countries programmes, approved for multi-year periods are funded from General Resources.

India received for 1996-1997 $71,600,000. The United States remained the largest donor to UNICEF, contributing a total of $129 million, while Sweden was the largest per capita donor, contributing almost $12.50 per person. The U.S. ranks 12th in per capita contribution.

Sweden continues to be the largest donor to supplementary funds, and the second largest to general resources, contributing a total of $110 million. The next countries were Netherlands, Norway, Denmark, Japan, U.K., etc.

5

THE PLANNING COMMISSION
(Five Year Plans)

Early History

The importance of Planning for carrying out the task of economic and social transformation had come to be emphasised in India from the early thirties. In 1934, Shri M. Visveswarya had published a Ten Year Plan with the objective of doubling national income. Five Year later in 1938, at a conference of the Provincial Ministers of Industries held under the Chairmanship of the then Congress President Sh. Subhash Chander Bose, a resolution was passed which stated that Industrialisation was essential for meeting the problems of poverty, unemployment, national defence and economic reorientation and a comprehensive scheme of national planning had to be formulated as a step towards such industrialisation. The Conference also recommended that a commission called the All-India National Planning Commission should be appointed for this purpose, and that it should consist of representatives of the Governments of Provinces and States in the country, the Federation of Indian Chambers of Commerce, and all India Village Industries Association. The Conference also decided to appoint a Planning Committee for doing parliamentary work regarding the preparation of a National Plan. A National Planning Committee was then constituted by the President of Congress with Shri Jawaharlal Nehru as Chairman, and Shri K.T. Shah was appointed Hony. General Secretary. The Committee discussed some basic issues and also appointed 29 sub-committees to study and report on different sectors of the economy and on certain special problems relating to national planning.

The work of the Committee was interrupted with the outbreak of the Second World War and the unrest and the imprisonment of the Chairman. A number of sub-committees prepared reports relating to their respective fields, some in 1939 and 1940 and some others in 1945 and 1946. These reports and the work of the Committee led to a considerable discussion and interest in the problems of national planning.

Another important development was the publication in 1944 by a prominent Indian Industrialists of "A Brief Memorandum" outlying a Plan of Economic Development for India. The object of memorandum was merely "to put forward, as a basis of discussion a statement in as concrete form as possible, of the objectives to be kept in mind in economic planning in India, the general lines on which development should proceed and the demands which planning is likely to make on the country's resources."

This document aroused a great deal of interest and helped further to emphasise the importance of planning for the economic betterment of the country. The memorandum also indicated that there should be under the Central Government, a National Planning Committee in which various interest concerned would be represented and to which the responsibility for drawing up the Plans would be delegated. The Actual execution of plans would be the function of a supreme economic Council working along side the national planning committee under the authority of the Central Government.

Two other documents that aroused some interest at that time were "The People's Plan" prepared by the Indian Federation of Labour under the leadership of Shri M.N. Roy and the "The Gandhian Plan" prepared by Shri Shriman Narayan.

Another significant development during the period was the increasing awareness shown by the Government of India of the importance of preparing development Plans for post-war reconstruction. Post-war Reconstruction Committees were appointed both by the Central Government and by the Provincial Governments and development plans were also prepared regarding the problems of development in different sectors.

The Government of India had also created in 1944 a Planning and Development Department for co-ordinating the work regarding post-war reconstruction.

The process of the transfer of power from Britain to India began with the appointment in September 1946 of an Interim Government under the leadership of Jawaharlal Nehru. An Advisory Planning Board was appointed by the Interim Government in October 1946, with Shri K.C. Neogy as Chairman for reviewing the work already done in Planning and to make recommendations for the future including the future machinery for Planning. The Board, in its report submitted in December 1946, recommended the appointment of a single, compact and authoritative organisation for the purpose of Planning. It also suggested that the proposed Planning Commission should be only advisory in character, the final decision resting with Government only in the allocation of scarce material resources was the Commission's decision to be final and subject only to an appeal to Government.

The Commission was a non-political body whose members would not fluctuate with change in political forthness. The proposed Commission can set-up Committees of Experts to assist it.

It was specifically recommended that a consultative body of 25-30 members should be setup which should meet half yearly or quarterly. The Congress and Muslim League Party had formed the Interim Government and no progress was possible regarding the setting up of a Planning Organisation because of the basic differences of approach between the Congress and the Muslim League wings of Government. The partition of the Indian Sub-continent at the time of Independence in 1947 and its aftermath created difficult problems for the new Government of India and this delayed any constructive and long-term approach to economic problems. Some initial steps towards development planning were taken through the setting up of Economic and Statistical Units attached to Cabinet Secretariat. The cabinet also appointed an Economic Committee of its, and to advise it, an informal committee of secretaries, also began to function.

Committees of Statisticians and economists working in Government departments were also set up to advice Government. However, no machinery for drawing up an overall plan for the country was created for over 3 years after the report of the Advisory Planning Board.

The idea that a planning organisation was needed in the country, however, gathered necessary support. The All-India Congress Committee had emphasised the importance of "Planned Central Directions" in a resolution passed by it in November 1947. The Economic Programme Committee appointed by this body under the Chairmanship of the Prime Minister Shri Jawaharlal Nehru, recommended in 1948 that a permanent Central Planning Commission should be appointed for the purpose of advising and assisting Congress Government in the practical steps that should be taken for implementing the programmes that the Committee had recommended. The working committee of the Congress party in a resolution passed in January 1950, recommended to the Government of India that a statutory Planning Commission should be set-up.

Dr. Soloman Trone, who was requested by Prime Minister to advise him on certain aspects of the Indian Economic problems made series of proposals in 1949, about the economic development in India. An important proposal was regarding formulation of a small expert body with authority to prepare a Five Year Plan under the Prime Minister's supervision, with number of regional and functional Planning groups organised throughout the country.

In a Press Conference addressed by Prime Minister early in January 1950 he mentioned about Dr. Trone's report to have a planning machinery which supported what the Government had been thinking for some time viz., that it was essential to create machinery for overall planning.

The Government's intention to establish a Planning Commission was announced in the President's Address to Parliament at the end of January 1950. Government also proposed to establish a Central Statistical Organisation. The actual announcement of the composition of the Commission was made by the Central Finance Minister in his budget speech on 28th February 1950.

The Planning Commission was established by a Resolution of the Government of India dated 15th March 1950. The Resolution said "For some years past the people of India have been conscious of the importance of planned development as means of raising the country's standard of living."

The Resolution further said "During the last 3 years the Centre as well as the Provinces have initiated the schemes of development but experience has shown that progress has been hampered by the absence of adequate co-ordination and of sufficiently precise information about the availability of resources."

"The needs for comprehensive planning based on a careful appraisal of resources and on an objective analysis of all the relevant economic factors has become imperative. These purposes can best be achieved through an organisation free from the burden of the day to day administration, but in constant touch with the Government at the highest policy level."

The resolution referred to the Constitution of India and especially to certain Directive Principles of State Policy and stated that in view of these and the "declared objectives of the Government to promote a rapid rise in the standard of living of people." A Planning Commission was set up with the following functions :

Planning Commission's Function

1. Make an assessment of the material, capital and human resources of the country, including technical personnel, and investigate

Enrolment of girls has been logging behind in Seventh Plan. The focus of effort will be on promotion of girls education through appointment of women teachers *attachment of pre-school centres* provision of incentives.

Seventh Plan will provide special funds for these programmes which will enhance the efficiency quality of this system preparation of teaching-learning material should be prepared and utilised.

FIVE YEAR PLANS FOR PRE-SCHOOL

Introduction

The Sargent Committee Report is practically the first document at the Government level in which we find a very helpful reference to the problems of pre-school education. One of the bold recommendations in this report was:

> "That the pre-schools should be agreed and no pains should be spared to make them as attractive as possible with the object of persuading parents to send their children voluntarily."
>
> "It is one of the many consequences of the general lack of educational planning in India that a very impressionable, plastic, and educational potent period of child's life has received very little attention."

First Five Year Plan (1951-56)

The importance of pre-school education is universally recognised as catering to the most plastic impressionable and educationally potent period of a child's life. Actually pre-school education has been rapidly gaining in popularity in the post-independence period, but only a fraction of the total population of 3-5 years old in India gets an opportunity to attend pre-school institution.

Second Five Year Plan (1956-61)

It marked another milestone in the history of pre-school programme in India. When a 'Child Care Committee' was constituted by the Ministry of Education for preparing a comprehensive plan for the young child (0-6 age group). This was a great step ahead in pre-school programme. (In India all schemes and programme for children of pre-school are (0-6) are bracketed with social welfare).

Third Five Year Plan (1961-66)

To promote pre-school education, the plan stressed the need to give facilities for pre-school education, improvement of existing Balwadis, opening new Balwadis and expansion of training programmes for Balsevikas. In this respect Indian Council for Child Welfare played an important role, to bring Child Welfare within the orbit of the plan and make planners realised importance of "Child."

Annual Plan (1966-69)

Programme started earlier were consolidated and considered annually.

Fourth Five Year Plan (1969-74)

Pre-school under-scored the vital role of the voluntary sector in developing pre-school education in the country. The Government's area of operation was limited to certain strategic fields such as training of teachers, evolving suitable teaching techniques and production of instruction material. Provision was made for setting up of Balwadis in rural and urban areas.

Fifth Five Year Plan (1974-79)

As regards Pre-school education the plan envisaged that children's play centres for the age group 3 to 6 would be attached to selected primary schools. Pre-school education was to be one of the components of ICDS scheme. Thus in India, pre-school moved into two parallel directions—as a part of education and as a part of Social Welfare Services.

Sixth Five Year Plan (1979-85)

The plan accorded high priority to schemes for welfare and development of children with an increased bias towards preventive and development services.

Seventh Five Year Plan (1985-90)

Early Childhood Education is important both from point of view of the personality, development of the child and for inculcating the children a healthy attitude to school-going to help increase their realisation rate in schools. This programmes will be developed with nutrition, health care and social welfare as a package within the broad framework of the programme of ICDS. Voluntary efforts to undertake innovative experiments in respect of early childhood education will be supported.

The Scheme of Integrated Education of disabled children was installed by Ministry of Social Welfare as a centrally Sponsored Scheme where handicapped children are sought to be integrated in normal school system with a view to promoting their psychological acceptance.

The scheme is now implemented by the Ministry of Education. Difficulty facing is lack of teachers in special education. In Seventh Plan great emphasis is laid on teachers training.

FIVE YEAR PLANS FOR SOCIAL WELFARE

> "Our century is called century of nuclear power and air and space travel. This is true of course but I would prefer to call it the century of Child."
>
> —*Indira Gandhi*

Introduction

In the Social Welfare, the planners must be able to understand and have vision of CHILD as the foundation of the country's future. If they had our country in these 50 Years of Independence, would have brought out more than one healthy educated generation.

In the Social Welfare plan for the third year plan child welfare was drawn up for the first time in the country. Whereas there is wide recognition of the importance of the child the fact that planning for children has been considered so late is an indication that this is a world of adults. Child Welfare as distinct from other aspects of Social Welfare is an integral part of Economic Plans. There is a difference in the concept of Social Welfare when it is applied to adults it is expenditure and when it is applied to child it is part of the investment. Thus planning of Child Welfare must cover all the needs of child, normal as well as special. Through different stages of growth.

First Five Year Plan (1951-56)

A provision of only Rs. 4 crores was made. All the programmes in this plan were undertaken by the Central Social Welfare Board (CSWB). These programmes including grants-in-aids to voluntary organisations, rendering welfare services for children, opening of welfare extension projects in rural areas where no voluntary welfare organisations existed.

The services were rendered through Balwadis, Creches, Mothers and Child Health Centres, Central Advisory Board of Physical Education and Recreation and establishment of Bal Bhavan Society.

Second Five Year Plan (1956-61)

Provision of Rs. 19 crores was made (Centre 12 crores and states 7 crores). During this plan activities of C.S.W.B. continued and strengthened by adding new schemes like Welfare Extension Projects (Urban), and Holiday Homes for children 10 to 16 age groups.

In this plan great concerned was shown for the handicapped children. It envisaged expansion of institutional programmes and creation of additional facilities such as model school, relationship, training of teachers for all types of handicap.

Third Five Year Plan (1961-66)

Provision rose to Rs. 31 crores (Centre 19 crores and States Rs. 12 crores).

A special provision of Rs. 3 crores was made for child welfare programmes. In the Central Sector, 17 Integrated Child Welfare Demonstration Projects were started in different states and union territories. The Committee on Child Care (1962) recommended several measures for expansion and strengthening of play and recreation facilities for young children. Welfare services for the handicap was considered very important stressed that they should be community and family oriented.

Annual Plans (1966-69)

Fourth Five Year Plan (1969-74)

All schemes Health, Nutrition, Education for children of Pre-school child welfare programmes received greater attention and the allocation was Rs. 93 crores (Rs. 81 crores in Central Sector and 12 crores in State Sectors). It was proposed to set up four National Institutes for the blind, deaf and dumb, mentally retarded and orthopaedically handicapped children.

Special emphasis was laid on the provision of facilities in backward areas and communities and also for girls. Pilot Schemes for integrated education of blind, partially blind and partially deaf were initiated. A scheme of Family and Child Welfare was started during this Plan. It also emphasise the importance of organising institutional and non-institutional services for destitute children and allocated special funds for this purpose.

Fifth Five Year Plan (1974-79)

Provision of Rs. 86 crores was made (Rs. 64 crores in Central Sector and Rs. 22 crores in State Sectors). The integrated Child Development Services scheme was formulated and started in 33 projects on an experimental basis during the Plan to provide a package of services. The State Government expanded their programmes of institutional services for the socially, physically and mentally handicapped children by setting up new institutions. For destitute children the Government was in favour of setting up institutions on the line of SOS children. State Government paid great attention to the need for enforcement of children's legislation and creation of necessary institutional services for this purpose.

Sixth Five Year Plan (1979-84)

The total allocation was Rs. 272 crores (Rs. 150 crores in the Central Sector plus Rs. 122 crores in State Sector). Child Welfare and Development Programmes continued to receive high priority in this Sixth Plan. The ICDS programme to be extended to 1000 projects by the end of Sixth Plan which will provide supplementary nutrition to 60 lakhs children, immunisation to 145 lakhs and pre-school education to 30 lakhs children in addition, some state governments have also started ICDS projects in the State Sector. Pre-school education component of the programme to continue and strengthened. Increasing emphasis on games and sports was put as recreation facilities exist for school-going children and leaves out many school age children not attaining formal education schools.

In this Sixth Plan the problems of working children and their welfare received the attention for the first time. They advocate corrective measures to minimise exploitation of child labour and improve working conditions. The Plan emphasises that appropriate programmes to be undertaken to improve the health, nutrition and educational status of this section of labour force. The committee on child labour which was set up in 1979 recommended a multiple policy approach in dealing with the problems.

Conclusion

The Programme of Child Welfare/Development in the last three decades show that the successive Five Year Plans have given importance to child and continue to give more and more attention to the needs and requirements of children. A variety of programmes having direct or indirect bearing on child development were launched in the sectors of health nutrition, education and Social Welfare. In Social Welfare Sector considerable resources were utilised as grants-in-aid to voluntary organisation which did result in the expansion of Child Welfare activities in voluntary sector which was not evenly distributed all over different parts of the country. The governmental programmes launched in different sectors achieved only limited coverage of child population of the country. The experience from the early plans helped to evolve the concept of integrated services for the development of children. This approach was welcomed and accepted, and became the nucleus of schemes like ICDS.

Through an overview of the schemes launched in the field of child development in the last 3 decades, however, reveal that there was discernible element of ad-hocism in child development planning in our country as evidenced in a series of experimental programmes pointing to a lack of long-term perspective. Therefore, it is time we draw up a long-term plan for 3 decades ahead so that we have a strong country.

Seventh Five Year Plan

Social Welfare Programmes in the Seventh Plan are essentially designed to supplement the efforts at human resource development. The objective is to improve the quality of life and to cater to the special needs of vulnerable sections like children, women and handicapped through organised and sustained development activities.

Strategy for the Seventh Plan

Social Welfare Services in the various facets are productive, promotive developmental and rehabilitative in nature. They are designed to enable the targeted sections of society to realise their full potential for growth. The programme of Social Welfare sections are wholly supplementary in nature, designed as they are to meet certain needs of the most deprived and vulnerable members of the society.

The welfare of children, women and the disabled is linked with the development of the family, the basic social unit. Child Welfare would be given the highest priority. The basic minimum child care services would be extended to the most vulnerable group, i.e., 0-6 year of age, specially age group 0-3, in order to reduce the high incidence of child mortality, morbidity and malnutrition in the country. More emphasis would be laid on enhancing the capability of the mother to look after the health and nutritional needs of the children. Effective coordination would be sought in the provision of health inputs, nutrition, education, water supply and other relevant services in order to maximise the returns from investments.

Seventh Plan Programme

The major programme of ICDS seeks to lay a solid foundation for the development of the national human resource by providing an integrated package of early childhood services. These consist of:

1. Supplementary nutrition
2. Immunisation
3. Health check-up
4. Referral Services
5. Nutrition and health education
6. Non-formal education to children below 6 years age and pregnant and nursing mothers in most backward rural and tribal blocks and urban slums. While the programmes would be expanded, emphasis will be on consolidation and improving the quality of services.

The health component of the programme viz., immunisation, health check-up, Vitamin 'A' Prophylaxis and iron and folic acid distribution, would be strengthened with stress on interrupted delivery of services. Necessary action would be initiated for maintaining the "Cold Chain" for the proper storage of vaccines. Efforts would be made that these services specially reach children below 3 years of age.

Greater stress would be laid on the training of functionaries as well as on their continued education through periodical refresher training courses.

Effective coordination between welfare of health department at Block levels would be strengthened. Community support and participation would be elicited in running the programme. Voluntary agencies and individual talent will be utilised in programme supervision, review and monitoring. They will be given financial and organisational support for the purpose.

The training programme in the children homes would be diversified and further vocationalised in order to provide larger employment opportunities to children when they have some degree of maturity. Special institutions for this purpose would therefore be avoided.

Social Welfare in State Sector

In State Sector, the Social Welfare programmes are variegated depending on the nature and magnitude of the prevailing social programmes in the different regions. In all these programmes, utmost importance would be given to education, training and rehabilitation services so as to enable the concerned target group to become self-reliant.

Institutional care will be provided only where it is necessary. Child Welfare will continue to receive high priority. The States/Union Territories would be engaged to undertake additional ICDS projects on Central Pattern to cover more children, pregnant women and nursing mothers with package of nutrition and health services.

Efforts would be continued to provide creche/Day Care Services for children of working women with emphasis on improvement of health and nutrition linkage.

The services envisaged under various legislations such as juvenile courts, children's homes, remand observation homes, certified schools, rescue homes, etc. would require to be strengthened, keeping in view the increasing problems of juvenile delinquency.

The States/Union Territories would be requested to adopt the programme features of the Central Government Children's Acts. Financial assistance would continue to be provided to voluntary organisations for undertaking institutional and non-institutional services for the affected groups. The States/Union Territories should develop suitable technical compliance at different levels so as to identify and assess the emergency, social problems in particular areas and suggest and devise ways to overcome such problems.

SEVENTH FIVE YEAR PLAN 1985-90

Labour

Since it is not feasible to eradicate the problems of child labour at the present stage of the economic development, attention has to be focussed on improving the working conditions of child labour and make it better and more acceptable socially.

Improved legislation coupled with better enforcement machinery are called for. Association of Voluntary Organisations and agencies with the task of providing child welfare with health care, nutrition and education will be desirable. Efforts can be made to bring non-formal education to child workers in large number of small factories and workshops in which they work. The ultimate goal of abolition of child labour can only be achieved when there is sufficient improvement in the conditions of the families where children are compelled to work.

For women to create creche facilities and family planning centres for women labour.

Seventh Plan has allocated fund for identification of bonded labour and also for projects for improvement of the conditions of child labour through a package programme of non-formal education, health care, nutrition and recreation.

TABLE 5.1: Percentage of Outlay on Social Welfare to Total National Plan Outlays in different Plans

Plans	*Total Public Sector Plan Outlay Rs.*	*Outlay in Social Welfare (in millions)*	*% of Outlay on Social Welfare to Total Plan*
First Plan	23,780	40	0.2
Second Plan	48,000	190	0.6
Third Plan	75,000	310	0.4
Annual Plan (1966-67 to 1968-69)	66.250 (Expenditure)	120 (Expenditure)	0.2
Fourth Plan	159,020	930	0.6
Fifth Plan	393,032	862	0.22
Sixth Plan	975,000	2,720	0.28
Seventh Plan	1800,000	10,124	0.56

Hence, although foremost attention is being provided to the child has been reiterated time and again by planners, this is not adequately reflected in their planning. Tasks are stupendous and the needs plenty. The claims on financial resources being numerous. It is the Social Service Sector which bears the brunt.

The approach towards the lot of children in successive plans remained largely sectoral. Trend has always been to tackle issues in separate sectors and compartments such as—education, health, family planning, nutrition, etc. After so many years of planned development, no direct mention is made of "Whole Child" in successive plans.

TABLE 5.2: Outlays on Social Services Sector (Concerning Child Development) in India (Central and State Sector) during Sixth and Seventh Five Year Plans 1980-90

Sl. No.	*Items*	*Sixth Plan (1980-85)*			*Seventh Plan (1985-90)*		
		Central Sector	*State Sector*	*Total*	*Central Sector*	*State Sector*	*Total*
	Total Public Sector Plan Outlays	47250.00	50250.00	975.00	95534.00	84466.00	180000.00
	Social Services	4453.42	9581.84	14035.26	10350.90	18999.56	29350.46
		(9.43)	(19.07)	(14.40)	(10.84)	(22.49)	(16.31)
1.	Education	737.45	1788.99	2526.44	2388.64	3994.01	6382.65
		(1.56)	(3.56)	(2.59)	(2.50)	(4.73)	(3.55)
2.	Health	601.00	1220.05	1821.05	897.34	2493.55	3392.89
		(1.27)	(2.43)	(1.87)	(0.94)	(2.95)	(1.88)
3.	Family Welfare	1010.00	—	1010.00	3256.26	—	3256.26
		(2.14)	—	(1.04)	(3.41)	—	(1.81)
4.	Social Welfare	150.00	121.97	271.97	799.97	212.39	1025.36
		(0.32)	(0.24)	(0.28)	(0.84)	(0.25)	(0.56)
5.	Nutrition	14.95	223.19	238.14	7.32	1732.86	1740.18
		(0.03)	(0.44)	(0.24)	(0.01)	(2.05)	(0.97)
6.	Labour & Labour Welfare	78.50	121.14	199.64	95.44	238.28	333.72
		(0.17)	(0.25)	(0.10)	(0.10)	(0.28)	(0.19)
	Total	2591.90	3475.34	6067.24	7444.97	8673.09	16118.06
		(5.49)	(0.92)	(6.22)	(7.79)	(10.27)	(8.95)

Note: Figures in parenthesis indicate percentage with respect to total Public Sector Plan Outlay.

6

THE EIGHTH AND NINTH FIVE YEAR PLANS

The Eighth Five Year Plan is being launched at a time of momentous changes in the World and in India. Planning has been one of the pillars of our policies since Independence, and our present strength derives from its achievements.

Human Development, in all its many fields, is the ultimate goal of the Eighth Plan. It is towards fulfilling this goal that the Eighth Plan accords priority to the generation—specially for control of population growth, universalisation of elementary education, eradication of illiteracy, primary health facilities to all, etc.

The success of development programmes can be multiplied manifold if the people are whole heartedly involved in their implementation. Therefore, implementation strategy for the Eighth Plan relies on making people active participants.

The Eighth Plan is financed mostly from domestic resources.

Salient Features of the Plan

The plan recognises "Human Development" as the core of all development efforts. It is only healthy and educated people who can contribute to economic growth and the growth in turn will contribute to human well-being.

The priority sectors of the plan that contribute towards realization of this goal are health, education, literacy and basic needs.

The Eighth Plan is an integrative plan and Government at the Centre and in the States will expand their role in this sphere. It is performance oriented and is flexible with scope for changes and adjustments.

The Plan attempts to correct the fiscal imbalances from which the Sixth and Seventh Plan suffered. This Human Development will be the ultimate goal of the Eighth Plan. It is towards this that population control, literacy, education, health, adequate food—Nutrition—are listed as the basic priorities. The provision of the basic elements, which help development of human capital will remain the primary responsibility of the Government.

Plan Allocation

Eighth Plan shows that nearly 81.7 per cent of the total budgetary support to the central ministries has now gone to the social infrastructure. This compares with 70 per cent in the Seventh Plan.

The total outlay of states, including area programmes will be Rs. 179,985 crores.

The total budgetary support to the state plans will be Rs. 78,500 crores (including normal central assistance).

What is planned for states is a little more than twice the Seventh Plan level.

Economic Development

The strategic importance of social sectors for achieving the basic objectives of economic growth, equity and self-reliance has been reflected in the process of economic reforms by increasing the investment in human capital development.

There is substantial increases in the Central Plan allocations for social sectors in the last 3 years budget.

For Education

Increased by 92 per cent over the past 3 years.

Outlay for Elementary Education going up by 129 per cent.

Outlay Adult Education increased by 95 per cent.

For Health

Allocation of Health was hiked by 122 per cent.

Several social sector programmes have been strengthened and reoriented in favour of weaker sections.

Family Welfare and Population

Population growth is one of the priority areas of the Eighth Five Year Plan.

The rate of population growth during 80's, though marginally slower than what it was in the 70's, was still around 20.1 per cent per annum, which implied an addition of around 18 million to the nation's population every year.

The country will cross 1 billion mark by the year 2001. If not halted it will never be possible to render social and economic justice to millions of our masses.

Therefore, Eighth Plan will make vigorous efforts to control the population growth.

The Central Plan outlay for Family Welfare programmes has been raised from 1000 crores in 1992-93 to Rs. 1581 crore in 1995-96, an increase of 58 per cent.

Total Fertility rate dropped from 5.2 in 1971 to 3.5 in 1993.

The Crude Death rate has declined from 19 per thousand population to 9.2 over same period.

Infant Mortality rate declined from 129 per thousand live births in 1971 to 73 in 1994.

In this great stress is placed on involvement of NGO's and organised sectors.

The percentage of India's population below the poverty line has declined from 25.49 per cent in 1987-88 to 18.96 per cent in 1993-94. This significant decline in the poverty ratio has occurred despite the major economic crisis of 1991-92.

Literacy and Education

Education is a process of development, therefore, an investment. This investment has to be done in time to deserve full benefits. Efforts in Kerala, some districts of Tamil Nadu and West Bengal, to achieve 100 per cent or nearby literacy are examples of what can be achieved through determination and people's achievement.

More efforts are required in States of Rajasthan, Haryana, U.P., Bihar, Madhya Pradesh, Orissa than in other states.

The intensity of the problems of education is due to the degree of lack of development in the rural areas, inequitable distribution of assets in terms of land-educational deprivation etc. Therefore, the broad priorities is to prepare grounds for the spread of literacy and primary education, remove traditional constraints on the states.

Primary Education

The Eighth Plan will aim at Universal Primary Education, both through full-time formal schools and part-time non-formal arrangement for working children and specially girls in particular. Also special programmes will be launched for education of tribal children, with due regard to tribal culture, economic problems, removal of disparities between tribal and non-tribal population group.

Yet number of primary schools increased from 2.10 lakhs in 1950-51 to 5.81 lakhs in 1994-95.

Upper Primary Schools increased from 0.13 lakhs in 1950-51 to 1.63 lakhs in 1994-95. To enhance the level of literacy among ST girls. A new scheme for the educational complex in low literacy pockets was started in 1993-94. Rs. 3.21 crore have been sanctioned to NGO's for opening 49 educational complexes.

A new scheme for vocational training in tribal areas was started in 1992-93, Rs. 5.28 crore have been sanctioned to states/U.T. for setting up 41 vocational training centres. In the last 4 years number of initiatives have been taken in the area of welfare of the Handicapped. Three new grants-in-aid schemes have been introduced.

Gross Enrollment Ratio (GER) in Primary Stage, i.e., class I—V, increased from 42.6 per cent in 1950-51 to 103 per cent in 1994-95.

Upper Primary Stage, i.e., class VI-VIII from 12.7 per cent to 65.5 per cent.

Providing access to schools—With 1 km. of walking distance to 8.25 lakh inhabitants covering 94 per cent of country's population. This has contributed to rise in overall literacy rate, i.e., literacy rate of country was 18.35 in 1951 and 52.2 per cent in 1991. About half of the children entering class I drop out, before reaching class V, and two-thirds before reaching class VIII. The drop out rate of girls is higher than boys at both primary and upper primary stage.

The enrollment of Schedule Castes (SCs) and Schedule Tribes (ST) has increased at Primary Stage, because of affirmative policies of government. Though the SC and ST is more or less in proportion to their share in population at Primary level, and the drop outs though declining are still large.

The National Literacy Mission (NLM) has been mandated to make 100 million persons literate in the age group of 15-35 by the end of the Eighth Five Year Plan.

The Total Literacy Campaign has become the principal strategy of the NLM in the eradication of illiteracy throughout the country. As on December 1995, 368 districts have been covered under the Total Literacy Campaigns either fully or partially. Similarly 157 districts have also been covered under the post-literacy campaigns either fully or partially.

Similarly 157 districts have also been covered under the post-Literacy Campaigns. Under all schemes of NLM, 49.89 million persons have so far been made literate as per NLM norms against an enrolment of 78 million.

Nutrition

The National Programme of National Support to Primary Education (Mid-Day Meal Programme) launched from 15th August 1995, intend to give a boost to universalisation of education, increasing enrolment, retention and attendance simultaneously, and improving on Nutrition of students in primary classes (I-IV). This programme is to be implemented through local bodies such as Panchayats and Nagar Palikas, and will cover children in primary classes in all Government schools, local bodies and government aided schools in all States/UT. In 1995-96 the programme will commence in all the 2368 Revamped Public distribution System (RGDs), Employment Assurance Scheme (EAS) blocks and 40 low Female Literacy blocks in States like Punjab where there is no EAS/RDS blocks.

The programme will commence in LFL blocks having low female literacy rates than the national average.

Health

By the end of Eighth Plan the Health facilities should reach the entire population.

The Health For All (HFA) paradigm must take into account not only the high risk vulnerable groups, i.e., the mother and child (as done so far) but must also focus sharply on the under privileged segments within the vulnerable groups 'Towards Health for the Underprivileged' may be the Key Strategy for the HFA by year 2000, a declaration to which India is a signatory.

Major efforts shall be initiated to expand educational facilities for those categories of health care providers where the existing numbers and the annual turn out are far below the desired level. Educational facilities for all categories of health professionals is essential.

Allocations of health was hiked by 122 per cent.

The structural framework for the delivery of Health programmes must undergo a meaningful orientation in a way that the underprivileged themselves become the subjects of the process and not merely its objects.

This can be done through emphasizing the community based systems. Such systems must provide the base and basis of health planning.

The Eighth Plan has focussed attention in promoting health care to the vulnerable sections of society through consolidating and operationalising the Primary health care infrastructure and strengthening referral systems through District Health care models.

Since introduction of economic reforms the Central Plan outlay for programmes of the Department of Health has been stepped up from Rs. 302 crores in 1992-93 to Rs. 670 crores in 1995-96. A substantial portion of plan outlay includes allocations for the control of major communicable diseases.

Under the safety Net Scheme to improve Maternal and Child Health (MCH) infrastructure, beginning with 90 poorly performed districts in a phased manner.

Immunization Programme

Universal Immunization Programme (UIP) was launched in 1985. From 1992-93, UIP has been strengthened and expanded with Child Survival and State Motherhood (CSSM).

Provision of Primary Health care facilities including immunization accessible to all villages and the entire population.

WHO has set up a global goal of eradication of poliomelis (Polio), a major crippling childhood disease by the year 2000 A.D.

The Government has taken up "Pulse Polio Immunization" (PPI) from year 1995-96. This would involve administration of OPU on the same day to about 75 million children aged 0-3 years in the country. Twice on 9th December 1995 and 20th January 1996. This will be repeated in the subsequent years.

Integrated Child Development Services (ICDS)

Integrated Child Development Services is a comprehensive scheme for the development of children, and expectant/nursing mothers. The Scheme has gradually been extended to 3945 Blocks/Projects.

There are about 4 lakh Anganwadis under ICDS. The beneficiary coverage of ICDS is as high as 1.80 crores children and 0.39 crore mothers.

Out of 3945 ICDS Projects, 755 projects are being implemented with the World Bank assistance in predominantly tribal and backward

TABLE 6.1: Eighth Plan (1992-97) Targets—Additional Enrolment/Elementary and Adult Education

(*Figures in 000's*)

Sl. No.	*State/Union Territory*	*Primary (Classes I-V)*		*Upper Primary Classes (VI-VIII)*		*Elementary Classes (I-VIII)*		*Adult Education age 15-35 years*
		Girls	*Total*	*Girls*	*Total*	*Girls*	*Total*	
1	2	3	4	5	6	7	8	9
1.	Andhra Pradesh	1475	2588	840	1400	2315	3988	7778
2.	Arunachal Pradesh	12	27	14	36	26	63	175
3.	Assam	244	500	384	800	628	1300	4500
4.	Bihar	4032	8400	1008	2100	5040	10500	9400
5.	Goa	3	6	5	9	8	15	100
6.	Gujarat	72	108	475	1100	547	1208	4300
7.	Haryana	173	275	180	300	353	575	5711
8.	Himachal Pradesh	58	125	29	66	87	191	800
9.	Jammu & Kashmir	62	150	85	227	147	377	600
10.	Karnataka	215	434	98	197	313	631	6000
11.	Kerala	129	252	42	80	171	332	980
12.	Madhya Pradesh	2310	3460	1796	2396	4106	5856	5500
13.	Maharashtra	600	1400	300	750	900	2150	9200
14.	Manipur	12	29	36.70	68.20	48.70	97.20	23
15.	Meghalaya	15	30	22	51	37	81	262
16.	Mizoram	12	25	12	29	24	54	32
17.	Nagaland	16	32	17.50	34	33.50	66	23

(*Contd.*)

TABLE 6.1 (*Contd.*)

1	2	3	4	5	6	7	8	9
18.	Orissa	247	600	142	416	389	1016	130
19.	Punjab	80	190	54	127	134	317	5000
20.	Rajasthan	2180	2647	621	1565	2729	4212	11000
21.	Sikkim	5	11	7	16	12	27	4
22.	Tamil Nadu	215	425	491	1142	706	1567	7800
23.	Tripura	13	25	36	89	49	114	400
24.	Uttar Pradesh	866	2480	530	1930	1396	4410	16700
25.	West Bengal	801	1638	1359	2788	2160	4426	8559
	Total (States)	**13775**	**25857**	**8484.20**	**17716.20**	**22359.20**	**43573.20**	**104977**
26.	A & N Islands	4.00	9.00	2.00	6.00	6.00	15.00	10
27.	Chandigarh	4.80	10.10	3.80	8.10	8.60	18.20	26
28.	Dadra & Nagar Haveli	0.05	0.11	0.03	0.13	0.08	0.24	15
29.	Daman & Diu	0.50	1.00	0.50	1.00	1.00	2.00	20
30.	Delhi	38.00	96.00	24.00	85.00	62.00	181.00	750
31.	Lakshadweep	0.05	0.20	0.05	0.10	0.10	0.30	12
32.	Pondicherry	3.00	6.00	1.80	4.00	4.80	10.00	30
	Total (UTs)	**50.40**	**122.41**	**32.18**	**104.33**	**82.58**	**226.74**	**863**
Total (States & UTs)		**13825.40**	**25979.41**	**8616.38**	**17820.53**	**22441.78**	**43799.94**	**105840**

Source: Eighth Five Year Plan, 1992-97, Planning Commission, Govt. of India, p. 319.

TABLE 6.2: Elementary Education: Projected Enrolment for Eighth Plan (1992-97)

(Figures in Crores)

Sl. No.	*Stage*	*Population by 1997*		*Population with overage/underage children*		*Enrolment achieved upto 1991-92*		*Addnl. Population to be enrolled by 1997*	
		Total	*Female*	*Total*	*Female*	*Total*	*Female*	*Total*	*Female*
1	2	3	4	5	6	7	8	9	10
1.	Elem. Edu.	16.64	8.09	19.14	9.30	13.53	5.54	5.61 (67%)	3.76
	(a) Primary (I-V)	10.53	5.12	12.11	5.89	10.09	4.24	2.02 (82.%)	1.65
	(b) Upper Primary (VI-VIII)	6.11	2.97	7.03	3.41	3.44	1.30	3.59 (59%)	2.11

Source: Eighth Five/Year Plan, 1992-97, Planning Commission, Govt. of India, p. 286.

TABLE 6.3 : Outlay and Expenditure During Various Years of the Eighth Plan

8th Plan	*Total*		*1992-93*		*1993-94*		*1994-95*		*1995-96*		*1996-97*	
	Outlay	*Actual (4 Years)*	*(BE)*	*(Actual)*	*(BE)*	*(Actual)*	*(BE)*	*(Actual)*	*(BE)*	*(Actual)*	*(BE)*	*(RE)**
Health and ISM&H	2848.30	1940.42	302.00	396.11	483.30	431.33	578.00	540.68	670.00	572.30	815.00	843.1
								Health -) }		550.30	791.81	820.1
								and				
								ISM&H -) }		22.00	23.19	23.1
Family Welfare	6816.00	5903.90	1000.00	1190.40	1270.00	1522.62	1430.00	1684.88	1581.00	1506.00	1535.00	1547.1

Source: Expenditure figures as provided by Deptt. of Health and Deptt. of Family Welfare.

@ Anticipated Expenditure.

* RE = Revised Estimate

areas of Andhra Pradesh, Orissa, Bihar, Madhya Pradesh providing certain additional services. ICDS has made substantial improvements in the nutrition and health status of children.

In 507 ICDS blocks services such as health, nutrition, etc. have been extended to adolescent girls in age group of 11 to 18 years, particularly school drop outs.

Other programmes for the development of children include Early Childhood Education, Balwadis, Nutrition Programmes, Special Nutrition Programmes etc.

Labour

For the elimination of Child Labour for hazardous employment, 63 National Child Labour Projects with an annual expenditure of Rs. 40-50 crores benefiting a total of 1.20 lack children in child labours endemic districts were sanctioned.

TABLE 6.4: Outlays on Central Sector Nutrition Programme in the Eighth Plan

(*Rs. in crores*)

Scheme	*Seventh Plan (1985-90)*		*Annual Plan (1990-91)*		*Eighth Plan (1992-97) Outlay*
	Outlay	*Expenditure*	*Outlay*	*Anticipated Expenditure*	
1	2	3	4	5	6
Central					
Fortification of milk with Vitamin-A	0.80	0.30	0.13	0.09	0.15
Research & Development	0.50	0.02	0.39	0.04	0.30
Quality Control	—	—	0.07	—	0.30
Mobile Food and Nutrition Extension Units	*	0.20	0.13	0.07	—
Integrated Nutrition Education Scheme	2.00	0.36	0.66	0 78	3.00
Mass Media Communication	*	0.21	0.42	0.12	0.50
Diet & Nutrition Surveys	0.10	—	—	—	—
Sub Total (A)	3.40	1.08	1.93	1.10	4.25
Centrally Sponsored					
Production/Promotion of Nutrious Food and Beverages	1.92	0.42	0.95	0.04	0.75

(*Contd.*)

TABLE 6.4 (*Contd.*)

1	2	3	4	5	6
Fortification of Salt with Iron	2.00	0.39	2.50	0.11	4.40
Food & Nutrition Extension Centres (FNECS)/Food Processing and Nutrition Centres (FPNCS)	0.85	0.28	0.41	0.06	0.60
Sub Total (B)	4.77	1.09	3.86	0.21	5.75
Total (A+B)	8.17	2.17	5.79	1.31	10.00

* Included under Nutrition Education Scheme.

Source: Eighth Five Year Plan 1991-97 Planning Commission.

TABLE 6.6: Pattern of Investment on Health, Family Welfare, Water Supply and Sanitation (plan outlays) in Different Plan Periods in Public Sector—Centre/States and UTs

(*Rs. in Crores*)

Sl. No.	*Period*	*Total Plan Investment Outlay (all heads of development)*	*Health*	*Family Welfare*	*Sub-Total*	*Water Supply & Sanitation*
1	2	3	4	5	6	7
1.	First Plan (Actuals) (1951-56)	1960.0 (100)	65.2 (3.3)	0.1 (-)	65.3 (3.3)	11.0 (0.6)
2.	Second Plan (Actuals) (1956-61)	4672.0 (100)	140.8 (3.0)	5.0 (0.1)	145.8 (3.1)	74.0 (1.6)
3.	Third Plan (1961-66)	8576.5 (100)	225.9 (2.6)	24.9 (0.3)	250.8 (2.9)	105.7 (1.2)
4.	Annual Plan (Actuals) (1966-69)	6625.4 (100)	140.2 (2.1)	70.4 (1.1)	210.6 (3.2)	102.7 (1.6)
5.	Fourth Plan (Actuals) (1969-74)	15778.8 (100)	335.5 (2.1)	278.0 (1.8)	613.5 (3.9)	458.9 (2.9)
6.	Fifth Plan (Actuals) (1974-79)	39426.2 (100)	760.8 (1.9)	491.8 (1.3)	1252.6 (3.2)	1091.6 (2.8)
7.	1979-80 (Actuals)	12176.5 (100)	223.1 (1.8)	118.5 (1.0)	341.6 (2.8)	387.6 (3.2)
8.	1980-81 (Actuals)	14832.4 (100)	269.6 (1.8)	141.9 (1.0)	411.5 (2.8)	517.4 (3.5)
9.	1981-82 (Actuals)	18210.9 (100)	346.5 (1.9)	183.9 (1.0)	530.5 (2.9)	640.2 (3.5)
10.	1982-83 (Actuals)	21282.9 (100)	386.9 (1.8)	288.3 (1.4)	675.2 (3.2)	729.6 (3.4)

(*Contd.*)

TABLE 6.6 (*Contd.*)

1	2	3	4	5	6	7
11.	1983-84 (Actuals)	25087.5 (100)	470.2 (1.9)	382.9 (1.5)	853.1 (3.4)	992.6 (4.0)
12.	1984-85 (Actuals)	29878.0 (100)	552.0 (100)	380.0 (1.3)	942.0 (3.1)	1097.7 (3.6)
13.	Total Sixth Plan (Actuals) (1980-85)	109291.7 (100)	2025.2 (1.8)	1387.0 (1.3)	3412.2 (3.1)	3977.6 (3.6)
14.	1985-86 (Actuals)	33059.9 (100)	579.9 (1.8)	479.8 (1.4)	1059.7 (3.2)	1181.1 (3.6)
15.	1986-87 (Actuals)	39149.1 (100)	641.8 (1.6)	561.1 (1.4)	1202.9 (3.0)	1292.5 (3.3)
16.	1987-88 (Actuals)	42920.6 (100)	724.3 (1.7)	607.4 (1.4)	1331.7 (3.1)	1469.3 (3.4)
17.	1988-89 (Actuals)	48069.8 (100)	831.0 (1.7)	671.8 (1.4)	1502.8 (3.1)	1541.7 (3.2)
18.	1989-90 (Actuals)	55530.2 (100)	911.6 (1.6)	800.7 (1.4)	1712.3 (3.1)	1608.5 (2.9)
19.	Total 7th Plan (1985-90) (Actuals)	218729.6 (100)	3688.6 (1.7)	3120.8 (1.4)	6809.4 (3.1)	7093.9 (3.2)
20.	1990-91 (Actuals)	58369.35 (100)	1040.8 (1.8)	782.2 (1.3)	1822.9 (3.1)	1834.0 (3.1)
21.	1991-92 (Actuals)	64751.2 (100)	924.8 (1.4)	1023.3 (1.6)	1948.1 (3.0)	2246.1 (3.5)
22.	1992-93 (Actuals)	72852.4 (100)	1213.9 (1.6)	1008.1 (1.4)	2222.0 (3.1)	2286.1 (3.1)
23.	1993-94 (RE)	92628.6 (100)	1435.5 (1.6)	1273.6 (1.4)	2709.1 (3.0)	2235.0 (3.0)
24.	1994-95 (Outlay)	112197.1 (100)	1819.1 (1.6)	1430.0 (1.3)	3249.1 (2.9)	3588.3 (3.2)

Note: 1. Figures in brackets indicate percentage to total (Col. 3)
2. R.E. = Revised Estimates

Source: Economic Survey 1994-95 and Planning Commission.

NINTH PLAN

APPROACH PAPER TO NINTH FIVE YEAR PLAN (1997-2002)

The Ninth Plan will be launched in the 50th year of Independence of our country. This is an opportune moment to take stock of the successes of our planning process as well as its failures, and to provide appropriate direction for the socio-economic development of the country. The principal task of the Ninth Plan will be to usher in a new era of people-oriented planning, in which not only the Governments at the Centre and States, but the people at large, particularly the poors, can fully participate.

TABLE 6.5: MCH Immunization

(*million*)

	1992-93			*1993-94*			*1994-95*			*1995-96*		
	T	*A*	%	*T*	*A*	%	*T*	*A*	%	*T*	*A*	%
DPT	24.29	21.98	90.6	24.79	23.0	93.1	24.30	21.8	90.2	24.78	22.0	11.1
Polio	24.29	22.10	91.0	24.79	23.2	93.5	24.30	21.9	90.9	24.78	22.2	19.1
BCG	24.29	23.45	96.6	24.79	24.0	96.9	24.30	23.0	95.0	24.78	23.6	95.4
Measles	24.29	20.84	85.9	24.79	21.9	88.5	24.30	19.9	82.6	24.78	20.4	82.9
TT (PW)	27.00	21.43	79.4	27.56	22.7	82.3	27.00	21.3	79.4	27.30	21.4	70.3

T = Target
A = Achievement
% = Achieved

Source: Expenditure figures as provided by Deptt. of Health and Deptt. of Family Welfare.

Although the macro-economy performed reasonably well in the Eighth Five Year Plan, some major weaknesses have also emerged. In particular, the growth pattern has not benefited the poor and the under privileged. The Ninth plan needs to be designed to remedy the weaknesses in such a manner as to ensure that the benefits of growth reach the poors.

The Objectives of the Ninth Plan

To mention some of them are:

(i) Ensuring food and nutritional security for all, particularly the vulnerable sections of society;
(ii) Providing the basic minimum services of safe drinking water, primary health care facilities, universal primary education, shelter, and connectively to all in a time bound manner;
(iii) Containing the growth rate of population;
(iv) Empowerment of women and socially disadvantaged groups such as Schedule Castes, Schedule Tribes and Other Backward Classes and minorities as agents of socio-economic change and development;
(v) Promoting and developing peoples participations like Panchayati Raj institutions, Cooperatives and self-help groups;
(vi) Strengthening efforts to build self-reliance.

However, the social indicators cannot improve merely through increased investment, but requires a significant change in social attitudes and behavioural responses of the people. In this process the role of women is critical. Though the process of empowerment of women at the political level has already begun, it needs to be carried forward into the social and economic spheres. It must be ensured, that the control of social infrastructure in the public domain is vested in women and women's organisations.

In the past, food and nutritional security has been largely interpreted to mean adequate availability of basic food products in the country. The concept of food security now needs to be broadened to include people's access to basic nutritional requirements, both physically and economically. This problem is particularly acute in the vulnerable sections of society and in the deficit and inaccessible regions of the country.

Labour

Abolition of child labour will be attempted through a multi-pronged approach involving identification and enumeration of child and their eventual emancipation.

Education

Following the directions given by National Policy on Education 1986 (and revised in 1992), Primary Education was given an over-riding priority in order to realise the goal of UEE during the Seventh and Eighth Five Year Plans. Despite this, backlog has continued in enrolment and drop out rate is still high. Two major initiatives taken during the Eighth Plan are District Primary Education Programme (DPEP) and the Nutrition support to Primary Education (Mid-day Meals) with a view to addressing the problem of equity, access, retention and quality at the primary stage. During this period the enrolment of girls, of Scheduled Castes and Scheduled Tribes has shown an increase at the primary stage and the drop out rates have shown a declining trend. However, there is a long way to go to achieve UEE. The National Literacy Mission (NLM) with a mandate to make 100 million people literate in the age group of 15-35 by the year 1997 has achieved (1996) a target of 56.1 million.

In the Ninth Plan, apart from carrying out the directions given by NPE (1992), and keeping in view the declaration of education as an aspect of fundamental human rights to life, making the nation fully literate by the year 2005 will be a committed goal.

The unfinished tasks of UEE will be completed with special focus on the backward states/districts, the girl child and other disadvantaged population groups, emphasising decentralised and disaggregated planning with the participation of non-government organisations (NGOs), the corporate sector and various other groups.

Population and Family Welfare

Containment of population growth was one of the six priority objectives of the Eighth Plan.

During the Ninth Plan every effort will be made to provide all the unmet need for spacing and terminal methods. The target of 100 per cent coverage of all the six vaccines preventable diseases (VPD) by 1997 though showing progress is unlikely to be fully achieved. There has been occasional slop ups in the programme resulting in morbidity and rare mortality. These will be eliminated during the Ninth Plan period. The initial success achieved in 1995-96 round of Polio programme, will be sustained until complete elimination of Polio from the country. This VPD surveillance and reporting will be improved.

The objectives during the Ninth Plan will include:

(i) Meeting all the needs of contraception.
(ii) Reducing the infant and maternal morbidity and mortality so that there is reduction in the desired level of fertility.

The strategies during the Ninth Plan will be:

(i) To assess the needs for reproductive and child health at PHC level and undertake area specified microplanning.
(ii) To provide need-based, client-centered, demand-driven high quality, integrated reproductive and child health care.

Health

The focus of the Eighth Plan on Health sector has been to improve access to health care for the under served and under privileged segments of the population.

These efforts have resulted in a discernible impact on mortality. However, the morbidity due to communicable and nutrition-related diseases has not shown a parallel decline; in addition, there is now an increasing morbidity due to non-communicable diseases and newly emerging infections such as HIV. In addition to new initiatives in these areas, rural health care for all through optimally functioning network of PHCs and sub-centres as a part of basic minimum services shall constitute an absolute and total commitment.

Communicable Diseases

Communicable diseases continue to be a major cause of morbidity and mortality in India. In addition to the existing bacterial, viral and parasite infections, there are newer additions such as HIV infection, re-emergence of some infections such as *Kala Azar*, so that the disease burden due to communicable diseases continue to be very high. There are national programmes for control of vector borne diseases, tuberculosis, leprosy and HIV infection. The performance in many of these have been sub-optimal mainly due to lack of key personnel. In the *Ninth Period* a major effort will be initiated for horizontal integration of these programmes at the district and below district level within the existing framework of primary health care infrastructure.

Increasing incidence of hospital acquired infections and accidental infections in health care providers and waste disposers, renders it imperative that programmes are initiated to improve infection control and waste management.

Disease Surveillance and Response

Until poor sanitation, contaminated water supply and lack of adequate facilities for solid and liquid waste management, both in urban and rural areas are corrected, it will not be possible to completely prevent periodic outbreaks of infectious diseases.

Urban Health Care

During the Ninth Plan period steps will be initiated to develop a well structured organisation of urban primary health care to ensure basic Health and Family Welfare services to all inhabitants within 1 to 2 kms. of their dwellings.

Increasing Involvement of ISM&H Practitioners

There are over 6.5 lakh of ISM practitioners in the country. They work in remote rural as well as urban slum areas and could play an important role in enhancing out reach of health care. There is need to improve pre-service training and provide periodic updating after graduation so that there is improvement in the quality of services.

It is important to increase the efficiency of the health system as also of all categories of health manpower during the Ninth Plan period. The recommendations contained in the National Education Policy on Health Sciences as approved by the Central Council of Health and Family Welfare in 1993 shall be implemented to ensure growth and development of appropriate mix of health manpower. Optimal utilization of the human resources for health will be made through:

(i) creation of a functional, reliable health management information system, training and deployment of health managers with requisite professional competence;
(ii) multi-professional education to promote team work;
(iii) skill upgradation of all categories of health personnel, as a part of structured continuing education;
(iv) increasing accountability and responsiveness to health needs of the people by assigning a rightful role to the Panchayati Raj institutions; and

(v) making use of available local and community resources.

Social Welfare

This sector covers the welfare, development and rehabilitative needs of persons with disabilities and other disadvantaged groups such as the aged, street children, the destitutes, the delinquent and those who come in conflict with law and who need special attention of the State. The strategy for the Ninth Plan in this sector will be as follows:

(i) A multi sectoral Community-Based Rehabilitation (CBR) strategy will be put into action for pooling the efforts of the *Disabled*, their communities in collaboration with the concerned departments of health, women and child development, nutrition, education, vocational training, labour and employment and welfare.

(ii) *Street Children* who are emerging as a significant social problem requires special attention during the Ninth Plan. The non-institutional basic services approach for the care, protection and education of these children will be continued.

(iii) Special attention will be paid to the welfare and development of *working children*, children of prostitutes, especially 'girl children', and also for the children whose parents suffer from infectious and contagious diseases like Leprosy, Tuberculosis etc.

(iv) The growth of *violence*, individual as well as collective, especially *towards the Girl Child* and other vulnerable groups has assumed serious proportions. The problem will be effectively addressed.

(v) The special problems of the *juvenile delinquents* and the children in difficult circumstances will be addressed by ensuring effective implementation of Juvenile Justice Act, 1986 and other curative and rehabilitative measures to reform the social deviants.

(vi) Efforts will be made to involve voluntary and corporate institutions in implementing the various schemes aimed at the welfare and development of the groups.

Empowering Children

There has been a significant shift in the approach towards the well-being of children from 'Welfare during fifties' to 'Development during Seventies' and to 'Empowerment during nineties'.

Human resource development being one of the major thrust areas in the Eighth Five Year Plan, all the developmental efforts were directed to empower both women and children besides mainstreaming them into the national development on equal footing along with their counterparts.

The main thrust in respect of children was to ensure their 'survival, protection and development' with a special focus on the girl child and the adolescent girl.

Children

Investment on child development will be viewed not only as a desirable societal investment for the nation's future but also as fulfilment of the right of every child to 'survival, protection and development' so as to achieve their full potential. In this context, the challenges are that of correcting adverse sex ratio at birth and of reaching every child with no gender or any other social discrimination.

The 'Convention of Child's Rights' ratified by the country in 1992 will become the guiding principle for formulating necessary policies and programmes of child development in the Ninth Plan. The existing National Policy for Children (1974) will be suitably reviewed.

Following universalisation of ICDS and ensured availability of basic minimum services for the overall development of the child, emphasis will be on consolidated and content enrichment of ICDS Priority will be accorded to focus attention on the child below 2 years. To achieve this ICDS will continue to be the mainstay of the Ninth Plan to promote all-round development of the young child.

Food and Nutrition Security

The Eighth Plan recognised malnutrition as a multifaceted problem requiring an inter-sectoral approach. Consistent with this, the Government adopted a National Nutrition Policy (NNP) in 1993 and initiated the National Plan of Action (NPA) in 1995. While the Inter-ministerial Coordination Committee continuously reviews and monitors these activities, the final direction and guidance is provided by the National Nutrition Council which is a forum for interaction at the highest level between the governmental and voluntary agencies to facilitate implementation of NNP.

Food and Nutrition Security has been recognised as one of the primary objectives of the Ninth Plan.

The following will be the approach for the Ninth Plan:

(i) Major emphasis will be on long-term measures which aim at eradication of hunger and starvation by ensuring availability, accessibility and affordability of balanced food and nutrition for all, thus eliminating mal-nutrition and under-nutrition from all segments of society especially the under privileged.

(ii) Special efforts will be made to universalise the supplementary feeding programmes viz., SNP for pre-school children, expectant and nursing mothers and MDM for school going children.

(iii) To tackle the problem of Protein Energy Malnutrition (PEM), the primary focus will be on the 'At Risk Groups' who are living below the poverty line and those who are nutritionally vulnerable viz., children and in particular, the girl child, the adolescent girl and children between 6-23 months. The plan will incorporate a special package of services with a combination of preventive cum curative cum rehabilitative components.

(iv) The micro-nutrient deficiencies of Vitamin-A, Iron and Iodine which are extremely important from the point of view of their serious health consequences and wide geographic prevalence will receive priority.

(v) Efforts will be made to cover all the remote and neglected pockets predominantly inhabited by Scheduled Tribes and Primitive Tribal Groups (PTGs). To those effect, the working mechanisms will revolve around the concept of Mini Anganwadis with redefined norms and conditions.

(vi) A Nutrition Monitoring and Surveillance System (NMSS) will be established to facilitate flow of data and information on a regular and a systematic manner based on the selected Nutritional Indicators for the purpose of planning and monitoring.

7

BRIEF HISTORY OF INDIAN COUNCIL OF CHILD WELFARE (ICCW)

The history of Indian Council of Child Welfare (ICCW) is of fairly recent origin. It was in 1952 that the Council actually came into existence as a registered Voluntary Organisation. The origin of child welfare, however, is as inspiring as any other great movement of the world. It is, therefore, imperative that its progress is studied against the wider international background of events which led to its birth.

The inspiration of one man is often the beginning of a great movement. In 1946 the Norwegian delegate to the U.N. General Assembly, Mr. Aske Ording moved by the tragic plight of children in war torn Europe, suggested the formation of an organisation for the care and protection of the children of the world. It was the intention, that governments would contribute 450 million dollars for this fund. But when this was not achieved, Mr. Aske Ording recalled how war-stricken areas in North Norway were helped by their Southern neighbours, by each contributing the proceeds of one day's work. Hence, he thought, why not use this same method to help the children all over the world. This was the stupendous world-wide drive for funds, launched in 1947 as The United Nations Appeal for Children (UNAC). Realising the humanitarian purpose and International unity it represented, the Government of India associated itself with the scheme. The history of ICCW can be divided into two distinct periods viz., 1947-1952 and from 1952 to-date.

I. 1947-1952

The ICCW is the successor of UNAC. During this period efforts were made to raise funds for the welfare of the children in India under a special agreement under United Nations. Raj Kumari Amrit Kaur the then Health Minister issued a special appeal for the purpose. The main land marks in the development of the Child Welfare movement during this period were:

(i) *Flower Day*

Accordingly on 5th November 1948, the first "Flower Day" was observed for the collection of funds through the sale of "flower tokens." The Army, under the direction of the Commander-in-Chief, General K.M. Cariappa, the schools and colleges all responded to the appeal. Governors of the Provinces, and Heads of the Princely States formed local committees to raise UNAC funds and were functioning in Delhi, Coorg, Channai, East Punjab, Ajmer, Bihar, Central Provinces and Berar, Mumbai, Orissa, Mysore, Cochin, Patiala, Tehri Garhwal, Jaisalmer, Baroda and Rajasthan. It was decided that 75 per cent of the collections made, may be retained for constructive programmes of Child Welfare where the money was collected.

(ii) *Children's Day (1949)*

On 30th July 1949, "Children's Day" was widely celebrated and publicity to children's needs was given through radio, special articles, cinemas, posters and hand bills. During the first-two years of its existence a sum of Rs. 10.5 lakhs was collected.

(iii) *International Child Welfare Exhibition*

From 7th to 14th August 1949, the Indian Committee of UNAC held an International Child Welfare Exhibition in New Delhi in order to stimulate public interest in the 'Care and Protection of Children'. The exhibition consisting of pictures, models and books on children from all over the world was the first of its kind, with the International and National sections in it.

(iv) *The Indian National Committee*

In this period, the United Nations General Assembly resolved that all UNAC funds must be paid into the International Children's Emergency Fund. The Indian National Committee faced with the enormous needs of India's children, felt compelled to severe its connection with the UN Body in order to retain control over the children's plans and finances.

This was the turning point in the History of the Child Welfare movement in India and in May 1950, the new organisation by the name of the *Indian National Committee for Children* came into being. In1950—The UNAC Committee was converted into the "Indian National Committee for Children" as an independent organisation.

II. Indian Council of Child Welfare (1952 to-date)

To save the Children's Fund Committee of the All India Women's Conference merged it with the Indian National Committee for Children and the new organisation was reconstituted into Indian Council for Child Welfare, and was registered as a separate body under the Societies Registration Act XXI of 1960, in May. The aims and objectives of the ICCW was to provide Welfare Services for the children (for details see Appendix I).

The ICCW set up affiliated branches in different states and Union Territories. The first President of the ICCW was Raj Kumari Amrit Kaur. During these formative periods many important events took place which laid sound basis for this National body. The main highlights of this period were:

From 1953

ICCW became the first organisation in India to become a full member of the International Union for Child Welfare (IUCW).

International Study Conference on Child Welfare

From 15th to 19th December 1953, for the first time in Asia, an International Study Conference on Child Welfare was held in Mumbai with Smt. Dhanvantri Rama Rao as Chairman, under the auspices of IUCW with ICCW as host. It brought together in the East, for the first time Child Welfare Experts from many parts of the world, and the East and the West joined in this great cause. A 'Continuation Committee' was constituted by the Mumbai Conference.

A Field Consultant Services

The important outcome of this conference was that ICCW entered into an agreement with IUCW and made its contribution with creation of a *Field Consultant Services in Asia.*

From 1952-1954

The major thrust was consolidation of Asian Child Welfare Movement by bringing various Asian countries together, Notable features of this period were:

(i) *Children's Bureau 1954*

ICCW established a 'Children's Bureau' with the assistance of Central Social Welfare Board. It served as Central Bureau of information on all matters, relating to child, to conduct Research and build up International contacts.

(ii) *All India Directory of Child Welfare Agencies and Service*

And a picture booklet on children welfare in India, listing over 518 institutions for the care of children, with complete details of their work, scope, objectives and personnel, was brought out with the help of Publications Division, Government of India.

(iii) *A Monthly Cyclostyled News Letter was Started by ICCW in 1954*

(iv) *Meeting of the Advisory Committee on Child Welfare of ICCW in 1955*

The first meeting of the Advisory Committee on Child Welfare of IUCW was held in Delhi, ICCW as its host Smt. Hanna Sen, a Founder Member of ICCW and its General Secretary and a moving spirit of the Council from its inception, was elected Vice-President of IUCW and remained so till her untimely death in 1957. Hence, after ICCW made rapid progress and a chronological review is given below:

1955-56 After Care Services

An extensive survey of the urgent need for "After Care Services" in all the States of the Union was made by ICCW under the Chairmanship of Shri M.S. Gore (ICCW standing committee member) under the auspices of Central Social Welfare Board (CSWB).

ICCW was entrusted with the starting of the HOME for young people in Delhi. Scheme was prepared by Smt. Hanna Sen and Shri V.M. Kulkarni, and Rs. 1,22,803 was sanctioned. A separate sanction was granted for Rs. 2 lakhs for a Production Centre, to be set up by the Ministry of Commerce and Industry.

1956 National Conference on Child Welfare

The National Conference on Child Welfare was organised at Delhi on the theme—"New Frontiers in Child Welfare." 71 organisations participated and there were 200 delegates and observers, besides representatives from Union and State Governments, voluntary agencies, CSWB, UN Agencies and Experts in the field, who all participated. At the Conference, an Exhibition of Juvenile Literature in 13 languages was the highlight and 800 books displayed were donated to ICCW to form a permanent Children's Library.

1957 Building

An important mile stone in the development of ICCW activities was providing a building for its important work since inception. ICCW from its small beginning with voluntary workers held its office in a single room in the Lady Irwin College Compound, New Delhi. Here Smt. Hanna Sen as Hony. General Secretary managed the Administration which functioned under her. The Hony. General Treasurer, Sir Gangaram Kaula carried the work also in his own office.

Later it was shifted in the Block 'A' Barrack 'B' Room 14-15, Janpath, New Delhi, where the offices of the Secretary and Treasurer came together under one roof. In the same year 1.4 acres land at Rouse Avenue was made available by Ministry of Works, Housing and Supply for ICCW Headquarters building. Ministry of Health gave Rs. 50,400 to cover the cost of the land.

On 14th November 1957, the President of India, Dr. Rajendra Prasad Laid the Foundation Stone of the ICCW Headquarters

At an impressive ceremony, in the presence of the Prime Minister Pandit Jawaharlal Nehru, Union Ministers, the Governor of Bengal, Diplomats and prominent Social Workers, the Building Sub-Committee was constituted which drew up plans for the Headquarters Building, appointing M/s Master Sathey Kothari as architects. A three storey building was planned to contain: Administrative Offices, Bureau and Research sections (with provision for extension), a Library and Reading Rooms, Conference and Committee room, Residential accommodation and short stay facilities for visitors.

1957, Children's Day 14th November

Under special Government Order, November 14th, was declared as the National Children's Day. This was announced at the time of the laying Foundation stone of the ICCW Headquarters Building at 4, Rouse Avenue (now renamed as 4, Deen Dayal Upadhyaya Marg). *Thus the Birthday of Shri Jawaharlal Nehru was given to the children of India.*

1957, Commemorative Stamp

To commemorate the Children's Day a special stamp was issued by the Posts & Telegraphs Department, which now is a regular event every year.

1957 National Awards for Bravery

The scheme for National Bravery Award was initiated by the ICCW, to be given to the children for their meritorious services, gallantry and courage. The awards were declared on the Children's Day 14th November every year and given during the Republic Day week in January by the Prime Minister at a function organised by ICCW. The children who received these awards participated in the Republic Day Parade with assistance given by Defence Ministry. (Up-to-date ICCW has conferred National Bravery Awards on 396 children of which 93 are girls and 303 are boys) (1990).

In the same year ICCW helped the Delhi Administration in conducting a survey of correctional institutions.

Holiday Homes 1957

Holiday camp is one of the means for providing recreational facilities to children away from their homes. Moreover, in big towns it is difficult for the parents to enable their children to make constructive and educative use of their vacation. Smt. Indira Gandhi, Vice-President, ICCW on her return from foreign tour, gave an outline of such a scheme to then Governor of Punjab, Shri C.P.N. Singh and as a result of the efforts of the Punjab Government and organisations like Red Cross Society, Bharat Scouts and Guides, the Indian Council for Child Welfare and individuals like Smt. Pratibha Singh, Sardarni Pratap Singh Kairon. Holiday Camp was started at various places in Punjab and a permanent Holiday Home at Tara Devi, Simla was set up under "Indira Holiday Home Scheme." A donation of a place at Anand Bhavan from Her Highness Maharani of Patiala made it possible to start a home there.

ICCW was requested by the Central Social Welfare Board to ask their various State Council to implement such Holiday Homes Scheme for the children during the vacation period.

1947-57—In these first ten years, the ICCW contributed substantially to the progress that had been achieved. Raj Kumari Amrit Kaur, Smt. Hanna Sen, Smt. Indira Gandhi, Smt. Kitty Shiva Rao, Sir Gangaram Kaula among many others were the dedicated pioneers of this movement.

1958

Smt. Indira Gandhi was elected President of the ICCW. During her Presidentship many important schemes were initiated and stress was mainly laid on arousing all sound consciousness amongst ministers and important individuals about Child Welfare. Among various steps taken for the above purpose were:

(a) *Special Stamp Cess 1958*

Suggestion was put up for *special stamp cess* to be levied, expressly devoted to the work for children all over the country.

(b) *National Commission for Children*

Smt. Ila Pal Chowdhary tabled a Resolution in Parliament, urging the establishment of a National Commission for Children, the underlying principles of which the ICCW strongly supported.

(c) *Press Conference by the President Smt. Indira Gandhi*

On 30th June 1958—A press conference was called by the President ICCW, Smt. Indira Gandhi who informed the Press that ICCW has initiated (a) the re-organisation of children's institution in Delhi, (b) Details of the programme for the Children Day, (c) ICCW's views on a "National Commission for Children" were expressed, (d) Shri B. Sen of the Supreme Court and legal Advisor to the Ministry of External Affairs, Government of India, was made Hon. Legal Adviser of the ICCW.

Policy Outlines

Smt. Indira Gandhi in her opening address at the Executive Committee meeting in 1958 said:

(i) "Children are still far from being the first priority in Governmental Planning or even in their thinking. This is evident from the fact that there is no planning for children on a nation-wide basis."

(ii) "True planning is impossible without the regular and adequate funds to implement the work; hence Child Welfare work in the country is carried on in an unplanned way through many different agencies, through the Ministries of Health, Education, Home and Community Development and others such as Red Cross, Central Social Welfare Board (CSWB), Voluntary Agencies and Institutions. No single body is entrusted with a specific task and no co-ordination has been possible."

(iii) "Let us however face the problem realistically. In India we do not lack plans and reports but when faced with large national problems there is a tendency to appoint a Committee and start again from the very beginning, Commissions are always advisory and our urgent need is for implementation."

(iv) "The ICCW has a National Headquarters and all India structure. It could take up both the Research and Planning as well as the implementation of Schemes, if funds are available."

Subsequently, copies of her address were sent to President, Prime Minister, Union Ministers concerned, Planning Commission and CSWB.

1958 Appointment of the Director

As a result of the above recommendations follow-up action were taken. On 11th July 1958, at the instance of ICCW a meeting was called in Ministry of Home Affairs, Recommendations of ICCW were accepted and a post of Director of Social Welfare was sanctioned. Shri D.V. Kulkarni was appointed as the first Director in January 1959.

(b) *Missing Persons Bureau*

ICCW's recommendation to the State Government to consider the alteration of the requisite section in the penal code to include exploitation and a maiming of children in Article 363 J.I.P.C. and on kidnapping. Thus a "missing persons bureau" was set up and many children have been restored to their homes.

(c) *1959 Canvassing for ICCW*

The President Smt. Indira Gandhi and the General Secretary Smt. Tara Ali Baig addressed meetings of the members of the Parliament to form a Pressure group in Parliament in favour of welfare programmes in the country and consider CHILD as the citizen of the first importance.

(d) *Third Five Year Plan*

ICCW took up the proposal of a child welfare plan to be included in the Third Five Year Plan with the Planning Commission. The planning was then entrusted to the Sub-group of CHILD WELFARE, which was chaired by ICCW.

(e) *1959 Appointment of Technical Expert*

June 1959 came madam IKA Paul Pont as a technical expert to the ICCW (under a bilateral agreement between France and India). She was the Chief of the International Division of the International Children's Centre, Paris. She was given one year absence to take up the work with the Council. The Atrone Co. France gave a car for her use in ICCW and sent it at their expense. The work of the export was to:

(a) to set up pilot project to demonstrate how total services for child can be established.
(b) to prepare preliminary material and draft syllabi for the training programmes for child welfare workers envisaged by the Education Ministry, ICCW & UNICEF.
(c) to visit State Council and advise in their programmes.

(f) *Pilot Project*

ICCW under its direct control started a Pilot Project at Tamia in Chhindwara District of Madhya Pradesh under the leadership of Dr. B.H. Mehta for the welfare of the Tribal Children of Madhya Pradesh with financial assistance from the Ministry of Home Affairs.

(g) *Deputy President of the IUCW (1960)*

President Smt. Indira Gandhi, ICCW was elected as Deputy President of the International Union for Child Welfare; first Asian to be elected.

(h) *Integrated Child Welfare Services (Demonstration Project) 1960*

On 17th December 1960, the above scheme was instated under the leadership and the then President Smt. Indira Gandhi, ICCW a high level meeting was called. It was attended by Cabinet Secretary, Secretaries of the Central Government Ministries dealing with Child Welfare Programmes in them. Social Welfare division, the Chief Commissioner and representative of all departments of the Corporation and NDMC, and representatives of Voluntary Organisations. At this meeting 2 important papers outlining the approach to the *Demonstration Project* for Child Welfare were discussed. Delhi Administration agreed that a Pilot Project should be set up for Third Five Year Plan in Delhi State. ICCW was named as the co-ordinating agency for setting up the Project and an intensive Survey of Mehrauli areas was chosen by Delhi Corporation to start the project, which would be undertaken by ICCW.

Schemes of *Integrated Child Welfare Services* (Demonstration Project) were initiated.

The Children Bureau was merged with the administrative offices of the ICCW.

(i) *Balsevika Training Programme 1961*

The need for trained field worker at grassroot level was felt early in the programme and the first Balsevika Training Centre (BST) was established at Delhi in 1961 and the second one in Chennai. It was realised that there was a necessity for trained workers at field level, who have understanding of the basic needs of the child and the knowledge of concept of integrated child welfare services. This child welfare workers/organisers role will be a link between the various services and the living environmental of the child. The training was multi-disciplined in its approach. Experts in Health, Nutrition, Education, Social Work were associated with it. It was first time in the history of India that efforts at experimental stage was made to provide integrated Child Welfare Services and a training of multi-disciplinary child welfare workers.

Till 1982 there were 38 training centres running in 22 States and Union Territories and 305 courses were completed. Of these 38 training centres, 18 Training Centres in 14 States were running along with it Anganwadi Training Courses also. Two B.S.T. Centres Kosabad (Rural) and Ajmer (Rajasthan) were under direct control of ICCW. These were started in 1963. In the current year 1983-84 only 277 centres in 14 States were running B.S.T. as others totally switched on to Anganwadi Training. Up-to-date (1985) 20,138 Balsevikas have been trained by ICCW.

Today B.S.T. such has been closed from March 1998 and some of them have been changed and converted to Middle Level Training Centres (MLTC) and some into AWTC (i.e., *Anganwadis*).

(j) *Other Activities 1962*

(1) ICCW started participation in the Children's International Summary Village Camps (CISV) by sending children in the age group of 11-12 years.
(2) In February 1962, services of Dr. D. Paul Chowdhary of CSWB were loaned to ICCW as Executive Director. He was succeeded by Margaret Naini in 1963.
(3) Lady Edwina Mountbatten Memorial Trust provided funds to ICCW to train suitable candidates every year in Child Welfare Services in United Kingdom. Up to 1978, 19 candidates with post-graduate qualification is Social Sciences were sent to U.K. to various universities. Lately, it was reviewed and decided that employees of ICCW State Councils and Union Territories should be selected and sent for "Service" training within the country.
(4) *Printing of Monthly Bulletin:* ICCW started printing its monthly Bulletin from its cyclostyled News Letters and also commenced bringing out an Annual Number on Children's day. Bulletins on different subjects were brought with technical data, facts, and figures and were in great demand at home and abroad. In-charge was Smt. Pramila Pandit Barooah who was the first assistant-secretary in the Council and continued for 9 years.
(5) *Orientation Courses:* ICCW organised on Orientation Courses for Child Welfare Organisers of the State Councils and the Balsevika Training Centre's Supervisors.
(6) *Appointment of an Officer on Special Duty:* 1962-64 Miss Sheroo Contractor was appointed officer on special duty.
    (i) *Adoption Programme 1963:* The Council started a new programme of giving children in adoption with a view to

eliminate profiteering and trafficking in children. The Supreme Court of India laid down guidelines in its judgement delivered on 16 February 1984 on intercountry adoption. It directed the Government of India to prepare a list of social child welfare agencies recognised for intercountry adoption by the Government in various foreign countries.

(ii) *Permanent Premises of ICCW:* ICCW shifted its office from Janpath Barracks to the rear portion of the ICCW Building at 4, Rouse Avenue which was completed. It was inaugurated by the then Vice-President of India Dr. Zakir Hussain.

(iii) *Deputy President IUCW:* Smt. Indira Gandhi was elected to the same post for the second term.

Scheme Undertaken during 1964

The Scheme of SOS Children's Village was taken up by the ICCW. The SOS Project Committee sponsored by the ICCW was constituted and registered under the Societies Registration Act XXI of 1860, (Punjab Amendment) Act, 1957 as extended to the Union Territory of Delhi under No. S-2429 of 1963-64 under the name of SOS Children's Villages of India. It is affiliated to the SOS Kenderdorf International and accepted as a full member of International Body at its Annual Conference held in Vienna in September 1964. Two members of ICCW were representatives in the Project Committee. The SOS Children's Villages of India is the Central Organisation responsible for developing the programmes in India. A plan for starting SOS Children's Villages for orphans and destitute children during Fourth Five Year Plan was submitted to the Department of Social Security Government of India through Indian Council for Child Welfare, Smt. Acchama John Mathai was its first Chairman and when she resigned, Smt. Tara Ali Baig, Vice-President ICCW was made its Chairman on 26th November, 1965. At present more than 25 SOS Children's Villages in the country are taking care of over 10,000 children."

Adoption of Children's Bill (1965)

ICCW organised a National Seminar on "National Policy for Children" at Hyderabad.

Exhibition of British Children's Paintings

ICCW with collaboration of Bal Bhawan organised an Exhibition of British Children's Paintings at Bal Bhavan.

Life Patron of ICCW (1966)

In 1966 Mrs. Indira Gandhi was made Life-Patron of ICCW and also Hony. President of IUCW.

Orientation Seminar on Bal Sevika Training Programme (1966)

The Council conducted the Orientation Seminar on Bal Sevika Training Programmes.

Children's International Summer Village Camp (CISV)

In 1967 ICCW formed the CISV (India) chapter, affiliated to CISV, U.K.

1968 Sponsorship Programme

ICCW introduced a new programme entitled "Sponsorship Programme" for the welfare of children.

1969 International Children's Fair in Delhi

(i) ICCW organised an International Children's Fair in Delhi under the Chairmanship of Shri Radha Raman and General Secretary Smt. Shyam Kumari Khan. It was inaugurated by the Prime Minister on 17.10.1969.

(ii) *Production and Supply of Educational Equipments and Toys:* ICCW chaired the Working Group set up by the Department of Social Welfare and Production and Supply of Educational Equipments and Toys for Children, under the Chairmanship of Kitty Shiva Rao.

In 1970 Dr. Phulerau Guha President ICCW and Smt. Shyam Kumari Khan, General Secretary, started new scheme.

(i) The first CISV Camp was held in India at Nagarjuna Sagar, Andhra Pradesh and nine countries sent their children to the camp.

(ii) *Learn to Live Together Camps:* A new scheme to encourage national integration called "Learn to Live Together Camp" was started both at national level and at State levels for children of low-income groups. For 10 days, 4 children (2 boys and 2 girls) with an escort came from all States to attend the Camp.

(iii) *Supervised Home Work Centre:* The scheme of "Supervised Home Work Centre" was started for the children of low income group families to provide help to them in their education all over the country. This Centre was organised in all States in the evenings after school hours. ICCW contributed Rs. 2000 to each State—these were in operation till 1979 (currently State Councils like Jammu & Kashmir, Chennai and Haryana etc. only few are running on their own).

(iv) *Seminar on Pre-School Education:* ICCW in collaboration with the International Children's Centre, France organised a Seminar on "Pre-School Education" at Chennai with support from the Government of India and the UNICEF.

1971 Good Friends Picture Albums

(i) In 1971 ICCW co-operated with "IE-NO-HIKARI" Association, Japan. It was world co-operative movement which aimed at building a peaceful co-operative society through children's paintings. Every year ICCW sent paintings selected from all over India received through our State Councils. They gave musical boxes to the winners and to all contestants "Good Friends Picture Albums" which consists of paintings of children from all over the world and India who are the winners. (This scheme was there till 1981).

(ii) *Nutrition Programme:* The Nutrition Programme commenced in the existing and New Balwadis run by the ICCW. There are in total 803 Balwadis in States and 2 Union Territories (currently only 795 are running).

(iii) *Programme for the Refugee Children of Bangladesh:* ICCW undertook a pilot emergency programme for the Refugee children of Bangladesh in Bengal in collaboration with IUCW and it was implemented by West Bengal State Council.

1972 Second International Summer Village Camp

The Second Children's International Summer Village Camp was held in Bhopal, Madhya Pradesh.

1973 Adoption of Children's Bill

ICCW along with All India Women's Conference, the Indian Council of Social Welfare and the Association for Promotion of Adoption, and also other prominent agencies submitted a signed Memorandum to the Prime Minister urging the early passage of the Adoption of Children Bill when Smt. Tara Ali Baig was President and Mrs. Pramila Pandit Barooah, General Secretary (and continued for 6 years).

1974 Formation of a Trust

ICCW Trust was registered as a separate Body with five Trustees of which Smt. Indira Gandhi as its Chair-person and President and Gen. Secretaries ICCW as ex-officio members. (Since the death of Smt. Indira Gandhi, the vacancy was filled by Late Mr. Rajiv Gandhi, who was then nominated as the fifth trustee and the Chairman of the Trust).

1975 Intensive Community Development Scheme (ICDS)

(i) On 2nd October 1975, the ICDS Project was launched by the Government.

(ii) *Anganwadi Training Centre:* Training of workers for the ICDS Project became an extremely crucial part of the Programme and ICCW was given the responsibility for organising Anganwadis Training Centres to start with. Today it has 118 training centres in 17 States and in Union Territories.

(iii) *Research:*

(a) *The Living Conditions of Working Children in Urban Delhi:* ICCW carried out Research Project on the living condition of working children in urban Delhi which was funded by Social Welfare Department.

(b) The family planning Foundation sanctioned a Research Project on "SEX Differences" in the Department of Child Development, Lady Irwin College.

(c) ICCW was given the authority by the Delhi High Court to carry out legal procedure for foster care and adoption.

1976 April 1975 CISV became Independent

A separate body was constituted and registered under Societies Registration Act, with Headquarters in Delhi under Chairmanship of Shri Radha Raman.

(i) ICCW organised a Seminar "Sex Education" in New Delhi.

(ii) A workshop was organised for the Child Welfare Organisers in collaboration with the National Institute of Public Co-operation and Child Development.

(iii) With the assistance from the Save the Children Fund, the ICCW undertook the immunisation programme of measles vaccine for 40,000 children with Delhi, implemented with the assistance of ICCW expert Dr. K.P.S. Verma, pediatrician from Willingdon Hospital. This was for the first time in India.

(iv) A rehabilitation Hostel and Home for the unsettled Gaddi Tribal children and epectant mothers was set up with the assistance of SCF in collaboration with the Himachal Pradesh State Council for Children Welfare at Mehla Village in Chamba District. SCF sanctioned Rs. 3.04 lakhs for the same.

Silver Jubilee Year of ICCW 1976

ICCW celebrated its Silver Jubilee Year by strengthening its 'on going' Programmes and taking new ones.

(i) Starting a rural project in four villages of each State and Union Territories to produce a package deal of welfare services (list in Appendix I).

(ii) On Children's Day it brought out special envelopes with Children's Day stamp, they were brought in great numbers by stamp collectors.

(iii) ICCW took up a special programme in the cyclone affected area of Andhra Pradesh by starting 43 Balwadis—31 in Krishna district and 12 in Guntur district. They were directly under ICCW, and the implementation and supervision was done by Life Member Smt. Seetha Kamaraj (who is doing so till today).

In 1977, Smt. Tara Ali Baig elected President IUCW, first person from the East.

In 1978 ICCW with assistance from Save the Children Fund took up relief work in Unnao and Barabanki districts of U.P. which were badly affected by the devastating floods and which have now permanent Day Care Centres. An amount of Rs. 1,19,531.45 was sanctioned and given 98 bags of milk and 40 bales of clothing.

(iv) In 1978 ICCW along with J&K State Council undertook relief for 1500 more children in Leh, Ladakh with the financial assistance of SCF and 31,000 blankets, 1,675 bottles of cod Liver Oil, 80 bales of clothing and it has now been converted to Leh Nutrition Project under the supervision of SCF directly.

(v) Organised a National Seminar on "Education of the Teachers for Pre-School Child in Delhi".

(vi) ICCW instituted two special National Awards in the memory of Geeta and Sanjay Chopra who were brutally murdered by miscreants inspite of their brave resistance.

1979 International Year of the Child

(i) Walking Crusade was organised by the ICCW to celebrate the International Year of the Child to bring awareness among the people about the Rights of the Child and their needs. About 1500 children from all over the country participated in the *Pada Yatra* and met in Delhi.

(ii) It sold special brass pins with the shape of ICCW emblem.

(iii) It brought out a special bulletin on its plan of action to be undertaken at headquarters and its affiliated bodies.

In 1980 ICCW entered into a new field by renewing its old scheme of printing and sale of Greeting cards to raise funds to strengthen and diversify its activities in the field of Child Welfare. Half of the income from the Project is utilised for ICCW sponsorship scheme and the other half goes in providing physical aids for handicapped children.

1981-82

(i) ICCW started organising a National Painting competition for children.

(ii) ICCW Library was reorganised and furnished and brought up-to-date with books and periodicals, with grant from Social Welfare Department up to 1985, the Library had 2,850 books, 55 magazines and journals are received regularly.

(iii) In the current year 115 prize winning entries from 10 states were received. Twelve paintings were selected by Expert Commission for National Awards.

1983-84

(i) Organised First Integration Camp for the Handicapped Children at national level in Delhi, at Gandhi Darshan Grounds, States participated and there were blind, deaf and dumb and physically handicapped.

On 31st October 1984, Smt. Indira Gandhi who was the only life-pattern of ICCW was assassinated and ICCW felt its great loss and held a Condolence Meeting on 13th November 1984.

1985-90

The work of the ICCW continued as before and the additional highlights during the period were—

(i) They got sanction for more creches and the total number of creches came to a total of 1574.

(ii) There were 57 creche workers training centres with 1842 trained workers.

(iii) There were 594 early childhood training centres.

(iv) A compilation was made of the ICDS Research study report based on 86 Anganwadi training centres.

(v) Child Labour Relief Projects made headway at the 4 centres in Madhya Pradesh and one in Tamil Nadu in Beedi Industry. Nine more were to be taken up in the glass and bangle industries at Ferozabad and ten centres for children employed in lock industry.

(vi) ICCW organised number of workshops/orientation courses in different areas during the period.

(vii) Started Sponsorship in the name of 'Ganga Hingorani' with the donation of Rs. 10,000 given by her husband, in her memory.

(viii) From 1987-88 the council instituted another award—the Bharat award for an exceptionally outstanding, meritorious and gallant deed. In 1988-89 three new awards with the Veer Bapu Gayadhani award were instituted.

From 1991-96: Anganwadis

In the beginning only a 3 months job training course was started for Anganwadi workers.

1985-86—a 15 day refresher training was introduced for them.

1987-88—13 day training of Anganwadi helpers was started.

1994-95—One week refresher course was introduced for Anganwadis helpers.

1995-96—During the year 6,145 Anganwadi workers were trained through 168 training courses.

Refresher training was provided to 5,042 Anganwadi workers through 139 courses. 7,786 helpers were oriented and 290 helpers provided with refresher training.

1995—A workshop for field officers was organised.

Balsevika Training Programme

Balsevika Training Programme started in 1961, to train multi-purpose child care workers, to look after the total development of children. This was 11 months training course.

Since beginning there were 708 courses which gave training to 36,096 balsevikas. 1995-96—25 BST institutes trained 1,195 Balsevikas.

To this time ICCW is running 1,633 creches. It has so far trained 5,780 creche workers through first course. Training creches were conducted for 269 creche workers.

Balwadi Nutrition Programme

They function for 4 hours daily for 270 days a year. There were 803 balwadis run by ICCW.

Early Childhood Education Programme was running in and 594 Early Childhood Centres functioned in 6 educational backward states of Assam, Bihar, Madhya Pradesh, Rajasthan, Uttar Pradesh and West Bengal.

As in the case of the Balwadi Nutrition Programme, the early childhood education programme too will be phased out, by the Government of India, with the universalisation of ICDS during the ninth plan.

Government of India formulated National Labour Policy on1987. Special schools for children were started in Glass and Bangle Industry, Ferozabad, Brassware in Moradabad, Lock industry in Aligarh, and 4 in Madhya Pradesh in Beedi Industry. ICCW was assigned with the responsibility for starting these schools.

Project for street children, started in 1994. So far 33 children between 6-18 age were given non-formal education, supplementary nutrition, preventive and curative health services, recreational and vocational training at the four centres located in different slums of Delhi. Some families were provided with counselling services.

Adoption Programme

479 cases were scrutinised in 1994-95, and 593 cases were scrutinised in 1995-96. Of these 254 were In-country and 339 were Inter-country.

Since Supreme Court of India authorized ICCW, it has scrutinised 880 cases of In-country cases, and 2,596 cases were of Inter-country. They represented in National Workshop on adoption, organised by the Bal Asha Trust in 1995 at Mumbai.

In 1996 at New Delhi, International Conference on Adoption was organised. Approximately representatives from various agencies from India and abroad participated.

Sponsorship

Total number of children covered under the programme are 532.

National Awards

* So far 485 children have received the awards.
* Geeta and Sanjay awards were instituted in 1978.
* Bharat award was instituted in 1987.
* Veer Bapu Gayadhani Awards in 1988.

National Painting Awards

* In 1994, 40 children were selected, of which 20 were normal and 20 were handicap children.
* In 1994-95, The Abhinav Award for environment was instituted.

National 'Learn to Live Together' Camp

The XXII camp in 1995 was held in collaboration with Andhra Pradesh State Council for Child Welfare. It was held in Hari Prasad Institute Campus. For the first time Mentally Handicapped children were included. A total number of 88 children and their escorts attended from 16 States/ U.Ts.

Indira Gandhi Scholarship Scheme

The Ministry of Health and Family Welfare reserved one seat in the MBBS course. J.I.P.M.E.R., Pondicherry while the Ministry of Human

Resources Development (Department of Education) reserved five seats (two in Degree and three in diploma courses) in Engineering for National bravery awardees during the year.

A total number of children, eleven in number, were studying in various technical institutions during 1995-96. Of these four children were enrolled in engineering course and seven in MBBS course. All these 11 children were provided financial assistance under the Indira Gandhi Scheme of ICCW. Each child is given Rs. 500 per month for the first year and Rs. 400 per year for the subsequent years of the course. A total number of 26 children have been covered under the programme since 1987. Twelve students in MBBS and in Engineering have so far completed the course. While three children left their studies mid-way.

The Government of India first reserved the seats for the recipients of awards in 1984.

Research and Development

In order to prepare a perspective action-cum research and development plan for ICCW, a meeting was organised by the R&D unit of the Council in January 1996. Representatives of various organisations—national and International participated and identified priority areas for research by ICCW. These included: a directory of NGOs, status report on the recipients of the national bravery awardees, identification of determinants of infant and child mortality in India and need based programmes for their reduction, strategies for rehabilitation of victims of polio etc.

Supervised Home Work Scheme

So far 22 centres functioned, 10 in Madhya Pradesh and 12 in West Bengal. In each centre, one teacher guides 40 children.

Library and Publication

The Library contains books on a variety of subjects pertaining to the child. The library receives a number of periodicals also.

Greeting Cards

A total number of 29,000 cards were printed in seven designs for Diwali and New Year during 1995-96. One of these was selected from the paintings sent for National Painting Competition. A total of 8,665 cards were sold from the new designs printed during the year. Also 7,328 old designs in addition. Thus accounting for a total sale of 15,993 cards during the year.

Annual Report

1981: Relief to Child at Work. The Council launched its "Relief to Child at Work" project with the starting of centres at Karnataka (for children engaged in rag picking) and Jammu & Kashmir (for children employed in the carpet weaving industry).

1981: International Conference on Child Welfare. An important event of the year was the International Regional Conference on Child Welfare organised by ICCW in collaboration with the International Union for Child Welfare.

1984: ICCW Appointed Scrutinising Agency. The Supreme Court of India authorised the Council to act as a scrutinising agency for all cases related to intra- and inter-country adoption.

1986: Creche Workers Training. The Creche Workers Training Programme was initiated.

1986: Seminar on Adoption. The first National Seminar on Adoption was organised by ICCW at New Delhi. Representatives from foreign agencies of adoption also participated in the Seminar.

1986-87: Centres for Working Children. The Council entered the area of providing relief to street and working children in a big way with the setting up of centres at Delhi. Subsequently the Ministry of Labour sanctioned the setting up of ten centres for the children employed in the glass and bangle industry in Ferozabad.

1986-87: Early Childhood Education Programme. Early childhood Education centres were started in the six educationally backward States listed by the Ministry of Human Resource Development.

1987-88: Research Study on ICDS. A research study on the ICDS components, to be carried out by ICCW run Anganwadi Workers Training Centres, was initiated.

1988-89: Enrichment Programme for Trainers. The Enrichment Programme for Trainers was initiated with the objective of enhancing their skills in order that they respond to the issues and problems prevalent in the field.

1989-90: Orientation Courses on Childhood Disabilities. Four regional level orientation courses on early detection and intervention of childhood disabilities were planned in collaboration with the National Institute for the Mentally Handicapped, Secundarabad.

1989-90: Exhibition—Helping Children Learn. For the first time the Council organised an exhibition—Helping Children Learn—on pre-primary education for teachers and parents. This was organised in collaboration with Centre for Learning resources, Pune.

1989-90: Workshop on Research and Documentation in Adoption. A national workshop on Research and Documentation in Adoption was organised. This workshop was the first of its kind.

1991-92: NGO Workshop on the Rights of the Child. A NGO Workshop on the Rights of the Child was organised at New Delhi in December 1991 to emphasise the importance of the voluntary sector in the formulation, implementation and monitoring of schemes related to child welfare/development.

1991-92: Evaluation of Balwadis. A research study on the Evaluation of Balwadis was started.

1992-93: Second International Conference on Adoption. The Council organised the Second International Conference on Adoption.

1992-93: NGO Consultation. A NGO Consultation on the implementation of the National Plan of Action was organised at New Delhi in December 1992.

1993-94: SAARC Friendship Camp. The first SAARC friendship camp for children was organised in February 1994.

1994-95: National Consultation on Rights of the Child. A national consultation on Rights of the Child was organised at New Delhi from November 21-23, 1994 to provide an input into the India country report to be presented to the UN Committee of experts.

1995-96: Workshop for Field Officers. A workshop-cum-orientation course was conducted for Field Officers in June, 1995.

In conclusion and in all fairness it must be mentioned that Pt. Jawaharlal Nehru and till late Smt. Indira Gandhi had been constant inspiration. With the dawn of Independence the late Prime Minister Pt. Jawaharlal Nehru had been giving the lead in many walks of life, but Every few will know and realise how vitally he influenced the workers of child welfare. He once indicated that "Our interest in the child and love for the child" are good qualifications for one who sincerely wants to deal with children and their problems and the State should consider itself responsible for at least every child if not every adult or grown up. He was deeply concerned always and did not remain blind to the magnitude of the problems, and emphasised the need for a sense of proportion and also of priorities regarding the work concerning children.

He advised that the problems of meeting the needs of children, should be tackled in simple way, so that any scheme may be capable of repetition all over the country. Therefore, he said "child welfare and how it deals with the child" should really be considered as of paramount importance in the states planning. Panditji's utterances, advice, statements still stand true today and give all of us food for thought.

APPENDIX-I

THE AIMS AND OBJECTS OF THE COUNCIL ARE

(a) To initiate, undertake or aid directly or through branches or affiliated bodies, schemes for furtherance of child welfare in India;

(b) To support wherever possible, and guide the progress of any approved scheme of child welfare which may already exist;

(c) To organise and maintain institutions for the training of child welfare workers and to encourage their employment for child welfare work;

(d) To help, wherever possible, in the extension of facilities for courses of special training in child welfare in the existing institutions;

(e) To establish a Central Bureau for the study and collection of data and statistics in respect of child welfare work;

(f) To public studies, treaties, books, periodicals, reports and other literature relating to child welfare;

(g) To promote dissemination of knowledge and information and to educate public opinion for child welfare programmes on a scientific basis;

(h) To arrange for the holding of periodical conferences and seminars on child welfare;

(i) To promote enactment of legislation and reform in existing laws relating to matters concerning children and their welfare and to work towards the formulation of a national charter for the children and implementation of its provisions;

(j) To promote generally the welfare of children in India having regard to their social, economic and other needs;

(k) To promote establishment or formation of State Council or Union Territory Councils with similar aims and objectives and to provide for their affiliation to the Council;

(l) To promote, establish and recognise societies or associations with similar objects within the territories of the Republic of India and to enter into agreements with other organisations for their affiliation to or amalgamation with the Council;

(m) To co-operate with national international organisations having similar objectives and to depute or receive representatives to and from such organisations;

(n) To co-operate with other agencies both Governmental and non-governmental in the organisation and administration of schemes and funds for furtherance of child welfare in India;

(o) To send delegates or observers to national and international conference on child welfare or allied matters;

(p) To receive grants, donations fees for subscriptions and to manage and administer the funds at the disposal of the Council;

(q) To acquire, receive and hold property both movable and immovable including securities and negotiable instrument;

(r) To purchase, construct, manage and alter buildings and to equip them suitably for the purpose of the Council;

(s) To manage, sell, transfer, pledge or otherwise dispose of or deal with property of any kind which may be at the disposal of the Council;

(t) To enter into contracts for and in connection with any of the purposes of the Council;

(u) To raise moneys and funds by borrowings or otherwise as may be deemed fit for and on behalf of the Council;

(v) To perform all such acts as may be necessary or proper for the achievement of any or all of the objectives of the Council.

The ICCW Emblem
&
Its Interpretation

Every child needs a few basic necessities that are his birthright. Necessities like food, clothing, shelter, medical care, education and love.

The Indian Council for Child Welfare strives to provide these necessities to the less fortunate of our children. With the help of people who are actively associated with ICCW, those children cannot look forward to a fuller happier future.

The symbol of ICCW is a graphic interpretation of its activities. The small "C" represents the unfortunate forsaken child, who looks to society for his well-being. He demands of society what his mother is unable to provide. Enclosing the letter "C" is a house, with walls and a mid-pointed roof-symbolising shelter and the protectiveness of a mother. Giving him an environment that stimulates his growth.

This, then, is what ICCW does. Pictured graphically in a symbol that protects the child—citizen of tomorrow.

8

UNIVERSAL CHILDREN'S DAY

Universal Children's Day (or World Children's Day, International Children's Day or simply Children's Day as it is called in some countries) has been observed in 149 countries and territories during the last so many years since it was established by the United Nations. There is now not a single month in the year when it is not on the calendar some where.

Origin

It was suggested by Eglantyne Jebb (Founder of IUCW) in 1923, in a letter to Ettienne Clousot (1st Secretary General to the Save the Children International Union, 1920-25) that a Children's Day be observed throughout the world. She thought, it should be the same day for all countries and suggested 1st June. This idea was followed 30 years later.

History of the Day

A world-wide 'Children's Day', the dedication of a day each year to the Children of the world, the rights and their needs was first proposed in 1952 by the International Union for Children Welfare (IUCW), a non-governmental organisation which had consultative status with the United Nation's Children Fund (UNICEF).

Thus in October 1953, 'Children's Day' was first celebrated internationally under the sponsorship of IUCW, and 40 countries and territories organised special ceremonies to strengthen the feeling of International Solidarity for the well-being of children.

The idea of a Universal Children's Day with UN Sanction was mooted by Indian delegate to the United Nations General Assembly, late Shri V.K. Krishna Menon when he was India's delegate to the 42nd Plenary Meeting of the United Nations General Assembly. On 14th November 1954, the United Nations General Assembly passed a

Resolution [836 (ix)] proposed by India, which recommended that "with effect from 1956, a Universal Children's Day shall be instituted by all countries, to be observed as a day for a world-wide fraternity and understanding among children's activity devoted to the promotion of ideals and objectives of the charter and the welfare of the children of the world, the strengthening and broadening of the efforts made by the United Nations in favour and on behalf of all the children of the World."

In accordance with this resolution, it assigned to UNICEF the responsibility for promoting this annual day and to take appropriate action. UNICEF joined hands with IUCW in sponsoring subsequent observances. United Nations agencies with special responsibilities such as:

The World Health Organisation (WHO), The International Labour Organisation (ILO), The Food and Agriculture Organisation (FAO), worked in partnership with UNICEF in those international programmes aimed at meeting the needs of the world's children.

Dual Purposes of the Day

1. *Educational:* It is an occasion when the public and governments are asked to focus on the needs and rights of children, through as many channels as possible, for example, radio and television programmes, exhibits, posters, community, newspapers and magazines, editorials, articles and special publications.
2. *Recreational:* It is an occasion for honouring children every where through celebrations and activities such as pageants, parades, sports' activities, the article productions, bazaars, film shows and orphanages, hospitals, community centres and children's homes.

Dual Theme of the Day

The General Theme

Each year is the "Universality of Children." The day fails in its purpose if it is regarded merely as an occasion to give a few children a party or to provide local politicians or celebrities a chance to be photographed kissing babies. Giving children's benefactors publicity are both valid aspects of the occasion, but to be truly significant, it must amount to more than that. It must provide an opportunity and focal point to increase public awareness of the needs and rights of children not only in one area or personal care, whom they know and love but all over the world, promoting a genuinely broad outlook. Because all children, no matter how rich or poor their parents are, no matter what religious group, political party, social class, nation or race they happened to belong to, have some needs and rights. Every child needs and deserve good medical care, education and food, protection from present dangers and preparation for the future.

Themes of the Universal Children's Day

Besides the general theme, a special theme for every year is proclaimed. The various themes since the inception of Children's Day have been

1957 -- "The hungry child must be fed."
1958 — "The Child that is sick must be nursed. The child that is physically or mentally handicapped must be helped."
1959 — "The maladjusted child must be re-educated. The orphan and the waif must be sheltered and succoured."
1960 — "The harmony of tomorrow's world depends upon the mental and physical health of to-day's children."
1961 — "Social services for children, especially adequate preventive work, safeguard a community from delinquency and maladjusted."
1962 — "The rights of every child, the responsibility of every adult and every community."
1963 — "National Policy for Children."
1964 — "Preparing children and their families for the changing of social pattern."
1965 — "The Child under Stress in a Changing World."
1966 — "Children and Peace."
1967 — "Challenge—good Nutrition for all Children."
1968 — "Good Health—a Human Right of Every Child."
1969 — "Training personal to project and prepare children."
1970 — "The Role of Education in Child Care."
1971 — "Young Human Resources: The key to National Development."
1972 — "A Better Life for Children in Slums and Shanty Towns."
1973 — "The Rural Child."
1974 — "A Future for Every Child."
1975 — "Today's girl tomorrow's woman."

1976 — "Reaching the Unreached" and "All children need basic services."
1977 — "Water for the children of the world."
1978 — "The Rights of the Child."
1979 — "Year of the Child."
1980 — "Children in the 1980s."
1981 — "First things First, Fighting child Disabilities with Clean Water."
1982 — "Cities and Children."
1983 — "Hungry Children—A challenge to the world's conscience."
1984 — "Youth and children together to looking forward to a new era."
1985 — "Community Participation."
1986 — "We are all one."
1987 — "The Child's Right to a Home."
1988 — "Happy Children—Chacha Nehru's Dream."
1989 — "Happy Child Nations Pride."
1990 — "Child Survival and Development First Call on the Society."
1991 — "Child's right to special care.
1992 — "Children and Environment.
1993 — "Children, Peace and Communal Harmony.
1994 — "Rights of the Child: A Commitment.
1995 — "Twenty Years of ICDS.
1996 — "Towards an Enabling Environment: Five decades of India—UNICEF partnership in the service of Children.
1997 — 50 years of Child Development : The Challenges ahead.

How the Day is Observed

A Promotional Kit is prepared and distributed each year by UNICEF containing press material, factual background information, and ideas for publicising and celebrating the day. This Kit is sent to UNICEF's regional and country offices around the world, to the National Committees of UNICEF, National affiliates of the International Centres, United Nations Associations and many non-government organisations. They adapt, reproduce, translate and disseminate material in the Kit for use by local organisations and individuals interested in children's welfare. The media and local groups are encouraged to use all appropriate material of special interest to their own communities.

Official Status of the Day

In some countries Universal Children's Day is an official holiday. Many countries have issued commemorative postage stamps in connection with the day. In other areas, the day's celebration is strictly voluntary, through leaders and schools, Scouts and other youth groups and all religious denominations.

When and Where the Day is Observed

Within a decade the concept of Universal Children's Day gained wide acceptance around the world. The development may be traced, in part of the Universal and Humanitarian feelings of responsibility for the well-being of the child.

The General Assembly resolution had also suggested that the Governments observe the day on the date and in a manner each consider most appropriate and convenient. There is, therefore, great variations as in some areas the sponsors are non-governmental, religious or educational groups, in others the day's events are organised and conducted by Government officials. When not otherwise noted the Ist Monday in October is the date on which the day is celebrated, this is the date recommended by the UN General Assembly.

In the list below is mentioned the month in which the day has been officially endorsed by the national government of respective country except in those countries in italics.

January — Egypt, Kuwait, Oman, Thailand, United Arab Emirates.
February — Burma.
March — Belize, *France, Iran*, Lebanon, Libya, Tunisia.
April — Jordan, Mexico, *Montserrat*, Turkey.
May — Burkina Fase, Israel, Jamaica, Korea, Maldives, Nigeria, *Solemon Islands*.
June — Afghanistan, Algeria, Angola, Antigua, Bulgaria, Byelorussion, Ṡ.SR., *Cape Verde*, China, Czechoslovakia, Denmark, Equador, Ethiopia, German Democratic Republic, Grenada, Guinea-Bissau, *Haiti, Indonesia, Ireland*, Lao People's Democratic Republic, *Malta*, Mangolia, *Mozambique, Netherlands*, Poland, *Portugal, Sao Teme, and Princip*, Seychelles, *Somalia*, St. Lucia, St. Vincent, Ukrania, S.S.R., U.S.S.R.
July — Cuba, *Liberia*.

August — Fiji, Nepal, Paraguay, *Tuvalu, Uruguay, Venezuela.*
September — *Costa Rica, Federal Republic of Germany, Guyana,* Honduras, United Kingdom, Vietnam.
October — *Austria*, Australia, Bangladesh, Barbados, Belgium, Botswana, *Burundi*, Canada, Cyprus, Dominica, Finland, Gambia, Ghana, Greece, Guatemala, Iraq, Lesothe, Luxembourg, New Zeland, Norway, Pakistan, Panama, Peru, Philippines, Singapore, *South Africa, Sudan, Swaziland,* Sweden, Trinidad and Tobago, Yugoslavia, Zambia.
November — Bahamas, Cameroon, Colombia, India, *Madagascar*, Sierra, *Leone*, Spain, *Uganda.*
December — *Bennian*, Central African Republic, *Congo*, Dominican Republic, Ivory Coast, Surinam, Tanzania, Togao, Zaire.

Dates and Months Unreported or Variable

Albania, Argentina (August or Oct.), Bahrain (Jan. or Oct.), Bolivia (April or Oct.), Brazil (Aug. or Oct.), British Virgin Islands, Chile (June or Oct.), El Salvador (Oct. or Nov.), Hungry (May or June), Italy (May, June, Oct. or Nov.), Japan (May or Oct.), Kenya, Malaysia, Mali, Mauritius (Nov. or Dec.), Morocco, Nicaragua, Niger, Papua, New Guinea (Aug. or Oct.), Rumania (May or June), *Rwanda, Samoa*, Senegal (March or June), Sri Lanka (May or Oct.), *Switzerland* (June or Oct.), Syria, Tonga (May or Oct.), U.S.A., Yemen.

Pattern of Celebration of Universal Children's Day as suggested by the International Union for Child Welfare:

1. *Children's Programmes:* Special 15 minutes or longer programmes are prepared on the themes related to Children's Day with Children participating both as performers and audience.
2. *Discussion Programmes:* Groups of prominent people in different fields of child-care are invited and discussed the theme of Children's Day with one person in charge to ask questions.
3. *Musical Programmes:* Recordings of music from different parts of the world—classical, folk and popular—are used effectively in the background or during programmes, breaks or as the basis of an entire programme, with brief entire commentary pointing out similarities and differences among culture, describing how

these affect the lives of children, leading to a meeting or discussion on Universal Children's Day.

4. *Service Programmes:* Children's Day material regarding child-care, domestic service, home economics or mother-craft or worked into radio talks or television talks in regular feature programmes, containing "Household Units" etc.
5. *Variety Shows:* Programmes, features, actors, musicians, singers, and other performers from different parts of the world are appropriately organised in connection with Children's Day.
6. *Miscellaneous Programmes:* These include skits performed by children, children's tableaux, puppet shows, paintings, drawings dancers and other visual entertainment, children's entertainments, discussion round-tables, musical recitals, quiz programmes and variety shows are also observed to celebrate Children's Day.
7. *School Projects and Activities:* These include classroom discussions concerning the needs of the children in economically deprived areas of the world, special classroom activities like debates, skits, spelling, and children's art projects involving drawings, paintings of portraits of children and for landscapes of other countries, toy making, clay modelling etc.
8. *Exhibits of Children's Toys from Many Countries:* These exhibits should show the contracts and similarities to be interesting and popular.

India

In India the Children's Day was known as "Flower Day" was observed first on 5th November in 1948, Later the Flower Day developed into Children's Day and was celebrated from 1949 on 30th July. On November 1957, under special Government Order, 14th November was declared as "Children's Day" in India, to be celebrated every year all over the country.

Thus the Birthday of Pandit Jawaharlal Nehru was given to the Children of India. This Government order was announced at the time of the laying the foundation stone of the Indian Council for Child Welfare Building Headquarters by the President of India, Dr. Rajendra Prasad at an impressive ceremony, and the Prime Minister Pandit Jawaharlal Nehru was present.

The Government of India, for the first time, issued three special stamps to commemorate the Children's Day. Every year a special stamp with the 1st Day Cover and Special Cancellation is issued at a special function organised by Indian Council for Child Welfare (ICCW), and released by a dignitary, ICCW also brings out a special "Children Day Annual" with emphasis on the theme of the year.

Since then, "Children's Day" is celebrated all over the country, by children, schools, organisations, State Councils of ICCW, Akashvani and Doordarshan Broadcast special programmes for the children and all leading newspapers bring out special features highlighting the importance of the day.

The State Councils for Child Welfare, affiliated bodies of ICCW organise variety entertainment, sports, dance, dramas, exhibitions and distribution of sweets on this day, and also undertake fund raising campaigns for the welfare of the children.

The Children Films Society has been organising Children's Film Week from 14th November every year to celebrate Children's Day. In many cities and towns all over India, hundred of Cinema Houses have held special shows for children films (produced by the Society) during the week. A special show of drills and dances is organised on a large scale, participated by various schools in the Stadium which is attended by many and inaugurated by the Prime Minister.

On the whole it must be remembered and realised that Universal Children's Day should be a spring board for lasting concern about children, rather than a past one time celebration. It is both a news event and a tool for development and education.

9

RIGHTS OF THE CHILDREN

The Children's Chapter

"There shall be peace on earth, but not until
Each child shall daily eat his fill,
So warmly clad against the winter wind
And learn his lessons with a tranquil mind.

And thus released from hunger, fear and need,
Regardless of his colour, race or creed,
Look upwards, smiling to the skies,
His faith in man reflected in his eyes."

(By permission of the McGraw-Hill Book Co.,
the above dedication by Dorothy Roight is
reprinted from "Ride with the Sun."
—*United Nations Children's Fund Booklet*)

Introduction

The peace for which all mankind yearns is much more than the mere absence of armed conflicts—that is simply its foundation. True peace means the opportunity to enjoy life and its blessings.

Therefore, when the Nations of the world after the holocaust of the First World War, hopefully established the League of Nations they attempted also to establish Standards according to which nations of the world would be pledged to live, to help build a truly peaceful and happy society.

How the Declaration was Born

In the year 1923, the need to set down principles of child protection to meet the situation obtaining at that time had been felt. A project for children's Charter was being studied by the Save the Children's Fund, London; a very detailed charter had been promulgated in Summer 1922 by the International Union Council of Women in Oslo; there were some international conventions relating to child labour and, in the same field, the International Union of Young Workers, the International Association of Socialist Youth and the International Federation of Trade Unions, published in 1922, a Socialist Charter governing the work of adolescents. Herbert Hoover had also endeavoured to condense the duties of mankind towards the child into a few phrases. Some of the texts quoted were very detailed, but they were programmes setting out minimum requirements rather than the statement of fundamental principles, whereas others were very restricted. At the Save the Children International Union (SCIU) the importance of establishing a Charter of the Rights of the Child, thus laying the basis of Child Welfare was realised, such a Charter had, first of all, to be easy to translate into all languages, and such, that it could be reproduced by the press and above all readily understood and adopted by all countries. Aimed at attracting the attention of all and bringing about a legislative change, and a revision of customs, a Charter is a valuable instrument of propaganda. The rights of child need to be proclaimed, but also and first of all the duties of adults towards children. How could these two concepts best be conciliated and united? Eglantine Jebb suggested that a short title should be adopted—"Declaration of Geneva"—followed by explanatory preamble laying down the Principles of the Rights and Duties.

The drafting proved long and laborious. Finally, on 17th May 1923, the Executive Board selected two drafts, one of which consisted of seven articles and the others five. The latter was adopted, the choice being unanimously approved by the General Council, the Sovereign Authority of the SCIU. A ceremony was held on 28th February, 1924 in Geneva, at the Art and History Museums in the presence of representatives of the authorities of the Communes and Canton of Geneva, the University, the technical and medical corps, the SWISS International Press, the League of Nations, the International Labour Office, the Red Cross etc., at which the Declaration of Geneva was solemnly presented by Georges Werner, who had helped to draft it to the archive of the Republic and Canton of Geneva.

The Declaration of Geneva met with almost unanimous approval by all sides and among the first to sign it were the Swedish Minister of Social Affairs, Prince Waldemer of Denmark and Elizabeth Queen of Belgium.

League of Nations Adopted the Declaration of Geneva

At its plenary session of 26th September 1924, the Fifth Assembly of the League of Nations unanimously adopted the following resolution:

> "The Assembly endorse the Declaration of the Rights of the Child, commonly known as *the Declaration of Geneva*, and invites the States, Members of the League to be guided by its principles in the work of Child Welfare." In endorsing the Declaration of Geneva, the Assembly of the League of Nations consecrated it as the "World Child Welfare Charter".

A copy of the Declaration which was originally written in French was translated in 37 languages and sent out to all members of the Assembly and many representatives.

The Declaration of Geneva was read from the radio-station on the Eiffel Tower, other countries also used their radios to proclaim the Declaration and make it better known. The communique sent to press were widely published.

Declaration of Geneva

1. The child must be given the means requisite for its normal development, both materially and spiritually.
2. The child that is hungry must be fed; the child that is sick must be nursed; the child that is backward must be helped; the delinquent child must be reclaimed and the orphan and the waif must be sheltered and succoured.
3. The child must be the first to receive relief in terms of distress.
4. The child must be put in a position to earn a livelihood, and must be protected against every form of exploitation.
5. The child must be brought up in the consciousness that its talents must be devoted to the services of its fellowmen.

But unfortunately in 1939, World War broke out once again, and rendered the League powerless. Its Declaration became mere "Scraps of papers".

Preparation for the Declaration of the Rights of the Child

In the aftermath of the Second World War, in 1946 a year after the United Nations was formed and it was recommended to the Economic and Social Council of the United Nations that the Declaration of Geneva be revived to "bind the people of the world today as firmly as it did in 1924".

Two years later, in 1948, the United Nations General Assembly approved the adoption of a Universal Declaration of Human Rights. In this Declaration the freedom and rights of children were implicitly included, but it was thought that this was not enough, the special needs of children justified an additional separate document. Therefore, in 1949, it drew up a preliminary draft of a new declaration of children's rights.

In 1948, the General Council of International Union for Child Welfare (IUCW) accepted the revised text counting seven points and including an additional clause on non-discrimination, based on race, nationality and religious faith—concept previously contained in the preamble—and another implying the concept that the child should be helped with due respect for the integrity of his family. Some further specifications were also added, mainly relating to provisions for Social Welfare and Security.

For the next few years however, further action was suspended, pending the formulation of this International Convents on Human Rights—one on Civil and Political Rights; one on Economic, Social and Culture Rights. It was not until 1959, a month after the adoption of the Declaration of Human Rights by the United Nations General Assembly, that the latter adopted the new ten points. Declaration of the Rights of Child, which incorporates all the principles set out in the Declaration of Geneva and which is included in entirety in the first article of the statutes of IUCW.

In 1957, the Human Rights Commission of the Economic and Social Council took up the question of adopting a Declaration of the Rights of the Child which would tie in with the Universal Declaration of Human Rights. After a preliminary discussion, this Commission drafted a declaration which it submitted to its 21 member-states, asking for their comments. Some of the members states said they would prefer a legally binding convention rather than a simple declaration, but the majority of the members favoured a brief declaration proclaiming general principles without providing methods of enforcing them.

The Commission then redrafted the declaration and, on October 19, 1959, the Third Committee of the United Nations General Assembly (the Social, Humanitarian and Cultural Committee) approved this revised draft. The vote was 70 in favour, none against, with Cambodia and the Union of South Africa abstaining.

Declaration of the Rights of the Child

On 20th November, 1959, the General Assembly with representatives of 78 countries meeting in plenary session—adopted the Declaration of the Rights of the Child . . . unanimously.

Preamble

Whereas the peoples of the United Nations have, in the Charter, reaffirmed their faith in fundamental human rights and in the dignity and worth of the human person, and have determined to promote social progress and better standards of life in larger freedom.

Whereas the United Nations has, in the Universal Declaration of Human Rights, proclaimed that everyone is entitled to all the rights and freedoms setforth therein, without distinction of any kind, such as race, colour, sex, language, religion, political or other opinion, national or social origin, property, birth or other status.

Whereas the child, by reason of his physical and mental immaturity, needs special safeguard and care, including appropriate legal protection, before as well as after birth.

Whereas the need for such special safeguards has been stated in the Geneva Declaration of Rights of the Child and in the statutes of specialized agencies and international organisations concerned with the welfare of children, whereas mankind owes to the child the best it has to give.

Now therefore,

The General Assembly

Proclaims this Declaration of the Rights of the Child to the end that he may have a happy childhood and enjoy for his own good and the good of society the rights and freedom herein setforth, and calls upon parents, upon men and women as individuals and upon voluntary organisations, local authorities and national governments to recognise these rights and strive for their observance by legislative and other measures progressively taken in accordance with the following principles:

Principle 1

The child shall enjoy all the rights setforth in this Declaration. All children, without any exception whatsoever, shall be entitled to these rights, without distinction or discrimination on account of race, colour, sex, language, religion, political or other opinion, national or social origin, property, birth or other status, whether or himself or of his family.

Principle 2

The child shall enjoy special protection, and shall be given opportunities and facilities, by law and by other means, to enable him to develop physically, mentally, morally, spiritually and socially in a healthy and normal manner and in conditions of freedom and dignity. In the enactment of laws for this purpose the best interest of the child shall be the paramount consideration.

Principle 3

The child shall be entitled from his birth to a nationality.

Principle 4

The child shall enjoy the benefits of social security. He shall be entitled to grow and develop in health to this end, special care and protection shall be provided both to him and to his mother, including adequate pre-natal and post-natal care. The child shall have the right to adequate nutrition, housing, recreation and medical services.

Principle 5

The child who is physically, mentally or socially handicapped shall be given the special treatment, education and care required by his particular condition.

Principle 6

The child, for the full and harmonious development of his personality, needs love and understanding. He shall, wherever possible, grow up in the care and under the responsibility of his parents, and in any case in an atmosphere of affection and of moral and material security: a child of tender years shall not, save in exceptional circumstances, be separated from his mother. Society and the public authorities shall have the duty to extend particular care to children without a family and to those without adequate means of support, payment of state and other assistance towards the maintenance of children of large families is desirable.

Principle 7

The child is entitled to receive education, which shall be free and compulsory, at least in the elementary stages. He shall be given an education which will promote his general culture and enable him on a basis of equal opportunity to develop his abilities, his individual judgement and his sense of moral and social responsibility, and to become a useful member of society.

The best interests of the child shall be the guiding principle of those responsible for his education and guidance; that responsibility lies in the first place with his parents.

The child shall have full opportunity for play and recreation which should be directed to the same purpose as educating society and the public authorities shall endeavour to promote the employment of the right.

Principle 8

The child shall in all circumstances be among the first to receive protection and relief.

Principle 9

The child shall be protected, against all forms of neglect, cruelty and exploitation. He shall not be the subject of traffic; in any form.

The child shall not be admitted to employment before an appropriate minimum age; he shall in no case be caused or permitted to engage in any occupation or employment which would prejudice his health or education, or interfere with his physical, mental or moral development.

Principle 10

The child shall be protected from practices which may foster racial, religions and any other form of discrimination. He shall be brought up in the spirit of understanding, tolerance, friendship among peoples, peace and universal brotherhood and in full consciousness that his energy and talents should be devoted to the services of his fellow-men.

The Significance of the Declaration

The Declaration of the Rights of the Child is not a mere "Scrap of paper", even though the rights it extols are not yet available to all—or even, unfortunately, to most children. The universal recognition that these rights exist is a very important first step in achieving them, and the fact that so many countries, of such diverse social conditions and cultural traditions, have agreed on the importance of these basic principles is an extremely encouraging omen of future progress.

Ancient, deep-rooted social problems and injustices die hard. There is an inevitable time lag between the recognition and acknowledgement of obligations and the ability to carry them out. But the unique value of every human being, even of the smallest and most helpless, is now officially acknowledged by almost every government in the world. All over the world it is now agreed that children need and deserve special assistance, and energetic efforts are, moreover, recognised as a duty of good government, not as an optional luxury.

In the modern world, with its highly, developed technology that makes possible destruction (and construction) on an unprecedented scale, peace is no longer a luxury either, but an increasingly urgent necessity. Children must be helped to enjoy the right to grow up healthy (physically, mentally, morally, spiritually and socially, in freedom and dignity as Right 2 of the Declaration asserts). If not, they will never be able to or willing to join together in helping to build a better world tomorrow, a safer and happier and more peaceful world, in which their children can enjoy their "rights".

When we protect and foster the rights of every child everywhere, we are protecting and fostering everyone's happiness and everyone's peace, including our own, racial, religious and any other form of discrimination. He shall be brought up in a spirit of understanding, tolerance, friendship among people, peace and universal brotherhood and in full consciousness that his energy and talents should be devoted to the services of his fellow men.

Finally, the General Assembly resolved that governments, non-governmental organisations and individuals should give this Declaration the widest possible publicity as a means of encouraging its observance everywhere.

Rights of the Child in India—A Review

India is a signatory to the Principle 2 of the Declaration of the Rights of the Child, which is the key provision of the Declaration has been included in the Directive Principles of the Indian Constitution in 1978, Article 39(F) has been from the Declaration and introduced into the Indian Constitution. Article 39(F) states—"Children are given opportunity and facilities to develop in a healthy manner and in conditions of freedom and dignity and that childhood and youth are protected against moral and material abandonment".

The primary concern for the interest and welfare of the child which from the fabric of the Declaration, have been the guiding principles in the judicial decisions as well as in the formulation of various child legislations, and also in the Resolution for the national policy for child welfare which was adopted in August 1974.

The "Child" has a subject matter of legislation in various laws—both penal and social. The Indian Penal Code, the Code of Criminal Procedure and various other laws prescribe a differential approach to children owing to their physical and mental limitations.

A survey of laws which have a bearing on the rights and privileges of children, reveals a four-fold classifications:

(1) The special aspects in the matter of culpability for crimes committed by children in relation to others. This matter is essentially dealt with by the Indian Penal Code.

(2) There is an adverse situation viz., where crimes are committed against children by others. In such cases the liability is determined in accordance with general principles of liability by the criminal law. The Indian Penal Code and other social legislations cover the above aspect.

(3) There are laws seeking implementation of social policy with the aid of criminal sanctions. This category consists of laws which through the underpinning of criminal sanctions, lend penal character to the commissions and omissions under law, with an evolved purpose of achieving a social policy in relation to the protection of children against social hazards of immoral trafficking, beggary, child marriage, and the like.

(4) There is a variation in procedure to determine the originality of children, and there are statutory provisions prescribing a different mode of custodial arrangement than what may be necessary for the adult.

Various enactments as well as statutory provisions have been brought into force to protect the rights and privileges of the child:

(1) The provision of child and maternal welfare services, i.e., health, education and nutritional services etc. have been included as an increasingly important aspects of the development plans. These services have been planned for at the Central as well as State levels, and strive to provide for some of the basic needs and rights of children as put down in the Declaration.

(2) A resolution on National Policy for Child Welfare was adopted in August 1974 strengthening and reinforcing the commitment to the goals prescribed in the Declaration. The resolution recognises the nations' children as a supremely important asset and states "we are also the part of the UN Declaration of the Rights of the Child. The goals set out in these documents can reasonably be achieved by judicious and efficient use of the available national resources".

(3) Constitution of National Children's Board subsequent to the adoption of the National Policy Resolution—a National Children's Board is constituted to ensure at different levels, continuous planning, review and coordination of all essential services. Similar Boards are to be constituted at the State level.

Apart from principle 3, despite genuine efforts made by the Government as well as private agencies the goals set down in the Declaration, still serve as inspiring beacons which remains largely to be achieved. Some of the reasons are:

(i) The sheer *magnitude* of the problems faced by the children of India.

(ii) Inadequacy of resources—both material as well as manpower, the latter being attributed largely to *lack of consciousness and availability of suitable personnel.*

(iii) With regard to legislature taking the example of legislations for child labour, the laws are deficient from the international standards as laid down by I.L.O. The reasons for:

  (a) Economic backwardness necessitating a family in India to augment its income by letting children seek employment;

  (b) Lack of educational facilities and the unorganised nature of the various economic sectors like agriculture and the smallness of manufacturing unit making machinery for implementation of the law inadequate.

(iv) Wherever suitable legislations have been enacted, for example in the case of education, the scheme of compulsory education had not been implemented by many states as the enforcement of compulsion is a costly affair. A very large proportion of children therefore do not attend schools. It has also been found that since the child is an economic asset to the family wherever schools have been provided, there is a very high dropout noted. Lack of a suitable enforcement machinery, as well as lack of consciousness on the part of parents serve as contributing factors.

(v) In the case of provisions for offenders and delinquents against one finds that the provisions in terms of remand homes/ observation homes etc. are inadequate resulting in over-crowding etc.

The above examples serve to illustrate the fact that lack of awareness couples with highly pressing economic factors are the main reasons for not having been able to realise the goals spelt out in the Declaration.

As principles, all the 10 principles of the Declaration are ideal and have universal applicability. Although great efforts have been made by governmental, non-governmental agencies the limitations of suitable material as well as manpower resources and the extremely large population however, make it extremely difficult to make these a reality. Thus for a large majority of the children of India these principles still remain a dream.

What is needed is not changes in the Declaration, but rather considerable thought as to the immense problems being faced by countries such as ours in making these principles a reality. The principles are universally applicable, provided they are actually implemented, it is important to take up indepth the response for the ineffective implementation of these principles, if they are to have any meaning at all, for a majority of children, ways of overcoming contribution factors such as illiteracy, lack of sufficient awareness particularly on the part of the parents, and a suitable enforcement machinery will have to be thought of. Evolution of an international enforcement possibly through a system of voluntary agencies or through the UN may be a possible solution. This would require the individual countries to act as members, and enlist a joint effort in terms of cooperation between the member-countries, as well as pressure on the Governments to implement the suggestions made to it.

The Convention on the Rights of the Child

Background

The question on the Convention on the Rights of the Child was first proposed in 1978 by the Government of Poland as one of the initiatives to be undertaken during International Year of the Child (IYC). The Economic and Social Council of the United Nations (ECOSOC), referred the proposal to the UN Commission on Human Rights, which created the "Open-Ended Working Group" in 1979. This working group met annually since then.

On February 5, 1988 the Open-Ended Working Group on the question of a Convention on the Rights of Child finished the first reading of the future UN Convention on the Rights of Child. The proposed Convention, one of the most comprehensive international instruments since the Universal Declaration of Human Rights, addresses economic, social, cultural, political and civil rights and defines the obligations of adults towards children. Agreement on these standards has been reached by international consensus—the result of 9 years of deliberations by representatives from more than 40 countries, supported by inter-governmental agencies of NGOs.

The draft Convention was subjected to a technical review. The review group identified overlap and repetition within and between articles, compared the standards established by the Convention with those in other human rights instruments, and check for the use of gender—neutral language and inconsistency in the text. The group also had to make editorial suggestions as to how these problems can be corrected. One of the needs of this review was to re-number the articles, eliminating the terms, "bister, quarter etc." which were used as a drafting device when provisions were added to the original Polish working document.

The Chairman of the working group, Prof. Adam Lopatka of Poland, ensured that the technical review be completed by August 1988, so that there can be discussions of the recommendations and a formal second reading by the Working Group either later in 1988 or in early 1989. Following the second reading, the proposed Convention will be forwarded to ECOSOC for discussion in May 1989, and then to the General Assembly for consideration in November 1989.

It was considered necessary and important to stress that special privileges and protection for children are included in many preceding international instruments. The novelty, however, was that the Convention's attempt to codify under one title those provisions of

International Law that pertain to children. So that the Convention is an important and easily-understood advocacy tool for those who work for the benefit of the children.

It was also necessary to stress that the Convention was not initiated by UNICEF of NGOs. It was an action by Governments for the benefit of their respective children. As internationalists, it was duty-bound to make the Convention meaningful for all the children of the world.

Obviously and very clearly, the Convention had an enormous potential for children throughout the world. When adopted by UN General Assembly and ratified by the requisite 20 member-states, the convention will provide a framework within which UNICEF and NGOs can more effectively define and promote their existing and future programmes and priorities. It will also assist in developing an alliance for action for the programmes of many diverse organisations—including UNICEF National Committee and Regional Offices, INGOs, other UN agencies and grassroot groups.

It was also important and crucial that public become aware of the Convention's existence and the provisions it contains. A need was felt to develop a broad coalition to demand that Governments support this critical initiative for children. The full text of the Convention comes to 32 pages in the official document (E/CN. 4/1988/WG. 1 WP/Rev. 1—dated 4th February, 1988).

Up-date Action and Follow-up

On 20th November 1989, more than 500 children from round the world were welcomed by UN to celebrate the 30th Anniversary of the UN Declaration of the Rights of Children. The children presented petitions and made statements in support of the Children's rights.

Also on this date the General Assembly was scheduled to vote on the historic Convention on the Rights of Child.

This convention modifies and consolidates the existing standards and introduced a range of relatively new issues of major importance. It is a comprehensive human rights convention drafted in full partnership between developing and developed countries, and, if and when adopted will represent the international community's first universal and binding policy statement on Children's rights.

The General Assembly's social committee began consideration of the Convention on 9th November, 1989.

Adoption of the Convention on the Rights of Child

The 54-Article Convention was adopted by the General Assembly on 20th November 1989 and is the first comprehensive and binding human rights instrument solely addressing the Rights of Children.

On 26th January 1990, sixty countries signed the Convention on the Rights of Child, in the signing ceremony at the UN Headquarters in New York. Opening the signing ceremony, Jan Martenson, Under-Secretary General for Human Rights, said "the Convention was an encouraging expression of the international community's faith in the future and a pledge to continue to strive for human world".

Mr. Martenson said "that the world community has to sincerely work and go quite far to make the world fit for children. It is so evident from the various problems affecting children, including the fact that the hundred million children had been abandoned by their families and left on the street to find their own ways, thus resorting to petty crimes and thefts, prostitution to beggary. Fifty million children round the world are forced to work under inhuman working conditions, and 3.5 million die each year from preventable diseases".

Mr. Martenson was convinced that the Convention could only be successful as countries' Institutions and individuals were willing to make it. He concluded by quoting the Secretary General Javier Perez de Cuellar, "that it was time to move on to make the principles embodied in the Convention a reality for every living child".

Purpose

The purpose of the Convention is to supplement and not replace the 1959 Declaration.

The Rights of the Child

Preamble

The preamble recalls the basic principles of the United Nations and specific provisions of certain relevant human rights treaties and proclamations; reaffirms the fact that children, because of their vulnerability, need special care and protection; and places special emphasis on the primary-caring and protective responsibility of the family, the need for the legal and other protection of the child before and after birth, the importance of respect for the cultural values of the child's community, and the vital role of international cooperation in achieving the realisation of children's rights.

Article: 1
Definition of a Child: All persons under 18, unless by law majority is attained at an earlier age.

Article: 2
Non-discrimination: The principle that all rights apply to all children without exception, and the State's obligation to protect children from any form of discrimination. The States must not violate any right, and must take positive action to promote them all.

Article: 3
Best Interests of the Child: All the actions concerning the child should take full account of his/her best interests. The State is to provide adequate care when parents or others responsible fail to do so.

Article: 4
Implementation of Rights: The State's obligation to translate the rights in the Convention into reality.

Article: 5
Parental Guidance and the Child's Evolving Capacities: The State's duty to respect the rights and responsibilities of parents and the wider family to provide guidance appropriate to the child's evolving capacities.

Article: 6
Survival and Development: The inherent right to life, and the State's obligation to ensure the child's survival and development.

Article: 7
Name and Nationality: The right to have a name from birth and to be granted a nationality.

Article: 8
Preservation of Identity: The State's obligation to protect and, if necessary, re-establish the basic aspects of a child's identity (name, nationality and family name).

Article: 9
Separation from Parents: The child's right to live with his/her parents,

unless this is deemed incompatible with his/her interests; the right to maintain contact with both parents if separated from one or both; the duties or States in cases where such separation results from State action.

Article: 10

Family Reunification: The right of the children and the parents to leave any country and to enter their own in order to be reunited or to maintain the child-parent relationship.

Article: 11

Illicit Transfer and Non-return: The State's obligation to try to prevent and remedy the kidnapping or retention of children abroad by a parent or third party.

Article: 12

The Child's Opinion: The child's right to express an opinion, and to have that opinion taken into account in any matter or procedure affecting the child.

Article: 13

Freedom of Expression: The child's right to obtain and make known information, and to express his/her views, unless this would violate the rights of others.

Article: 14

Freedom of Thought, Conscience and Religion: The child's right to freedom of thought, conscience and religion, subject to appropriate parental guidance and national law.

Article: 15

Freedom of Association: The right of children to meet with others and to join or set up associations, unless the fact of doing so violates the rights of others.

Article: 16

Protection of Privacy: The right to protection from interference with privacy, family, home and correspondence, and from libel/slander.

Article: 17

Access to Appropriate Information: The role of the media in disseminating information to children that is consistent with moral well-being and knowledge and understanding among peoples, and respects the child's cultural backgrounds. The State is to take measures to encourage this and to protect the children from harmful materials.

Article: 18
Parental Responsibilities: The principle that both parents have joint primary responsibility for bringing up their children, and that the State should support them in this risk.

Article: 19
Protection from Abuse and Neglect: The State's obligation to protect children from all forms of maltreatment perpetrate by parents or others responsible for their care, and to undertake preventive and treatment programmes in this regard.

Article: 20
Protection of Children without Families: The State's obligation to provide special protection for children deprived of their family environment and to ensure that appropriate alternative family care or institutional placement is made available to them, taking into account the child's cultural background.

Article: 21
Adoption: In the countries where adoption is recognised and/or allowed, it shall only be carried out in the best interests of the child, with all necessary safeguards for given child and authorization by the competent authorities.

Article: 22
Refugee Children: Special protection to be granted to children who are refugees or seeking refugee status, and the State's obligation to cooperate with competent organisations providing such protection and assistance.

Article: 23
Handicapped Children: The right of handicapped children to special care, education and training designed to help them to achieve the greatest possible self-reliance and to lead a full and active life in society.

Article: 24
Health and Health Services: The right to the highest level of health possible and to access to health and medical services, with special

emphasis on primary and preventive health care, public health education and the diminution of infant mortality. The State's obligation to work towards the abolition of harmful traditional practices. Emphasis is laid on the need for international cooperation to ensure this right.

Article: 25
Periodic Review of Placement: The right of children placed by the State for reasons of care, protection or treatment to have all aspects of that placement evaluated regularly.

Article: 26
Social Security: The right of children to benefit from social security.

Article: 27
Standard of Living: The right of children to benefit from an adequate standard of living, the primary responsibility of parents to provide this, and the State's duty to ensure that this responsibility can be fulfilled, and then fulfil, where necessary through the recovery of maintenance.

Article: 28
Education: The child's right to education, and the State's duty to ensure that primary education at least is made free and compulsory. Administration of school discipline is to reflect the child's human dignity. Emphasis is laid on the need for international cooperation to ensure this right.

Article: 29
Aims of Education: The State's recognition that education be directed at developing the child's personality and talents, preparing the child for active life as an adult, fostering respect for basic human rights and developing respect for the child's own cultural and nationa! values and those of others.

Article: 30
Children of Minorities or Indigenous Populations: The right of children of the minority communities and indigenous populations to enjoy their own culture and to practice their own religion and language.

Article: 31
Leisure, Recreation and Cultural Activities: The right of children to leisure, play and participation in cultural/artistic activities.

Article: 32
Child Labour: The State's obligation to protect children from engaging in work that constitutes a threat to their health, education or development, to set minimum ages for employment, and to regulate conditions for employment.

Article: 33
Drug Abuse: The child's right to protect from the use of narcotic and psychotropic drugs and from being involved in their production or distribution.

Article: 34
Sexual Exploitation: The child's right to protection from sexual exploitation and abuse, including prostitution and involvement in pornography.

Article: 35
Sale, Trafficking and Abduction: The State's obligation to make every effort to prevent the sale, trafficking and abduction of children.

Article: 36
Other Forms of Exploitation: The child's right to protection from all other forms of exploitation not covered in Articles 32, 33, 34 and 35.

Article: 37
Torture and Deprivation of Liberty: The prohibition of torture, cruel treatment or punishment, .capital punishment, life imprisonment, and unlawful arrest or deprivation of liberty. The principles of appropriate treatment, separation from detained adults, contact with family and to legal and other assistance.

Article: 38
Armed Conflicts: The obligation of States to respect and ensure respect for humanitarian law as it applies to children. The principle that no child under 15 takes a direct part in hostilities or be recruited into the armed forces, and that all children affected by armed conflict benefit from protection and care.

Article: 39
Rehabilitative Care: The State's obligation to ensure that child victims

of armed conflicts, torture, neglect, maltreatment or exploitation receive appropriate treatment for their recovery and social re-integration.

Article: 40
Administration of Juvenile Justice: The rights of children alleged or recognised as having committed an offence to respect for their human rights and, in particular, to benefit from all aspects of the due process of law, including legal or other assistance in preparing and presenting their defence. The principle that recourse to judicial proceedings and institutional placement should be avoided wherever possible and appropriate.

Article: 41
Respect for Existing Standards: The principle that, if any standards set in national law or other applicable international instruments are higher than those of this Conventions, it is the higher standard that applies.

Article: 42—45
Implementation and Entry into Force: The provisions of Articles 42-45 notably foresee:

(i) The State's obligation to make the rights contained in this Convention widely known to both adults and children.
(ii) The setting up of committee on the rights of child composed of ten experts, which will consider reports that State Parties to the Convention are to submit two years after ratification and every five years thereafter. The convention enters into force.
(iii) States Parties are to make their reports widely available to the general public.
(iv) The Committee may propose that special studies be undertaken on specific issues relating to the rights of the child, and may make its evaluation known to each State Party concerned as well as to the UN General Assembly.
(v) In order to "foster the effective implementation of the Convention and to encourage international cooperation" the specialised agencies of the UN (such as ILO, WHO, UNESCO) and UNICEF would be able to attend the meetings of the Committee. Together with any other body recognised as "competent," including NGOs in consultative status with UN and UN organs such as UNHC, they can submit pertinent

information to the Committee and be asked to advise on the optimal implementation of Convention.

The First World Summit for Children attended by world leaders represented a commitment at the highest level to build a world order that would guard the most precious resource of the human race—its children. The commitment also assured top priority to the welfare of children and mothers and ensured that their rights are not violated.

Convention on Children's Rights came into force on 2nd September, 1990. With its entry into force, the Convention becomes binding international law for those states that are party to it. Twenty-nine (29) States ratified the Convention, two States (2) have acceded to it and one hundred and five (105) States signed it.

The Convention on the Rights of the Child is unique. One of the main doctrines of the Convention is that the 'Child' is not alone; it considers the basic role of the parents and family for the welfare, care and protection of the children, also the need for special protection of children who are separated or are without families. It considers the role of community and State when required and the crucial contribution that can be made by international organisations and international co-operation. Moreover, the Convention provides a framework within which the child can make the difficult transition from infancy to adulthood.

The document which has been signed provides ten (10) point programme to protect the rights of child, to improve their lives and plans of action at national and international level by the year 2000. The national Plan of course will depend on that particular country social and special need and requirements.

The document considers and urgently calls for action in:

1. Infant and maternal mortality to be reduced.
2. Completion of primary education covering 80 per cent of primary school age children.
3. Improve protection of children.
4. Reduction of server and moderate malnutrition of children under age of five (5).
5. Universal access to safe drinking water.
6. Sanitary means of disposal of excreta.
7. Improving status of women which will lead to better child care.
8. Within a decade it envisages:

   (a) Global eradication of poliomyelitis.

(b) High level immunization of children under one year old with a coverage of 90 per cent children.
(c) Reduction by 95 per cent of measle cases.
(d) Reduce 50 per cent of deaths in children under 5 years old due to diarrhoea.
(e) Reduce 1/3 deaths due to respiratory infections in children under 5 years old.

9. Universal access to safe drinking water, sanitary conditions, reduction in pollution, protection of environment and increase in food production.
10. The Convention also seeks to balance the rights of child with the rights and duties of parents and others who have responsibility or child survival, development and protection.

The 20th Century will be recorded as an era of extraordinary change for children, and among those changes, the convention on the Rights of the Child holds perhaps the greatest potential. The angularly powerful and wide-ranging legal instrument promotes and protects the full spectrum of human rights for children.

The Convention, which entered into force in 1990, reflects a watershed in the way our world looks at children. The work of a few decades has overturned traditions that date back millennia: children have been transformed in the realm of justice from powerless charges into human beings with legal rights of their own; from 'object' to 'subject' of the law; from chattel to personhood.

Emblematic of this sea-change in perception was the 1990 World Summit for children at which 71 Heads of the Government adopted specific goals to substansively improve the lives of children by the year 2000. That such a high level summit came together around the subject of children would have been unthinkable even a few years before.

As of December 1995, all but eight countries in the world had ratified this treaty—propelling it towards becoming the first Universal Law in history. Already its ratification by 185 nations at year end has surpassed the record for any other human rights treaty.

The promises made by the international community at the World Summit for Children have been strengthened by commitments made to fulfil the obligations of the Convention. The ratification of the Convention by each government adds the force of law to the principle that States have a requirement to act in the best interests of the children. Now the countries have to be reminded that putting children first is now a legal obligation, not simply a matter of charity and compassion.

The Government of India ratified the Convention on the Rights of the Child on 12 November 1992. Accordingly the Government took various initiatives to review the National and State legislations and bring it in line with the provisions of the Convention, develop appropriate monitoring procedures to assess progress in implementing the Convention, involve all relevant Government/Ministries, departments, International agencies, Non-governmental organisations and the legal profession in the implementation and reporting process to publicise the Convention and seek public inputs for the frank and transparent reporting (p. 10 Report).

No matter how progressive and rosy the Convention looks on paper and sounds fantastic, no matter how many countries have signed or ratified it, the change will depend how it is put into practice. Improvement in the daily life of children and their welfare will depend largely on how it is implemented.

10

NATIONAL INSTITUTE OF PUBLIC CO-OPERATION AND CHILD DEVELOPMENT (NIPCCD)

The Central Institute of Research and Training in Public Co-operation, was sponsored by the Planning Commission on the recommendation of the National Advisory Committee on Public Co-operation. It was registered on February 28, 1966 as an autonomous organisation under Societies Registration Act of 1960.

Its headquarters is situated in the midst of picturesque surroundings of the ancient Siri Fort, 5, Institutional Area, Hauz Khas, New Delhi-110 016.

In 1967 the Planning Commission decided to wind up the Public Co-operation Division to make it purely advisory body.

On 1st January 1968 the Institute was placed under the administrative control of the Union Department of Social Welfare with the Minister in charge of the Department, as the Chairman of the Institute and President of its General Body.

On 4th July, 1975, the Institute was re-organised and renamed as National Institute of Public Co-operation and Child Development (NIPCCD). This was done, keeping in view the thrust in the Fifth Five Year Plan, on early Childhood Care Services and their projected expansion. Hence, the Department of Social Welfare proposed to add a Separate Child Development Division to the Institute. Main object is to take comprehensive view of child development and to develop and promote programme in pursuance of the national policy for children, to develop measures of co-ordination of government and voluntary action.

In April 1979, the Family and Child Welfare Centre which was previously run by the Jamia Millia Islamia, was also merged with the Institute.

Since 1985, NIPCCD which is an autonomous organisation is under the administrative jurisdiction of the Department of Women and Child Development, Ministry of Human Resource Development, with the Headquarters in New Delhi.

Objectives

The objectives of the Institute are:

(i) to develop and promote voluntary action in social development;
(ii) to take comprehensive view of child development and to develop and promote programmes in pursuance of the National Policy for Children;
(iii) to develop measures for coordination of governmental and voluntary action in social development; and
(iv) to evolve framework and perspective for organising children's programmes through governmental and voluntary efforts.

Functions

The main functions of the Institute are:

(i) Research and evaluation of studies in voluntary action and Child Development,
(ii) Training of Government and Voluntary Sector personnel engaged in social action, Child Development and allied activities,
(iii) Dissemination of information pertaining to Child Development and voluntary action through documentation and publication,
(iv) Technical advice to Central and State Government and other agencies in promotion and implementation of policies and programmes for Child Development and Voluntary Action, and
(v) Liaison with research institutions, Universities and technical bodies engaged in activities similar to those of the Institute.

Regional Field Units

In order to cater to the specific field level requirements of training research, consultancy and documentation in different regions of the country, the institute has set up Regional Centres. It also identified a number of Institutions to cater to the training needs of child care workers in different States and Union Territories.

The Institute has so far set up Regional Centres and they are located at:

1. *Guwahati-Assam:* was established on 14th November, 1978, for the North-Eastern States of India—viz., Assam, Manipur, Meghalaya, Nagaland, Sikkim, Tripura, Mizoram and Arunachal Pradesh.
2. *Bangalore-Karnataka:* was established in 1980 for the Southern States viz. Andhra Pradesh, Karnataka, Kerala, Tamilnadu and Union Territories of Pondicherry and Lakshadweep.
3. *Lucknow-Uttar Pradesh:* was established in October 1982, to meet the needs of the Hindi speaking States of Bihar, Madhya Pradesh, Rajasthan and U.P.

Each Regional Centre is headed by a Regional Director assisted by Professional and Administrative Staff, and to evoke in social development and perspective for organising children's programmes through Government efforts.

Constitutional Bodies

The Institute has two main Constitutional Bodies, namely, The General Body and the Executive Council.

The General Body is responsible for formulating the overall policy of the Institute.

The Local membership of the General Body includes representatives of all State Governments and Union Territories, nominees of various departments of Union Territories, representatives of institutional members, nominated experts and representatives of academic bodies and faculty of the Institute and nominees of the President.

The Executive Council is responsible for management and administrative of the Institute. The Executive Council comprises of the Chairman (The President of the General Body), the Vice-Chairman and members nominated by Government departments, representatives of institutional members and the faculty of the Institute and nominees of the President.

The Executive Council set-up Committees from time to time to discharge different functions.

The Union Minister of State for Youth Affairs and Sports, and Women and Child Development is the President of the General Body and is also the Chairman of the Executive Council.

Administrative Structure of the Institute

The Institute functions under the overall executive control of the Director who is both the academic and the administrative head. Its activities are divided into five broad divisions each headed by a Deputy Director, who is assisted by faculty members, consisting of specialists, research associates, research assistants, research investigators etc.

(i) *Public Co-operation Division* which has six units, namely—Social Welfare, Management, Rural and Scheduled Tribes, Women and Family Welfare and Children's Institutions.

Each unit is headed by a Specialist, assisted by Research Associate(s) and Research Assistant(s).

(ii) *Child Development Division*, has four units, namely, Child Health, Child Nutrition, Pre-School Education and Socio-psychological Development of the Child. Each unit comprises a Specialist Research Associate(s) and Research Assistant(s).

(iii) *Training Division*, has four units, namely, Planning, Co-ordination and Monitoring, Training Technology, Communication Support and Programme Planning. Each unit, except Programme Planning Unit consists of a Specialist, Research Associate(s) and Research Assistant(s). Programme Planning unit comprises of a Programme Officer and Research Investigators.

(iv) *Monitoring and Evaluation Division* which has been set-up for monitoring and evaluation of social components of ICDS, namely, non-formal pre-school education, health and nutrition education and community participating.

The Library and documentation services units which cater to the entire Institute are currently under the Administrative Charge of the Division.

(v) *Common Services Division*, offers supportive services to programme divisions at the Headquarters as also to the Regional Centres of the Institute. It is mainly concerned with financial, personnel, management and house-keeping functions of the Institute. It also looks after financing, co-ordination and monitoring of projects undertaken with UNICEF, assistance under Master Plan of Operations (MPO), publications, re-prography and implementation of official language policy.

(vi) *Field Demonstration Services* to strengthen its training and research programmes, provide field experiences to trainees and its academic staff as well as to develop innovative models, the Institute has set up three field demonstration services, namely, Child Care, Child Guidance and Nutrition Extension.

Programmes and Activities

The central focus of the Institute is the Integrated Development of the child and mother in its most comprehensive and varied form. The activities of the Institute are carried out through the following Divisions:

(i) Public Cooperation
(ii) Child Development
(iii) Training
(iv) Monitoring and Evaluation
(v) Women's Development
(vi) Common Services

Each Division is grouped under two Departments, namely, the Department of Mother and Child Development and the Department of Common Services and Training.

Achievements

Since its inception, the institute has organised many training courses, seminars and orientation courses and workshops. These programmes have been organised at the international, national and regional levels.

The Institute has had many research projects and conducted good number of studies which received nationwide publicity. It also undertook studies sponsored by International Organisations.

The Institute prepared the draft of the National Plan of Action for observance of the International Year of the Child in India, at the request of the Ministry of Social Welfare, Government of India.

It organised National Seminar (April, 1979) to discuss and review the implementation strategy of IYC in India.

It has brought out many publications based on research and evaluation—studies and reports of seminars and workshops.

The Documentation and Information Centre (DIC) was established in 1983, to provide comprehensive perspective about the status, needs and welfare/developmental programmes of women and children and to fill in information gaps in these areas. It is a specialised information Centre on children and women and other disadvantaged groups.

It is engaged in the collection, storage, retrieval and dissemination of information (at both national and international levels) about child welfare development and public cooperation. It prepares bibliographies and research inventories.

It brings out every month a list of selected articles from periodicals subscribed by the Institute. It has a Specialised Library with more than 20,000 books and subscribes to about 250 professional journals.

Earlier "NIPCCD" new letter was published in English only. Since 1985-86, a Hindi edition has been started and it is a bimonthly publication.

Institute's activities are multiplying and have been beneficial to all who care and work for the "Child" in the country. It has wide recognition and has been awarded Maurice Pate Memorial Award by UNICEF in recognition of its outstanding contribution during 1975-85 in the field of Child Development.

Support from UN Agencies and Other International Agencies

1. UNICEF
2. World Bank
3. DANIDA (Danish International Development Agency)
4. IFAD (International Fund for Agriculture Development).

11

NATIONAL POLICY FOR CHILDREN

Background

Nearly 47 years ago, the Indian Constitution made special provisions for the care, protection and prevention of exploitation of children. These provisions (Articles 24, 39 and 45) in the Constitution laid the basis for legislation and action, but unfortunately action-oriented programmes were slow to follow. It was realised that while on the one hand there was a fair amount of realisation of the needs of the children and the problems confronting them, or the other, there was absence of a clear and well co-ordinated policy and action programmes.

In October, 1967, the Government of India appointed a Committee under the Chairmanship of Sri Ganga Saran Sinha to go into the full extent of the problems facing the children, assess their needs during the various stages of development and support programmes to meet these needs. The Committee in its report identified areas requiring action and suggested appropriate action programmes. The Committee observed that a comprehensive national policy for child welfare was necessary to take an integrated view of the different needs of children and assign priorities. It recommended the Constitution of a high level committee on Child Welfare under the Chairmanship of the Prime Minister to take a unified view of the needs of children in the perspective of economic and social development at home and abroad, consider various aspects of national policy for child welfare and promote and co-ordinate governmental and private agencies engaged in implementing Child Welfare programmes and formulating criteria for servicing reasonable allocations in the National Plan for Child Welfare Programmes.

National Policy for Children

Accepting the recommendations of the Committee to formulate a National Policy for Children, the Government of India proclaimed the

National Policy Resolution. This Policy has been enunciated in Government Resolution No. F.1-14/74-CDD, dated August 22, 1974 which was tabled in both the Houses of Parliament on August 26, 1974 which was discussed and accepted. To lay down a policy, by itself is a great achievement, as very few countries have taken this step.

Resolution

No. F.1-14/74-CDD—The Government of India have had under consideration the question of evolving a national policy for the Welfare of Children. After the consideration, it has been decided to adopt the policy enunciated below:

The Nation's children are a supremely important asset. Their nurture and solicitude are our responsibility. Children's programmes should find a prominent part in our national plans for the development of human resources, so that our children grow up to become robust citizens, physically fit, mentally alert and morally healthy, endowed with the skills and motivations needed by society. Equal opportunities of development to all children during the period of growth should be our aim, for this would serve our larger purpose of reducing inequality and ensuring social justice.

Goals

The needs of children and our duties towards them have been expressed in the Constitution. The Resolution on a National Policy on Education, which has been adopted by Parliament, gives direction to State Policy on the educational needs of children. We are also party to the UN Declaration of the Rights of the Child. The goals set out in these documents can reasonably be achieved by judicious and efficient use of the available national resources. Keeping in view these goals the Government of India adopts this Policy and measures.

It shall be the policy of the State to provide adequate services to children, both before and after birth and through the period of growth to ensure their full physical, mental and social development. The states shall progressively increase the scope of such services so that, within a reasonable time, all children in the country enjoy optimum condition for their balanced growth. In particular, the following measures shall be adopted towards the attainment of these objectives:

Objectives

(i) All children shall be covered by a comprehensive health programme.

(ii) Programmes shall be implemented to provide nutrition services with the object of removing deficiencies in the diet of children.

(iii) Programmes will be undertaken for the general improvement of the health and for the care, nutrition and nutritional education of expectant and nursing mothers.

(iv) The State shall take steps to provide free and compulsory education for all children up to the age of 14 for which a time-bound programme will be drawn up consisted with the availability of resources. Special efforts will be made to reduce the prevailing wastage and stagnation in schools, particularly in the case of girls and children of the weaker sections of society. The programme of informal education for pre-school children from such sections will also be taken up.

(v) Children who are not able to take full advantage of formal school education shall be provided other forms of education suited to their requirements.

(vi) Physical education, games, sports and other types of recreational as well as cultural and scientific activities shall be promoted in schools, community centres and such other institutions.

(vii) To ensure equality of opportunity, special assistance shall be provided to all children belonging to the weaker sections of the society, such as children belonging to those Scheduled Castes and Scheduled Tribes and those belonging to the economically weaker sections, both in urban and rural areas.

(viii) Children who are socially handicapped, who have become delinquent or have been forced to take to begging or are otherwise in distress, shall be provided facilities for education, training and rehabilitation and will be helped to become useful citizens.

(ix) Children shall be protected against neglect, cruelty and exploitation.

(x) No child under 14 years shall be permitted to be engaged in any hazardous occupation or be made to undertake heavy work.

(xi) Facilities shall be provided for special treatment, education, rehabilitation and care of children who are physically handicapped, emotionally disturbed or mentally retarded.

(xii) Children shall be given priority for protection and relief in times of distress or natural calamity.

(xiii) Special programmes shall be formulated to spot, encourage and assist gifted children, particularly those belonging to the weaker sections of the society.

(xiv) Existing laws should be amended so that in all legal disputes, whether between parents or institutions, the interests of children are given paramount considerations.

(xv) In organising services for children, efforts would be directed to strengthen family ties so that full potentialities of growth of children are realised within the normal family, neighbourhood and community environment.

Priority in Programme Formation

In formulating programmes in different sectors, priority shall be given to programmes relating to:

(a) Preventive and promotive aspects of child health;

(b) Nutrition for infants and children in the pre-school age along with nutrition for nursing and expectant mothers;

(c) Maintenance, education and training of orphan and destitute children;

(d) Creches and other facilities for the care of children of working or ailing mothers; and

(e) Care, education, training and rehabilitation of handicapped children.

Implementation

The most vital and important requirement for implementing the policy are resources. The Policy stipulates that Government shall endeavour that adequate resources are provided for Child Welfare Programmes and voluntary organisations shall continue to develop services for children. Provision of resources for the various programmes, however, is through the State Governments who have major responsibility for implementing children's programmes and the Government of India. Actually the implementation of the Policy, suitable action programmes need to be undertaken and this leads to commitment, dedication and determinant.

Constitution of National Children's Board

During the last two decades significant process have been made in the provision of services for children on the lines detailed above. There has been considerable expansion in the health, nutrition, education and welfare services. Rise in the standard of living, wherever it occurred, has indirectly met children's basic needs to some extent. But all this work needs a focus and a forum for planning and review, and proper co-ordination of the multiplicity of services striving to meet the needs of children. A National Children's Board shall be constituted to provide this focus and to ensure at different levels continued planning, review and co-ordination of all the essential services.

Similar Boards may also be constituted at the State level.

Role of Voluntary Organisations

The Government shall endeavour that adequate resources are provided for child welfare programmes and appropriate schemes are undertaken. At the same time, voluntary organisations engaged in the field of child welfare will continue to have the opportunity to develop either on their own or with State assistance in the field of education, health, recreation and social welfare services. India has a tradition of voluntary action. It shall be the endeavour of the State to encourage and strengthen voluntary action, so that State and voluntary efforts complement each other. The resources of voluntary organisations, trusts charities and religious and other endowments would have to be tapped to the extent possible for promoting and developing Child Welfare Programmes.

Legislative and Administrative Action

To achieve the above aims, the State will provide necessary legislative and administrative support. Facilities for reason and training of personnel will be developed to meet the needs of the expanding programmes and to improve the effectiveness of the services.

People's Participation

The Government of India trust that the policy enunciated in this statement will receive the support and cooperation of all sections of the people and of organisations working for children. The Government of India also calls upon the citizens, State Governments, local bodies, educational institutions and voluntary organisations to play their part in the overall effort to attain these objectives.

12

NATIONAL CHILDREN'S BOARD

An integrated approach to child development requires considerable expansion in the health, nutrition, education and welfare services. Therefore, a need was felt for a focus and a forum for planning and review and proper co-ordination of a multiplicity of services striving to meet the needs of children. Para 5 of the Government Resolution, dated August 22, 1974, on National Policy for Children, states that a National Children's Board should be constituted to provide this focus and to ensure at different levels continuous planning, review and co-ordination of all the essential services.

The Government of India, therefore, constituted a National Children's Board under Government Resolution No. F.1-14/74-CDD, dated December 3, 1974.

The National Board was Inaugurated on September 15, 1975.

Resolution

Sub: Constitution of a National Children's Board.

No. F.1-14/74-CDD: In recognition of the supreme importance of children as a national asset, the Government of India have adopted the Resolution No. F.1-14/74-CDD dated August 22, 1974 on the National Policy for children. This Resolution urges that the programmes for the development of children should be a prominent part of our national plans and that all children should receive equal opportunities for their growth and development. Through such programmes of action, there will emerge in due course, generations of citizens endowed with mental and physical qualities to build and strengthen the country, Para 5 of the Resolution emphasises the need for a focus and a forum for planning, review and coordination of a multiplicity of services striving to meet the needs of children and stipulates the constitution of a National Children's Board to provide this focus and such a forum.

Constitution

The President is, therefore, pleased to constitute a National Children's Board, consisting of the following members:

(1) Prime Minister—President.

(2) Minister of Education and Social Welfare—Working Chairman.

(3) Minister of Health and Family Welfare—Member.

(4) to (10) Seven Social Workers with experience of Child Welfare Services—Members.

(11) to (23) Ten persons nominated by State Governments and three persons by U.T. Administrations, in rotation, from among those who are concerned with Child Welfare Services—Members.

(24) to (26) Two Members of Lok Sabha and one Member of Rajya Sabha to be nominated by the Speaker and the Chairman respectively—Members.

(27) Chairman, Central Social Welfare Board—Member.

(28) Director, Central Institute of Research and Training in Public Operation—Member.

(29) Secretary of the Government of India, Department of Social Welfare—Member-Secretary.

Functions

The functions of the Board shall be:

1. To create and sustain public awareness of the needs of children in general.
2. To coordinate and integrate the efforts made by different governmental and private agencies engaged in implementing, programmes for the welfare of children.
3. To review periodically the progress made in the different programmes.
4. To locate gaps in the existing services and suggest measures of eliminating such gaps, and
5. To suggest from time to time any chances needed in the priorities accorded to the different programmes.

The functions of the Board will be advisory and coordinational.

Standing Committee

The Board will have a Standing Committee, consisting of the following members:

(1) Minister of Education and Social Welfare—Chairman.
(2) Chairman, Central Social Welfare Board.
(3) A representative of the Ministry of Health.
(4) to (8) Five other members elected by the Board for a period of one year.
(9) Secretary to the Government of India in the Department of Social Welfare—Member-Secretary.
(5) A unit in the Department of Social Welfare will form the Secretariat of the Board.
(6) The term of office of the non-official members on the Board will be two years.
(7) The Board shall ordinarily meet once a year and the Standing Committee twice a year.
(8) The non-official members of the Board and the Committee will be eligible for T.A. and D.A. as provided under the rules.

Articles in the Constitution of India Regarding Welfare of Children

Article 24: *Prohibition of Employment of Children in Factories, etc.*— No child below the age of fourteen years shall be employed to work in any factory or mine or engaged in any other hazardous employment.

Article 39: *Certain Principles to be followed by the State*—The State shall, in particular, direct its policy toward securing—

(e) that the health and strength of workers, men and women and the tender age of children are not abused and that citizens are not forced by economic necessity to enter avocations unsuited to their age or strength,
(f) that childhood and youth are protected against exploitation and against moral and material abandonment.

Article 45: *Provision for free and compulsory education for children*— The State shall endeavour to provide, within a period of ten years from the commencement of this Constitution, for free and compulsory education for all children until they complete the age of fourteen years.

Professor S. Nurul Hasan, Minister of Education, Social Welfare and Culture in his Welcome Speech, said that:

Madam Prime Minister,

In the midst of your heavy and pressing engagements, you have able to find time to inaugurate the first meeting of the Board. The National Children's Board of which you are the President, symbolises your personal interest in the welfare of the children. The emergence of the Board coupled with the adoption of the Resolution on the National Policy for Children provide the high watermark or the Nation's concern for the welfare of children. The emergence of these two—the Resolution and the Board—are a milestone in our planned process of nation-building. Some twenty years ago Pandit Jawaharlal Nehru had said:

> "For somehow the fact that ultimately everything depends on the human factor gets rather lost in our thinking of plans schemes of national developments in terms of factories and machinery and general schemes—it is all very important and we must have them, but ultimately, of course, it is the human-being that counts, and if the human-being counts well, he counts more as a child than as grown-up."

You have, Madam, not only shared Panditji's love and concern for Children, but have given the policy of care for children a new dimension. In 1969, you gave a call for the adoption of 'Charter for Children', you initiated the special nutrition programme for children, particularly those belonging to the weaker sections of the community. These, along with the other measures fostered by you have found expression in the National Policy for Children, in the establishment of this Board to oversee its implementation, and in the new Scheme of Integrated Child Development Services Scheme which is to start soon.

The magnitude of the problem will be evident from the fact that 42 per cent of 236 million of our total population is comprised of children below the age of 15 years, each year, approx. 22 million children are born, while some 3 million perish before they are one year old. The net addition is estimated at 19 million per annum. Many of them suffer from one handicap or another in the shape of cerebral palsy, an orthopaedic deformity, mental retardation, blindness or deafness. Some of them are born to the leper population of 3.7 million. And in any case 80 per cent of them belong to the homes of our weaker and poorer sections.

This picture speaks for itself and brings out the grim reality and the baffling diversity of the task that lies ahead in building the future and in rearing the human material. In spite of the enormity of the undertaking, I have no doubt that the people of India, under your leadership, will face the future with fortitude and courage.

Madam Prime Minister, the National Policy for Children whose origin and formulation owes so much to your personal initiative and encouragement embodies a 15-Point programme to attain the balanced growth of children. It also stipulates a 5-Point priority guideline to formulate schemes in the various sector to meet certain urgent needs of children. The great task envisages coordination of a number of activities among Departments such as Health, Family Planning, Education, Social Welfare, Rural Development, Works and Housing and so on. The entire work of child development demands an integrated view. We have to work for a combination of efforts by the various departments, so that acting in symbiosis, their services may strengthen and support the growth of a child. This is vital to success because there is an inherent unity of the child's personality. We must consider the young in their complexity and recognise their physical, emotional, intellectual and social needs.

Madam Prime Minister, I would like to take this opportunity of extending my thanks to the Ministers of Health, Rural Development, Works Housing, Finance and the Planning Commission who have given their full cooperation and support in the planning and implementation of a number of programmes aimed at giving effect to the Policy Resolution. The enthusiastic response of the State Governments who have to implement the programmes, augurs well for the future. I would also like to mention that in this fascinating adventure of promoting child welfare, it is not only the Government sector but also the people who have a vital role. Our voluntary agencies have for the decades, now been devotedly engaged in running child care centres of various types. Their experience and suggestions have been a great help to Government in propounding new spheres of work to look after children. I extend my warm thanks to them and look forward to their continuing partnership in awakening the community to our common cause. In the coming years, non-officials and officials will have to play their part as team. Officials should bring the experience of training and disciplined service. The non-officials should represent and bring that popular urge and enthusiasm which gives life to a movement. Both are essential and both have an inspiring ideal to stimulate them.

Madam Prime Minister, while expressing the need of family planning you had underlined the importance of child welfare in the following words:

> "We need family planning not because we are against children, but because we want every child to have the best opportunity possible in life."

With the national focus, which the National Policy for Children and the Board provides, we have, Madam Prime Minister every hope to realise your words in practice. This Board, under your Presidentship, will have the benefit of your advice and ideas to devise newer paths to provide increasingly improved services for the proper all-round development of children. We have on this Board distinguished members who have long experience in the upbringing of children. It is my privilege to welcome them to this first meeting. We have a big task and a great responsibility, but only meagre financial resources. Our success—for succeed we will—will have far-reaching effect on the building of a new nation of tomorrow. It is an exhilarating thought and an inspiring venture. It will call for the best in us, in whichever sphere we may be working.

Madam Prime Minister, we now look forward to your Inaugural Address.

Prime Minister's Inaugural Address

Inaugurating the first meeting of National Children's Board, the Prime Minister, Shrimati Indira Gandhi, said here today—

We have so many boards that I am a little wary of yet another one and I can only hope that this one will not remain a mere forum for talking but will be able to get down to the grassroots of some of the problems which we face.

Mr. Minister, you have quoted some statistics of the handicapped, the ailing and so on. But anybody who deals with children must realise that they are not statistics. Each child is an individual and unless our education recognises him as such, we will be compounding the mistake which we have so far made in education.

In most of our educational institutions—perhaps this is true of most other countries as well, it is not an Indian phenomenon—there is tendency not only for the child but for the adult also to be just the statistics—so many women, so many men, so many in this religion or that religion or caste or some other kind of grouping. There is obviously a necessity to have an integrated programme to deal with all aspects of the welfare and development of the child. But unless a proper foundation is laid, all these programmes will only be linked up at the top and so far all the coordination we have been doing, whether in child welfare or in other spheres of national activity—even governmental activity—has been coordination at top. You all, are very experienced people but even now I do see that some important educational experimentation is completely unrepresented in this body and, I would say largely the people are those who stand for the conventional existing education. Do we think this is the right education for India? We ourselves—the Minister, myself and other people have been shouting from the house-tops that it is not, that we must make a major effort to change the structure of education.

But we must make a beginning. We have vast problems, but I believe that we have vast opportunities. And I think that it would be better if this Board, instead of merely, dealing with the problems side of it, looks at the opportunities side of it, what is the positive, not the negative side of the work for children. And here I don't think I need repeat that the children are the foundation of any society and of the future of this country. So our primary aim must be to see how we enable the child to fully develop his personality, a personality which is not narrowed down in any way. If I have a grouse against education that we, are giving to our children, it is that while allowing the talent of a child to blossom, we quite often suppress the child's spontaneity and originality and even vision.

Most saints or great religious heads of any religion have come down to some basic simple values. So we have to deal with this problem as explorers in a way not as people who already know what has to be done, but who have to try and search what is the right way. First of all I don't think that we can make any changes in our welfare services or in our educational structures or system unless we are prepared to cast off a lot of preconceptions, a lot of superstitions. Amongst the major problems in this country I do not think it is number of children who suffer, it is the attitude of the society towards children and towards these problems.

There have been a number of special years announced by the United Nations. We have Population Control Year, we are in the middle of International Women's Year, but none of these has really helped to find a way out. With regard to Women's Year I have said on almost every occasion that I do think that the women needs to be liberated but I do think that men also need to be liberated equally and therefore woman's liberation is part of the larger liberation of men and women, and by liberation it means not that we can do many things which we perhaps are not allowed to do because of customs, but because we imprison ourselves in our superstitions, in our habits and customs and Indian society in spite of many changes which are taking place is still very much in the old rut. Now if we are dealing with children we have to go down to this basic fact. How are we taking the child out of this rut and enabling him to be a free human-being?

We all know of course that freedom does not mean licence. Freedom is that from the beginning the child learns to distinguish and it is not at all difficult. If you talk to a child like a reasonable human-being, the vast majority of children understand and they do have that self-restraint, and even discipline without any disciplining having to be undertaken. So I think that one of the primary aims of this Children's Board should be made to see that children are not the victims of superstition or any type or narrow thinking. Children with all their charm and lovable qualities can be cruel.

We know here, and in other countries also, they can be very clear to somebody who is different—child who is handicapped for instance. A child who is different in religion, if there is a child of a minority community. In India itself we have experience that he has had to suffer from taunts from other children. Now this is not natural to children. This is something that they have picked up from the adult atmosphere. And unless we can help to solve this in any institution which deals with children and not just help but be very firm about such matters—we cannot create a good citizen of India.

I would like to lay stress that details of programmes are very important and you all will deal with them, as there is the general programme, there are specific programmes for special age groups of handicapped and you have to have special projects for specific needs of different groups or areas. You have to concentrate on nutrition, on sanitation which is essential for health. But unless you have the right sight, unless you and the parents and teachers have the right attitude of mind towards children and enable the children to grow up in that sort of atmosphere, you will not be helping them in mental health. This is the sort of development which we have to pay far greater attention. Obviously, no matter what an institution or a school it is for the child, unless his home atmosphere is conducive to proper growth, the institution cannot be successful. Therefore, it means the involvement of parents and guardians in any programme which you take up. A broader view of the programmes must be taken not only how they complement on another. There may be gaps. But we need not wait for the gaps to fill up before linking up the programmes and seeing how they can help one another. But for every programme the basis must be thus of broader point of view.

We have far too many people in our country who are constricting growth. I hope this Board will play some part in trying to break through these barriers. The broader view is not only of improving general welfare which has a great deal to do with the general material uplift, higher standards of general education but also certain basic values for which this country has stood. So we want to produce citizens who are capable of understanding these problems and who have the courage—moral, intellectual and physical—to stand up for our high ideals. This means developing the scientific temper of mind, by which I do not mean merely knowledge of science although that is important in itself and also is conducive to the development of the temper, but a way of thinking a more rational way of thinking. I think that our old thinking was very rational. It had a broadness of vision. It had a depth of thinking which is rare to find anywhere in the world. But it was rational. How many today who speak in the name of religion have gone away from that rationally and have imprisoned religion itself in routine or superstition. We have to liberate it from all these bonds.

If the problems are great with regard to the urban child, in some ways they are greater for the rural child. The problem of providing them proper facilities is a large one. Schools exist but I find still that greater importance is given to the building to see whether it has a corrugated iron roofing rather than the quality of the teaching. As Gurudev Ravindranath Tagore and many other teachers in our country taught us that you can learn anywhere and in any conditions.

What is more important is the teacher, the attitude of the teacher and the attitude of the parents and of the society surrounding a child. And I hope that this will be taken cognizance of. Of course, there are the problems of the handicaps. Now, I don't know to what extent we can afford today to give them the attention and the care and the treatment which is their due. That is why we have been trying to encourage voluntary organisations to do more for them. Again, this does not mean Government should ignore them, but I personally feel the Government should help voluntary organisations, but society should try to take up this burden as far as possible on itself because until we have better conditions for the normal child, it will never be possible to give better conditions to one who is abnormal. They have our full sympathy because their burden is far greater than the other but I don't think that we will be able to serve them unless the attitude of society changes towards them and the normal child has a better chance and is also willing to help. I think a great deal can be done is schools and other institutions by some children looking after other children. They are capable of it and it gives them the first experience of being useful. Nothing gives the child a greater pleasure than feeling that it is useful or doing something. Most children want to do work of what their mothers or their fathers are doing. Now this feeling should be channelised in a way that is useful for the child's growth and can be useful to society also.

Recreational facilities are also important. They don't mean that we must have dolls of various specific types of things. Perhaps you have read that in later years, the most popular play grounds in the richest countries abroad are junk-yards. They collect things which are not needed by anybody and the children enjoy playing with them, it encourages their imagination and they are very much happier than with the made dolls because the made dolls are sometimes things with which the child gets very quickly bored. While it is new, it is exciting, but after a while you are bored with it, but in things which you can endow your qualities through imagination, they are limitless because there can be different things as time goes on. So we must try to make everything more simple and I think that through that you will not be depriving the child, rather you will be adding the richness to his personality because it will be his effort to make something out of whatever there is and in this way I would say that some of our rural children do have a richer personality than some of the slum children because they have a greater opportunity of not only helping in the field and in the house but in making dolls with things, which develops certain worthwhile qualities.

Hope that this Board does not follow the routine pattern as most Boards do and, becomes a mere talking shop. All experiments do not turn out well but it is only by experimenting and searching for the truth that we can have something worthwhile. I sincerely hope that this Board will be successful in this and I give it my best wishes.

National Plan of Action

Many speakers made their observations on the measures taken to implement the national policy for child as well as proposals contained in the Plan of Action.

Election of 5 Members to the Standing Committee

The Board unanimously resolved that the Prime Minister, President of the Board, may nominate 5 members of the Board to work as members of the Standing Committee.

Appointment of the Secretariat of the Board

The Board noted that a Child Development has been created in the Department of Social Welfare with effect from September 3, 1975 and that this Division, in addition to directing and coordinating the programmes relating to children, will constitute the secretariat of the Board.

Concluding Remarks by the Minister of Education, Social Welfare and Culture

The Chairman (Minister of Education, Social Welfare and Culture) expressed his remarks to all the members for their contribution and the enthusiasm shown by them for the work of the child welfare. At his suggestions, the following decisions were taken:

(a) The National Policy for Children which has been adopted by the Central Government and has the general support of the Parliament and the State Governments, should be popularised. It should be brought to the notice of the young people as well as the elder generation and used as a lever for securing suggestions and encouraging initiative of the community and people's participation. The Central Government should request the State Governments, voluntary agencies and educational institutions to carry this message, so that more and more initiative will be forthcoming.

(b) The Plan of Action, which was circulated to the Board, was endorsed, subject to the valuable suggestions and points made by the speakers which might necessitate some change or modification in emphasis.

The Chairman referred to the proposal for establishing Bal Kendras and observed that this is an important programme and should be implemented effectively. There is a Bal Bhavan in Delhi and there should be more Bal Bhavans in other places so that, with the minimum of expenditure, a large number of children can be benefited. He referred to the Prime Minister's emphasis on the development of the child's personality and observed that we cannot have many paid teachers to look after every child and that, therefore, we have to involve the youth, educated women and elder children through newer ways, to meet the needs of children.

The Chairman complimented the Secretary and his colleagues for the excellent documentation and expressed the hope that, in the next meeting, the Board will have not only a report on the Central Government but complete reports from different State Governments. The Chairman stated that though it has not been possible to include all the States/Union Territories as members of the Board because that would have considerably enlarged the Board, all the States/Union Territories will serve on the Board by rotation and each State Government/Union Territories Administration will be requested to send a representative to each meeting of the Board so that all State/Union Territories have an opportunity for participating in the discussions and in making contributions as well as informing the Board about what is happening in their respective areas, how they have been solving their difficulties and whether there has been interesting ideas or suggestions which can be taken note of.

13

NATIONAL CHILDREN'S FUND

In pursuance of National Policy for children as "The nation's supremely important assets" the Government of India decided to constitute the National Children's Fund.

The National Children's Board in the meeting on 22nd July, 1978, under the Presidentship of Prime Minister passed a resolution approving the proposal to set-up a National Children's Fund at the Centre and similar funds at the State level. It will be a standing fund and is to be utilised by voluntary organisations for extending various child welfare services including rehabilitation of destitute children, according high priority to Scheduled Castes, Scheduled Tribes and other backward classes.

Objectives

The objectives of the National Children's Fund shall be:

(i) To administer and apply the funds of the children fund to pay grant-in-aid to voluntary organisations at national, state and district levels to implement programmes for the welfare of children including rehabilitation of destitute children, particularly, pre-school children.

(ii) To do all other things that are incidental to the above objects.

The fund started with a contribution of rupees one lakh made by the Government of India. A donation of rupees five lakhs has been received from the Prime Minister's National Relief Fund. Thereafter, contributions are expected from the general public, voluntary organisations, State Governments, industry and business etc. for which an appeal has been issued by the Prime Minister. There have also been some touching spontaneous reasons from individuals. A copy of Government of India Notification in this behalf is:

Notification

In the Matter of the Charitable Endowments Act, 1890 and in the Matter of the National Children's Fund, New Delhi

S.O. 120(E). Whereas the Secretary to the Government of India, Ministry of Education, Social Welfare and Culture, Department of Social Welfare, being the person who proposes to apply the funds of the National Children's Fund, New Delhi, in trust for charitable purposes, has applied for vesting the funds mentioned in Schedule A annexed hereto in the Treasurer of Charitable Endowments for India for the settlement of a scheme for the administration of the said funds,

Now, therefore, the Central Government, in exercise of the powers conferred by Sections 4 and 5 of the Charitable Endowments Act, 1890 (6 of 1890), and upon the application, as aforesaid, and with the concurrence of the Secretary to the Government of India, Ministry of Education, Social Welfare and Culture, Department of Social Welfare, do hereby order that the moneys set out in Schedule annexed hereto shall, as from the date of publication of this notification, be vested in the Treasurer of Charitable Endowments for India to be held by him and his successors in office upon trust to hold the said moneys and the income thereof in accordance with the trust and terms set out in the Scheme set forth in Schedule B, annexed hereto for the administration of the said funds;

And it is hereby notified that the Scheme setforth in Schedule B annexed hereto has, under sub-section (1) of Section 5 of the said Act, been settled for the administration of the said funds and under sub-section (3) of the said Section 5 of the said Act, it is hereby further ordered that it shall come into force with immediate effect.

Schedule 'A'

Contribution of rupees one lakh made by Government of India towards the funds of the National Children's Fund.

Schedule 'B'

Scheme for the administration of the National Children's Fund, New Delhi.

The objects of the National Children's Fund (hereinafter referred to as the Fund) shall be:

(i) to administer and apply the funds of the Fund to pay grants-in-aid to voluntary organisations of National, State and District level, to implement programmes, for the welfare of children, including rehabilitation of destitute children, particularly pre-school age children.

Programmes for welfare of children belonging to Scheduled Castes, the Scheduled Tribes and other backward classes will receive priority consideration:

(ii) to do all other things and the incidental and conducive to the above objects.

2. The objectives of the Fund shall extend to the whole of India except the State of Jammu and Kashmir.
3. For the management and administration of the Fund, a Board of Management (hereafter referred to as the 'Board') shall be constituted consisting of the following members, namely:

Chairman (Ex-Officio)

(a) Union Minister of Education and Social Welfare.

—Working Chairman

(b) Union Minister of State for Education and Social Welfare.

—Members

(c) Joint Secretary, Ministry of Finance, Government of India.
(d) Secretary, Department of Social Welfare, Government of India.
(e) Director, National Institute of Public Co-operation and Child Development.
(f) Chairman, Central Social Welfare Board, New Delhi.
(g) Six Non-official Members to be nominated by the Chairman.

—Secretary-Treasurer

(h) Joint Secretary, (Nutrition and Child Development), Department of Social Welfare, Government of India.

4. Not less than seven members shall form a quorum. Every matter shall be determined by a majority of votes of the members present and voting on questions. In case of quality of votes, the chairman shall have a casting vote.
5. The Board may function notwithstanding any vacancy in its Constitution.
6. subject to the provisions herein contained, the Board may frame, and vary, from time to time, as they think fit, rules for the conduct of their business: Provided that the Central

Government shall make the first rules for the conduct of business of the Board.

7. The funds of the Fund shall be vested in the Treasurer of Charitable Endowments for India.
8. (i) The Board may make Rules for the regulation, management, and for any other purpose connected with the execution of the funds of the Fund.
   (ii) The Board shall invest the proceeds of the sale or other disposal of the property as well as any moneys or property not immediately required to be used for the objects of the Fund in any one or more of the modes of investment for the time being authorised by law for the investment of the trust moneys as the Board may think proper.
9. The Board may appoint a Working Committee for each State/ Union Territory in India and such officers and staff as they may consider necessary.
10. The Board may delegate any of their powers to any of the Working Committees constituted in respect of the State/Union Territories or any one or more members of their body.
11. The Board may also delegate to one or more of the members such of their powers as may, in the opinion of the Board, are merely ministerial acts and involve no discretion or are necessary and comfortable to common usage.
12. Regular accounts of the moneys in the funds shall be kept by the Secretary-Treasurer.
13. All contracts and other assurance shall be in the name of the Board and signed on their behalf by a least one of the Members or Secretary-Treasurer.
14. The Board may receive any endowment, donation or other contribution in augmentation of any of the objects and general purpose of the Fund. They may also receive endowments, donations, or other contributions for any special purposes connected with the charity not inconsistent with or calculated to impede the due working of, the provision of this scheme.

March 2, 1979

Rules for the Administration of the National Children's Fund, New Delhi

In pursuance of the powers conferred by the provision to para 6 of Schedule B of Notification No. 120(E), dated 2nd March, 1979, the

Central Government makes the following rules for the conduct of business of the Board of Management of the National Children's Fund:

1. *Short-title*—These rules may be called the Administration of the National Children's Fund Rules, 1979.
2. *Definitions*—Unless there is anything repugnant to the subject or the context of the scheme for the administration of National Children's Fund as laid down in Schedule B of Notification No. 120(E), dated the 2nd March, 1979 (hereinafter referred to as the said Notification)—

    (a) "Fund" shall mean the National Children's Fund, New Delhi;
    (b) "Board" shall mean the Board of Management constituted for the administration of the Fund in pursuance of para 3 of Schedule B to the said Notification;
    (c) "Secretary-Treasurer" shall mean the Secretary-Treasurer of the Board;
    (d) "Year" shall mean the financial year ending on the 31st March.

3. *Authorities of the Fund*—For the management and administration of the Fund, a Board as set out in para 3 of Schedule B to the said notification shall be constituted with powers and functions as laid down in the said Schedule.
4. *Duration of Membership*—(i) A nominated member of the Board shall hold office for a period of two years, (ii) A member of the Board shall cease to be member if he dies, resigns his membership or becomes of unsound mind or insolvent or is convicted of a criminal offence involving moral turpitude; (iii) The resignation of membership shall be tendered to the Chairman of the Board and shall become effective from the date of its acceptance or on the expiry of thirty days after the date of resignation, whichever is earlier.
5. *Vacancies on the Board*—Vacancies on the Board shall be filled in the manner in which the Board was originally constituted.
6. *Meeting of the Board*—The Board will meet as often as it is necessary to do so for the transaction of business of the Fund, but in any case at least once a year.

7. *Powers and Functions of Secretary-Treasurer of the Board*—It shall be the duty of the Secretary-Treasurer:

   (a) to be the custodian of all records of the Board;
   (b) to conduct the official correspondence on behalf of the Board;
   (c) to issue all notices for convening the meeting of the Board;
   (d) to keep minutes of all meetings of the Board and of such bodies the responsibilities for convening whose meetings rests with him;
   (e) to manage the properties and funds of the Fund, to maintain accounts and execute all contracts on behalf of the Board; and
   (f) to exercise all other powers and execute such other functions as may be assigned to him by the Board from time to time.

8. *Assets of the Fund*—(i) In addition to the moneys, particulars of which are given in Schedule A to the said notification, the assets of the Fund shall include all such grants and contributions, recurring from the Central and the State Governments, local bodies or any other statutory or non-statutory bodies set up by the Central or the State Governments as well as voluntary donations and endowments from any other sources, whenever received, (ii) All assets of the Fund shall vest in the Board of the Fund.
9. *Allocation of Fund*—The Board may, from time to time, determine the proportion of the total funds at its disposal which shall be applied for the purposes of the Fund in a particular year.
10. *Deposit of Fund*—All money of the Fund shall be credited initially to the account of the Board of the Fund to be opened in the State Bank of India or any of its subsidiaries or any other Scheduled Bank approved in this behalf by the Government of India.
11. *Withdrawal of Funds*—Withdrawal of funds from the accounts of the Fund shall be regulated in a manner to be determined by the Board. Such withdrawals shall be made by the cheques or requisitions (as the case may be) signed by the Secretary-Treasurer in the case of amounts not exceeding rupees one

thousand and signed duly by the Secretary-Treasurer and another member of the Board to be nominated by the Board in other cases.

12. *Administrative Expenses*—Administrative expenses incurred by the Board, such as expenditure incurred on salaries and allowances and T.A. and D.A. of their officers and staff, and T.A. and D.A. of the members, shall be a legitimate charge on the funds of the Fund.

13. *Appointment of Staff*—The Board may appoint such staff as they may consider necessary for the discharge of their functions. The terms and conditions of service of the staff may be determined by the Board.

14. *Remuneration to Members and Officers*—(i) No remuneration shall be paid to any of the members of the Board except travelling and daily allowance at rates to be determined by the Board, (ii) Official members of the Board will draw travelling and daily allowances at the rates admissible to them from the source from which they draw their salaries, (iii) Officers and staff of the Fund may draw such remuneration and T.A. and D.A. to which they may be entitled under the rules applicable to them.

15. *Accounts and Audit*—Regular accounts shall be kept of all money and properties and income and expenditure of the Fund and shall be audited by a firm of Chartered Accountants or any other recognised authorities as may be appointed by the Board. The Auditors shall also certify that the expenditure from the funds of the Fund has been correctly incurred in accordance with the objects of the Fund. Copies of the annual accounts of the Fund duly audited and certified by the auditor shall be submitted by the Secretary-Treasurer of the Fund to the Government of India every year.

16. *Annual Report*—An annual report on the working of the Fund shall be prepared by the Secretary-Treasurer of the Board and shall, after approval of the Board, be presented to the Government of India.

17. *Repeal and Saving*—The Board shall, within the framework of the scheme of the Fund, as laid down in Schedule B to the said notification, have full powers to repeal, aimed or revise any or all of these rules, whenever, in the opinion of the Board, it is expedient to do so.

14

INTERNATIONAL YEAR OF THE CHILD (IYC)

Introduction

In 1976, Economic and Social Council recommended that General Assembly may proclaim 1979 as the "International Year of the Child." Thus 1979 observance of the IYC generated a great interest and concern with the problems of children and much new activity along with the growing recognition among governments of the need for a regular review of the starvation of children and of the policies and programmes affecting them. The United Nations' General Assembly designated UNICEF as the "lead agency" of the UN. System responsible for co-ordinating and developing aspects of the follow-up activities of the year.

Declaring 1979 to be the International Year of the Child, the UN General Assembly Resolution A/31/169 of 21st December, 1976, set out its general objectives as follows:

(a) to provide a framework for advocacy on behalf of children and for enhancing the awareness of the special needs of children on the part of decision-makers and the public;

(b) to promote recognition of the fact that the programmes for children should be an integral part of economic and social development plans, with a view to achieving in both the long-term and the short-term, sustain activities for the benefit of children at the national and international levels.

In sharpening the world's focus on the child the International Year of the Child (IYC) triggered worldwide action towards the Year's main goal: increased long-term services benefiting children.

The year received widespread support. Over 150 countries set up high-level IYC National Commissions often with leadership at the highest levels.

Most countries examined the situation of their children and some launched both short-term and long-term programmes to improve conditions for their children. Such for example India, Egypt and Colombia.

Support for the Year came not only from Governments but especially from professional groups—lawyers, architects, doctors and journalists; from other non-governmental organisations, and from individuals. The media produced stories dramatizing the poverty, deprivation, exploitation and the problems affecting children. In reference to the global objectives of the International Year of the Child 1979, the Indian Plan of the action, had been attuned to the guidelines laid down by the UN General Assembly. India has been supporter for declaring 1979 as the International Year of the Child and was the *first country* to announce its contribution of Rs. 9,00,000 to UNICEF for the purpose. The National Plan was prepared by the National Institute of Public Co-operation and Child Development (NIPCCD) in pursuance of the general agreement that 1978, the Year proceeding IYC, shall be devoted to advocacy and preparatory work in connection with programmes of Child Welfare/ Development, consolidation and strengthening of ongoing programmes for children and introduction of new ones where needed, so that a series of action programmes could be launched to realise concrete objectives laid down for the observance of the year.

IYC 1979—India

India's Symbol for the Year was depicting a male and female child, with sun and a slate. The sun signifies health and strength; the slate stands for the importance of education for the future of children

The symbol was designed by Shri Saliesh Modi, of Ahmedabad, and was selected on the basis of a competition for an award of Rs. 3,000. The Hindi Version *Bachhe ki Muskan Rashtra ki Shan* India's slogan for IYC was: "Happy Child—Nation's Pride" (coined by Shri Narendra Kumar Sinha, of Ranchi). He won a prize of Rs. 2,000.

India's General Theme was: "Reaching the Deprived Child." The Government of India has already formulated a National Plan of Action. The National Children's Board was set up under the Chairmanship of the Prime Minister to guide the nation in observing IYC.

Objectives

The specific objectives of the observance of the International Year of the Child in India were as under:

(a) To make concerted efforts to significantly reduce the incidence of maternal and child mortality and morbidity by providing effective programmes and services for their health and nutritional needs;
(b) To promote community awareness and education about the crucial importance of the healthy development of the child and a happy family life as the foundation for the child's security and well-being;
(c) To facilitate optimum psycho-social development of pre-school children so as to prepare them for schooling by providing a

network of Balwadis/Anganwadis/creches/day-care centres/ nursery schools;

(d) To strive for the speedy realisation of the goal of universal elementary education and to substantially reduce the rates of school drop-out;

(e) To secure the basic rights of children and to protect them against neglect, cruelty, hazards and exploitation by promoting effective implementation of existing legislation and enacting new ones where necessary; and

(f) To secure entitlement of all children in the poverty groups born on/after 1 January, 1979 to public assistance for their survival, growth and development.

The Approach Strategy

The objectives of the IYC are of a global nature encompassing all children in the age-group of 0-14 years and call for massive inputs and viable infrastructures. However, in view of our resource constraints and differential degrees of ecological deprivation, our approach must be endowed with a certain focus and realism. The following guidelines may be kept in view while formulating action programmes for the observance of the International Year of the Child in this country:

(a) The general theme of IYC in India shall be "Reaching the Deprived Child."

(b) The IYC should not be construed as a one-year programme. It should be viewed as a spring-board for vigorous and continued action during the residual part of the century. The goals and objectives as spelled out should positively be achieved by the end of the Century and to this end, a perspective plan for the next two decades (1979-99) should be evolved.

(c) The emphasis during this period shall be on children of weaker sections of society, namely, Scheduled Castes and Scheduled Tribes and other poverty groups located in rural areas and urban slums. Within this regret group, greater attention should be bestowed on children in the age-group of 0-16 years, primary school children as also pregnant and nursing mothers. It has been estimated that out of 115 million children (1971 census) between the ages of 0-6 years in India, at least 46 million are below the poverty line. Of these, 9.2 million live in the teeming urban slums, 2.8 million in tribal areas, and 34 million in rural areas, often inaccessible and affected by drought, flood and other hazards of marginal existence;

(d) Since it will be difficult to cover, during IYC, all children under health and nutrition programmes, priority should be given to cater to the needs of children below the age of 6 years, pregnant and nursing mothers.

(e) During the IYC, an attempt should be made to reduce maternal and infant mortality rate by about five per cent.

In the light of the objectives and approach strategy as outlined above the action plan has been divided into the following six broad heads, each spelling out concrete measures to be undertaken in respective fields, followed by guidelines for their implementation:

1. Health and Nutrition including environmental sanitation and supply of safe drinking water.
2. Education including pre-school, elementary and community education.
3. Social Welfare.
4. Legislation.
5. Publicity.
6. Fund raising.

Guidelines for Implementing the National Plan for IYC

The entire plan of operation for the International Year of the Child will be co-ordinated by the National Children's Board, recently reconstituted by the Government of India and headed by the Prime Minister of India, and the Department of Social Welfare.

The conditions of the children and their problems vary from region to region. It is not possible to have a uniform plan of action for the entire country. The National Plan of Action, therefore, should be considered as a general guide on a series of actions, which could be implemented at various levels in accordance with the genius, needs and resources of the implementing agencies and the people.

The role of Co-ordination Committees at the Nation, State, District and Block levels could be as under:

(i) Making available to the field personnel the latest information on health nutrition and child-care;

(ii) Providing teaching aids (materials);
(iii) Helping in the preparation of resource units;
(iv) Organising special short-term courses for health workers and community workers (volunteers);
(v) Providing means for field demonstration;
(vi) Enriching the programme content through resource personnel, consultation and teaching aids;
(vii) Interpreting the educational programme and unmet needs of children to the community; and
(viii) Launching fund raising campaigns for child welfare programmes in a concerted manner.

A Perspective Plan for Children—1979-99

It is recommended that the Planning Commission should prepare a perspective Plan for Child Development for the period for 1979-99 as an integral part of the national development plan for the residual part of this century.

It is obvious that the plan would call for massive resources which would not be immediately available. It is, therefore, suggested that priorities be given to children in the following groups/areas:

(a) Children of weaker sections including those in poverty groups; and
(b) Children in ecologically deprived areas such as drought-affected areas, coastal areas, hilly, tribal and backward areas.

UNICEF document on background and guidelines for the International Year of the Child 1979 recommended that:

> "That Government of participating countries may wish to create some sort of central point for planning, co-ordinating and implementing IYC activities. Where applicable, these are called 'National IYC' Commissions and agencies, official and private, should be mobilised to participate. To be effective, the commissions must have a permanent secretariat."

Accordingly, the National Children's Board was designated as the national level IYC Commission and its permanent secretariat is located in the Union Department of Social Welfare.

It is hoped that wherever State and Union Territory Children's Boards exist, they would function as State/Union Territories level committee for the observance of IYC; alternatively. Special Committees may be constituted for this purpose where necessary.

The State Level Committee on the basis of National Plan of Action, may plan and implement a State Level Plan on the following lines:

(i) Promote advocacy and publicity for the cause of the child;
(ii) Finalise a State Level plan to meet the special needs of the area in the light of IYC national guidelines; and
(iii) Consider launching new programmes and services for the child and mother:

State Sector,
Voluntary Sector.

(iv) Consider strengthening existing programmes and services:

State Sector,
Voluntary Sector.

(v) Legislation—Children's Act:
Working Conditions of Children, Enforcement of Legislation.
(vi) Encourage and promote research and evaluation studies by academic institutions and support them with funds.

Role of Voluntary Social Welfare Organisations

Voluntary organisations in India constitute a reckonable force in view of their number, long and established tradition of social service, high level motivation and rapport with the people. The large organisations are generally of a national character and have their branches/affiliates at the State and local levels, whereas small ones are of a local character and operate only at the community level. Some of these organisations are directly engaged in the field of child welfare/development whereas some others indirectly. Voluntary organisations by virtue of their background can perform a wide spectrum of roles in the promotion of child welfare/development viz., advocacy, supportive, supplementary operational, innovative and pioneering. More specifically, their roles and functions may be as under:

(i) Education and preparation of local community for immunisation against diseases like small-pox, tetanus, polio, diptheria, tuberculosis through individual and group approaches;

(ii) Large scale distribution of health aids like vitamins, minerals and medicines;
(iii) Propagation of scientific practices relating to community health, hygiene and sanitation;
(iv) Education of expectant and nursing mothers on scientific practices relating to child rearing and child-care;
(v) Detection and treatment of disease and "at risk" cases; and
(vi) Healthy baby competition.

Nutrition

(i) Supplementary nutrition programmes for children of weaker sections;
(ii) Mid-day-meal programmes in elementary schools and provision of equipment for the same;
(iii) Supply of food material for supplementary nutrition programme;
(iv) Community education on production, preparation and preservation of nutrition food;
(v) Distribution of nutrition supplements; and
(vi) Educating the community on health-promoting dietary habits.

Education

(i) Setting up of *Balwadis* and *Anganwadis* in areas inhabited by weaker sections;
(ii) Setting up of Parents-Teachers Associations in schools;
(iii) Generating community awareness in favour of compulsory schooling;
(iv) Promoting school enrolment and reducing drop-out;
(v) Production of children's literature;
(vi) Distribution of educational material and uniforms to needy children;
(vii) Organisation of functional literacy classes for mothers and non-formal education for non-school going children;
(viii) Setting up of pre-vocational/vocational training centres for children of weaker sections; and
(ix) Running of coaching classes for children weak at studies.

Recreation

(i) Organisation of games and sports for normal, pre-delinquent, as well as handicapped, school-going as well as non-school-going children and also for institutionalised children;

(ii) Organisation of visits to zoo, museum and picnic spots etc.;
(iii) Organisation of holiday camps;
(iv) Organisation of talents competitions;
(v) Opening of recreation and play ground centres, specially in slum areas; and
(vi) Organisation of film shows and exhibitions.

Social Welfare

(i) Opening of creches and day-care centres for children of working mothers;
(ii) Expansion of SOS type of villages for children needing care and protection;
(iii) Promotion of foster care and adoption services;
(iv) Orienting the community towards problems of handicapped and institutionalised children with a view to facilitating their care and rehabilitation; and
(v) Launching social action programmes in areas like untouchability, child marriage, child abuse, child labour, child exploitation etc.

Social Legislation

(i) Creating awareness in the community about the existing Act; and
(ii) Extension of support for effective enforcement and implementation of the existing Act.

Family Welfare

(i) Promoting of population education;
(ii) Educating the community about the small family norm; and
(iii) Setting up of family welfare centres.

Research and Training

(i) Identifying researchable problems relating to children and referring them to research bodies;
(ii) Conducting micro-research where technical expertise is available;

(iii) Identifying training needs of their functionaries including volunteers;
(iv) Conducting training programmes for child welfare/development workers at the grassroot level; and
(v) Utilising to the full measure, existing governmental training infrastructure for the training of their functionaries.

Participation of Professional Organisations and Associations

The IYC theme and action plan should be widely discussed and disseminated through sub-regional, regional and national conferences and meetings and efforts should be made to reach professional organisations of teachers, lawyers, engineers, doctors, students' organisations, service agencies like Rotary Clubs, Lions, Masons etc. and many other voluntary associations. These organisations should be encouraged to make IYC the theme of their meetings and activities and persuaded to lend their organisational, financial sponsorship and other supports to IYC action programmes.

It may also be noted that this document has laid stress on what needs to be done for children during the IYC and the following years to ensure their survival growth and development. Involvement of children has not been, by and large, touched upon in this plan. As such involvement can only be generated at the micro-level, it is hoped that realistic plans would be developed to secure individual and collective participation of children for:

(i) Their own betterment;
(ii) Assisting other children in greater need; and
(iii) Participation in the development of their schools and neighbourhoods.

While the action plan does envisage the participation of children in drawing, painting, elocution, essay, poetry, music, dance, handicrafts, games and sports competitions at various levels, the full unfoldment of their natural abilities and creative potentialities would also call for their participation in ventures oriented in improving their schools, neighbourhoods and eco-system around them.

Child Welfare Fund Raising

It was also suggested that during the International Year of Child (1979), the following measures may be taken to raise the Child Welfare Funds at National level and the States:

(a) A levy of 5 paise on postal articles may be imposed as Child Welfare Cess, during the IYC.
(Action: Ministry of Communications, DGP&T and Ministry of Finance).

(b) Donations to National Children's Fund and State Children's Fund may be exempt from Income-Tax from the year 1979-80 onwards.
(Action: Department of Social Welfare and Ministry of Finance).

(c) A day's collection on cinema tickets may go to the Children's Fund.
(Action: Ministry of Information & Broadcasting and State Governments).

(d) A levey of Rupee one may be imposed on all tickets for airship, first class railways/luxury bus travel during the IYC.
(Action: Ministry of Railways, Civil Aviation and Shipping & Transport).

(e) A nation-wide fund raising drive may be launched during IYC and in later years through sale of IYC seals by authorised voluntary agencies.
(Action: Department of Social Welfare, National/State/District Level Child Welfare Organisations/State Coordination committees).

IYC International

IYC National Commissions in most countries have reviewed the situation of their children and helping to prepare long- and short-term measures to benefit children. They looked into the health, nutrition, and education of children; and such areas as the special problems of handicapped children, the problems of street children, drug abuse, children abandoned or abused by their families, delinquency children and violence, mental health, play and cultural activities and the impact of television and other media on young children. They also engaged in advocacy and fund-raising for children. In some countries, these National Commissions became permanent bodies advising the President's or Prime Minister's Office.

As 1979 was the twentieth anniversary of the United Nations Declaration of the Rights of the Child, many countries have reviewed existing legislation to bring it more into the line with the declaration. Other countries realised that their laws relating to children, though adequate, need to be better enforced.

The Year produced a realisation of the basic universality of children's needs. While the child's survival needs—basic services such as food, clean water, clothing, shelter and health care—are more urgent and compelling in developing countries, they are also relevant to industrialised countries where children in isolated rural areas or urban ghettoes often live in conditions of severe poverty and deprivation.

Similarly, developing countries also confront the problems generally associated with more affluent societies: drug and alcohol addiction among the young; child abuse; teenage pregnancy; prostitution and delinquency. In responding to the needs of children in the years ahead, it is becoming clear that developing and industrialised countries may be able to learn a lot from each other.

Support to the work of IYC was given by the specialised agencies of the United Nations system and its regional bodies such as the economic and social commissioners; by other inter-governmental organisations; and by 130 international non-governmental organisations which have formed an IYC Co-ordinating Committee. The IYC Secretariat, set up within the administrative structure of UNICEF to provide a focus for international activities worked out of New York and Geneva. It produced and distributed basic information and core material including discussion papers on major issues concerning children, and meeting a large volume of requests for technical information or support of specialised meetings, workshops, symposia and research in child related areas. The Special Representative for IYC visited more than 60 countries to stimulate interest in IYC and to help generate programmes of lasting benefit for children.

At its 1979 session, the UNICEF Executive Board considered the implications of IYC on UNICEF's work. While acknowledging that UNICEF might have represented international concern for all children of the world more deliberately, the Board stressed that UNICEF must retain as its principal function the co-operation with developing countries. However, UNICEF might for example, facilitate the exchange of experience and information between all countries on politics and programmes benefiting children, and stimulate children related research and encourage its dissemination. The Board decided to consider further at its 1980 session appropriate UNICEF support of the follow-up of IYC in both developing and industrialised countries.

The success or failure of IYC will ultimately be measured by the extent to which it succeeds in extending and strengthening policies and services benefiting children, and making them an integral part of national development. It will be the responsibility of UNICEF and other organisations concerned with the well-being of children to see that the momentum generated during 1979 is not lost.

As the International Year of the Child (IYC) was the question asked and must be answered. But, behind all the special events publicity, what has actually been done. In fact, despite the rather modest objectives cited originally by the General Assembly—to provide a framework for advocacy on behalf of children and to promote government recognition of the need for programmes of lasting benefit what has already been accomplished during IYC can only be regarded as spectacular.

The results so far are all the more impressive for the fact that most are initial core projects preparing the way for much broader programmes which will benefit children far beyond IYC. During early preparations, IYC Planners often emphasised the potential catalytic effect the year could have in terms of heightened public awareness and commitments to eventual comprehensive programmes benefit children.

What has been compiled here, moreover, is just the beginning. Every week the IYC Secretariat receives reports of new efforts and accomplishments by groups and governments. Every week, the number of such reports multiplies, as does the number of announcements of programmes to start within the next year or so as a result of research done during the IYC?

Some 170 countries and territories representing some 1.5 billion children are participating in IYC. Existing efforts, programmes and institutional structures and responding to the needs of children vary widely in scope, quality and sophistication. By the same token the problems of needs and children vary widely according to region, country and locality. Enumerating the number of countries studying, initiating or expanding programmes dealing with one of the concerns of IYC can be as a consequence somewhat misleading unless it is kept in mind that the figures indicate additional, not total programmes benefiting children, and do not attempt to quantify the number of programmes within the countries. On the other hand, such a list provides a useful way of measuring and highlighting the concrete success which national and international cooperation can produce when concerted attention is given to a common concern during an international year such as IYC.

While most of the projects and programmes initiated in IYC have been developed and are taking place at national and community levels in line with IYC's central concern for maximum effective and lasting participation, numerous members of the UN family have also been active in promoting the rights, assessing the needs, and defending the cause of children everywhere.

UNICEF: The United Nations Children's Fund has acted as the lead agency for IYC, providing the necessary additional resources through, for instance, the PREPAC programme for comprehensive National Commissions information efforts, some 40 media missions of its own to 60 countries, the supply of documentaries, etc. for national broadcasting media, special IYC information kits for journalists, governments and non-governmental groups, and support of various fund-raising events involving public participation, such as the "Music for UNICEF" television special which has been shown in 60 countries to an estimated audience of 250 million.

FAO: The Food and Agriculture Organisation set-up a network of departmental/divisional co-ordination officers for IYC at the end of 1978, and instructed all FAO country-level representatives to intensify efforts directly benefiting children in 54 FAO field projects. Studies and documents have been prepared on "Prospects for rural children", "the food situation and children", "Rural children", and "what is the meaning of food in the daily life of children and how it affects their future". The FAO's inter-departmental working group on IYC is reviewing selected on-going projects in the field of nutrition and home economics, promotion of day-care centres, preparation of training materials for rural women and youth, applied nutrition and supplementary feeding, school forestry and school gardening, production of small animals, the Freedom from Hunger campaign, and the money and medals programmes.

ILO: The International Labour Organisation has focussed on the five issues of prohibition of child labour, formulation of "transitional policy measures" to protect working children, attacking the basic causes of child labour, adaptation to future work life and protection of the children of working mothers. Action has included expanding support of non-formal education programmes, encouraging governments to implement comprehensive standards on the minimum age of admission to employment, making an extensive study on working children in Argentina, Greece, India, Indonesia, Italy, Mexico, Nigeria, Pakistan, Peru and Thailand, designing two projects on "Maternal Employment and the Basic Needs of Children" and "Children at World: Profiles from developing countries" and studying new programme orientations based on the 1965 recommendations on women with family responsibilities, maternity, protection legislation and its impact on children, migrant children's special needs of vocational training and apprenticeship schemes, and national measures to improve the conditions of work and life of children.

ITU: The International Telecommunication Union has conducted an information campaign organisation, with some 50 member-countries offering the free use of telecommunication circuits for a live television project underlining the university of communications in the context of the world's children.

UN: With the United Nations: The Department of International Economic and Social Affairs has undertaken a global study on the training of para-professional social welfare personnel working with children and families, a study on the changing role of women and the implications for family and child welfare services, and reports for the UN Secretary General on the co-ordination of the social components of IYC and on adoption and foster placement. Other activities planned include a study on alternative models for providing comprehensive family services in the context of the UN Decade for Women, a study on ways of monitoring the situation of children, a study on the problems of child abuse, a review and analysis of formal and customary laws affecting the rights of children, and a declaration of social and legal principles relating to adoption and foster placement of children.

The Division of Human Rights is working on a draft convention on the human rights of children and preparing an "Inventory of international standards and related activities in the field of the rights of the child." Ongoing activities include providing the services of experts to assist Government in devising policies and measures aimed at ensuring the rights of children, and particularly those of indigenous children subject to slavery and such practices as the forced marriage of young girls.

UN regional organs, such as the Economic and Social Commission for Asia and the Pacific, the Economic Commission for Latin America, Economic Commission for Africa, has each undertaken regional surveys on the needs of children and have established coordinating units for an information exchange and programme co-operation benefiting child.

UNDP: The United Nations Development Programme, through its field staff, is expanding its work with governments to assure that programmes of rural development, and to support the participation of women in development, education and training, primary health-care and other services.

UNDRO: The Office of the United Nations Disaster Relief Co-ordination has reinforced its relief co-ordination and preparedness activities concerning the special needs of children including education in disaster preparedness in primary schools.

UNEP: The United Nations Environment Programme is focusing on children's basic needs through features in its publication, a symposium on "Environment, education and the child," scientific studies on malaria and schistosomiasis with emphasis on children, World Environment Folder on child development, a compilation of research studies on "The environment and child development in Africa," the preparation of the information component of the UNEP/UNICEF water project in Swaziland. Pilot studies on formal and non-formal environmental education for children, comparative studies on an integrated approach to slum improvement with emphasis on children, and a theme paper for IYC on the environment for children of the future.

UNESCO: The United Nations Education, Scientific and Cultural Organisation has completed an in-depth study on "UNESCO and the Child" and a pursuing, among numerous IYC activities, the publication of "The right of the child to education," case studies on pre-primary education suited to socio-demographic conditions and cultural traditions a handbook for training pre-primary school personnel and parents, a 62-country survey of the effects of various types of school life on the development of the child's personality, regional case studies on the early detection of handicaps in children and the problems of special education, a comprehensive report on the effects of educational television on psychological development in early childhood, a study of international human rights instruments with regard to handicapped children, and a study of effective and inexpensive ways of producing children's book and toys. It is in addition co-sponsoring a symposium on "Trends in social science research on children a symposium and supporting the production of reading materials in Braille by the Lesotho National Commission as well as reading promotion campaign in Brazil, Panama and the Philippines."

UNFDAC: The United Nations Fund for Drug Abuse Control and the division of Narcotic Drugs have published a comprehensive report on "Children and Drugs" for IYC, as well as varied media materials on "Freedom from drug dependence: a child's right." Also supported in a special IYC project focusing on the determination of the incidence of drug abuse and addiction among children in Malaysia, on the hazards and advisability of using amphetamine-type drugs in the therapeutical management of hyperactive children, and on the various behavioural and patho-physiological effects on the foetus of opiate addiction in the mother.

UNFPA: The United Nations Fund for Population Activities is supporting a research project to develop illustrative approaches to a population strategy giving more attention to reducing infant and child mortality through the documentation of population trends. It also jointly sponsored at end-1978 a meeting of 50 international journalists with a panel of demographers, biologists, economists, public health specialists and administrators of population programmes which looked at child health and infant mortality worldwide as an introduction of IYC efforts.

UNHCR: The United Nations with High Commissioners and Office for Refugees has worked in the context of IYC for the increase in protection of refugee children through a new campaign for ratification of the 1961 Convention on the Reduction of Statelessness, and improved application of the 1951 Convention on the Status of Refugees particularly in relation to schooling, family reunification, and naturalisation. The UNHCR has also made a new IYC connected push in the fields of health, nutrition and general welfare which has succeeded among other things in obtaining 243 new visa to Belgium for unaccompanied Vietnamese children, the field of new fund-raising, the UNHCR's compendium of projects. The refugee child has to date attract $3 million for specific projects benefiting refugee children for instance Australia, Belgium, Canada, Denmark, Finland, France, Italy, Japan, Sweden, the UK, Yugoslavia, Botswana and Thailand, and for the resettlement of the children of "boat people" families.

UNIDO: The United Nations Industrial Development Organisation is pursuing programmes to establish textile industries providing school-age children with school uniforms and other garments, food processing and weaning food industries to meet the protein and other requirements of pre-school and school-age children, and leather industries needed to provide school children with proper footwear.

UNRWA: The United Nations Relief and Works Agency for Palestine Refugees in the Near-East has produced a health education calendar for free use among the 307,000 primary and preparatory pupils who are refugees in Lebanon, Jordan and Syria. It has also produced a report on UNRWA's work among children in the area of education, health, nutrition and overall welfare services for those in special hardship.

UNVP: The United Nations Volunteers Programme has reinforced ongoing programmes assisting children in the fields of nutrition, health care of mothers and children, clean water supply and education.

WFC: The World Food Council has augmented its activities for children in the line with the 1978 Mexico Declaration, launching major campaigns to prevent vitamins a deficiency and endemic goitre as part of national IYC activities, and encouraging government to pay special attention to malnutrition, the development of local food-stuffs and supplementary feeding programmes in the context of IYC and in future national rural development goals.

WFP: The World Food Programme has worked out a long-term strategy directed at especially vulnerable groups such as nursing mothers and pre-school children for nutrition rehabilitation, long-term intervention aimed to socio-economically deprived groups of children facing meddler degrees of malnutrition, and enhanced supplementary feeding programmes which ensure that rations intended for young children and expectant or nursing mothers are not consumed by other family members.

WHO: The World Health Organisation has carried out an extensive study on the present status of maternal and child health and trends in the development of relevant services, in the context of overall national health and socio-economic planning. Plans emerging from a review of issues and priorities by the six WHO regional offices include, for example, special attention to immunisation against the five major childhood diseases, the strengthening and development of appropriate technology for the care of the mother and new born, a large-scale study of oriental mortality, and the establishment of national teacher-training programmes in maternal and child health care in three regions. Additionally WHO has either initiated or strengthened activities in the areas of pre and perinatal care, reduction in the number of low-weight births, eradication of neo-natal tetanus, abolition of Vitamin 'A' and 'D' deficiency diseases, reduction in the death rate due to diarrhoeal diseases and promotion of breast feeding and proper infant and young nutrition.

World Bank: The International Bank for Reconstruction and Development has compiled and published a World Atlas of the child, providing full statistical information on the economic and social conditions of children in nearly all the countries and regions of the world.

Inter-Governmental Activities have provided Co-ordination and Support to IYC Activities on a Variety of International Fronts

EEC: The European Economic Community is making a community-wide public opinion survey specially designed for IYC on attitudes and behaviour towards children and children's needs as well as preparing a booklet in six languages on the little citizens of Europe. Guidelines on toy security are being prepared. Studies are being conducted on the child and publicity. A campaign has been launched to sensitize children to environmental problems and consumptions. Credits of the European Social Fund have been increased and allocated to programmes for the children of migrant workers. Anti-poverty programmes and special education programmes, for migrant workers' children, pre-schools, and handicapped children have been developed, as well as programmes to promote equality in status and educational opportunities between boys and girls. The EEC European Fund for Development has financed new medical services and nutrition centres in a number of developing countries.

Council of European Representatives have Held Round Table with NGOs on ill-treatment and child labour, and underprivileged children. Reports are being prepared on the legal position of the child, medical care, and child labour in preparation for the drafting of a European Charter on the Rights of the Child. Special education programmes for the children of migrant workers and a series of studies on pre-school education are being undertaken along with preparation for a conference on "From birth to right": young children in European society in the 1980's followed by a seminar on "present-day cultural provisions for children in Europe." Also to be studied are the role of school health services measures against the prostitution of minors, the criminal aspects of ill-treatment of children, the social integration of children and two draft conventions on the custody of children and an International Tribunal to settle child custody disputes.

OECD: Organization for Economic Co-operation and Development is reinforcing its ongoing support for programmes benefiting children of the developing world. A study on early childhood will be published during IYC as well as on the demographic situation and children's position in 20 industrialised countries, a document on policies towards early childhood with a view to their future development, a study on social services for children and a study on governmental costs with regard to policy programmes for the child. Inter-Governmental conference and seminars on policies and services for children as well as a meeting of donor countries on the effects of external aid for the benefiting children in developing countries have also been organised.

IPU: The Inter-Parliamentary Union has initiated new efforts for the elaboration of laws and measures favouring children. Moves are also under way to provide continuing support to UNICEF and other groups involved in family and child protection. Consideration is also being given to permanent links between various Parliamentary groups and international bodies dealing with the welfare of children.

What has been achieved in IYC

What has been Accomplished in IYC . . . By Non-governmental Organisation

One of the most important effects of the IYC has been the mobilisation of over 220 International NGOs through the Non-governmental Organisation's Committee on the International Year of the Child. In this respect, IYC has unlocked unprecedented possibilities for communication, co-operation and joint programming on the needs of children both between these groups and between NGOs and involved governments NGO groups have been active at almost every level in almost every one of the 170 countries and territories participating in IYC. Characterised by many small-scale initiatives, often unrecorded, NGO activities have been the force behind countless local initiatives responding to specific local needs and lending themselves to expansion to overall national action.

The NGO/IYC Committee has sponsored formal working groups preparing studies, materials and programmes on "The handicapped child," "The right of the child," "Children of the Fourth World," "Education," "The Children's movements." The League of Red Cross societies has initiated for reinforcing numerous national and international programmes in social welfare, education, the arts, health and public information. The Save the Children Fund has funded numerous IYC projects, including an Overseas Poliomyelitis Eradication scheme providing technical and material support in several countries. The Baptist World Alliance in co-operation with the Brother's Brother Fund is supporting special child health projects including the immunisation of approximately 1 million children in Grenada and Liberia against the five major childhood diseases. The international Planned Parenthood Federation has supported national programmes and programme development dealing with the rights of the child, health and nutrition, information education, communicating youth and women's development and child welfare. The International Board on Books for Young People has worked with several governments and national NGOs to establish guidelines, develop activities, select book titles and make surveys. The World Council of Men's Clubs has six international projects for children. Jaycees International is in the second year of a three-year IYC programme on "Opportunities for Children."

The International Federation of Women Lawyers has made legal protection of the child, the theme of its 20th International Convention including projects on the employment of minors, children in trouble with the law, child abuse, custody, support and inheritance rights. Amnesty International has issued reports on the situation of children living under regimes violating the First Principle of the Declaration of the Rights of the Child. The International Commission of Jurists has published a report on "The detention of children in South Africa." The International Catholic Migration Commission has been working with affiliates on refugee children and especially on the acceptance on unaccompanied minors from refugee camps in Southeast Asia.

The Mayors of major cities held a working conference on a better life for the child in the city, and the United Towns Organisation is distributing a booklet outlining possible action on "The rights of the child in the town." The Social and Educational Association of Seafarers have collected information on the children of seafarers and established a new international organisation called children of the sea. The World Council of Churches is working with member churches to learn from the pro-called—"The people of this world belong together. The World Association of Girl Guide Scouts has developed IYC programmes in more than 90 countries, has inaugurated 34 New SOC Children's villages throughout the world to mark IYC. National NGO affiliates have initiated or expanded action and information programmes spanning every area of IYC concern in a total to date 104 countries. The number carrying out major work in specific fields included (and this unavoidable is only a partial tabulation) 5 in the field of adoption, 14 in the arts, 4 on blind children, 56 on children's book and publications, 11 on child care, 11 on child development, 4 on child labour, 13 on children's activity programmes, 3 on destitute children, 2 on drug abuse, 63 on early childhood education, 49 on education in general, 18 on the environment, 21 on the family, 11 on family planning, 3 on children's films, 5 on the gifts children, 15 on handicapped children, 46 on health, 5 on housing, 11 on institution such as shelters and diagnosis centres, 17 on inter-cultural exchange and understanding, 9 on legislation, 14 on the media, 13 on migrants and refugees, 22 on nutrition, 14 on the parent education, 23 on protective services, 8 on recreation, 28 on basic research, 31 on the rights of the child, 12 on the rural situation, 23 on the status of women, 14 on the urban situation and 8 on violence. In addition, 74 have held major meetings.

International Year of the Child (IYC)

What has been accomplished through . . . towards legislation on Children's Rights

The legal rights of a child have been or are the object of new programmes of study and research aimed a changing related legal codes and statutes in 18 countries in Africa, 8 countries, in Asia, 6 countries in Latin America, and 13 countries in Europe, North America and elsewhere. New Comprehensive legal codes and statutes dealing with various aspects of the rights of the child have been or are being drafted or enacted in 12 countries in Africa, 7 countries in Asia, 13 countries in Latin America, and 8 countries in Europe, North America, and elsewhere.

What has been accomplished . . . towards Child Welfare

New research and study into the overall social welfare of children and mothers with the objective of changing appropriate programmes and institutional mechanisms has taken or is taking place in 19 countries in Africa, 22 countries in Asia, 13 countries in Latin America, and 21 countries in Europe, North America, and elsewhere.

The number of countries which have changed or are in the process of changing or introducing comprehensive programmes and institutional mechanisms dealing with various aspects of the overall social welfare of children include 10 countries in Africa, 12 countries in Asia, 10 countries in Latin America, and 13 countries in Europe, North America and elsewhere.

What has been accomplished . . . in special areas of children's needs

New studies and research into the problems of such disadvantaged children as abandoned delinquent, and street children have been or are being carried out in 7 countries in Africa, 4 countries in Asia, 5 countries in Latin America and 9 countries in Europe, North America and elsewhere. Actual programmes for such children are being established, expanded or improved in 10 countries in Africa, 8 countries in Asia, 7 in Latin America and 5 in Europe, North America and elsewhere. The special needs of physically and mentally handicapped children have been or being newly studies especially for IYC in 7 countries in Africa, 2 countries in Asia, 5 in Latin America and 6 in Europe, North America and elsewhere. New or expanded programmes have been or are being initiated in 9 countries in Africa, 10 countries in Asia, 3 in Latin America and 12 countries in Europe, North America and elsewhere.

The needs of nomadic, migrant and refugee children and their families have been or are being of new study and research in 9 countries in Africa, 3 countries in Asia, 2 in Latin America and 3 in Europe, North America and elsewhere. Special programmes and centres to deal with the specific needs of under-privileged urban or rural children have been or are being studied in 5 countries in Africa, 3 in Latin America and 2 countries in Asia, 4 countries in Europe, North America and elsewhere. Programmes have been or are being established, expanded or improved in 8 countries of Africa, 5 countries in Asia, 2 countries in Latin America and 4 countries in Europe, North America and elsewhere.

What has been accomplished . . . in regard to basic services . . .

The basic services by which essential services are extended to children through trained workers from the community explicitly or implicity undergirds, virtually all the IYC programmes dealing with the overall social welfare of children in the developing world. Special attention however, has or is being given on strengthening the introduction or implementation of the basic services approach in 7 countries in Africa, 5 countries in Asia, 3 in Latin America and 3 countries in Europe, North America and elsewhere.

What has been accomplished in IYC . . . In the fields of nutrition and health . . .

Detailed research into child nutrition, proper diet, and improvement of nutrition services benefiting children has been completed or is under way in 13 countries in Africa, 12 in Asia, 8 countries in Latin America, and 5 in Europe, North America and elsewhere.

Comprehensive child nutrition programmes, including for instance increased food supply, school lunches, and supplementary feeding programmes have been initiated to expand in 15 countries in Africa, 19 countries in Asia, 5 countries in Latin America, and 8 in Europe, North America and elsewhere. A review of and research into the needs, scope and quality of child health-care with the aim of introducing, extending, or improving local and national health services for children, has been completed or is under way in 13 countries in Africa, 9 countries in Asia, 9 countries in Latin America, and 8 in Europe, North America and elsewhere.

New programmes establishing extending, or improving comprehensive local and national health services for children have been introduced of are being introduced in 17 countries in Africa, 20 countries in Asia, 3 in Latin America and 14 countries in Europe, North America and elsewhere.

Sanitation and clean water programmes have been or are being studied, established, extended or improved in 13 countries in Africa, 10 in Asia, in Latin America and 5 countries in Europe, North America and elsewhere.

What has been accomplished . . . in education for children and parents . . .

New studies and research into establishing, expanding or improving local and national pre-school or primary education programmes have been completed or are under way in 15 countries in Africa, 11 countries in Asia, 9 countries in Latin America and 6 in Europe, North America and elsewhere.

Newly established expanded or improved programmes of pre-school or primary education have been or are in the process of being instituted in 8 countries in Africa and 17 in Asia, 8 countries in Latin America and 10 countries in Europe, North America and elsewhere.

New programmes of basic and non-formal education including vocational education for children, have been or are being studied in 5 countries in Africa, 2 countries in Asia, 5 countries in Latin America and 2 countries in Europe, North America and elsewhere, while the number of action programmes, being established, expanded or improved include those 13 countries in Africa, 10 in Asia, 5 in Latin America, North America and 10 countries in Europe, North America and elsewhere.

The development of new books, reform of textbooks and establishment or expansion of libraries for and about children have been or are being studied in 2 countries in Africa, 6 countries in Asia, 2 in Latin America, and 4 in Europe, North America and elsewhere. But actual programmes having been or being established include those in Africa, 15 countries in Asia, 6 countries in Latin America and 10 countries in Europe, North America, and elsewhere.

New research and study into the right to play, educational games, toy development, and new or improved playgrounds and recreational programmes has taken or is taking place in 4 countries in Africa, 2 in Asia, 5 countries in Latin America, and 5 countries in Europe, North America and elsewhere, while actual programmes have been or are being initiated in 14 countries in Africa, 8 countries in Asia, 9 countries in Latin America and 17 in Europe.

What has been accomplished in IYC . . . in regard to the needs of women and girls . . .

New research and study into the situation, role opportunities and need for women has taken or is taking place in 5 countries in Africa, 2 countries in Latin America and 9 countries in Europe, North America and elsewhere. Action programmes have been or are being established of women and girls in 5 countries in Africa, 5 in Asia, 3 in Latin America and 3 countries in Europe, North America and elsewhere.

The establishment and expansion of day-care centres has been in the object of new study in 3 countries in Africa, 2 countries in Asia, 2 countries in Latin America, and 2 in Europe, North America and elsewhere. While actual programmes for establishing, expanding, or improving day-care centre facilities have been or are being initiated in 16 countries in Africa, 12 countries in Asia, 10 countries in Latin America, and 8 countries in Europe, North America and elsewhere.

Henry R. Labousie, Executive Director of UNICEF said:

> "The International Year of the Child 1979 will be considered if it sets in motion plans and programmes that will improve the fate of generations of the children to come. It will have reached its goal if it spreads knowledge not only that the problems of children are urgent and immense, but the wisdom and the wealth to solve them are at our command. The task is manageable in both scope and time. We know that the world has the means. The question is: Do we have the .will"?

15

THE CHILD IN INDIA TODAY

India's present population according to 1981 Census is 685.185 million (which includes provisional population of Assam) and 720 million as of 1983. (Rural population 508 million and urban 158 million) and of 1988 figure it crossed 800 million.

Every seventh person in the world is an Indian with 2.4 per cent of the global area, India accommodates 15 per cent of the world's population and over 20 per cent of the world's developing countries. Though it ranks second to China, it overtakes it in population growth.

In India population is increasing by about 15 million every year. As per 1981 Census the total child population in the age group of 0-14 years of age is 263 million, i.e., 38.8 per cent of the total population. 205 million or 78 per cent are in the rural area and 58 million or 22 per cent are in urban area.

This size of child population is growing faster than the general population in India, and it has grown from 90 million in 1901 to 263 million in 1981, an increase of 192 per cent. At this rate it may be 333 million in the year 2001.

Total population of children in the age group of 0-14 is 263,107,050 of which children between 0-4 years is 83 million. Males 42 million and females 41 millions.

Children between 5-9 years is 93 million, males 48 million and females 46 million.

Children between 10-14 years is 86 million, males 45 million and females 41 million.

In the rural areas 205 million or 78 per cent (excluding Assam).

Of the total population, children in the age group of 0-14, males are 106 million, females 99 million.

In urban areas the total population of children in the age group of 0-14 is 58 million or 28 per cent (excluding Assam) male children 30 million, females 28 million.

In Tribal areas the total population is 51,628,638, or 7.76 per cent.

There are 532 Scheduled Tribes in India from the percentage distribution of scheduled tribes population (1981)—(Assam excluded). Also it is to be noted that no tribes were scheduled by the President of India for Haryana, Jammu & Kashmir, Punjab, Chandigarh, Delhi and Pondicherry.

Out of the total scheduled tribes population, i.e., 51,628,683 (7.76%). In this child population is:

0-9 years age, males are 90,495,837 and females are 86,700,346

10-14 years age, males are 45,265,292 and females are 40,646,075

15-19 years age, males are 34,026,988 and females are 30,111,819

According to the statement of the Planning Minister in Parliament in February 1981, 118 million children are living below the poverty line, and these are the children who need services related to health, nutrition, education, access to safe water supply etc.

Scheduled Castes

"Scheduled Castes are defined in Article 366(24) of our Constitution to mean such castes, races or tribes or sections or parts of or groups within such castes, races or tribes as are deemed under Article 341 to be scheduled castes for the purpose of this Constitution."

When the Constitution of India was drafted, noticing the sad condition of the depressed sections of the society, special privileges and facilities for the socio-economic upliftment of these groups was incorporated into the Constitution. Through the Presidential order of 1950 regarding Scheduled Castes, the President has specified in the Schedule of Constitution who are the Scheduled Castes.

Specific Provisions in the Constitution for the Scheduled Castes

1. Article 15(4) empowers the Government to make special provisions for the advancement of the Scheduled Castes.
2. Article 16(4) authorises the State to make provisions for reservations of appointments or posts in favour of any backward class of citizen not adequately represented in the services under the State.
3. Article 17 abolishes "Untouchability." Its practice is forbidden and is made an offence punishable under Law.

4. Article 46 directs the State to promote with special care the interests of Scheduled Castes to protect them from social injustice and exploitation.
5. Article 164 (1) provides for appointment of Ministers in certain States for the welfare of Scheduled Castes, Scheduled Tribes and Backward classes.
6. Article 330 provides for reservation of seats for Scheduled Castes and Scheduled Tribes in the House of People according to the proportion in population.
7. Article 332 provides reservation of seats for Scheduled Castes and Scheduled Tribes in Legislative Assembly.
8. Article 334 provides for cessation of reservation of seats for Scheduled Castes and Scheduled Tribes and special representation to Anglo-Indians' community in the House of People and in the Legislative Assemblies of the States after 40 years from the commencement of the Constitution.
9. Article 335 recognises the claims of Scheduled Castes and Scheduled Tribes to services and posts connected with the affairs of the Union or States.
10. Article 338 provides for appointment by the President of a special officer for the Scheduled Castes and Scheduled Tribes to investigate all matters relating to the safeguards provided for them under Constitution.
11. Article 34 empowers the President to specify Castes, Races and Tribes to be the Scheduled Castes.

The Scheduled Castes today are at different levels of Socio-Economic Development. A substantial proportion of Scheduled Castes and Scheduled Tribes women are employed as agricultural labourers. During 1961-1971 the number of females rose from 24 to 50 per cent of the total female working population. According to 1981 census the figure decreased to 45 per cent.

Traditionally these women perform strenuous tasks of agriculture which involve hours of walking and bending. In addition to the outdoor work they have to do necessary indoor work plus cooking for the family, which is not considered as productive work and the contribution goes unnoticed.

In Urban areas 75 per cent were concentrated in 19 occupations, apart from 20 per cent who were teachers, nurses and clerks. Majority were in occupation which required no education—such as domestic servants, construction workers, unskilled labourers, Delhi Municipal Corporation is one of the biggest employers of sweepers. Though the formal policy is to employ men and women in the quota of 75 : 25, still in actual fact the appointments are 50 : 50 in favour of women. Due to this pre-condition 'Child' exists. There are restrictions imposed on them. They start working early and a differential treatment of boys and girls exist throughout.

There are about 474 individual Scheduled Castes and they constitute 15.75 per cent of the total population.

Scheduled Castes total population is 104,754,623, i.e., 15.75 per cent. Out of these males are 15.75 per cent and females are 15.73 per cent.

In the *Rural* the Scheduled Castes population is 17.34 per cent.
Males are 17.44 per cent and females are 17.23 per cent.
In the *Urban* the total Scheduled Castes population is 10.63 per cent.
Males are 10.56 per cent and females are 10.71 per cent.

(These figures exclude Assam and no Castes were Scheduled by the President of India for Nagaland, Andaman and Nicobar Islands and Lakshadweep).

Scheduled Tribes

The tribals of India live in the forests and hills and naturally isolated regions and known by different names.

The popular names are:

Vanvasi (Inhabitants of Forests)
Vanyajati (Castes of Forests)
Adimjati (Original Communities)
Adivasis (First Settlers)
Janjati (Folk People)
Anusuchit Janjati (Scheduled Tribes), and so on.

Among these all terms *Adivasis* is known most extensively, and the *Anusuchit Janjati*—Scheduled Tribes is the constitutional name covering them all.

At the time of 1971 census the major tribes computed to 39 million, but the tribal population increased to 52 million according to 1981 census, with the Amendment Act of 1976 when the area restriction within the States was removed. This population follows a distinct life style identified as tribal culture. It is tied up with land and forests and characterised by their own language and heritage, love for freedom and self-identity.

Tribal History

Coming to the tribal history, we find that the tribals are an integral part of the Indian civilization. Various elements in the ancient civilisation of India were contributed by the tribals. It is believed that they were the earliest among the present inhabitants of the country.

Four main races and cultures welded together into one people.

(i) *The Austro-Asiatics*, in their primitive form are represented by the Kols or Mundas, Khasis and the Nicobarese.
(ii) *The Mongoloid* speaking dialects of the Sino-Tibetan family who are found largely among the Sub-Himalayan regions and who are represented by the Nagas, Bodos, the Kuki, Chins etc.
(iii) *The Dravadians* consist of the Malers, the Oraons, the Gonds and the Khonds who speak tongues of the Dravadian families.
(iv) *The Aryans* are the last to come to India.

All the four racial and cultural elements made a contribution to the formation of the Indian people.

Major Scheduled Tribes in India

There are 532 Scheduled Tribes in India. The tribal section of the Indian population is characterised as isolated in ecology, demography, economy, politics and other social behaviours from other ethnic groups.

In the North Eastern region, they are in Arunachal Pradesh, Meghalaya, Nagaland, Manipur, Tripura and Mizoram.

In Assam they are—Boro, Boro Kachari, Chakma, Dhimsa, Devari, Hozai, Haflong, Kachari Sonwal, Lalung, Mech, Mikir, Burmans in Cachar and Rabha.

Tribals

There are 532 Scheduled Tribes in India, and the total population is 51,628,638, they constitute 7.76 per cent of the total population of the country—

Males are 7.57 per cent and Females are 7.96 per cent.

Rural—9.54 per cent, out of which males are 9.37 per cent and Females are 9.72 per cent.

Urban—2.0 per cent out of which males are 2.00 per cent and Females are 2.07 per cent.

Out of the total population, children age-wise are:

	Age Group	*Males*	*Females*
Total	0-9	90,495,337	86,700,346
	10-14	45,265,292	40,646,075
	15-19	34,026,988	30,111,819
Rural	0-9	71,023,470	68,075,299
	10-14	35,080,837	31,384,678
	15-19	25,003,133	22,317,499
Urban	0-9	19,471,867	18,625,047
	10-14	10,184,456	9,261,397
	15-19	9,023,754	7,794,320

The Scheduled Tribes are considered as special groups of agriculturists, but a few among them still take out an existence through hunting, fishing and food gathering.

This percentage distribution of Scheduled Tribes Population (1981)—Assam is excluded. Also it is to be noted that no tribes were Scheduled by the President of India for Haryana, Jammu & Kashmir, Punjab, Chandigarh, Delhi and Pondicherry.

Religion

India is a multi-lingual country where as many as 179 languages, 544 dialects and 1942 mother tongues are spoken, even though only 15 national languages are enlisted in the Constitution.

However, our Constitution based on secularism provides for freedom of worship and equality of all religions, creeds and castes in the states. So there is a need to develop mutual tolerance of religions, respects for the religious beliefs of others and to understand the basic similarities in all religions.

In the population of the country one of the important characteristics is religion. India is a secular state, as several religions have thrived from time immemorial and the data given provides an interesting picture of religions followed by the people. This data is useful to every common man and also to a scholar or for a research purpose.

According to 1981 census the growth of major religious communities are:

1. Hindus—549,779,481 (82.64 per cent of total population), an increase since 1971 by 24.15 per cent:

   Rural — 429,116,124 (84.54%)
   Urban — 120,663,357 (76.52%)
   Males — 284,392,942
   Females — 265,386,539

2. Muslims—75,512,439 (11.35% of the total population), an increase since 1971 by 30.59 per cent:

   Rural — 49,835,389 (9.82%)
   Urban — 25,678,050 (16.28%)
   Males — 38,989,763
   Females — 36,522,676

3. Sikhs—13,078,146 (1.96% of the total population), an increase since 1971 by 26.15 per cent:

   Rural — 10,245,347 (2.02%)
   Urban — 2,832,799 (1.80%)
   Males — 6,957,891
   Females — 6,120,255

4. Christians—16,165,447 (2.43% of the total population), an increase since 1971 by 16.77 per cent:

   Rural — 11,450,802 (2.25%)
   Urban — 4,714,645 (2.99%)
   Males — 8,113,569
   Females — 8,051,878

5. Buddhists—4,719,796 (0.71% of the total population), an increase since 1971 by 22.52 per cent:

   Rural — 3,209,752 (0.63%)
   Urban — 1,510,044 (0.96%)
   Males — 2,416,780
   Females — 2,303,016

6. Jains—3,206,038 (0.48% of the total population), an increase since 1971 by 23.60 per cent.
7. Other religions—2,466,285 (0.42% of the total population), an increase since 1971 by 26.16 per cent.
8. Religion not stated—60,271 (0.01% of the total population), an increase since 1971 by 66.88 per cent.

Religion Oneness

Having too many religions in the country, the very thought or word "Religion" brings division when preaching is same, yet the effect brings an opposite reaction. The child actually does not internalise what he/she learnt from preaching, but takes it what others attitude is. Because he neither reads, neither he understands the original text or of these problems at that stage of life. Therefore, the attitude of family, educational institutions and the total environment is responsible for his attitude.

It is said that once Akbar who in his interest wanted to find out whether religion is inborn in child when born. He isolated a group of infants, as they grew up, they were questioned about their religion and religious beliefs, all were found to be dumb.

Actually there is no difference in the fundamentals of religions, e.g., we may consider few basic teachings of all major religions.

> "Hatred ceaseth not by hatred, hatred ceaseth by love. This is the ever-lasting law"—*Buddha.*

> "If anyone says I love God, and yet hate his brother, he is liar, because who ever does not love his brother whom he has seen, he cannot love God whom he has not seen. God has made of one blood all nations of man"—*Jesus Christ.*

> "Let us all in unison like true friends, invoke upon God, best known in his revealed law (of nature) for our protection and help in all our battles of life"—*Rig Veda:* 30, 7.

> "No one is a true believer until he loves for his brother that which he loves for himself"—*Koran.*

> "Regard your neighbour's gain, as your gain, and regard your neighbour's loss as your own loss"—*Tao.*

> "That nature is not good when it shall not do to others whatever is not good for its own self."—*Zoraster.*

"In happiness and sufferings, in joy and grief, we should regard all creatures as we regard our own self and should therefore, refrain from inflicting upon others such injury as would appear understandable to us if inflicted upon ourselves".—*Jainism.*

"As you treat yourself so treat others. Then you shall become partner in heaven. Regard all men as equal since God's light is contained in the heart of each".—*Guru Nanak.*

Hence it will be noted from above sayings, and it reveals that all religions are complementary and nothing could be termed as contradictory. Such teachings and information should be inculcated in the minds of children. Respecting and understanding of all religions can bring in National Integration and thus a scientific approach to religion in its totality will bring in vigour and vitality.

Thought for Children

In the prevailing environment the attitudes developed by the children towards other religions during their formative years will be carried for the rest of his life. Their influence on human mind will last longer. In the absence of positive introduction to the other religion, the exclusive, confined thinking and worship of one's own religion, the unreasonable high estimation of the religious beliefs in other religions, the general grudges, hatreds, prejudices, intolerance, psychological imbalance within the personality, results in dislike of other religion and it is different, the physical failures, political unrest, uneven economic development, poverty brings unrest with the human mind and it reacts with the people, who are different either by caste, culture and religion. The children, when they are ushered into this life should be given training in areas of tolerance, understanding and respect for the other religion and its people. This will enhance, national integrity, development and unity in the communities. All these factors will also strengthen the political life of the Nation.

A serious thought must be given to this problem as to what steps may be taken for understanding, accepting and tolerating other religions in our secular State and bring in national integration.

Religion which is a way of life our society influences the young easily and quickly. The growth of many religions in the country has many advantages and disadvantages on the growth of the young. Religious faith of dogmatic nature gets hold on the young mind comparatively more than the adult. The religious environment of the Indian children are manifolded. The children in our country are born with caste, in addition to the acquired religion by birth. The Indian Constitution while, discouraging the caste and colour, ensures the religious freedom of each citizen. Having a constitutional sanction by the State all the Social Institutions primarily first the family, then school and next other religious institutions are free to teach the young ones, their religion and encourage to practice it irrespective of caste, creed and colour, sex, and their political ideology. The Child is influenced by all the above institutions, soon after he/she begins his/her life and comes to know the world.

In practical religious life, traits like purity, truth, compassion, universal love, forbearance, humanity spirit of brotherhood, absence of anger, self-denial, selfless service and sacrifice form the bond of universalism and it is equally applicable to all religions of the world. All religions are based on foundation of right conduct and therefore moral rectitude and ethical perfection form yet another bond of universalism. Religions are only different ways of life.

Hence, Home and School can help in building up toleration, understanding and respect for each other, though children for a better future.

Latest Health Statistics according to 1991 Census

Health

Article 24 of the Convention on the Right of the Child states with urgency the child's right to the enjoyment of the highest attainable standard of health. Again Article 6 of the Convention asserts that the States should recognise that every child has the inherent right to life.

In the Indian context health is a constitutional mandate. The Constitution of India in the Directive Principle of State Policy states that State shall regard the raising of the level of Nutrition and Standard of living of its people in the improvement of public health as among its primary duties [Article 39(e) & (f), and Article 47].

The National Policy for Children spells out in clear terms the Constitutional provisions—"It shall be the policy of the State to provide adequate services to children, both before and after birth and through period of growth, to ensure their full physical, mental and social development. The State shall progressively increase the scope of such services so that, within reasonable time, all children in the country enjoy optimum conditions for their balanced growth".

Good health is the birth right of every individual and health care is the basic need. High fertility combined with rapid decline in mortality and immigration has increased rate of growth of population. The rural birth rate dropped from 38.9 in 1979 to 34.8 in 1981. While the urban birth rate fluctuated from 29.7 in 1970 to 27.3 in 1981. Mortality death rate declined steadily from 1970 to 1981, which was 12.5 per 1000 live births, in Rural areas it was 13.7 per cent and in Urban areas it was 7.9.

Infant Mortality 47 per cent occur in age groups of 0-4 and about one-third in the first year, about one-fifth approximately in the first month of life and one-tenth of all deaths are in the first week. The reson for high fertility in Inida is because of girls getting married very young.

In the age group of 1-14 the females deaths on the whole is more than the males. According to 1987, estimates, the infant mortality rate per thousand live births was 95, which is still considered very high and is due to many causes.

The task of providing health care to ensure holistic development of the 300 million children (0-14 years) in India where one-third of them live in condition of abject poverty and neglect, is an enormous challenge. The National Health Policy (1983) has given highest priority to launching special programmes for the improvement of maternal and child health. India is committed to attain the goal of Health for All by 2000 A.D. through universal provision of comprehensive primary health care services.

The specific programmes of the Ministry of Health and Family Welfare are geared towards Child Health are Universal, such as— Immunisation Programme, Oral Rehydration Therapy, and Prophylactic Schemes against Nutritional Anaemia among Pregnant Women, against Blindness due to Vitamin A deficiency. The on-going MCH programme of the country has been strengthened by launching Child Survival. The programme is going in phases to cover all districts in the country by 1997. The additional intervention proposed are expansion of the programme for control of Acute Respiratory infections for children below 5 years of age.

To maximise the reach of health services, there has been an increase in the number of PHC's and sub-centres. At present, a network of 21,040 PHC, 1,31,471 sub-centres and 3,297 Community Health Centres provide the health services to the target population.

The development of health facilities and use of integrated approach of packaging National Child Health Care with nutrition, education, water and sanitation etc. has paid dividends.

There has been significant drop in the infant mortality rate, from a level of 119 deaths per thousand live births in 1981 to 74 in 1993. The age specific child mortality rate has also declined for all age groups 0-4 and 5-14 years. In the age group 0-4 years, the decline was from 41.2 in 1981 to 26.5 in 1991, whereas in the age group 5-14 years the mortality rate declined from 2.9 in 1981 to 2.1 in 1991. The improvement in the survival of children can also be attributed to successful coverage of all the districts for immunisation. By March 1994 were: 83 per cent immunisation in three antigens—DPT, OPV and BCG; 88 per cent in measles, there was reduction in deaths due to diarrhoea of new born babies from 9.5 per cent in 1983 to 9.0 per cent in 1990.

Four Leading Causes of:

Health

Infant mortality rate (per 1000 live births)	73 (1994)
Neonatal mortality rate (per 1000 live births)	47.2 (1993)
Perinatal mortality rate (per 1000 live births)	44.3 (1993)

Source: Sample Registration (41-43) System, Office of the Registrar General, India, New Delhi.

Maternal mortality rate (per 1000 live births)	4.2 (1992-93)

Source: National Family Health Survey, (1992-93)

1. Infant Mortality:

Causes	*Per cent*
(a) Prematurity	46.4
(b) Respiratory Infection of New Born	4.4
(c) Diarrhoea of New Born	8.0
(d) Cord Infection	4.5

Source: Survey of Causes of Death (Rural) 1993, Office of the Registrar General of India.

2. Child Mortality (1 to under 5 years)

Causes	*1993 Per cent*
(a) Coughs (Disorders of Respiratory System)	25.6

(b)	Fevers	21.2
(c)	Abortion	18.8
(d)	Accident and Injuries	8.9
(e)	Crude Death Rate (per 1000 population)	9.2 (1994)

Source: Survey of Causes of Deaths (Rural), 1993, Office of the Registrar General India.

Four Leading Causes of:

1. Infant Morbidity

	Causes	*Per cent*
(a)	Diarrhoeal Diseases	NA
(b)	Acute Respiratory Infection	NA
(c)	Malnutrition	NA
(d)	Low Birth Weight	NA

Pre-school Morbidity
(1 to under 5 years)

	Causes	*Per cent*
(a)	Malnutrition	NA
(b)	Diarrhoeal Diseases	NA
(c)	Respiratory Infection	NA

In India—Elimination of guinea worm disease as on 31.3.95
No. of villages/hamlets free for past 2 years.

	1992	*1993*
Out of number of village as in endemic areas	1244	2592

Immunization

About 20 to 30 per cent of deaths in children are due to 6 common immunisable childhood diseases. In India 5 million children die every year and equal number become disabled due to non-protection against the preventable diseases. Immunisation is the most important, simple and cost effective programme in India, which was launched in 1978 and there are 20 million children every year to be immunised.

During 1982-83 actual coverage was as follows:

D.P.T. ... 38.2% Polio ... 17.7% B.C.G. ... 8.8%

For the first time in 1977, 10,000 vaccines for measle were donated to Indian Council for Child Welfare by SAVE the Children Fund, London. It was given to the children of Delhi with the help of a group of Pediatricians, and was a very successful programme. In India now immunisation programme for measle has started since 1985-86.

Immunisation has made significant progress in the country. By August 1980 the target achieved were as follows:

Triple Antigen (D.P.T.)—over 5 million of this 18.06 lakhs children in the age group of (0-2) were vaccinated.

Bivalent Immunisation (D.T.)—Nearly eight million out of which 19.98 lakhs children in the age group of 3-8 received it.

Tetanus	...	Nearly 5 million got it.
Polio	...	Over 5 million got it.
B.C.G.	...	Over 11 million got it.
Smallpox	...	Nearly 7 million. But now it is totally wiped out.
Typhoid	...	Nearly 2 million.

Lately the programme has been given the status of Immunisation Mission. Ministry of Health and Family Welfare will be nodal agency. The mission is one of the five technical missions under the Advisor to the Prime Minister of India.

Prophylaxis against:

Blindness—Through administration of Vitamin 'A'. This programme has been very effective. Solution is being given orally to children 1-5 years of age every 6 months up to age of 5-6. Till 1982 over 65.22 lakhs of children covered.

Nutrition Anaemia —Up to 1982, 35.90 lakhs of children were covered.

Coverage of Children < 1	*1994-95*	*1990*
(a) DPT %	92.0	(99.2)
(b) Measles %	83.5	(89.1)
(c) Polio %	92.3	(98.9)
(d) Tetanus % pregnant women	81.0	(78.2)
Elimination of Neonatal Tetanus	*1994*	
Annual number of cases	4688	(11241)
Reduction of Measles		
(Children < 5) Annual number:		
(a) Deaths	646	(303)
(b) Cases	61381	(79655)

Progressive Eradication of Polio	*1994*	
Annual number of cases	7028	(8670)

Polio Immunisation campaign was taken up throughout the country targetting 75 million in the 0-3 age group on the 9th December, and followed up on the 20th January 1996. The target was fully achieved.

Oral Rehydration Therapy (ORT)

Diarrhoeal diseases are major health problems in the country especially among children below 5 years of age. One hundred million children below 5 years of age suffer about 300 million episodes of diarrhoea of which 10 per cent, i.e., 3 million may face death. To reduce the death rate by 4.50 per cent this scheme ORT is taken up. There has been training of medical personnel. Funds have been provided to all states for purchasing ORS packets at Rs. 3,500 per P.H.C. Thus ORS is available in remote areas and corners of the country. By the end of Seventh Five Year Plan all the districts and PHC are expected to be totally covered.

Nutrition

Nutrition is seldom mentioned as a human right in the UN declaration, and Convention finds a prominent place in Article 24 and Article 27 of CRC (Convention of Rights of Child), nutrition is explicitly mentioned. A staggering 250 million or more Indians suffer from varying degree of malnutrition. It is more acute among infants, pre-schoolers, children and expectant and nursing mothers of poor socio-economic groups.

As estimated 30 per cent of all infants born in India are Low Birth Weight (LBW) babies. A study in rural areas of some states reports that 37 per cent of children suffer from mild nutrition, 43 per cent are moderately affected and 8.7 per cent suffer from extreme forms of malnutrition.

Roughly 56 per cent of pre-school children and almost 50 per cent of expectant mothers in trimester of pregnancy suffer from iron deficiency anaemia. All the states in India show prevalence of iodine deficiency. It accounts for 90,000 still births and neo-natal deaths every year.

Close to 2.2 million children are afflicted with cretinism and about 6.6 million are mildly retarded and suffer from various degrees of motor handicaps. Around 60,000 children become blind due to deficiency of Vitamin A coupled with Protein Energy Malnutrition (PEM). Field experience highlights continuing gender disparity in intra-familial distribution of food. Children continue to be vulnerable to seasonal food shortage. Each episode leaves the child vulnerable and less able to recoup.

In India, various programmes have been launched by the Government to combat the exiating levels of malnutrition and also to prevent malnutrition in vulnerable groups.

The most extensive nutrition programme is ICDS, which is the largest nutrition programme in the world, covering 16.2 million children in age group of 0-6 years, as well as 5 million pregnant and nursing mothers. The programme provides package of services comprising supplementary nutrition, immunisation, pre-school education for children below 6 years of age, health check-ups and referral.

The programme of the Food and Nutrition Board (FNB) of the Department of Women and Child Development are also directed towards improving the Nutrition through Nutrition Education and Extension; Development and Promotion of Nutrition Foods; and Fortification of Foods.

The other Nutrition interaction programme of Government are Special Nutrition Programme, Wheat Based Supplementary Nutrition Programme, Tamil Nadu Integrated Nutrition Programme and Mid-Day Meal Programme for school children. The Government of India has also adopted the National Nutrition Policy in 1993 to tackle the problem of malnutrition.

Proportion of low-birth weight babies (< 2.5 kg.) 30%

Source: Nutrition Trends in India, 1993.

Percentage of Mothers exclusively breastfed their babies for the first four (4) months 51%

Source: NFHS, 1992-93.

Proportion of infants malnourished:

(1-3 Years)

	Severe	10.97
	Moderate	45.30
	Mild	34.90

Source: NNMB Survey Report, 1993.

Proportion of Pre-school children malnourished

(3-5 years)

Weight for age:	Severe	11.1

Moderate	44.9
Mild	38.4

Source: NNMB Survey Report, 1993.

Weight for height	—

Source: National Evaluation of ICDS, NIPCCD, 1992, New Delhi.

Proportion of Pregnant women suffer from anaemia	25-30%
Proportion of Population with Goitre	63 millions (1993-94)

Proportion of children under 5 years with Vitamin A deficiency:

Night Blindness	NA
Keratomalacia	NA
Others (specify) Bitot Spot	0.7%

Virtual elimination of Vitamin A deficiency:

Children < 5 receiving	
(a) Vitamin A supplement	83.5%
(b) Vitamin A fortified food	NA
Virtual elimination of iodine deficiency	
Proportion of Salt manufactured/imported adequately iodised	52%
Proportion of pregnant women receiving iron supplement (IFA)	85.8% (1994-95)

To overcome the micronutrient malnutrition, the Department of Women and Child Development has taken up the following programmes:

(i) Fortification of Milk with Vitamin 'A'
(ii) Fortification of salt with iron and iodine.

At present 67 dairies in 17 States and 1 UT are implementing the scheme of fortification of milk with Vitamin 'A'.

Foods and Nutrition Board (FNB) promotes setting up of nutritious food units through State Governments and NGOs for producing low cost nutritious foods for supplementary feeding programmes. Five food plants are in operation in the States of Madhya Pradesh, Andhra Pradesh, Rajasthan, Sikkim and Delhi.

Education

A Directive Principle of the Indian Constitution (Article 45) lays down that the State shall endeavour to provide free and compulsory education for all children until they complete 14 years of age. In 1960 Parliament enacted Delhi Primary Education Act and several State legislations have been modelled on the same.

In each successive Five Year Plans the outlay on elementary education increased. There were 97.7 children in the age group of 5 to 14 years in 1971, and nearly 43 million out of school children in the 6 to 14 years ranged in 1977-78. The educational systems have not been able to generate any skills in 94 per cent India's rural population and 87.9 per cent of urban population.

In 1981 the total enrolment in primary grades (I-V) for children in the age group 6-11 years old was 83 per cent (73 million) and for grades (VI-VIII) in the age group 11 to 14 years was 40 per cent (19.8 million).

In 1981-82 the number of primary schools were 495,007 (an increase of 136 per cent since 1950-51 when there were 206,671 primary schools).

The middle schools (VI-VIII class) rose 13,596 in 1950-51, to 119,560 in 1981. 90.5/8 of primary schools and 33 per cent of middle schools are in rural areas. 80 per cent of the children enrolled in schools in the age of 5-8 years old, are majority boys. 20.5 per cent who do not attend schools are mostly girls.

Enrolment of boys and girls from scheduled caste and tribes is low in proportion of the total enrolment. Girls from these communities are much lower than that of boys. While scheduled caste is 15 per cent of the total population, their total primary level enrolment is only 11 per cent, while the scheduled tribes population is 8 per cent of the total population, their total enrolment is only 5 per cent. Their position in middle schools is even worse. Only 56 per cent of scheduled caste population and 78 per cent of scheduled tribe population has facilities for primary schooling, and may not have access to it. At middle schools level only 13 per cent of scheduled castes and 21 per cent of scheduled tribes has facilities.

Latest Education Statistics according to 1991 Census

Article 28-1 (a) of the Convention state that primary education be made compulsory available for free for all.

More than four decades ago, the Constitution of India made an even bigger commitment. Its Article 45 (as mentioned earlier) states "The

State shall endeavour to provide, within a period of 10 years from the commencement of the Constitution of free and compulsory education, for all children until they complete the age of 14 years".

The National Policy on Education (NPE) 1986 and Programme of Action (POA) 1992 have perceived education as fundamental to all round development of children and stipulates free and compulsory education of satisfactory quality to all children upto 14 years of age before the turn of century.

NPE also had emphasized that "It shall be ensured that all children who attain age of 11 years by 1990 will have had 5 years of schooling or its equivalent through the non-formal stream. Likewise by 1995 all children will be provided free and compulsory education upto 14 years of age." The policy aims to fulfil the objective of "Education for All" by providing early childhood care and education, universalising elementary education through formal and *Non-formal Methods.* About 5.7 million children had been receiving non-formal education in 0.32 million Non-formal Education Centres till March 1994.

The Department of Education has introduced various programmes to achieve the goal of universalisation of Elementary education. The programmes in operation are—Operation Blackboard, Minimum Levels of Learning, Scheme of Operationalising Micro-planning and Scheme of Non-formal Education.

Under the scheme 'Operation Blackboard', 91 per cent of primary schools have been covered till 92-93. Under Minimum Levels of Learning (MLL) about 15 per cent NGOs are sanctioned to implement programme to cover 2000 schools. The concept is to ensure a child centred approach to teaching and assessment, than the syllabus. But there are problems as it tends to focus more on *Literacy and Numeracy* rather than integrated education. Teachers finding it difficult to implement it, special stress is placed on teachers training.

The scheme for Non-formal Education is being implemented in 18 States/UTs. It is particularly for *dropouts, working children* in habitation without schools and *girls* who cannot attend formal schools and focus mainly on disadvantage groups and girl child.

Leisure should also be an integral part of education.

Pre-school Education

The value of Pre-school education has not been very well recognised and accepted. But till recently they existed due to voluntary efforts and private agencies. It has not been recognised as a part of Article 45 of the Constitution. In 1978 it was estimated that there was 12,000 nursery schools for urban children and over 44,000 recognised and unrecognised balwadis. The I.C.D.S. Scheme covered 40,00,000 children getting pre-school education through 95,000 Anganwadis and Balwadis and there were 10,800 pre-primary schools run by Ministry of Education.

Early childhood education has come to be viewed as a coaching period for entrance to primary schools. While the actual need for children is to be able to talk, play, explore, observe, inquire and be happy and enjoy whatever they do, is overlooked.

The Indian education is far from child-oriented though the National Policy on Education 1986 advocates child centred approach. Even the Central Advisory Committee on Education has recommended that the main objective of "Early Childhood Education" should be to provide young Children with social experience rather than formal instruction.

Therefore, a serious thought needs to be given to the concept and practice of Early Childhood Education from the prevalent distortions and to ensure that nursery schools, Kindergartens, *Balwadis*, *Anganwadis* or Play centres provide ample opportunities for the development of cognitive, effective and social growth of children in national environment.

With the commitment to universalisation of education by 1995, the National Policy on Education has looked at Early Childhood Education as a supporting programme for universalisation of elementary education. It is within this framework one must plan and find ways and means to reach the young child.

Early Childhood Care and Education (ECCE)

ECCE has been accorded a high priority in NPE. Early Childhood programme seeks to improve the children communication and cognitive skills as a preparation for entry into primary school. This programme is implemented in the country in 9 backward States, which are Andhra Pradesh, Assam, Bihar, Jammu & Kashmir, Madhya Pradesh, Orissa, Rajasthan, Uttar Pradesh, West Bengal. Till March 1994, NGOs numbering 190 were assisted to run 4,365 ECCE Centres.

Early Childhood Education

Constitutes a vulnerable period in life because infants and young children cannot survive without the active assistance of adult caretakers. Infants are more vulnerable to developmental retardation, if not parmanent damage, from neglect and deprivation.

The State has or must have a responsibility for the survival and development of every child born. The state of infants in a nation is a good indicator of the Rights of Children being honoured.

Early Childhood intervention programmes are an attempt to enhance the course of their development. The provision of child care and development services ensures a safe setting as well as an interesting one in which infant can spend a large part of the day.

Supplementary nutrition, health check and immunisation are also provided. It will be discontinued and wound up after 1998.

Creches

Creche/Day care is expected to provide an environment which is livelier and better than if she/he is left alone at-home or with immatured sublings or old grand parents.

Even where laws for the provision of creches have been enacted they are only for the organised sectors, factories, mines and plantations. Few women workers fall under this definition especially since a minimum number of women are stipulated in the conceived establishment.

In 1975 the Department of Women and Child Development started the scheme of *Creche/Day Care Centres* for children of working and ailing mothers, to provide day care services for children of these women who are sick or incapacitated due to sickness or suffering from communicable diseases, are also covered under this scheme. Services include supplementary nutrition, immunisation, etc. During 1993-94 12,470 were provided serving about 3000,000 children.

To meet the increased demand for new creches a *National Creche Fund* has been set up by the Department of Women and Child Development with a corpus amount of Rs. 19.90 crores.

This fund will be utilised to set up new creches as well as for conversion of some of the existing Anganwadis into Anganwadi-cum-creches.

In ICDS there are already creches, hence if any separate creche has been started, they will be shifted to non-ICDS areas.

Balwadi

Since 1970-71, The Balwadi Nutrition Programme (BNP) is being implemented through Central Social Welfare Board (CSWB) and 4 National level Voluntary Organisations. Basic aim of the programme is to provide supplementary Nutrition to children in the age groups 3-5 years attending Balwadi/Day Care Centres. There are more than 5,641 Balwadis run in the country. It will be wound up after 1998.

To help working women, there have been Hostel Buildings for *Working Women with Day Care Centres*. Under this scheme, working women with children upto age of 8 years of age are eligible to live in a separate hostel where Day Care facilities are provided for children. So far the facilities have been provided for more than 5,907 children in 229 hostels, i.e., till 1994.

Balwadis and BNP will continue according to government's decision till the end of Ninth Plan.

The Anganwadi

The Anganwadi (AW) literally a courtyard play centre, is a child care located within the village or the slum area itself. It is the focal point for the delivery of services at community levels to children below 6 years of age, pregnant women, nursing mothers and adolescent girls.

Besides this, the AW is a meeting place or ground where women and mothers groups can come together, with other frontline workers, to promote awareness and joint action for child development and women empowerment.

All ICDS services are provided through the Anganwadis (AW) in an integrated manner to enhance their impact on children. Each Anganwadi is run by an Anganwadi Worker (AWW) supported by a helper in integrated service delivery.

The population coverage through Anganwadi is approximately 1000 in rural and urban areas and 700 in tribal areas. Services for children are limited to those below 6 years of age. This is because the early years are the most vulnerable and critical years. They contribute to the unfolding of almost three-fourth of the total potential for the physical, social, and mental development of an adult personality. In fact, by the end of second year of life, most of the growth of the human brain is already complete. The mother plays a key role in the overall development of the child.

Till June 1994, there were 10.4 million children in the age group 3 to 6 years had been receiving pre-school Education in Anganwadis under ICDS projects.

Integrated Child Development Services (ICDS)

Integrated Child Development Services (ICDS) in India's response to the challenge of meeting the holistic needs of the child, launched initially in 33 blocks (33 projects), on October 2, 1975. In 1995 there were 3,907 projects.

Today, the Integrated Child Development Services (ICDS) is one of the world's largest and most unique outreach programmes for early childhood care and development. It symbolises India's commitment to its children. ICDS is designed to promote holistic development of children under six years, through the strengthened capacity of care givers and communities and improved access to basic services, at the community level. The programme is specificially designed to reach disadvantaged and low income groups, for effective disparity reduction.

The programme provides an integrated approach for converging basic services for improved childcare, early stimulation and learning, health and nutrition, water and environmental sanitation—targetting young children, expectant and nursing mothers and adolescent girls' groups. They are reached through nearly 300,000 trained community structures/women's groups—through *Anganwadi* centre, the health system and the community.

The programme helps achieve major national nutrition and health goals, embodied in the National Plan of Action for children, 1992. Poised for universal coverage by the turn of century, ICDS today reaches out to 3.8 million expectant nursing mothers and 17.8 million children (under 6 years of age) of disadvantage groups. Of these 10.2 million children (3 to 6 years of age) participate in centre based pre-school education activities. The network consists of 3,907 projects, covering nearly 70 per cent of the communities development blocks and 260 urban slum pockets.

ICDS is the reality of today, on which our vision for tomorrow is founded.

Its Objectives are :

1. Improve the nutritional and health status of children below the age of 6 years;
2. Lay the foundation for the proper psychological, physical and social development of the child;
3. Reduce the incidence of morality, morbidity, malnutrition and school dropouts;
4. Achieve effective coordination of policy and implementation among various departments to promote child development; and
5. Enhance the capability of the mother to look after the normal health and nutritional needs of the child through proper health and nutrition education.

There are 5,239 CD Blocks in Total. 3,663 CD Blocks covered by ICDS and 1,576 were uncovered as on 31 March 1995.

I.C.D.S. was started on 2nd October, 1975 as a miniature programme in a small number of 33 blocks covering less than 0.5 per cent of India's population. Integrated Child Development Services (ICDS) is one of the world's largest and most unique outreach programmes for early childhood care and development. It symbolises India's commitment to its children. The early years are the most crucial period in life, when the foundations for cognitive, social, emotional, language, physical/motor development and lifelong learning are laid. Recognising that early childhood development constitutes the foundation of human development, ICDS is designed to promote holistic development of children under 6 years.

During the two decades of its existence, the programme has expanded to cover about four-fifths of its population. Today—March 1995—the programme covers 21.6 million children, pregnant and nursing mothers and 3.9 lakhs adolescent girls through 3,907 projects in rural and tribal areas and urban slums, covering nearly 70 per cent of country's community development blocks and 260 urban slum pockets. They are reached through nearly 300,000 trained Anganwadi workers and equal number of helpers, supportive community structure/women's groups—through the Anganwadi centre, the health system and in the community.

As ICDS it stands at the threshold of the universal coverage by the turn of the century. It is the reality of to-day, on which our vision for tomorrow is founded. Thus ICDS has covered 3,663 of the total 5,239 community development blocks in the country through 3,907 projects. ICDS reaches out to 3.8 million expectant and nursing mothers and 17.8 million children (under 6 years of age), of disadvantage groups. Of these, 10.2 million children (3 to 6 years of age) participate in centre-based pre-school education activities.

ICDS has several important characteristics which can be summarised as follows:

(i) It seeks to achieve the aim of child development through health, nutrition and early childhood education services;

(ii) It has the village centre as the focal point for the delivery of services to ensure maximum participation of pre-school children, pregnant mothers and lactating mothers;

(iii) It started in the most backward areas and expanded to cover more and more of such areas on priority basis;

(iv) It took conscious decision to create a minimum new staff structure focused on better utilization of the existing infrastructure of primary health centres, medical institutions, and other organisations;

(v) For the first time in any national programme, the local woman has been identified as a key functionary at the Anganwadi centre for delivery of the mother care and child development services;

(vi) It has the unique feature of a very large number of honorary functionaries. This includes the Anganwadi workers, health and paramedical staff and academicians of medical institutions;

(vii) It has established a systematic and well planned optimal cost of monitoring, training and evaluation system for the very beginning.

(viii) It has started the process of coordination and team work amongst administrators, health staff, academicians and voluntary workers.

Well beyond the stage of experimentation, ICDS is here to stay and today it stands out as the world's largest programmes reaching the most disadvantaged and vulnerable sections of the society.

Disabled Child

A disabled child includes partially or totally blind, partially deaf, orthopaedically handicap, mentally retarded, the slow learner and those affected by multiple handicaps.

"Article 23 recognises the special needs of the disabled child and enjoins on the State the responsibility of ensuring the child's fullest possible integration and development. Article 2 also specifies the inclusion of the disabled child in every other category, with respect to each of the rights enshrined in the Convention."

The Convention on the Rights of Child makes specific mention of the disabled children. The disabled children are distinct from other groups of children with special needs. The child has specific needs and problems requiring special interventions and the fact that their needs continue through life.

It is estimated that 10 per cent of the population world-wide is disabled. The extrapolation that 35 million children are disabled is conservative. Most Indian children are disabled because of poverty and its correlates. Protein malnutrition, iodine deficiency and Vitamin A deficiency are the major causes of mental retardation and blindness. Major childhood hearing handicap and untreated middle ear infections are widespread. National Vitamin-A Supplementary programme has achieved some results but coverage needs to be improved. Lack of early detection and treatment leads, in most cases, to major and stressful secondary handicaps of physical function, intellectual handicap and social and emotional behavioural problems. The vast majority of disabled children lead lives singularly lacking in stimulation; they know no difference between childhood, maturity or old age.

The situation is further exacerbated by the lack of basic service. The few services that exist are mostly in cities, and mainly accessed by the middle and upper classes. Rehabilitation strategies focus largely on literacy and academic goals. The few assistive devices produced are suited to the aspirations of financially well off urban Indians; mass produced mobility aids are suitable only for urban terrain, and the focus of the aids resource allocations for the visually handicapped is on braille devices for literacy and academic achievement. And estimated 98 per cent of rural and 95 per cent of urban disabled children have no access to services.

	per 100,000	*Urban*	*Rural*
2.5 lakhs totally blind children	0-4	25	39
	5-11	87	66
100 lakhs partially handicap			
2.5 lakhs deaf . . . *per100,000 population*			
	0-4	540	435
	5-14	718	676
40 lakhs impaired hearing . . .	. . .	244	314
Dumb. . .	. . .	429	411
5 lakhs severe orthopaedic disabled	0-4	540	435
	5-14	718	676
20 lakhs mentally retarded in age 0-14 years.			

To cater to the needs of such large number of children, there are only 600 agencies:

200 for the blind,
150 for the deaf,
150 for the orthopaedically handicap, and
180 for the mentally retarded children.

In the voluntary sector, there are approximately 600 agencies and 200 welfare and rehabilitation work.

The handicap Welfare Division in the Ministry of Welfare is responsible for all the programmes for the Welfare of disabled in the country.

Four National Institutes under the Ministry are there. The Rehabilitation Council was set up in January 1986 to enforce uniform standards in training programmes.

Working Children

In 1991 alone, through 23 special employment exchanges for the handicapped persons and 55 special cells in normal employment exchanges, 307 blind, 287 deaf and 3,997 orthopaedically handicapped were given placements. Some rural development organisations in South India have facilitated the formation of village level organisations of the disabled people. These "Sangams" have effectively assumed responsibility for the needs of disabled people in those villages.

Approximately working children constituted 10.7 per cent (7.9 million boys and 2.8 million girls) of the total population in 1971. By 1981 there were about 14.5 million below the age of 14 years or 5.5 per cent of the total population. In Rural areas 6.30 per cent and Urban 2.5 per cent. Actually in 1983 the Child Labour force was as high as 17.4 million, but the actual figure was estimated to be 30 million. Majority, i.e., 93 per cent of child labour is in rural area and 7 per cent in urban area. Most of the children employed worked for longer hours and low wages, and they work on an average for 211 days a year. Children are kidnapped, tortured and forced to work in sub-human conditions in the carpet industry of Mirzapur. A survey ordered by the Supreme Court found that 41 per cent of carpet weavers in U.P. are under the age of 14 and 48 per cent of these receive no wages, but only food. The rest get Re. 1 to Rs. 5 per day. The kind of work they do causes eye problems, skin problems, filaria, Asthama, T.B., enlarged lymph glands.

The diamond cutting units of Surat employing about 2 lakh workers of whom 15 per cent are children. They live and work in squalid ill-ventilated factory premises for 12 to 15 hours a day. Eye strain, headache, T.B., and skin diseases, viral and urinary infections is their reward and they are paid on an average Rs. 15 per day. In Sivakashi the production of matches are entirely non-mechanical. 50,000 children work here who are below 15 years of age. Between 3 a.m. and 5 a.m. children are woken up and about 22 hundred of them are put in a bus and taken to factories, and they return between 6 to 9 p.m. Most children are below

7 years of age and girls outnumber boys—3 to 1. The working conditions are detrimental to health and they earn Rs. 2 to 7 per day.

In Balloon factories children work for 9 hours a day in the atmosphere with a thick pall of dust and chemicals filling the small unventilated rooms. In return they have pneumonia, breathlessness and heart failure.

At Ferozabad, in the glass bangle factories there are 40,000 children under 14 years age and receive Rs. 9 to 16 per day. They are not paid extra for overtime. It takes only 3-4 years to destroy their lungs and their life span in reduced by one-third, as they are exposed to 1300 degrees celsius heat every day. This leads to cancer, anaemia, retardation of growth, muscle cramps, respiratory ailment. Their are 15,000 children working in the powerloom industry in Biwandi in Maharashtra. The cotton dust causes fibrisis of the tissues in the lungs. The Slate industry where children work and they have to cut slates gives them lung diseases worse than T.B. and most of them generally choke to death.

Unfortunately the labour laws that deal with the child labour are concerned with children in the organised sectors, but the unorganised sector remains totally uncovered by the legislation. Moreover, the working conditions for child labour are usually harsh. It has been found that children between the ages 4-14 years work for almost 12 hours a day in some industries and that also in hazardous conditions.

India has the largest child labour force in the world. The Anti-slavery Society in its report to the sub-commission of the UN Human Rights Commission informed that the child labour force is 16.5 million children between the ages of 5-14 years, old working in rural and urban areas. The society noted that the situation was due to economic condition and therefore, children should be allowed to work but at the same time protected. Accordingly to a study in India, these children contributed 23 per cent to the family income.

The level of illiteracy is very high among the child workers (65 per cent males and 75 per cent females). Nearly 16 per cent children in the Urban and 10 per cent in the Rural areas are literate without any educational level. Census figures show that illiteracy is very high among female child workers—81 per cent Urban and 90 per cent Rural areas.

Child workers in the U.T. of Delhi are nearly 4 lakhs. Out of these approximately

30,000 work in the shops, Dhabas,
20,000 work in Scooter and Car Repair Shops,
30,000 assistants in non-eating establishment,

40,000 labourers,
1,00,000 as maids.

Working hours of jobs differ and are from 3-18 hours a day. These children work for low or no wages, prolonged working hours. No weekly rest or avail holidays with 'pay'. They are punished, abused humiliated and neglected on the slightest pretext. They are redused to greater subservience and are subjected to exaggerated forms of control and exploitation.

The poor working and living conditions degrade the quality of life of whole workers. A good proportion of working children are runaways from there homes (8%). They abandon their families due to maltreatment and they are mostly from poor families. Staying on pavement or slums which lack basic amenities like water, toilet etc. They are vulnerable to the anti-social elements, such as pick-pockets, thieves, smugglers, drug peddlers, gamblers, homo-sexuals etc. These children fall an easy victim of these elements.

While the Indian Laws attempt to regulate some of the conditions, they do not consider conditions in which children work and the specific needs of the children. The problem of child labour is more acute in cities due to influx of rural poor. About 80 per cent of children migrants work as compared with 19 per cent of urban children. Due to legislation there is decrease in child labour in factories, but great increase in the unorganised sector.

There are more than dozen laws regulating the employment of children. Unfortunately, the laws are variance with one another in manifold respects, and hence their enforcement and implementation leave much to be desired. The existing laws needs to be consolidated into one single legislation and also need to be extended to unorganised sector.

Child Labour

In India though undesirable, child labour persists on account of socio-economic compulsions. The number of working children was estimated at around 17 million according to the 43rd round of the National Sample Survey (1987). This figure has been extrapolated to reach an estimate of 20 million working children by the year 2000.

Article 32 of the Convention states "State parties recognise the right of the child to be protected from economic exploitation and from performing any work that is likely to be hazardous or to interfere with the child's education, or to be harmful to the child's health or physical, mental, spiritual, moral or social development."

In India there has been provisions for protection of children from the type of work which is beyond their capacity, or involves long hours of work interfering with their education, recreation, rest and overall physical and mental development under the Constitution itself, and by various industrial acts and labour laws enacted from time to time. The Child Labour (Prohibition and Regulation) Act of 1986, therefore, has tried to prohibit their employment in jobs that are hazardous to their lives and health. It prohibits engaging children in night shifts, making them work in more than one shift, prevents their working near dangerous machinery, handling hazardous chemicals, also prohibited from working at ports or railways, picking cinders, and clearing ash pits where their safety is jeopardised. They may not work in industries such as bidi-making, carpet weaving, cement manufacture, bag making, carpet printing, dyeing and weaving, manufacture of matches, explosives, and fireworks, mica-cutting and splitting, shellac manufacture, soap manufacture, tanning, wool-cleaning, building and construction industry. The Act also ensures that they have adequate hours of rest and holidays.

Number of initiative and programmes have been undertaken. The formulation of a National Child Labour Policy, the enactment of the Child Labour (Prohibition and Regulation) Act, 1986, the setting up of Task Force on child labour and the adoption of the Convention on the Rights of the Child have all formed a part of this process. A provision is being considered under the Minimum Wages Act, for providing equal wages to children and adults, thereby removing the economic incentive to employ child labour on lower wages.

A Child Labour Cell, which was set up in 1979, is now a part of the Labour Ministry. It formulates, co-ordinates and implements policies and programmes for the welfare of child labour. The Cell has financed four major projects for agricultural child labour near Aurangabad (Maharashtra)—(Indian Institute of Rural Workers), Urban Child Workers in Calcutta (Institute of Psychological and Education Research), Child Workers in Ahmedabad (Self-employed Women's Association), and rag-picker children in Bangalore (Karnataka State Council for Child Welfare).

India has the dubious distinction of having the largest number of child labourers in the world. The *Operations Research Group* (1983) estimated it to be 44 million. Government figures claims it is no more than 17.4 million. Manila's *Balai Data Bank* puts it at 111 million or almost 1 in every 3 children.

The general Indian attitude towards child labour is indifference and helplessness. The inadequate, irrelevant and often inaccessible education system is a crucial factor which decides whether or not a child is put to work. Most often the lack of schools and facilities leaves children with no option but working. A recent survey found that "there are 5 lakhs formal schools in India for a population of 329 million; 14 per cent have no school building; 38 per cent have no blackboards; 30 per cent have only one teacher for the whole school; 58 per cent have no drinking water. The result 4 out of 5 children do not even enter school and 70 per cent of children drop out before they enter Class IV." 86.4 per cent of the child labourers are employed in agriculture and allied activities in the rural sector.

A large number of children work in hazardous industries, in areas for Carpet weaving in Jammu and Kashmir, Pottery in Khujra, Gem polishing in Jaipur, Lock industry in Aligarh, Glass in Ferozabad, Mines in Meghalaya, Carpet weaving in Mirzapur, Stone quaries in Mandsaur and Markapur and Kerala, Hosiery in Tirupur, Fishing in Kerala, Handlooms in Trivandrum, Match and fireworks in Sivakashi, Balloon factories of Dahanu (Maharashtra). Children who work here have to inhale ammonia, acetic acid fumes and french chalk for more than 8 hours a day for 6 days a week. Inhalation of such acids over time, burns the respiratory lining and causes pneumonia, broncho-pneumonia, cough, breathlessness and even heart failure.

Putting a child in school has been shown to be one of the most effective ways of keeping her/him out of labour force. As an "illiterate child can never become an artisan."

Totally Shocking but Absolutely True

Child labour contributes to 20 per cent of the National Product (GNP) which subsidises higher education for privileged children.

A country like India which cannot find jobs for 60 million adults can find space for 111 million child labourers.

Over 90 per cent labourers belong to the Schedule Castes, Backward Classes and the Muslim community. Also it must be noted that the domestic child labourer is not in any way better off. Domestic child labour cannot be considered non-hazardous by any standards. They are exposed to many dangers.

Kerala has the lowest incidence of child labour and Andhra Pradesh the highest.

Flouting legislation and campaigns, Assam's flourishing tea estates continue to exploit children while the State turns a blind eye. (*Source:* Article 'Nipped in the Bud' author Hemanta Barman—Guwahati based journalist).

Tea is one of the most profitable industries, and Assam has a major share in its production and export. During the pre- and post-independence era, spread over one and a half centuries of plantation industry here, millions of children have worked in every area of tea production. There were 9,86,781 child workers (in the tea industry) in India in 1990 (*Tea Statistics, 1990-91*, Tea Board).

"The 638-odd tea gardens in the state employed 53,127 child workers as on December 1994." This was based on yearly returns submitted by the management of the tea gardens to the labour department.

The UNICEF and Ministry of Labour and Social Welfare, Government of India sponsored report, Ms. Vasanti Raman quoted the Assam Governments statistics and confirmed the existence of child workers in tea plantations. Nothing is being done to ameliorate the conditions that they have to live in and work. Basic human needs are not catered to and many of them live in appealing conditions. The residential area of tea workers are characterised by a complete lack of civic amenities—roads, drainage, electricity, drinking water and toilets and their kuccha or pucca houses are not adequately ventilated.

Unhygienic living conditions, extreme poverty and hard work render child workers prone to malnutrition, anaemia, and diseases like malaria, TB, and filaria. About 416 qualified doctors have to look after 6,98,185 tea garden workers and their families (Labour and Employment statistics (1991-92). According to Labour department sources in 1991, there were 1,06,816 tea workers children between the ages of 6 to 12 years in Assam of which only 34,400 attended school only 32 per cent attended school and 68 per cent were deprived of primary education.

Thousands of children work in Tea Industry in the State for a daily wage of Rs. 8.91 or slightly more. Some even get less. Without increasing the income levels of tea workers and providing them basic needs, merely, banning or regulating child labour on paper is not enough.

Child labour continues under inhuman conditions in Orissa, where children earn much less compared to the number of hours and quality of service they render. They don't have fixed hours for working, they do not get paid holidays and their jobs are not secure. Moreover, children are not included in muster rolls of their employer and are exposed to dangerous operation without any adequate safety education.

Out of a total of 86.3 lakh working force in the State, 5.97 per cent or 5,15,347 were children. The projected figure for the 1991 census in the state is estimated at 6 per cent of the total work force or about 6 lakhs.

82 per cent child labour is in the agrarian sector. The remaining 18 per cent of the force is in other industries, including mining. It is estimated that 94.86 per cent of the child labour in the State is engaged in rural sector and the remaining 5.14 per cent in the urban sector. Of the total force 75.25 per cent are males and the remaining 24.75 per cent are females.

Apart from agriculture and construction work, children are mostly engaged in forest operations beedi making, weaving and brick klins in rural sector and hotels, and eating houses, garages and workshops in the urban sector.

The Law vs. Child Labour

Several laws have been passed with regard to child labour, the earliest one being the Factories Act of 1881 and the most recent one being the Child Labour Prohibition and Regulation Act of 1986.

This Act lists 11 industries as hazardous (bidi making, carpet weaving, cement manufacture, cloth printing, dyeing and weaving, manufacture of matches, explosives and fireworks, mica-cutting and splitting, shellac manufacture, tanning, wool cleaning and the construction industry) prohibiting employment in the same and regulating the conditions of work in certain other occupations.

Limitations of the Act

That it did not 'define' child labour. Failed to cover the agrarian sector which constitutes 86.4 per cent of the total child labour force. It does not prohibit night employment of children. It did not 'Legitimised' child labour in occupations not listed as hazardous such as zari-weaving, rag picking, clearing sewers etc. which are in reality highly harmful. It also did not provide for welfare or preventive measures.

Problems in the Enforcement of the Act

Few errant employers of child labour are ever booked under the Act. Only 7 State Governments have framed the rules for the Act. Which means that in the remaining states, even if the employers are arrested under the Act, the case cannot be heard in the court. (Though the Act has empowered the State Governments to frame their own rules. There are not enough labour inspectors to police factories and ensure that children are only doing safe jobs. Also when enforcing labour laws, the officials give child labour laws the lowest priority. The penalty for employing children is ridiculously low Rs. 50 to 500.

Another Lease of Childhood

Children below 14 forced to take employment in the Capital have received another lease of childhood and a chance at education with the Supreme Court ordering their employers to pay compensation ranging from Rs. 2,000 to 25,000. Joint survey conducted by the Labour Department, Directorate of Social Welfare and Delhi Police from March to September 1996 have identified 1,740 children below 14 employed in 1,330 commercial units across the Capital. An eight years old was the youngest child found employed and 80 per cent of the labour force falling into the age group of 10-11. Their presence in the commercial units violates the Shop and Establishment Act under which children below the age of 12 are not to be employed, and the Factories Act under which children below 14 are barred from employment. Delhi also had its share of children employed in hazardous industries like the electroplating units in Subhash Nagar.

The compensation as it is being worked out now is to be paid through schools, as the court wants the children to be taken off the place of their work and given at least primary education. The package is drawn out based on the employers ability to pay. This is the first time in the Capital that the children have been compensated. There is no such clause under the existing law, but due to Supreme Courts initiative has strengthened the issue.

TABLE 15.1 : Estimates of Child Labour in Selected Cottage and Small Scale Industries

Industries	*Child Labour*
(1)	(2)
Carpet Weaving (Bhadoi, Mirzapur and Zaipur)	95,000
Cotton Hosiery (Tiruppur, Tamilnadu)	8,000
Powerloom (Bhiwandi, Maharashtra)	15,000
Art Metalware (Moradabad, Uttar Pradesh)	24,000
Semi Precious Stones (Jaipur, Rajasthan)	7,000
Wood Carving (Saharanpur, Uttar Pradesh)	10,000

(Contd.)

TABLE 15.1 (*Contd.*)

(1)	(2)
Silk/Zari Embroidery (Varanasi, Uttar Pradesh)	50,100
Other Handicrafts (Kashmir, J&K)	87,200
Fish Processing (Kerala)	20,000
Hotels/Dhabas (Delhi, Mumbai)	110,000
Match,Fireworks (Sivakashi, Tamilnadu)	50,000
Quarries (Meghalaya and Kerala)	48,000
Glass (Ferozabad, Uttar Pradesh)	50,000
Bidi (Karnataka and Andhra Pradesh)	50,000
Slate (Mandsaur, Madhya Pradesh)	1,000
Various Handicrafts (J&K)	92,000

Source : Indian Social Institute, 1993.

Destitutes

In the country, the problem of destitution persists inspite of a network of institutional and non-institutional programmes and services being provided by the Government and Voluntary Organisations. For the development of destitute children in a family setting, SOS children's villages were started in the country in 1964.

Disaster management should respond to the needs of destitute children in crisis situations. A pilot project has been undertaken by 'Shishuadhar', in Pune based NGO, to introduce the non-institutional services like sponsorship, foster care, guardianship and family assistance to the orphaned and destitute children in Latur. This is an attempt to provide alternate family care to the children instead of institutionalization. This 'rehabilitation package" has helped in assisting many children who would otherwise have been sent to institutions.

The National Policy talks about the family as being the best environment for a destitute child but there are very few schemes and programmes to promote the non-institutional approach to child welfare.

Children are the most vulnerable part of the society. Within this segment are children who are destitutes, orphans, neglected, abused or those who are in conflict with law. This number is increasing due to parents inability to look after them or care for them and discharge their responsibility and to their duty, due to poverty and many other reasons such as bad health. More than anything these children need to be protected, guided, taken care of an trained, to avoid them becoming a liability to the community and society as a grown up. Besides being abandoned or orphaned there are also children who have no family support. Therefore, Ministry of Welfare decided to rehabilitate destitute and neglected children by launching a scheme in 1974-75. "Services for the welfare of the children in need of care and protection". Since 1979-80 it has been implemented as a centrally sponsored scheme. Presently 40,000 children have been covered through 900 voluntary organisations in the States/U.Ts. Adoption is considered the best method of rehabilitating a destitute or orphan child. As regards Inter-country adoption the Indian agency must arrange at least 25 per cent of its total placements of its children within the country during 1989 and the level to be raised to 50 per cent by 1991.

A vocational training for Destitutes has been set-up with the assistance of UNICEF by SOS Children's Village Association, Panchkula, Haryana. Here vocational training facilities will be provided within the Institute for destitute children, also for working and street children. Also for programme development and monitoring programmes related to child welfare in States/U.Ts., during 1988-89. UNICEF will provide assistance for setting up "Programme Development and Monitoring cells in States of Assam, Bihar, Gujarat, Kerala, Punjab, Orissa, Madhya Pradesh, Uttar Pradesh, and U.T. Delhi.

UNICEF will also assist in setting up a model "Child Care Institute" in each of the State for development a model Institute for training of functionaries.

Child Abuse

Article 34 and 35 of the Convention, the State's parties shall undertake to protect the child from all forms of sexual exploitation and sexual abuse.

Child abuse is increasingly coming out in the open, being exposed, reported, drawing more attention, concern and condemnation. There is also an acknowledgement of the importance of specific focus on the problems of children (specially of girl children) related with their abuse and neglect. The Indian Constitution (1950) provided the framework within which provisions were available for protection, development and welfare of the children, much earlier than the UN Convention of the rights of the child. However, child abuse and neglect within the family has been highlighted as a part of advocacy under the convention. Another legal obligation of significance that has been included is safeguarding children from sexual exploitation and abuse, and action to prevent the abduction and sale of children in any form. Again the Convention assigns the primary responsibility to both parents for the children's upbringing.

Traditionally, the family and community in India have been insulated, authoritarian and patriarchal, with parent(s) guardians/caretakers having full right over their children, to treat them in whichever way they deem fit. Child rearing practices accept physical force or punishment as means of discipline. Child battering, corporal punishment or maltreatment by parents/guardians or even teachers are considered to be in the "interest of the child."

The term "Child abuse" encompasses a broad and wide range of acts and maltreatment of children. About child abuse there is no consensus about its forms, which can include child battering, extreme punishment, hard labour, emotional abuse, sexual abuse, including incest and exploitation, and abandonment. There is hardly any data base with regard to child abuse. Yet from statistics on children being admitted to the institutions due to abandonment, running away from home etc.; from the number of children apprehended under the Juvenile Justice Act on cases of exploitation, victimization and as child beggars; and from the newspaper reports of minor girls becoming victims of prostitutions and sexual assaults etc., it is clear that child abuse is a serious problem in the country.

Child battering and injuring the child physically by the parents, teachers and others in authority is very much relevant in India. Sexual abuse is the least reported form of child abuse despite its high incidence and the fact of its occurring in all economic and ethnic groups. Some estimates show that in 30 to 50 per cent incidents, the offenders are family members, close relatives, neighbours and friends and 80 per cent of children know their attackers. According to Crime in India (1992), (the Report of the National Crime Records Bureau) child rape victims in the age group of 0-10 and 10-16 years went on increasing from 1988 to 1991 but declined in 1992. Out of 301 cases reported in all Union Territories, Delhi recorded 276 (19.7%) cases while Lakshadweep was free from this form of crime. The incidence of rape, torture and sexual harassment recorded increase in 1992 over its previous year, while cases of kidnapping, abduction and molestation have declined.

Rape is covered in Sections 375, 376 of Indian Penal Code (1860). Sexual intercourse with female with or without her consent when she is under 16 years of age amount to rape and the offender is punishable upto imprisonment for life (Section 375 of the IPC).

The procedural details are great hurdles in the speedy trial of child rape cases. Total number of cases in which trial were completed, only 41.5 per cent ended in conviction in 1990, 34.2 per cent in 1991 and

33.8 per cent in 1992. Thus the percentage of cases acquitted is showing upward trend over the years. The disposal of cases in courts was 23.9 per cent in 1990, 18.6 per cent in 1991 and 18.1 per cent in 1992. On the average 80 per cent of the cases remained pending.

The Supreme Court has directed the State Government to immediately implement the provisions of the Indian Penal Code on the issue of child rape in strict manner, specially with the child below the age of 16 years.

Juvenile

Juvenile Justice Act 1986, which provides for the care, protection, treatment, development and rehabilitation of the neglected or delinquent juveniles came into force from October 2nd, 1987, throughout the country except in the State of Jammu & Kashmir. It was enacted by the Parliament in December,1986 replacing Children Act in the States/U.T. In order to implement the Act effectively, scheme for "Prevention and Control of Juvenile Social maladjustment was formulated by Ministry of Welfare and came into operation since 1986-87. The scheme is centrally sponsored providing assistance for setting and upgrading services for Observation Homes/Juvenile Homes/Special Homes/After Care Homes and for training of functionaries. By 31st December, 1988 there were in 18 States, 222 Observation Homes, with a capacity for 7,135. In 16 States there were 231 Juvenile Homes with a capacity for 12,200. In 15 States there are 42 Special Homes with a capacity of 3,005. In 6 States there are 16 After Care Institutions with a capacity of 870. From 10 States/U.Ts. no information was available and in two states the Act has not been enforced.

Over the years, the process of social development in India not only led to changes in the family structure and values, but has also resulted in an increase in social problems like destitution, and Juvenile delinquency. The Government of India has introduced various legislations and programmes to minimise these social problems. In the country, a well planned Juvenile justice system is in operation comprising Juvenile Welfare Boards, Juvenile Courts, Observation Homes, Juvenile Homes, Special Homes and After Care Organisations.

Juvenile Justice Act 1986 which came into force in 1987, which provided a uniform pattern of justice to Juveniles throughout the country has brought a change in the upper age limit of Juveniles to 16 years for males and 18 years for females, as per the earlier limit of 21 years for both males and females. The Act provides for the care, protection, treatment, development and rehabilitation of neglected and delinquent juveniles, and lays down a uniform legal framework to ensure that no child under any circumstances is lodged in jail or kept in police lock-up. The Act provides for a different approach in the processing of the neglected Juveniles vis-a-vis the delinquents. While neglected children are produced before Juvenile Welfare Boards, the delinquents are dealt with by the Juvenile Courts.

As follow-up measure contemplated under the Juvenile Justice Act, the Scheme for Prevention and Control of Juvenile Social Maladjustment is being implemented by the Ministry of Welfare since 1986-87 to provide financial support to States/UTs for setting up or upgrading of services for Observation Homes/Juvenile Homes/Special Homes/After Care Organisations and training of functionaries.

As a result of these efforts, the Juvenile crime in India has declined over the years and during 1992 accounted for 0.7 per cent of all the crimes under the Indian Penal Code. Sex-wise and age-group-wise distribution of Juvenile apprehended during 1991 indicates that the age group 12-16 years is comparatively more susceptible for criminal activities.

Since 1974-75, the Ministry of Welfare is implementing the Scheme for Welfare of Children in Need of Care and Protection to take care and rehabilitate abandoned, neglected, orphaned and homeless children. The welfare services being provided under the scheme include food, shelter, education, health, vocational training etc.

In short the whole attention is shifted from mere correction to the growth, development and rehabilitation of children in distress.

The enactment of the Act was a major step ahead in ensuring uniform, progressive, preferential treatment to neglected and delinquent children throughout the country. This act lays down not only specialised approach towards such children, but make sure that their treatment will be different from that of the adult offenders. In short, it will be seen that under no circumstances they will be kept in police lock-ups or in jails. Whole attention is shifted from mere correction to the growth, development and rehabilitation of child in distress.

16

INDIGENOUS MEDICINES

The Indigenous Indian System of Medicine, developed against a rich back-ground of social, cultural and philosophical principles prevailing in India between 600 B.C. and 700 B.C. Its three great contributors were Charaka, Sushruta and Vagbhatta, who were influenced by the Sankhya and Yoga philosophies, and discussed not only bodily illness, but also psychosomatic disorders. This system is based on the principle that human beings are constituted from the same basic elements as the universe. These elements were familiar to European medicine of the Middle Ages as "Humours" which were held to account for different types of health disorders, not only physical but also mental. Even in *Rigveda* some of the medicinal plants have been mentioned and in our country we have more than 15,000 species of medicinal plants.

In India, an elaborate system was evolved for the selection of students, codes of conduct, methods of training and examinations. Practitioners had a high standard of social behaviour and were strictly disciplined. At the beginning of the Christian era, Ayurveda the indigenous Indian system influenced medicine in Arabia, Egypt, Greece and Rome. The advent of Muslim rule in India brought with it the Unani or Arabic system of medicines, and both were used in popular health care. All these indigenous practices suffered a decline under the British Rule. In good old days the knowledge of these indigenous medicines used to descend from one generation to the next. The grandmother used to be instrument and home doctor. With the advancement in industry, change in life, increasing methods of communication, the grandmother system is slowly vanishing. The house wife is thus at the mercy of a doctor even for minor ailments. By the end of the 19th Century, the indigenous system had become static, having fallen mainly into the hands of untrained persons, incompetent to practice Ayurvedic medicine properly.

Dr. K.V. Panse, Nutritionist and Dietician, Pune (Maharashtra) enlightened us on the facts and giving us the original knowledge which according to him is in Sanskrit. Since there are so many local languages, he has made an attempt to give local names of these indigenous medicines. The ocean of thousands of herbal and indigenous medicines was churned and he brought out one hundred important ones. He classified them into five groups: (1) Infants, (2) Children, (3) Pregnancy and after Delivery, (4) Nursing Mothers, (5) Women. In this chapter mainly those concerning infants and children have been included and few from other groups.

Also a small information has been included and added from the M.Sc. thesis done by Smt. Kanchan (Barooah) Deshpande, which enlightens us on the use of indigenous material and methods used in diet of Nursing Mothers from medical point of view in Assam.

Hope this information will be of great benefit for all parents, teachers and prove useful for the children and mothers.

(1) FOR INFANTS

1. **Vasaka**

Botanical Name: *Adhota Vasica Nees.*

Indian Names: Hindi: Adusa; Bengali: Vasaka; Assamese: Bahaka; Gujarati: Aldusa; Kannada: Adulsoge; Marathi: Adulsa; Tamil: Adadorai; Telgu: Adasaramu.

Medicinal Importance: It softens the thick sputum, facilitates its coming out. It gives quick relief in bronchitis.

Purpose: For infants during cough and lung disturbances.

Method of Preparation: (1) Get the juice from the leaves. One teaspoonful of juice mixed in one teaspoonful of honey. Put the paste on the tongue of the infants. To be administered thrice a day. (2) Put the leaves in boiling water in a kettle and let the child inhale the steam coming out from the nozzle. Available commercially also.

2. **Hyoscyamus**

Botanical Name: *Hyoscyamus Niger.*

Indian Names: Bengali, Gujarati, Hindi: Khurasani Ajvain; Marathi: Khurasin Ova; Assamese: Joni.

Medicinal Importance: It is useful for relieving pain due to indigestion. It relieves stomach pain and flatulence. It helps to assimilate milk.

Purpose: For infants during stomach disturbances.

Method of Preparation: Heat this and convert it into powder. Mix the powder in water and jaggery. One teaspoon at a time, four times a day.

3. **Bal Ghutti**

Bal Ghutti consists of the following medicines:

(a) Jaiphal,
(b) Maiphal,
(c) Balhirda,
(d) Behada,
(e) Murudsheng,
(f) Kharik.

This has been the tradition in India for ages together.

(a) From 12th day to 9 months—Boil the water then cool it. Take this water on the home stone (Sahan) and have 4 rounds of each Jaiphal and Maiphal and reduce to two rounds of other items. Gives this to infants morning and evening. Same thing can be done without water, by taking mother's milk one teaspoon.
(b) If there is diarrhoea have 8 rounds of Jaiphal and Maiphal and only two rounds of others.
(c) If there is constipation, have 8 rounds of Balhirda and Behada and two rounds of others.

Medicinal Importance: Hirda is the real doctor of the infant. It helps digestion of the infant. It is a very good combination of plant medicines. These save the infant from cold, cough, diarrhoea, and constipation. These are very mild in action and suitable to infants.

4. **Rice-Pop Rice**

Botanical Name: *Oryza Satira.*
Indian Names: Hindi: Chowla; Tamil: Arisaiaval; Telgu: Atukulu; Marathi: Salichya Laya; Assamese: Akhoee.

Medicinal Importance: This is prepared from paddy. It is rich in Vitamin B. It is very much useful in assimilation. Infants digest it very easily. It is good for children after weaning. It is rich in minerals particularly Iron. This can be used if the faeces of infants are watery and not formed.

Purpose: For infants after weaning period.

Method of Preparation: (a) Make flour of this and mix it with honey and put this on the tongue of the infants. When the children are in position to chew, this can be given directly. (b) Mix the flour of Pop Rice with jaggery and ghee. Give this for formation of good faeces.

5. **Sugarcane Preserves**

Indian Names: Tamil: Karuppan Char; Telgu: Charakarasam; Kannada: Kakaunbi; Marathi: Kakvi; Bengali: Chini Shira.

Medicinal Importance: It contains good amount of minerals particularly iron and Vitamin-B. It helps in digestion. Children always need something sweet. Chocolates, lemon drops, peppermint, etc. Spoil the health and create cavities in the teeth of the children. This is good substitute for sweet.

Purpose: For children as sweet substitute.

Method of Preparation: At the time of meals two teaspoonful can be taken. Sherbat with this can be prepared. Where there is a need of white sugar this can be very well replaced.

6. **Honey**

Botanical Name: *Apes Melifica.*

Indian Names: Tamil: Theu; Marathi: Madh; Kashmiri: Maanch; Assamese: Moee.

Medicinal Importance: It has extreme case of assimilation. It is digested in 20 minutes. Hence medicines are given in honey. So as to reach all the parts of the body immediately. If there is pain to the nipple of the breasts, due to sucking or biting by infants, honey is applied. For getting sound sleep honey in the water before going to bed is advised, specially for children. Honey in water is good for indigestion, cough, and sore throat. It is also a very good tonic for children. Honey is highly alkaline.

Purpose: For children during indigestion, cough and for sound sleep. For lactating mothers for application to nipples and for general health.

Method of Preparation: Add 2 to 4 spoonfuls of honey in a cup of water. Addition of lemon juice is a good combination.

7. Dry Ginger

Botanical Name: *Zingiber Officinale.*
Indian Names: Hindi: Adrak; Tamil: Inji; Telgu: Alam; Bengalee: Ada; Marathi: Saunth; Gujarati: Adu; Assamese: Adda.

Medicinal Importance: The powder mixed with honey is very good for diarrhoea. This is good for cold and cough and also for stomach pain. It works very well when there is flatulence or dysentery.

Purpose: For infants and children in diarrhoea, dysentery, cold and cough and also distansia of stomach.

Method of Preparation: Powder of dry ginger mix it with ghee and honey. Sometimes it can be mixed with dry and powdered leaves of Bel. It can be given with ghee and sugar also.

8. Kokam

Botanical Name: *Garcinia Indica.*
Indian Names: Hindi: Kokam; Marathi: Amsule.

Medicinal Importance: It is rich in vitamins particularly 'C'. The ripe fruits are good for urticaria. They are good to reduce thirst in summer. This is good for itchings of the skin. Its oil is used for massage and helps to make skin soft. This oil is generally used in winter. One teaspoonful of oil taken in one cup of milk is useful for dermatitis.

Purpose: For infants for skin. Also oil is good in winter for dermatitis.

Method of Preparation: Put the ripe fruit cut in pieces in water. Squeeze them, add sugar and prepare sherbat. The fruits can be dried and used all the year round.

9. Nutmeg and Mace

Botanical Name: *Myristica Fragraus.* Mace is leaves and Nutmeg is fruit.
Indian Names: Tamil: Jathi pathiri, Jathikai; Oriya: Jaitri, Jaiphal; Marathi: Jaypatri, Jaiphal; Bengali: Jayatri, Jaiphal; Kashmiri: Jalwatur, Jaiphal.

Medicinal Importance: The properties of Mace and Nutmeg are the same. However, nutmeg induces sleep and cautiously used. This is very good for diarrhoea and particularly to summer diarrhoea to infants. It is good to induce sleep and useful in headaches.

Purpose: For infants in diarrhoea, and for headaches and for inducing sleep to women.

Method of Preparation: Roast the Nutmeg powder and mix it with honey. One-fourth teaspoonful 5 to 6 times in a day and continuously after every 15 minutes till the diarrhoea stops. For headache, put one teaspoonful of milk on stone grinder and have six rounds of nutmeg in the same. Apply to the head.

10. **Fennel**

Botanical Name: *Foeniculum vulgare.*
Indian Names: Hindi: Badisonf; Gujarati: Variyali; Marathi: Badishope.

Medicinal Importance: It is customary to eat this after meals. It helps to reduce gases and flatulence. It helps during teething period from diarrhoea. The extract is given to infants during stomach pains and flatulence.

Purpose: For infants for teething and stomach ache and for others for gases and flatulence.

Method of Preparation: For children—take 3 gms. of this, crush a little and add one cup of water. Boil it till it is reduced to one-eighth. Give this along with sugar, one teaspoonful thrice a day. For gases—powder it and take it with hot water.

10. **Indian Spinach**

Botanical Name: *Basella Alba* and *Rubra.*
Indian Names: Marathi: Mayalu, Mayphal, Ponchi Bhagi, Velboudi.

Medicinal Importance: This is good in colds and watery soapy faeces of infants.

Purpose: For infants in cold and watery soapy faeces.

Method of Preparation: Put one teaspoonful of milk on the home stone grinder and have 5-6 rounds of the fruit. Give this one-fourth teaspoonful thrice in a day for three days.

12. **Pomegranate**

Botanical Name: *Punica Granatum.*
Indian Names: Hindi: Anar; Tamil: Medalam pazham; Telgu: Dannima pandu; Kannada: Dalimbari; Oriya, Marathi; Bengali and Assamese: Dalimb; Gujarati: Dalam; Kashmiri: Daan.

Medicinal Importance: It is very good for the cough of infants. It helps in indigestion. It is useful in diarrhoea. It is used whenever there is bleeding from the nose.

Purpose: For infants in cough and diarrhoea. For others in indigestion.

Method of Preparation: For infants one teaspoonful fruit juice mixed in the same proportion with sugar or honey. Apply steadily the paste to the tongue of infant. For indigestion powdered skin of the tree mixed with jaggery should be given.

13. **Holy Bezil**

Botanical Name: *Osimus Sefuptum.*
Indian Names: Hindi: Tulsi; Gujarati, Marathi, Assamesse: Tulsi.

Medicinal Importance: This is one of the most important plants. It purifies the atmosphere and it is good for palpitation. It is good for skin diseases. It is good in malaria, and is used in ear and tooth ache. It is a good tonic. It is useful in reducing teething troubles in children.

Purpose: For children in teething troubles and is also a good tonic. For women for skin and other use.

Method of Preparation: For palpitation—one teaspoonful juice mixed with same proportion of ginger juice and sugar. For Malaria Fever—put 20-25 leaves in a cup of water and boil and reduce to one-fourth. Take this four times a day. For skin trouble apply the juice. For Tonic—take the seeds, soak them in water over night. Next day cook them in hot milk, add sugar to taste.

14. **Indian Yellow**

Botanical Name: *Yellow Indica.*
Indian Names: Hindi: Kuvar; Gujarati: Kuvar Patha; Marathi: Korphad.

Medicinal Importance: Inside the leaves there is a paste which is medicinal. It helps appetite and digestion particularly of infants. It is customary in India to give Kuwari Asar to infants. The main ingredient in this is Indian Yellow. It is good tonic for spleen and liver.

Purpose: For infants for the age of one year.

Method of Preparation: "Kuwari Asar" for infants is available in the market for infants. Take the juice of this and mix it with the same amount of honey. One teaspoonful thrice a day. For constipation of infants—one teaspoonful of juice mixed on the same quantity of honey, castor oil, and give before going to bed.

15. Brahmi

Botanical Name: *Bacopa Monneri.*
Indian Names: Hindi: Brahmi, Safed Chamni; Gujarati: Jal Brahmi, Jaluvri; Malayalam: Barna; Marathi: Brahmi; Tamil: Sanbra neelaye.

Medicinal Importance: It is a tonic for nerves and is prescribed in nervous disorders and mental diseases. It acts as a diuretic, i.e., prompts urination. It is used for infants in bronchitis. It is good in rheumatism and its oil is famous.

Purpose: (i) Good for infants in bronchitis. (ii) Women for diuretic and as hair oil.

Method of Preparation: Powder dry leaves 5 gms. and mix in the same quantity of honey. Good as brain tonic. For Diuretic—take juice mixed with sugar.

16. Castor Oil Seed

Botanical Name: *Ricinus Communis.*
Indian Names: Hindi: Arandi; Assamese and Bengali: Eri; Gujarati: Diveli; Malayalam: Avanakka; Marathi: Arandi; Oriya: Jada; Tamil: Amanakkam; Telugu: Erandamn.

Medicinal Importance: The seeds are poisonous but the oil obtained from the seeds called 'castor oil' is used as purgative. A new born infant is given this oil and honey. The oil is used in ointments as a soothing agent and in eye drops. The castor oil was used to facilitate child birth. A gel prepared from this oil is used in dermititis and in eczema.

Purpose: For infants and children as purgative.

Method of Preparation: Take the seeds and roast them, powder them and allow it to boil after putting some water. After some time, oil will be collected on the top. Castor oil is available in the market.

17. Calamus

Botanical Name: *Acorus Calamus.*
Indian Names: Hindi: Bach, Ghorabach; Assamese: Theinepril; Bengali: Bach; Gujarati: Gandhilovoj; Kannada: Bajegida; Malayalam: Vasambe; Marathi: Vakaud; Tamil: Vasambu; Telgu: Vasa.

Purpose: For infants after bath. For others on flatulence.

Method of Preparation: The dried barks are to be powdered. To be taken along with hot water.

(2) FOR CHILDREN

18. **Kamela**

Botanical Names: *Kamala.*

Indian Names: Hindi: Kamela, Shenduri, Rohini; Assamese: Gangeal; Bengali: Kamala, Raini; Gujarati: Kapila; Kannada: Kesalai, Ronati; Malayalam: Kapila; Marathi: Sendri; Oriya: Kamalagundi; Tamil: Kapila podi; Telugu: Kuukumma.

Medicinal Importance: It is used to destroy tapeworms. It is used externally for skin diseases and scabies.

Purpose: For children in tapeworm.

Method of Preparation: The red portion of the fruit is removed. This is to be taken with sugar and honey.

19. **Wheat Germ**

Botanical Name: *Tritucum Aestivum.*

Indian Names: Hindi: Gehukar Satva; Tamil: Godumai; Kannada: Godhi; Marathi: Gavachestava; Bengali: Gome asta.

Medicinal Importance: Due to germination of wheat, all the nutrients Vitamin B, E are increased and more assimilated. Germinated wheat is later on dehydrated by roasting. Thus there is no chance of fermentation. Roasting brings an easy digestion.

Purpose: For the children of 1 to 10 years it is good tonic.

Method of Preparation: Soak wheat in water over night. Next day hang it in a cloth tied. There is full germination 1 inch long in 24 to 48 hours. After drying roast the germinated wheat. Convert it into flour. Add one to three spoonful in milk depending on age.

20. **Ragi Malt**

Botanical Name: *Eleusine Coracana.*

Indian Names: Hindi: Maudal Okra; Tamil: Ragi; Marathi: Nachani; Gujarati: Ragi Bhar; Telugu: Ragalu Chollu.

Medicinal Importance: Ragi contains a good combination of protein, iron and calcium. These very nutrients are responsible for the growth of children. Ragi has a very high biological value. The outer covering is hard and is full of bran and hence malting is a must.

Purpose: For children1 to10 years age it is the best tonic.

Method of Preparation: Soak Ragi in water for twenty-four hours and allow them to dry. White sprouts will come out. Germination will be complete within 24 to 48 hours. Remove the outer covering by lightly beating with wooden hammer. Roast in iron pan along with sand. After this convert the germinated Ragi into flour. During this process, add sugar, essence to your taste. Give 2 to 3 tea spoonfuls in milk to your children.

21. **Karwanda**

Botanical Name: *Carrisa Carandas.*
Indian Names: Hindi: Karond; Oriya: Kendu; Marathi: Karwand; Bengali: Karamcha; Gujarati: Karwanda.

Medicinal Importance: It is very good source of iron. It has ease of assimilation. It is good for articaria.

Purpose: (i) Children for articaria. (ii) As tonic.

Method of Preparation: For articaria, juice of this mixed with sugar is given.

22. **Horsegram**

Botanical Name: *Dolichos bifflorus.*
Indian Names: Hindi: Kulthi; Tamil: Kollu; Telugu: Ulavalu; Marathi: Kuleeth; Bengali: Kulthi Kalia; Gujarati: Kuleeth.

Medicinal Importance: It is a rich source of proteins and all minerals, particularly rare minerals such as sodium, potassium, copper, sulphur, chlorine. It has good assimilation. Soup from this helps to reduce the weight in obesity. Soup is also useful in kidney stones. It is very good after delivery as it helps to clear uterus. Flour of this is used as soup, as it helps to reduce sweating.

Purpose: Tonic for children. Good for women after delivery.

Method of Preparation: Prepare soup from this. The best preparation is to take 50 gms. of horsegram, add 100 ml of water and boil till the water is reduced to one-fourth 250 ml. Take this soup.

23. **Cholam Flakes**

Botanical Name: *Sorghum Vulagare.*
Indian Names: Hindi: Juar; Tamil: Cholam; Telugu: Jounalu; Marathi: Jwari; Bengali: Juar; Gujarati: Juar.

Medicinal Importance: It is a good source of protein and minerals, including rare minerals like manganese, sodium, potassium. This is a mild laxative and has an ease way of assimilation. Cholam Flakes flour into milk or butter milk is an ideal tonic for children. Cholam Flakes flour remains in good condition for a long period.

Purpose: A good tonic for children.

Method of Preparation: Soak Cholam in water and then roast it in hot iron pan with sand. White big flakes will be ready. This can be eaten mixed with salt and pepper or flour can be prepared.

24. **Gingeey Seeds**

Botanical Name: *Sesamum Indicum.*
Indian Names: Hindi: Til; Tamil: Ellu; Telugu: Nuvvulu; Marathi, Bengali, Assamese: Til.

Medicinal Importance: It is a good source of proteins, unsaturated fatty acids, Calcium, phosphorus, and iron. It is very good for message. It is enriched with Vitamin D if kept in sun. One tea spoonful of oil taken before meal reduces acidity. It is useful in duodenal ulcer. Children many times want to eat always, 10 to 15 drops of this oil in sugar given twice will reduce this. One ounce of this oil can be used for children as enema. Gingelly seed, groundnut and jaggery is the best tonic for children. This helps to reduce constipation.

Purpose: Oil is good for message for children and infants. Also a good tonic.

Method of Preparation: Gingelly seeds and groundnut are roasted. They are converted into flour by hand pounding. One part of gingelly seed in one part of ground nut and two parts of jaggery is mixed along with ghee. This is ideal tonic for children, and is very useful in winter.

25. **Safflower Oil**

Botanical Name: *Carthamus Tinctorius.*
Indian Names: Hindi: Kardai; Tamil: Sendurkan; Telugu: Kusumbha; Marathi: Kardai; Gujarati: Kusumbo.

Medicinal Importance: Safflower leaves is a very good leafy vegetable. It has ease of assimilation and is for intestinal disorders.

Safflower seed flower kept once in water is generally given to children suffering from measles. Massage with the oil is good in dermitis and joint pains. This oil is useful in hypertension and heart diseases and it helps to reduce cholesterol.

Purpose: For children in measles and massage. For women in intestinal disorders.

Method of Preparation: 10 gms. of safflower seeds flour kept in 2 cups of cold water overnight. Give it to children after straining when they are suffering from measles, four times a day.

26. **Coriander Seeds**

Botanical Name: *Coriandrum Sativum.*

Indian Names: Hindi: Dhania; Tamil: Kothamalli, Virai; Telugu: Dhaniyalu; Kashmiri: Daaviwal; Gujarati: Kothniri; Marathi: Dhaniabeer.

Medicinal Importance: It is rich in potassium and hence very good for heart. This is very good for heart patients if taken along with sugar. This helps to get rid of worms in children. It helps to reduce heat trouble in summer if applied to forehead and back of the ears.

Purpose: Good for worms for children.

Method of Preparation: For heart patients, take equal amount of seeds and sugar and chew. For children for worms mix the powder in sugar or honey, give one teaspoonful 4 times a day.

27. **Onion**

Botanical Name: *Allum Cepa.*

Indian Names: Hindi: Pyaz; Tamil: Periya, Vengayam; Telugu: Pedda Nirulli; Marathi: Kanda; Bengali: Barapyaj; Gujarati: Dungli; Kashmiri: Gandu.

Medicinal Importance: There are two varieties, red and white. White is better in medicinal properties. It is good for scurvy, and induces sleep. It is good in piles. It helps in increasing height in children, and is good for general growth. Few drops are useful in inflammation in ears. It is used in swelling in feets. It is given for smelling when the blood oozes out of the nose.

Purpose: It is good for children for general tonic. To women for general use in insomnia.

Method of Preparation: Take 500 gms. of grinded onion and mix it with 500 gms. of honey. Keep this packed for 40 days. Then take 2 tea spoonfuls per day. This is a very good tonic. For insomnia eat onion along with curd at dinner.

28. Figs

Botanical Name: *Ficus Carica.*
Indian Names: Hindi: Anjeer; Tamil: Athi paxham; Telugu: Athipollu; Oriya: Dimiri; Marathi: Anjeer, Bengal: Dumoor; Gujarati: Anjir; Kashmiri: Anjeer.

Medicinal Importance: It contains good amount of fibre. It is Alkaline. It is a good liver tonic. It helps to remove constipation, particularly of infants and children.

Purpose: A good tonic. Relieves constipation.

Method of Preparation: Use fresh ripe figs. If dry figs are to be used, they must be cut into pieces and soaked in water for 24 hours. Take these with one cup of milk at bed time.

29. Bengal Gram Roasted and Dehusked

Botanical Name: *Cicer Arietinum.*
Indian Names: Hindi: Bhuna Chana; Tamil: Pottukadalai; Telugu: Putnalu; Marathi: Futane; Bengali: Bhajaboot; Gujarati: Futana.

Medicinal Importance: It has taste and cripness. It is rich in proteins, calcium, phosphorus, iron and Vitamin A and Vitamin B. Combined with jaggery, it is good tonic particularly for lungs and heart. If taken before going to bed, without drinking water, it helps to cure cold. Flour being very soft mixed with milk and used as a soup for infants. A liquid is collected by spreading cloth early morning on bengal gram shrubs. This when mixed with sugar is very useful in collitis, diarrhoea and dysentery.

Purpose: (i) Tonic for children. (ii) For curing colds in children and adults. (iii) For collitis, diarrhoea and dysentery in children.

Method of Preparation: Soak in water and roast in iron pan along with sand. Roast the flour in little ghee and mix this in the same amount of jaggery.

30. Banana

Botanical Name: *Musa Paradisiaca.*
Indian Names: Hindi: Kela; Tamil: Nandran Vazhai; Telugu:

Aratipandu; Kannada: Bale; Oriya: Kadali; Marathi: Kele; Bengali: Kala; Gujarati: Kele; Assamese: Kaul.

Medicinal Importance: It is alkaline and helps to increase HB in the blood. It acts as a mild purgative. It is a good tonic. It is good in piles and eczema. It is good in white discharge in women.

Purpose: (i) Mild Purgative and good tonic for children. (ii) Alkaline to others.

Method of Preparation: For children make a fine gruel of fine ripe bananas and ask them to take slowly by spoon. For mild discharge the juice of the skin must be taken. It is taken mixed in the sugar, one tea spoonful morning and evening. After the juice take one ripe banana along with ghee, morning and evening.

31. **Dates**

Botanical Name: *Phoenix Dactylifera.*

Indian Names: Hindi: Khajur; Tamil: Pericham, Pazham; Telugu: Kharjooram; Kannada: Kharajee; Oriya: Khajuri; Marathi: Khajoor; Bengali: Khejur; Gujarati: Khajur.

Medicinal Importance: It is very good in calcium and iron. These minerals are necessary for the growth of child. Hence, best tonic for children. It is alkaline and it is very much assimilable. It helps to reduce the enlargement of spleen.

Purpose: As a regular tonic for children.

Method of Preparation: Soak 5-6 dates (seeds removed) in water over night. Mix them in same water thoroughly and give them as drink after adding salt and pepper. If soaked 5-6 dates (seeds removed) for 4 hours in water, take them out, put in a cup of milk and add honey as a sweetening agent. (No sugar).

32. **Sensative Plant**

Botanical Name: *Mayahosa Pudika.*

Indian Names: Hindi: Lajvanti; Gujarati: Risamani; Marathi: Lajalu.

Medicinal Importance: If you touch the leaves, they close themselves. It is good in whooping cough amongst children. It is used for piles.

Purpose: (i) For children in whooping cough. (ii) For others in piles.

Method of Preparation: Take the juice of the leaves and mix it in honey. One tea spoonful morning and evening.

33. **Amla**

Botanical Name: *Phyllanthus Emblica.*

Indian Names: Hindi: Amla; Tamil: Nellikai; Telugu: Usiri Kayi; Kannada: Nellikayi; Oriya: Amla; Marathi: Avala; Bengali and Assamese: Amlaki; Gujarati: Amla.

Medicinal Importance: It is very good source of Vitamin-C. It helps to reduce acidity. It is good tonic specially in summer. Its oil is useful for black and long hair. It is one of the important ingredients of famous Ayurvedic medicine "Triphala" (for constipation) and "Chyavanprash" (general tonic).

Purpose: (i) For children as tonic.

(ii) For women as general tonic.

Method of Preparation: Amla can be cut into pieces (after removing the seeds) dried in the sun and mixed with salt. This dried pieces can be soaked in water for overnight and water can be mixed with sugar.

34. **Groundnut**

Botanical Name: *Arachis Hypogea.*

Indian Names: Hindi: Mungphali; Tamil: Nilakkadalai; Telugu: Veri-Sangakaji; Kannada: Kadale Kaji; Oriya: China Badam; Marathi: Bherimung; Bengali: China Badam; Gujarati: Bhoising.

Medicinal Importance: Groundnut soaked in water overnight and eaten slowly by proper chewing is best tonic giving proteins, Vitamin A and unsaturated fatty acids. Groundnut milk is on par with the cows milk. It is good for rickets. Groundnut cake is good source of cheap proteins.

Purpose: For children as tonic.

Method of Preparation: For children—10 gms. groundnut soaked in water over night. Remove red skin, Eat slowly. Groundnut milk—soaked groundnut in water for three hours. Remove skin and make a paste on stone grinder. Add 15 times water, one tea spoonful of lime water. Allow it to settle. Pass it through muslin cloth and the groundnut milk is ready.

35. **Linseed Seeds**

Botanical Name: *Linumussitatissimum.*

Indian Names: Hindi: Alsi; Oriya: Pesi; Marathi: Juwas; Bengali: Tishi; Gujarati: Alsi; Malayalam: Cheruchannavithu; Kashmiri: Alish.

Medicinal Importance: It is good in cold and cough. It is used to wash eyes. It helps in constipation. It can be used for poultice. Before 'Antiflogistin' this was used to remove the cough in children. It helps to reduce colic pain.

Purpose: For children for cold and cough. For others used for constipation or poultice.

Method of Preparation: For eyes—Soak the seeds in water and use this water for washing eyes in eye glass. For cold and cough. Take 100 gms. of seed and soak in 100 ml. of water, then rub the seeds in water, heat the same and take the water, 2 tea spoonful mixed with honey in the morning. For constipation take this water 2 tea spoonful before going to bed.

36. **Rough Chep Tree**

Botanical Name: *Pireayus Opsera.*
Indian Names: Hindi: Chirchira; Gujarati: Adhedo; Marathi: Aghada; Kannada: Uttarani; Bengali: Aparg.

Medicinal Importance: It is very good for cough. Many times infants have liquid type faeces, this is very useful in such cases.

Purpose: For children in loose motions and cough.

Method of Preparation: Burn the wood of this tree. The ash of this is mixed in honey. Put the leaves in boiling water and take the vapour from this. In the case of loose motions take the root of this tree and rub on home stone grinder in water, and give one teaspoonful thrice a day.

37. **Fig Tree**

Botanical Name: *Fecus Clomireta.*
Indian Names: Hindi: Gular; Gujarati: Umar; Marathi: Umbar; Kannada: Ahimaram; Bengali: Yadua, Odumbar.

Medicinal Importance: It has cool effect. It is good in inflammation of the inside of the mouth. It is used in kidney stone. It is used in diarrhoea.

Purpose: Good for children.

Method of Preparation: If the tree is cut by pointer, a white juice or sap oozes out. This is applied to the cheeks. For inflammation there are pin points on the leaves of this tree, these are to be eaten. For kidney stone the skin to be rubbed in water and mixed in honey and to be taken one tea spoonful thrice a day.

38. **Kurchi**

Botanical Name: *Holarrhena Autidysenerica.*

Indian Names: Hindi: Indrajav, Korai, Kurci; Assamese: Dutkhuri; Bengali: Kurchi; Gujarati: Kuda; Kannada: Hale; Marathi: Gal, Dudheri; Oriya: Khurni; Punjabi: Kewar; Tamil: Indraban; Telugu: Pala Kodsa.

Medicinal Importance: Its leaves and bark are used. This is mainly used in amoebic dysentery. The seeds are called "Indrajav." It is good in cough and acidity.

Purpose: For children and others for amoebic dysentery.

Method of Preparation: For amoebic dysentery—extract the juice of the bark and mix it with honey in equal proportion. For cough the seeds are used, powder them and adding it with water, allow it to boil till it is reduced to one fourth.

39. **Grapes Blue Dry**

Botanical Name: *Vitis Labruscana Vinifera.*

Indian Names: Hindi: Angur; Tamil: Nila Drakshi; Telugu: Nalla Draksha; Kannada: Kari Drakshi; Marathi: Manuka; Bengali: Angur; Gujarati: Draksha; Kashmiri: Dach.

Medicinal Importance: Black raisins are best. This is mild purgative. This is best tonic for liver for children. This helps to reduce acidity. It is good for teething troubles and it purifies blood.

Purpose: (i) For children as Liver Tonic and Purgative. (ii) For others as general tonic and for acidity.

Method of Preparation: For liver tonic—Soak 8-10 black raisins in lemon juice. Next day morning add sugar or honey, stir the same and take it. For milk purgative—Soak 8-10 black raisins in water for 12 hours. Take this mixed in half cup of milk before going to bed. For general tonic soak 8-10 black raisins in water. Mix them thoroughly and drink the water.

40. **Datura**

Botanical Name: *Datura Stramoniumt.*

Indian Names: Hindi: Datura; Bengali: Shet Datura; Gujarati: Dholo Datura; Malayalam: Ummattai; Marathi: Dhotra; Punjabi: Dhatura; Tamil: Ummatai; Telugu: Datturamu.

Medicinal Importance: The medicinal principle is hyoscyamine. The drug is used as Bellodonna. It is useful in bronchitis and asthama. It is poisonous and not to be used or taken orally.

Method of Preparation: For tooth ache put a small piece in the mouth, or apply its oil to the paining tooth. For women after pregnancy and heavy discharge, powder the same and mix it with sugar, take one teaspoonful, four times a day. For diarrhea one-fourth tea spoonful powdered cinnamon with one dessert spoon curd, one tea spoonful jaggery to be mixed and given morning and evening.

(3) DURING PREGNANCY AND AFTER DELIVERY

41. Bajra Porridge

Botanical Name: *Pennisetum Typhoidenm.*

Indian Names: Hindi: Bajra; Tamil: Cambu; Telugu: Cambu; Marathi: Bajri; Bengali: Bajra; Gujarati: Bajari; Kashmiri: Bajri.

Medicinal Importance: This is good source of iron. Women after delivery due to loss of blood need iron. It helps to increase lactation. Ten days after delivery this is given for one week.

Purpose: For women after delivery and for lactation.

Method of Preparation: Soak 20 gms. of Bajri in water for overnight. Next day in the morning make a paste on a home grinder. Cook it in one cup of milk and add sugar to taste.

42. Badam Porridge

Botanical Name: *Prunus Amygdalus.*

Indian Names: Hindi, Tamil, Telugu, Marathi, Bengali, Gujarati: Badam.

Medicinal Importance: Women after delivery need unsaturated, easily assimilated fatty acids. It is rich in those fatty acids. For small infants also, it is very easily digested if given in small amounts.

Purpose: (i) Women after delivery. (ii) For lactating mothers for increase in milk. (iii) Good tonic for children and infants specially.

Method of Preparation: Soak 10 seeds in tepid water. Next day morning remove the skin. Make a paste on home stone grinder, and cook it well in one and a half cups of milk, and add sugar to taste. For infants soak one seed in water, remove the skin, put little milk on home grinder stone and rub one seed slowly on it for 10-12 times. Give the milk with badam mixed this way.

43. Garden Cress Seeds

Botanical Name: *Lepidium Sativum.*
Indian Names: Hindi: Halim; Tamil: Alivirai; Telugu: Adityalu; Marathi: Ahalir; Bengali: Halim; Gujarati: Asalio.

Medicinal Importance: It is very good source of proteins, unsaturated fatty acids, calcium, phosphorus, iron and nicotinic acids. This is very good after delivery, and it helps to increase the milk of nursing mothers.

Purpose: (i) Women after delivery. (ii) For lactation.

Method of Preparation: Put 25 gms. of cleaned garden cress seeds in water just sufficient to soak, overnight. Next day morning add one and a half cups of milk and boil. Add sugar after removing from the fire and when it is cooled down. "Ladoos" also are made and prepared by mixing it with ghee and jaggery.

44. Fenugreek Seeds

Botanical Name: *Trigonela Foenum Graeccum.*
Indian Names: Hindi: Methi; Tamil: Venthayam; Telugu: Menthulu; Marathi: Methi; Bengali, Gujarati: Methi; Malayalam: Uluva.

Medicinal Importance: This is good source of proteins, calcium, phosphorus, iron, and vitamin choline. In 100 gms. of these seeds the choline content is 1,161 mg. After delivery the women do not do physical exertion and hence finds difficulty in digestion. This helps in digestion. The infants fed on mothers milk suffer, but this acts as a purifier of mothers milk.

Purpose: Women after delivery.

Method of Preparation: Soak the seeds over night in water. Prepare laddoos by powdering it and mixing it with ghee and jaggery.

45. Omum

Botanical Name: *Trachyspermum Amnic.*
Indian Names: Hindi: Ajwan; Tamil: Omum; Telugu: Vamu; Marathi: Ova; Bengali: Joan; Kashmiri: Ja Awem; Assamese: Joni.

Medicinal Importance: This is good source of minerals, and vitamins. This helps to reduce disturbances due to indigestion and flatulence. This brings good appetite. Some elderly children have a tendency to wet their beds in the night, this helps to cure this tendency.

Purpose: Good for infants and children.

Method of Preparation: Heat omum on light fire and then powder the same. Use this powder mixed with water in milk. Elders can drink water after the powder.

46. Cumin Seeds

Botanical Name: *Cuminum Cyminum.*
Indian Names: Hindi: Zira; Tamil: Jeergam; Telugu: Jeelakara; Marathi: Jire; Gujarati: Jiru; Kashmiri: Zyur.

Medicinal Importance: It is good for digestion and acidity. It is useful in amoebic dysentery. There is tendency of vomiting in during pregnancy. This is useful in preventing the nausea. It is also good for pregnant women for the proper development of foetus. It is very good for children suffering from rickets.

Purpose: (i) Good in Pregnancy. (ii) Good for children suffering from rickets.

Method of Preparation: Powder the cumin seeds and mix it with sugar in the same proportion. One teaspoon thrice a day. For children mix it with honey.

47. Garlic Dry

Botanical Name: *Allium Sativum.*
Indian Names: Hindi: Lehsun; Tamil: Ullipundu; Telugu: Vellulli; Marathi: Lasson; Bengali: Lashun; Gujarati: Lasan; Kashmiri: Ruanan.

Medicinal Importance: If included everyday in diet, a person is generally free from diseases of eyes, throat, lungs, heart, and digestive system. This is good for loose and frequent motions, and too much sneezing. It is good for worms. In case of infants, the garlic dry is to be taken by mothers. For skin irritations garlic juice is rubbed on the skin. If there is pus in the ears, garlic juice may be put in the ear with a dropper.

Purpose: (i) Women after delivery for general health. (ii) For children for skin trouble.

Method of Preparation: In boiling oil 10-15 garlic dry are put for a very short duration and used. Juice can be taken out.

48. Turmeric

Botanical Name: *Curcuma Domestica.*
Indian Names: Hindi: Haldi; Tamil: Maujal; Telugu: Pasupu; Marathi: Halad; Bengali: Halud; Gujarati: Haldar.

Medicinal Importance: It is antiseptic. It purifies blood. Whenever there is a bruise and wound it is applied. It is good for cough and voice. It is good for skin. Whenever there is sprain, it is applied mixed with oil. It is given to women after delivery.

Purpose: (i) As antiseptic and for sprain. (ii) For cough and voice. (iii) For skin. (iv) After delivery to be taken by mother.

Method of Preparation: As antiseptic it is applied on wound. For sprain add this with oil, heat the same and then apply to the part concerned. For cough and voice problem, mix one tea spoonful in hot water and drink the same. For skin mix it with milk and apply to the skin at bed time. Take a good bath next morning.

49. Drum Stick

Botanical Name: *Moriuga Olefera.*
Indian Names: Hindi: Sajjan; Tamil: Muruugaikai; Telugu: Mulagakada; Marathi: Shevaga; Bengali: Saijna; Gujarati: Saragavo.

Medicinal Importance: Its leaves and flowers are used as vegetables. It is a rich source of calcium, iron and Vitamin A. It is used in ulcer and acidity. It brings the uterus to its normal size after delivery. It is used in belching and pain in the waist.

Purpose: (i) For women after delivery. (ii) For children as tonic.

Method of Preparation: The vegetable of this is good in ulcer and acidity. The outer portion of the tree is boiled in water and reduced to ¼. This is used for back ache and uterus problems. It is taken four times a day. The juice of leaves is taken for belching.

50. Gum

Botanical Name: *Gum of Akasia.*
Indian Names: Hindi: Gonda; Marathi: Dink; Gujarati: Gunder.

Medicinal Importance: This contains good amount of calcium and manganese. After delivery there is a loss of energy and pain in the waist. This helps to decrease the pain and acts as a good source of energy. Hence gum ladoos are always given after delivery. It helps to reduce burning sensation at the time of urination.

Purpose: For women after delivery.

Method of Preparation: Ladoos mixed with dry dates, jaggery, ghee etc. are prepared. Wheat suji, flour of gram dal, powdered gum taken in same proportion and roasted in ghee and mixed with sugar is a very good tonic.

51. **Poppy Seeds**

Botanical Name: *Papaver Semhinferum.*
Indian Names: Hindi: Poshts; Marathi and Gujarati: Khas Khas.

Medicinal Importance: A good tonic. It induces sleep. The porridge prepared from this is given to women after delivery. It also helps to create more milk.

Purpose: For women after delivery.

Method of Preparation: Soak it overnight in water. Then grind the same at the stone grinder in home. Mix it in milk, boil and add sugar to taste. Sometimes it is mixed with gingelly seed and sugar.

52. **Cinnamon**

Botanical Name: *Cinnamomum Zeylamicum.*
Indian Names: Hindi: Dalchini; Gujarati: Taj; Marathi: Dalchini.

Medicinal Importance: It helps to reduce tooth pains. It is good in diarrhoea with mucus. It helps to bring uterus in normal position after delivery. It is good for women getting discharge during periods. It is good for colds and headache.

Purpose: (i) For women after delivery. (ii) For children for colds and diarrhoea.

Method of Preparation: For toothache put a small piece in the mouth, or apply its oil to the paining tooth. For women after pregnancy and heavy discharge, powder the same, mix it into sugar, take one tea spoonful, 4 times a day. For diarrhoea one-fourth tea spoonful powdered cinnamon with one dessert spoon curd, one tea spoonful jaggery to be mixed and given morning and evening.

53. **Betel Leaf**

Botanical Name: *Piper Betel.*
Indian Names: Hindi: Panvel; Gujarati: Nagvel; Marathi: Vidyachipane.

Medicinal Importance: It contains good amount of calcium, which is necessary after delivery. Hence, women after delivery should take this regularly. It helps in digestion. If there is more cough in the chest, this helps to reduce. It is good for cold and headache. The leaves are used in poultice.

Purpose: For women after delivery.

Method of Preparation: For women after delivery a pan with lime, betelnut, cardamom etc. is to be prepared. There is a special way of preparing this pan. For removing the cough, take the juice of 4-5 betel leaves. For cold and headache eat 4-5 betel leaves or take the juice.

54. **Indian Gum Tree**

Botanical Name: *Akesia Arebika.*

Indian Names: Hindi: Babul; Gujarati: Baval; Marathi: Babhul; Kannada: Karjali; Bengali: Babulgach.

Medicinal Importance: Its leaves, tender shoots, roots, skin, fruit and gum are medicinal. Tender shoots are used for cleaning teeth. It is used for cracks in bones. It gives energy. It is used in acidity. Gum is useful for giving energy after delivery.

Purpose: For women after delivery.

Method of Preparation: For cracks in bones, powdered seeds be taken into honey and ghee. For acidity boil the leaves in water till it remains one-fourth and take this after mixing it with sugar. For Gum Laddus—250 gms. gum fried in good ghee mixed with 50 gms. Almonds 50 gms. dried dates, 100 gms. dry coconut, 60 gms. choroli seeds, 60 gms. poppy seeds (Khuskhus) and jaggery for taste.

(4) FOR NURSING MOTHERS

In most countries, there are certain foods (herbs, or other concoctions or dietary practice) which are believed to improve lactation. Probably most lactogogues have no real beneficial action, but when taken with faith in their values, or in the herbalist that prescribes them, they do have beneficial effect. Garlic is one of these. Although there is no significant increase in an already satisfactory production or in lactation failure. It has been shown to be a source of plant oestrogans and small doses are claimed to help lactation by preventing normal enlargement of the breast, due to over secretion of milk.

LEAFY VEGETABLES AND THEIR USE SPECIALLY IN ASSAM

55. Bhedalata

Botanical Name: *Hydytos Scandens* (Family Rubiaceae).

Medicinal Importance: It is said to be an appetite stimulant. It reduces the frequency of stools and relieves grips, abdominal pains, and muscular pains. Local belief is that it counteracts diarrhoea, cleans liver and helps the uterus to contract.

56. Hukoloti

Botanical Name: *Thunbergia Grandiflor* (Family Acanthacese).

Medicinal Importance: Corrects constipation and flatulence and stimulates liver function. Aids digestion. Local belief is that it prevents intestinal complications and helps contract the uterus.

57. Bhutmula (Murraya Koengi)

Botanical Name: *Guandropsis Gyandra* (Family Capparidaceae).

Medicinal Importance: It is Antihelminic and also same as No. 56.

58. Narasingha (Curry Leaf)

Botanical Name: *Fam Rutaceae.*

Medicinal Importance: Stimulates the appetite and promotes activities of the organs concerned with digestion. Also helps blood secretion, eliminates worms and destroys ova. Local belief is that it cleanses the intestines.

59. Mani Muni (Indian Pennywort)

Botanical Name: *Centella Asiatica* (Family Amaranthaceae).

Medicinal Importance: Used in common diarrhoea of non-specific origin, in chronic colitis etc. Rapidly reduces frequency of stools and returns the consistency to normal. Relieves griping, tenesmus and gastroenteritis and heals the intestinal mucous membrane. Contains Vitamin C and D mainly. Local belief is that it prevents anemia and increases energy and appetite. It also helps contract the uterus, regulates the stomach and cures ulceration of the ovum.

60. **Dahikasu Pat (Leaves of Colocasia)**

Indian Names: Assamese: Colocasia; Bengali: Kochu; Hindi and Marathi: Arvi (See No. 62).

61. **Jatilau Pat (Leaves of bottle gourd)**

Indian Names: Assamese: Lau (Bottle Gourd); Hindi: Laoki; Marathi: Bhopla.

62. **Kathalu Pat**

Indian Name: Leaves of white yam.

Medicinal Importance: These above three—60, 61, 62 relieve pain. They are usually applied locally as a paste for inflammation of muscles and are often used for stopping bleeding. Local belief, these keep the head cool. They are mild laxatives and relieve pain.

Certain vegetables such as cabbage, red pumkin, squashes are considered taboo as they may produce gas and causes indigestion.

MISCELLANEOUS

63. **Mango Ginger**

Medicinal Importance: Stimulates appetite and promotes enzyme secretion enhances blood circulation, relieves constipation and corrects liver functions. Local Belief: It removes pain and prevents cough and colds.

64. **Banana Flower**

Medicinal Importance: Establishes normal bowel habits and corrects diarrhoea and loose motions. It is also given to the mother after delivery on the 11th day only. The mothers body is believed to be thoroughly cleansed and all the bad blood been excreted, so a mashed preparation is given which helps to stop bleeding.

65. **Garlic**

Medicinal Importance: This also stimulates the appetite, acts as a digestive, relieves flatulence and eliminates toxins. It is a mild stimulant and very effective for muscular and joint pains. It heals muscular damage and inflammation. Contains mainly iron and calcium.

66. Black Pepper

Medicinal Importance: Black peppers are ground in a banana leaf and baked in an oven. This is then removed and salt, mustard oil and two cloves of garlic are added. This mixture is made into paste, mixed with rice and eaten. And this also helps and it is believed to help in contraction of the uterus and relieves pain in the body. It helps also in milk output. This is given to mothers after delivery from the second day, twice a day.

FISHES

67. Kaoi (Climbing Perch)

Indian Names: In English: Arabas; Assamese: Kaoi (Climbing perch); Bengali: Koi.

Medicinal Importance: It has many thorns. It is recommended to eat after sickness and also after delivery, specially for nursing mothers.

68. Magur

Botanical Name: *Clearias Batrachus.*

Indian Name: Assamese: Magur.

Medicinal Importance: It has only one bone and it is very good for health.

69. Goroi

Botanical Name: *Ophiciphlus Punctalus.*

Indian Names: Assamese: Goroi (snake headed fish). It is also commonly known as Bhelki or Lata Toshi. Considered good for health.

Medicinal Importance: This is termesees 'Air beathing fishes' owing to an amphibious mode or respiration—they are able to exist for length of periods out of water and can travel over moist ground. They can live on the most semidried mud of tanks during summer. They are of good food value as they contain a high percentage of protein and a low percentage of fat—this also makes them easily digestible. The average weight of one fish is 100-150 gms. And each 100 gms., contain 10 gms., fat 15 gms., protein, 210 gms., calcium and 74 gms., iron.

Local Belief: They clean stomach and improve concentration of breast milk.

(5) FOR WOMEN

70. Cloves Dry

Botanical Name: *Syzigium Aromaticum.*
Indian Names: Hindi: Laung; Tamil: Kirambu, Lavangam; Telugu: Endu-Lavangaln; Marathi: Lavang; Bengali: Sukna Labanga; Gujarati: Laving; Kashmiri: Ruang.

Medicinal Importance: It is good for digestive and breathing system. For infants its effect is seen through mother's milk. Hence, mothers are to be given this and not infants directly. It is useful in cough, creates appetite and is useful in headache in cold season. Its oil is used for relieving pain in tooth ache when applied.

Purpose: (i) For women in cough and cold. (ii) For infants in cough and cold to be taken by mother.

Method of Preparation: Powder 4-5 dry cloves and mix it in sugar in the same proportion. Take only one pinch (one-fourth of tea spoonful) four times a day.

71. Cardamom

Botanical Name: *Cardamomum.*
Indian Names: Hindi: Iliachi; Tamil: Elakki; Telugu: Elakkay; Marathi: Veldode; Bengali: Elachi; Gujarati: Elaychi; Kashmiri: Elathari.

Medicinal Importance: It is used for relieving flatulence or feeling of overfulness of stomach, i.e., to promote digestion. Powdered with cloves, ginger, and caranay it is good in indigestion. It is used in flavouring agent. It produces cold action in the body. It is mixed in many other medicines.

Purpose: For women and children in indigestion.

Method of Preparation: The seeds are taken out of the fruit and powdered or eaten as such.

72. Cucumber

Botanical Name: *Cucumis Sativus.*
Indian Names: Hindi: Kakri; Tamil: Kakkarikkai; Telugu: Dosakaya; Marathi: Kakadi or Khire; Bengali: Sasha; Gujarati: Kakdi; Kashmiri: Laar.

Medicinal Importance: This contains rare minerals like magnesium, sodium, potassium, copper, sulphur, chlorine. It acts as a diuretic and has cold effect in the body. It is very good for the inflammation of the throat and also good for skin.

Purpose: Women as diuretic and of glossy, lusturous skin. For children for inflammation of throat.

Method of Preparation: The seeds are boiled in water along with coriander seeds, water reduced to one-fourth. This water is given to children one tea spoonful four times in a day for inlflammation of throat. The slices are rubbed on the skin for glossy and lusturous skin.

73. **Asafoetida**

Botanical Name: *Ferula Foetida.*

Indian Names: Hindi: Hing; Tamil: Perungayam; Telugu: Inguva; Kannada: Hingu; Oriya: Hingoo; Marathi: Hing; Bengali: Hing; Gujarati: Hing; Kashmiri: Yangu.

Medicinal Importance: It helps digestion. It is good for cough. It is used to relieve stomach pain. It is good for worms. It is given to women bearing tendency of abortion. It is good for cramps and pain in stomach during M.C.

Purpose: (i) For children for cough and cold. (ii) For women to regular menstruation.

Method of Preparation: It is to be given in very small quantity. It is roasted and then given.

74. **Mustard**

Botanical Name: *Brassica Juncea.*

Indian Names: Hindi: Lalsarso; Kannada: Sasive; Gujarati: Rai; Marathi: Mohori; Telugu: Aavalu.

Medicinal Importance: This is used in our foods. When the chest is full of cough, this is powdered and spread over a cloth and the cloth is kept on the chest. It is very strong hence direct contact is harmful. Whenever there is back pain or joint pain mustard powdered paste is applied. This is good in colds.

Purpose: For back ache and joint ache.

Method of Preparation: Powder it on stone grinder by adding little water and prepare the paste.

75. **Karveseeds**

Indian Names: Hindi: Shyjeera; Gujarati: Shyajeera; Marathi: Shahajira.

Medicinal Importance: It is one of the items amongst condiments. It is good for skin. It is good for children for diarrhoea.

Purpose: (i) For women for skin trouble. (ii) For children for diarrhoea.

Method of Preparation: For skin grind it in milk on the home stone grinder. Apply the paste to the mouth and keep it overnight. Next day wash the face with hot water. For children for diarrhoea, roast it on iron pan and then powder the same. Use only one pinch (one-fourth of tea spoonful) mixed in honey.

76. **Pepper Dry**

Botanical Name: *Piper Nigrum.*

Indian Names: Hindi: Kalimirch; Tamil: Milagu; Telugu: Miriyalu; Kannada: Vena menasu; Marathi: Mire; Bengali: Sukna; Golmirch; Gujarati: Mari; Kashmiri: Maruts.

Medicinal Importance: It helps to create appetite and is good for digestion. It is good for indigestion trouble. It is good for colds. It helps in curing amoebic dysentery.

Purpose: For all in creating appetite and help in digestion.

Method of Preparation: For appetite digestion take powder of 10 to 15 peppers and take the same mixed with honey half an hour before meals. For indigestion take the same mixture after meals. For Amoebic dysentery, take the powder of 10 to 15 peppers dry in buttermilk thrice a day for four days.

77. **Coconut**

Botanical Name: *Cocos Nucifera.*

Indian Names: Hindi: Nariyal; Tamil: Thengai; Telugu: Cobbari Kaya; Kannada: Thangu; Oriya: Paida; Marathi: Naral; Bengali: Narikal; Gujarati: Nariyal.

Medicinal Importance: Water of the tender coconut is the best diuretic and used in kidney stones problems. This water also reduces acidity. Coconut milk is an energy giving tonic. Dry coconut powder and turmeric mixed with ghee is used as poultice for sprain.

Purpose: (i) As Diuretic and kidney flushing for all. (ii) As poultice for sprain of children.

Method of Preparation: Water of the tender coconut must be taken immediately. For sprain, put coconut powder and turmeric in a cloth, tie it properly and heat the same on iron pan and apply the heat from outside. Repeat the same several times.

78. **Tamarind**

Botanical Name: *Tamarindus Indica.*
Indian Names: Hindi: Imli; Tamil: Puli; Telugu: Chintha Pandu; Kannada: Hunisehannu; Oriya: Tentuli; Marathi: Chincha; Bengali: Tentul; Gujarati: Amli; Kashmiri: Tamber; Assamese: Titali.

Medicinal Importance: Its leaves are used as vegetables. It is good for constipation and inflamation of intestine. It is digestive. It is used to reduce stomach pain.

Purpose: For all as a good "Sherbat" in reducing acidity and helping digestion.

Method of Preparation: For sherbat one part of pulp to be mixed in 20 parts of water or milk. Pulp, dates and milk in the proportion 1:1:40 is good combination for sherbat. Tamarind soup 1:64 is very good.

79. **Dogsteeth**

Botanical Name: *Sainodou.*
Indian Names: Hindi: Durva; Gujarati: Dharo; Marathi: Durva; Assamese: Dubari.

Medicinal Importance: It is good in any type of skin allergy. It is good in colds and ear pain. It is useful in irregular menstruation. It is purifier of blood.

Purpose: For women for menstruation and skin allergy.

Method of Preparation: For skin allergy—One tea spoonful juice to be taken once in a day. Juice may be applied to skin as well. For colds put the juice a few drops in the nose. For ear pain—take 5 gms. of juice and mix it with 20 gms. of cow's ghee and heat the same. Put this in the ear once a week.

80. **Bel**

Botanical Name: *Aele Marmeloscorrea.*
Indian Names: Hindi: Bel; Bengali: Bel; Gujarati: Bili; Kannada: Bilpatre; Marathi: Bel; Tamil: Vilvam; Telugu: Maredu.

Medicinal Importance: It is valuable for its mucilage and pectin. It is good in chronic diarrhoea particularly with constipation. It improves appetite and digestion. Its leaf, skin has medical properties. It is good in palpitation and heart diseases. It is good in white discharge amongst women.

Purpose: (i) For Children for diarrhoea. (ii) For women for palpitation; heart and white discharge.

Method of Preparation: For diarrhoea—give juice of leaves, in honey one tea spoonful 5-6 times a day. In palpitation and heart trouble, powder the skin of the tree and take it in the honey. For white discharge—dry the leaves and powder them. One tea spoonful powdered leaves to be taken in one cup of milk, morning and evening.

81. **Pimpal**

Botanical Name: *Feens Religlosa.*
Indian Names: Hindi: Pimpal; Gujarati: Pimalo; Marathi: Pimpal.

Medicinal Importance: It is said that this increases intelligence. It is given to below par and stammering children. It is good for regular and adequate menstruation. It is helpful in sterility. It helps to reduce the effect of heat on skin. It is useful if blood oozes through faeces.

Purpose: (i) For children for heat effect. (ii) For women for menstruation.

Method of Preparation: For intelligence—Take the skin of the tree and rub it in water on home stone grinder. One tea spoonful during the day. For regular menstruation, skin of pimpal, Babool and Tamarind tree and rub them on stone grinder and take the same along with honey, twice a day.

82. **Neem Tree**

Botanical Name: *Azadirachta Indies.*
Indian Names: Hindi: Neem; Bengali: Nim; Gujarati: Limbra; Oriya: Nim; Tamil: Vepa; Marathi: Limba; Kannada: Beru; Telugu: Vepu; Malayalam: Vepa.

Medicinal Importance: It is useful in fever. It is good for skin diseases. Eating 10-12 leaves per day is very good for health. It is useful in malaria. It breaks the periodic fever. It is very bitter and cannot be used by children.

Purpose: For women for fevers and skin diseases.

Method of Preparation: The skin of the tree is put in the boiling water and reduced to one-fourth. This is very useful in fevers and skin diseases. For skin trouble, the juice of the leaf is applied.

17

STATISTICS ON CHILDREN IN INDIA

TABLE 17.1 : Child Population (Census 1991)

India, State/ Union Territory	*Total/ Rural/ Urban*	*Area in sq.km.*	*Total Child Population in the age group 0-6*		
			Persons	*Males*	*Females*
(1)	(2)	(3)	(4)	(5)	(6)
India	**Total**	**3,065,027**	**150,421,175**	**77,322,151**	**73,099,024**
	Rural		**116,828,332**	**59,963,100**	**56,865,232**
	Urban		**33,592,843**	**17,359,051**	**16,233,792**
States					
Andhra Pradesh	Total	275,045	10,964,388	5,551,959	5,412,429
	Rural		8,223,818	4,154,898	4,068,920
	Urban		2,740,843	1,397,061	1,343,509
Arunachal Pradesh	Total	83,743	182,625	92,156	90,469
	Rural		162,168	81,643	80,525
	Urban		20,457	10,513	9,944
Assam	Total	78,438	4,421,511	2,238,599	2,182,912
	Rural		4,072,276	2,059,951	2,012,325
	Urban		349,235	178,648	170,587
Bihar	Total	173,877	17,764,186	9,065,869	8,698,317
	Rural		15,775,776	8,046,360	7,729,416
	Urban		1,988,410	1,019,50	968,901
Goa	Total	3,702	137,316	69,910	67,406
	Rural		81,218	41,190	40,028
	Urban		56,098	28,720	27,378
Gujarat	Total	196,024	6,830,357	3,543,374	3,286,983
	Rural		4,635,328	2,393,808	2,241,520
	Urban		2,195,029	1,149,566	1,045,463
Haryana	Total	44,212	3,125,173	1,663,350	1,461,823
	Rural		2,429,267	1,294,035	1,135,232
	Urban		695,906	369,315	326,591
Himachal Pradesh	Total	55,673	840,421	430,666	409,755
	Rural		779,971	398,91	381,052
	Urban		60,450	31,747	28,703

(*Contd.*)

TABLE 17.1 (*Contd.*)

(1)	(2)	(3)	(4)	(5)	(6)
Karnataka	Total	191,791	7,477,611	3,815,832	3,661,779
	Rural		5,378,741	2,740,028	2,638,713
	Urban		2,098,870	1,075,804	1,023,066
Kerala	Total	38,863	3,836,900	1,959,527	1,877,373
	Rural		2,881,664	1,471,560	1,410,104
	Urban		955,236	487,967	467,269
Madhya Pradesh	Total	443,446	13,091,570	6,706,104	6,385,466
	Rural		10,408,924	5,320,985	5,087,939
	Urban		2,682,646	1,385,119	1,297,527
Maharashtra	Total	307,713	15,504,536	6,939,044	6,565,492
	Rural		8,795,484	4,504,724	4,290,760
	Urban		4,709,052	2,434,320	2,274,732
Manipur	Total	22,327	306,617	155,308	151,309
	Rural		227,375	115,120	112,255
	Urban		79,242	40,188	39,054
Meghalaya	Total	22,429	393,729	198,261	195,468
	Rural		336,815	169,339	167,476
	Urban		56,914	28,922	27,992
Mizoram	Total	21,081	128,273	65,141	63,132
	Rural		72,561	36,786	35,775
	Urban		55,712	28,355	27,357
Nagaland	Total	16,579	207,487	104,102	103,385
	Rural		170,348	85,148	85,200
	Urban		37,139	18,954	18,185
Orissa	Total	155,707	5,347,501	2,719,219	2,628,282
	Rural		4,712,217	2,393,321	2,318,896
	Urban		635,284	325,898	309,386
Punjab	Total	50,362	3,306,245	1,763,452	1,542,793
	Rural		2,353,703	1,253,102	1,100,601
	Urban		952,542	510,350	442,192
Rajasthan	Total	342,239	8,859,492	4,622,750	4,236,742
	Rural		7,013,109	3,655,361	3,357,748
	Urban		1,846,383	967,389	878,994
Sikkim	Total	7,096	74,647	37,994	136,653
	Rural		69,595	35,385	334,210
	Urban		5,052	2,609	224,443
Tamilnadu	Total	130,058	7,448,059	3,823,011	3,625,048
	Rural		5,069,400	2,606,230	2,463,170
	Urban		2,378,659	1,216,781	1,161,878
Tripura	Total	10,486	497,122	252,724	244,398
	Rural		440,461	223,798	216,663
	Urban		56,661	28,926	27,735
Uttar Pradesh	Total	294,411	28,199,623	14,627,899	13,571,724
	Rural		23,117,483	11,992,665	11,124,818
	Urban		5,082,140	2,635,234	2,446,906

(*Contd.*)

TABLE 17.1 (*Contd.*)

(1)	(2)	(3)	(4)	(5)	(6)
West Bengal	Total	88,752	11,562,297	5,879,284	5,683,013
	Rural		9,290,292	4,717,307	4,572,985
	Urban		2,272,005	1,161,977	1,110,028
Union Territories					
Andaman & Nicobar Islands	Total	8,249	46,349	23,497	22,852
	Rural		35,821	18,154	17,667
	Urban		10,528	5,343	5,185
Chandigarh	Total	114	95,770	50,431	45,339
	Rural		12,136	6,353	5,783
	Urban		83,634	64,078	39,556
Dadra & Nagar Haveli	Total	491	28,337	14,075	14,259
	Rural		26,469	13,133	13,336
	Urban		1,868	945	923
Daman & Diu	Total	112	15,778	8,060	7,718
	Rural		9,514	4,922	4,592
	Urban		6,264	3,138	3,126
Delhi	Total	1,483	1,607,396	839,421	767,975
	Rural		198,378	104,403	93,975
	Urban		1,409,018	735,018	674,000
Lakshadweep	Total	32	9,464	4,877	4,587
	Rural		4,339	2,224	2,115
	Urban		5,125	2,653	2,472
Pondicherry	Total	492	110,395	56,252	54,143
	Rural		43,681	22,248	21,433
	Urban		66,714	34,004	32,710

(As on 1-10-1995)

Total Population	919,98 million
Male	477,47 million
Female	442,51 million
Urban	236,71 million
Rural	683,27 million
Tribal	67,8 million

Child Population	*Estimated Number (in million)*	*Proportion of Total Population*
Infants (under 1 year 1995-96)	24.86	2.70%
Per-school (1 to under 5 years)	92.83	10.09%
School (5 to under 16 years)	223.56	24.34%

Source : Annual Report on Situation Analysis of Children for 'SAARC' countries, India 1995.

TABLE 17.2 : Projected Child Population (0-14) by Sex in India and Major States, 1981-2001

India and Major States	*1981*		*1986*		*1991*		*1996*		*2001*	
	M	*F*	*M*	*F*	*M*	*F*	*M*	*F*	*M*	*F*
India	**140,321**	**131,679**	**148,151**	**140,415**	**152,784**	**144,965**	**157,998**	**149,670**	**157,606**	**149,556**
Andhra Pradesh	10,370	10,136	10,787	10,617	10,792	10,528	11,240	10,882	10,911	10,553
Assam	4,475	4,215	4,850	4,547	5,060	4,794	5,288	5,035	5,459	5,186
Bihar	14,941	14,209	15,912	15,370	16,497	16,059	18,157	17,529	19,100	18,612
Gujarat	6,876	6,475	7,067	6,734	7,050	6,789	6,889	6,612	6,554	6,297
Haryana	2,830	2,531	3,089	2,815	3,195	2,932	3,179	2,907	2,828	2,588
Karnataka	7,412	7,285	7,878	7,675	8,081	7,758	8,127	7,723	7,710	7,366
Kerala	4,505	4,454	4,632	4,498	4,686	4,528	4,707	4,500	4,613	4,474
Madhya Pradesh	10,869	10,418	11,655	11,140	12,139	11,391	12,689	11,864	12,263	11,501
Maharashtra	12,179	11,492	12,630	12,970	12,135	11,474	11,839	11,078	11,474	10,731
Orissa	5,246	5,243	5,456	5,344	5,518	5,285	5,707	5,369	5,651	5,318
Punjab	3,277	2,927	3,378	3,056	3,228	2,965	3,016	2,825	2,808	2,650
Rajasthan	7,572	7,074	8,418	7,930	9,239	8,746	10,231	9,724	10,806	10,293
Tamil Nadu	8,537	9,295	8,804	8,480	8,866	8,486	8,886	8,475	8,602	8,196
Uttar Pradesh	24,907	21,929	26,784	24,061	28,150	25,605	30,418	27,974	32,244	29,944
West Bengal	10,704	10,483	11,111	10,840	11,352	11,030	11,714	11,176	11,352	10,801

Source : Census of India 1981, Occasional Papers No. 4 of 1988, Report of the Expert Committee on the Population Projections.

TABLE 17.3 : Percentage Distribution of Population by Broad Age Groups, Sex and Residence, India, 1992

Residence	Sex	Broad age groups (years)					
		0-4	5-9	10-14	0-14	15-59	60 & above
Combined	Persons	13.1	11.8	11.1	36.1	57.8	6.2
	Male	13.2	11.9	11.2	36.3	57.8	5.9
	Female	13.0	11.8	11.0	35.8	57.7	6.5
Rural	Persons	13.6	12.0	11.3	36.9	56.8	6.3
	Male	13.8	12.1	11.4	37.3	56.7	6.0
	Female	13.5	11.9	11.1	36.6	56.8	6.6
Urban	Persons	11.2	11.2	10.6	33.0	61.2	5.7
	Male	11.1	11.2	10.6	33.0	61.7	5.3
	Female	11.3	11.2	10.6	33.1	60.7	6.2

Source : Sample Registration System, 1992, Office of Registrar General, India.

TABLE 17.4 : Percentage Distribution of Population by Broad Age Group, for India and Major States, 1992

India and Major States	Broad age groups (years)					
	0-4	5-9	10-14	0-14	15-59	60 & above
India	**13.1**	**11.8**	**11.1**	**36.1**	**57.8**	**6.2**
Andhra Pradesh	11.6	11.5	10.9	34.0	59.4	6.6
Assam	12.2	12.7	11.2	36.1	59.4	4.5
Bihar	15.4	12.5	12.0	39.8	54.1	6.1
Gujarat	11.4	11.6	11.2	34.2	59.7	6.1
Haryana	14.9	12.5	11.1	38.5	56.1	5.5
Himachal Pradesh	13.1	12.3	11.4	36.7	55.7	7.5
Kerala	9.8	9.8	9.8	29.3	62.3	8.3
Karnataka	11.7	11.6	11.5	34.8	59.1	6.1
Madhya Pradesh	14.2	12.0	11.6	37.7	56.4	5.8
Maharashtra	12.8	11.5	10.5	34.9	58.6	6.5
Orissa	12.8	10.7	10.8	34.3	59.7	6.0
Punjab	11.7	11.5	10.6	33.8	59.1	7.1
Rajasthan	14.2	12.6	11.5	38.3	56.2	5.4
Tamil Nadu	10.3	10.2	10.4	30.9	62.2	6.9
Uttar Pradesh	14.8	12.8	11.8	39.4	54.5	6.0
West Bengal	12.7	11.6	10.1	34.4	59.9	5.7

Note : Excludes Jammu & Kashmir.
Source : Sample Registration System, 1992, Office of Registrar General, India.

TABLE 17.5 : Number of Institutions and Enrolment in Pre-primary/Pre-basic Stage in States/Union Territories, 1993-94

States/Union Territories	*Pre-Primary/ Pre-Basic Schools*	*Enrolment as on 30th September 1993*		
		Boys	*Girls*	*Total*
States				
Andhra Pradesh	18	33,693	25,221	58,914
Arunachal Pradesh	299	9,510	7,132	16,642
Assam	482	10,678	8,617	19,295
Bihar	1	20,920	11,347	32,267
Goa	0	0	0	0
Gujarat	2,380	90,506	65,781	156,287
Haryana	27	5,864	4,156	10,020
Himachal Pradesh	15	3,300	2,740	6,040
Jammu & Kashmir	0	10,828	7,625	18,453
Karnataka	5,336	184,674	159,192	343,866
Kerala	261	7,870	7,120	14,990
Madhya Pradesh	634	68,903	49,428	118,331
Maharashtra	2,507	191,965	168,248	360,213
Manipur	1	48,510	43,490	92,000
Meghalaya	0	70,720	62,899	133,627
Mizoram	0	0	0	0
Nagaland	0	36,913	33,547	70,460
Orissa	0	0	0	0
Punjab	2	13,136	9,706	22,842
Rajasthan	33	81,000	59,000	140,000
Sikkim	723	9,263	7,866	17,129
Tamil Nadu	22	2,176	2,481	4,657
Tripura	3,410	82,311	81,485	163,796
Uttar Pradesh	45	22,854	14,683	37,537
West Bengal	0	0	0	0
Union Territories				
Andaman & Nicobar Islands	23	2,403	1,977	4,380
Chandigarh	0	7,004	5,555	12,559
Dadra & Nagar Haveli	0	129	100	229
Daman & Diu	12	410	303	713
Delhi	760	34,810	37,519	72,329
Lakshadweep	9	520	536	1,056
Pondicherry	172	6,928	5,132	12,060
India	**17,172**	**1,057,806**	**882,886**	**1,940,692**

Source : Selected Educational Statistics, 1993-94.

TABLE 17.6 : Enrolment Ratio at Primary and Middle Level by Sex in States/Union Territories, 1993-94

States/Union Territories	*Classes I-V (6-11 years)*			*Classes VI-VIII (11-14 years)*		
	Boys	*Girls*	*Total*	*Boys*	*Girls*	*Total*
States						
Andhra Pradesh	116.4	100.1	108.4	73.9	53.1	63.7
Arunachal Pradesh	132.5	99.2	115.8	62.5	46.3	54.5
Assam	134.4	125.3	130.0	89.3	65.5	77.7
Bihar	95.9	54.4	76.1	47.4	21.0	34.7
Goa	102.3	93.7	98.0	104.3	88.6	96.4
Gujarat	131.4	106.0	119.1	82.8	55.5	69.6
Haryana	109.7	95.4	102.8	81.8	59.2	70.9
Himachal Pradesh	126.8	111.5	119.1	124.4	97.9	111.2
Jammu & Kashmir	104.3	72.6	88.8	79.7	48.8	64.7
Karnataka	124.3	115.2	119.9	72.4	57.2	65.0
Kerala	103.8	100.8	102.3	108.3	105.7	107.0
Madhya Pradesh	116.7	91.3	104.5	82.5	50.0	66.9
Maharashtra	123.6	115.0	119.4	89.0	71.9	80.7
Manipur	100.3	96.0	98.2	77.9	68.4	73.2
Meghalaya	77.8	71.8	74.8	42.7	38.3	40.5
Mizoram	138.6	138.3	135.6	111.7	103.2	107.5
Nagaland	110.9	101.6	106.3	70.1	68.9	69.5
Orissa	116.8	77.5	96.8	67.5	46.9	57.0
Punjab	92.9	88.1	90.6	71.8	63.4	67.8
Rajasthan	119.5	60.9	91.0	76.8	28.9	53.9
Sikkim	128.8	111.1	117.6	59.9	59.3	59.6
Tamil Nadu	149.0	140.8	145.0	111.3	91.0	101.4
Tripura	141.3	119.1	130.3	92.9	72.2	82.8
Uttar Pradesh	103.9	72.8	89.3	72.2	35.4	55.0
West Bengal	124.7	123.0	123.9	98.2	89.1	93.8
Union Territories						
Andaman & Nicobar Islands	101.5	85.5	93.2	84.4	75.2	79.9
Chandigarh	65.5	64.0	64.8	62.2	63.3	62.7
Dadra & Nagar Haveli	125.7	92.6	109.9	58.3	36.7	48.0
Daman & Diu	—	—	—	—	—	—
Delhi	86.3	87.4	86.8	81.6	78.0	79.9
Lakshadweep	153.6	129.3	141.5	125.2	96.5	111.3
Pondicherry	146.4	133.7	140.1	138.8	125.5	132.2
India	**115.3**	**92.9**	**104.5**	**79.3**	**55.2**	**67.7**

Source : Annual Report, 1994-95, Govt. of India, Department of Education, 1995, Ministry of Human Resource Development, New Delhi.

TABLE 17.7 : Progress of enrolment at Primary and Middle level by Sex in India, 1950-51 to 1993-94

(*Million persons*)

Year	*Primary Level (Class I-V) (Age 6-11 Years)*			*Middle Level (Class VI-VIII) (Age 1-14 Years)*		
	Boys	*Girls*	*Total*	*Boys*	*Girls*	*Total*
1950-51	13.8	5.4	19.2	2.6	0.5	3.1
1960-61	23.6	11.4	35.0	5.1	1.6	6.7
1970-71	35.7	21.3	57.0	9.4	3.9	13.3
1980-81	45.3	28.5	73.8	13.9	6.8	20.7
1990-91	57.0	40.4	97.4	21.5	12.5	34.0
1991-92*	59.2	42.4	101.6	21.4	13.0	34.4
1992-93*	60.5	44.9	105.4	23.7	15.0	38.7
1993-94*	61.8	46.4	108.2	24.2	15.7	39.9
Enrolment as percentage of the corresponding age-group						
1950-51	60.0	24.8	43.1	20.6	4.8	12.9
1960-61	82.6	41.4	62.4	33.2	11.3	22.5
1970-71	92.6	59.1	76.4	46.5	20.8	34.2
1980-81	99.0	66.2	83.1	52.1	27.2	40.0
1990-91	115.3	86.0	101.0	73.4	46.1	60.1
1991-92*	116.6	88.1	102.7	74.2	47.4	61.2
1992-93*	118.1	92.7	105.7	80.5	53.8	67.5
1993-94*	115.3	92.9	104.5	79.3	55.2	67.7

* Provisional

Source : 1. *A Handbook of Educational and Allied Statistics*, 1987.
2. Selected Educational Statistics, 1985-86 to 1993-94.

TABLE 17.8 : Growth of Recognised Educational Institutions, 1950-51 to 1993-94

Year	*Primary*	*Upper Primary*
1950-51	209,671	13,596
1960-61	330,399	49,663
1970-71	408,378	90,621
1980-81	494,503	118,555
1990-91	560,935	151,456
1991-92*	565,786	152,077
1992-93*	572,541	153,921
1993-94*	572,923	155,707

* Provisional.

Source : Annual Report 1994-95, Part 1, Govt. of India, Department of Education, 1995, Ministry of Human Resource Development, New Delhi.

TABLE 17.9 : Growth of Persons in Educational Institutions, 1950-51 to 1993-94

(*in Thousands*)

Year	*Primary*			*Upper Primary*		
	Male	*Female*	*Total*	*Male*	*Female*	*Total*
1950-51	456	82	538	73	13	86
1960-61	615	127	742	262	83	345
1970-71	835	225	1,060	463	175	638
1980-81	1,121	342	1,363	598	253	851
1990-91	1,143	473	1,616	706	353	1,059
1991-92*	1,194	499	1,693	718	354	1,072
1992-93*	1,189	493	1,682	736	346	1,082
1993-94*	1,196	507	1,703	710	370	1,080

* Provisional.

Source : Annual Report, 1994-95, Part-1, Govt. of India, Department of Education, 1995, Ministry of Human Resource Development, New Delhi.

TABLE 17.10 : Drop-out Rates at Primary and Middle Stage by Sex in States and Union Territories, 1993-94

States/Union Territories	*Primary Classes (I-V)*			*Middle Classes (VI-VIII)*		
	Boys	*Girls*	*Total*	*Boys*	*Girls*	*Total*
(1)	(2)	(3)	(4)	(5)	(6)	(7)
States						
Andhra Pradesh	42.48	41.78	42.18	59.94	66.46	62.82
Arunachal Pradesh	60.09	61.09	60.52	69.62	67.45	68.72
Assam	38.65	39.55	39.05	63.81	71.80	67.55
Bihar	61.85	66.20	63.36	76.70	82.73	78.74
Goa	7.95	3.09	2.57	8.57	16.34	12.28
Gujarat	42.05	51.39	46.25	54.65	66.46	59.97
Haryana	1.60	6.81	3.93	17.57	32.05	23.91
Himachal Pradesh	24.64	28.16	26.28	13.11	27.39	19.74
Jammu & Kashmir	53.12	42.35	48.66	45.25	72.73	56.46
Karnataka	37.50	44.42	40.78	56.83	69.72	62.98
Kerala	5.35	3.05	4.23	1.24	0.57	0.91
Madhya Pradesh	23.43	34.96	28.36	38.12	54.15	44.68
Maharashtra	24.10	31.63	27.62	44.02	56.30	49.79
Manipur	68.02	68.53	68.26	72.41	72.26	72.34
Meghalaya	29.96	34.43	32.06	58.14	57.11	57.65
Mizoram	56.73	58.54	57.58	58.05	50.60	52.44
Nagaland	37.56	24.13	31.65	36.71	39.58	38.13
Orissa	52.78	52.23	52.54	62.64	59.04	61.21
Punjab	20.69	22.94	21.74	36.15	42.78	39.22
Rajasthan	45.70	55.63	48.93	62.34	72.34	65.43

(*Contd.*)

TABLE 17.10 (*Contd.*)

(1)	(2)	(3)	(4)	(5)	(6)	(7)
Sikkim	63.18	61.19	62.27	78.83	77.93	78.43
Tamil Nadu	16.39	18.35	17.30	32.15	41.20	36.34
Tripura	60.57	66.95	63.49	66.28	70.92	68.39
Uttar Pradesh	19.86	20.08	19.94	31.99	47.63	37.51
West Bengal	36.17	45.76	40.43	48.82	43.96	46.67
Union Territories						
Andaman & Nicobar Islands	9.26	10.34	9.77	25.25	29.62	27.32
Chandigarh	20.31	9.04	14.90	5.96	12.79	9.09
Dadra & Nagar Haveli	40.50	55.19	47.00	57.77	67.93	62.21
Daman & Diu	7.32	2.97	5.32	0.00	0.00	0.00
Delhi	19.25	28.83	25.74	19.89	31.24	25.35
Lakshadweep	12.55	18.75	15.51	47.18	57.43	52.16
Pondicherry	7.86	8.20	8.02	7.71	7.23	7.49
India	**35.05**	**38.57**	**36.32**	**49.95**	**56.78**	**52.80**

Source : Annual Report, 1994-95, Part-1, Govt. of India, Department of Education, 1995, Ministry of Human Resources, New Delhi.

TABLE 17.11 : Percentage Distribution of Specific Causes under the Group of "Causes Peculiar to Infancy"—India (Rural) 1984-1992

Sl. No.	*Specific causes under group diseases peculiar to infancy*	*Percentage Deaths*								
		1984	*1985*	*1986*	*1987*	*1988*	*1989*	*1990*	*1991*	*1992*
1.	No. of deaths under the group diseases peculiar to infancy	1,948	1,772	1,923	2,056	2,256	2,096	2,063	2,317	2,516
2.	Prematurity	45.3	41.4	41.0	43.9	45.8	48.2	49.59	48.2	50.5
3.	Respiratory infection of new born	15.5	13.5	14.5	16.6	17.2	14.7	13.23	15.4	13.5
4.	Malnutrition	—	—	—	—	—	—	—	—	—
5.	Diarrhoea of new born	8.9	11.3	10.2	10.0	8.6	7.3	9.0	6.8	6.9
6.	Convulsions	—	—	—	—	—	—	—	—	—
7.	Others	30.3	33.8	34.3	29.5	28.4	29.8	28.18	29.6	29.1
	Total	100.0	100.0	100.0	100.0	100.0	100.0	100.0	100.0	100.0

Source : Survey of Causes of Deaths (Rural), 1984-92, Office of the Registrar General, India.

TABLE 17.12 : Year-wise Vaccination Performance for Years 1975-94

(*Figures in millions*)

Year	*T.T. (Preg. Women)*			*(D.P.T.)*			*D.T.*			*Polio*		
	Target	*Achievement*	*Percentage Achievement*	*Target*	*Achievement*	*Percentage Achievement*	*Target*	*Achievement*	*Percentage Achievement*	*Target*	*Achievement*	*Percentage Achievement*
(1)	(2)	(3)	(4)	(5)	(6)	(7)	(8)	(9)	(10)	(11)	(12)	(13)
1975-76	3.02	1.45	46.3$	5.03	2.41	47.0$	5.73	1.28	22.0$	—	—	—
1976-77	5.00	2.14	42.0$	10.00	4.02	39.6$	5.00	2.72	54.2$	—	—	—
1977-78	6.94	3.51	50.7$	10.90	7.81	71.6$	6.96	6.54	94.0$	—	—	—
1978-79	5.00	3.72	74.5$	8.94	6.80	76.2$	7.93	7.21	91.1$	—	—	—
1979-80	6.00	4.75	79.4$	12.00	6.88	57.6$	10.00	10.84	108.7$	—	—	—
1980-81	6.84	5.28	77.3$	13.55	7.15	52.8$	11.37	10.23	90.1$	3.83	1.61	42.2$
1981-82	7.96	7.11	89.5$	15.97	9.23	57.9$	12.57	10.81	86.1$	2.40	2.93	123.8$
1982-83	9.00	7.64	84.9$	13.97	10.34	74.0$	12.50	10.25	82.0$	5.24	4.55	87.0$
1983-84	11.50	8.25	71.70	14.50	11.23	77.50	13.00	10.63	81.7	7.50	8.03	107.1
1984-85	13.03	9.36	71.90	14.51	12.43	85.70	13.06	11.45	87.6	12.00	9.89	82.4
1985-86	12.86	10.36	80.60	14.04	15.18	108.10	11.19	12.53	112.0	14.04	13.19	93.9
1986-87	15.20	11.73	77.2	15.30	12.99@	84.09	12.10	10.80	89.2	15.30	11.14@	72.8
1987-88	16.93	14.96	88.3	17.21	16.69@	97.0	13.00	10.47	87.5	17.21	14.27@	82.9
1988-89	22.66	16.19	71.4	18.04	16.81@	93.2	18.94	12.47	65.84	18.04	15.90@	88.1
1989-90	25.12	17.83	71.0	19.14	19.19@	100.2	18.75	13.84	76.89	19.14	19.04@	99.5
1990-91*	17.13	13.68	79.9	22.34	22.46@	100.5	17.13	13.68	79.9	22.34	22.46@	100.5
1991-92*	26.13	19.87	77.3	22.72	20.72@	91.2	16.70	12.56	75.9$	22.72	20.76	91.4
1992-93*	27.01	21.44	79.4	24.29	21.91@	90.2	17.55	12.91	73.5$	24.29	22.01	90.8
1993-94*	27.55	—	82.1	24.79	—	92.8	—	—	—	24.79	—	93.2

(*Contd.*)

TABLE 17.12 (*Contd.*)

(1)	(14)	(15)	(16)	(17)	(18)	(19)	(20)	(21)	(22)	(23)	(24)	(25)
1975-76	—	—	—	—	—	—	—	—	—	—	—	—
1976-77	—	—	—	—	—	—	—	—	—	—	—	—
1977-78	—	—	—	—	—	—	—	—	—	—	—	—
1978-79	—	—	—	—	—	—	—	—	—	—	—	—
1979-80	—	—	—	—	—	—	—	—	—	—	—	—
1980-81	—	—	—	—	—	—	9.82	1.62	16.5	—	—	—
1981-82	—	—	—	—	—	—	10.00	2.63	26.6	—	—	—
1982-83	15.00	4.12	27.5	—	—	—	10.00	5.02	50.8	—	—	—
1983-84	15.00	4.47	29.8	—	—	—	10.00	6.23	62.3	4.00	2.75	83.7$
1984-85	14.51	5.36	37.0	—	—	—	11.00	7.35	66.9	5.01	3.64	72.8$
1985-86	14.04	6.62	47.3$	—	—	—	11.19	7.87	70.3	5.54	4.53	82.0$
1986-87	15.30	11.81	77.2	5.70	3.71	67.5$	12.10	7.88	65.1	6.70	5.29	79.0
1987-88	17.21	16.35	95.0	11.21	10.05	89.7	13.00	8.43	64.9	7.80	7.00	89.7
1988-89	18.04	17.44	96.6	15.76	12.43	78.9	N.A.	N.A.	N.A.	9.75	8.29	85.0
1989-90	19.14	20.38	106.5	19.14	15.94	83.3	N.A.	N.A.	N.A.	18.08	10.59	58.6
1990-91*	22.34	22.98	102.9	22.34	20.21	90.5	N.A.	N.A.	N.A.	15.47	10.83	70.0
1991-92*	22.72	21.37	94.1	22.72	19.51	85.9	N.A.	N.A.	N.A.	15.19	9.79	73.5$
1992-93*	24.29	23.43	96.5	24.29	20.83	85.8	N.A.	N.A.	N.A.	16.05	10.45	73.1$
1993-94*	24.79	—	96.7	24.79	—	88.3						

Notes :* Figures are provisional.

$ Worked out after excluding the targets of those States/UTs for which figures have not been received.

Figures pertaining to DPT, Polio, BCG, Measles are pertaining to below 1 year.

NA = Not Available.

— Nil

@ Date relate to third dose only.

Sources : 1. Year Book, 1990-91, Ministry of Health and Family Welfare.

2. Annual Reports, 1993-94 and 1994-95, Ministry of Health and Family Welfare.

TABLE 17.13 : Reported Coverage Level under Immunization of Women and Children in Different States, India, 1993-94

States	*Achievement as %age of estimated infants and pregnant women*				
	DPT	*OPV*	*BCG*	*MSL*	*TT(PW)*
Larger States					
Andhra Pradesh	107.67	102.76	109.81	98.08	104.61
Assam	88.93	88.94	101.46	92.33	82.52
Bihar	77.77	78.27	66.17	71.04	60.32
Gujarat	99.98	100.87	102.15	94.96	94.68
Haryana	85.69	88.23	100.56	79.58	70.55
Karnataka	93.64	93.60	102.38	88.93	93.84
Kerala	99.68	99.16	107.98	88.43	93.28
Madhya Pradesh	88.55	88.61	92.64	88.81	78.53
Maharashtra	96.51	97.28	101.79	90.02	85.51
Orissa	88.68	88.92	96.61	87.58	76.89
Punjab	109.29	109.29	115.03	105.75	102.50
Rajasthan	91.28	91.60	91.79	88.26	84.44
Tamil Nadu	103.69	104.12	114.14	102.72	100.67
Uttar Pradesh	97.21	97.39	96.65	93.41	78.28
West Bengal	84.57	85.10	96.38	73.84	79.78
Smaller States					
Himachal Pradesh	94.51	94.37	94.32	89.61	76.82
Jammu & Kashmir	74.99	75.77	93.89	67.21	35.55
Manipur	99.95	99.17	100.79	77.38	94.56
Meghalaya	49.63	49.22	56.96	34.62	40.99
Nagaland	42.00	41.34	45.17	28.33	30.97
Sikkim	85.47	78.79	93.54	70.71	46.81
Tripura	78.92	79.16	106.26	77.52	51.62
Andaman & Nicobar Islands	100.16	100.16	101.08	93.02	80.66
Arunachal Pradesh	63.32	62.27	66.73	47.99	36.95
Chandigarh	115.46	119.67	130.20	103.34	100.77
Dadra and Nagar Haveli	100.12	100.12	96.33	91.07	83.52
Delhi	91.83	93.40	134.68	90.37	74.69
Goa	106.81	108.08	112.00	101.40	94.32
Daman & Diu	129.68	130.04	104.84	100.18	100.29
Lakshadweep	103.36	110.53	99.39	107.71	85.55
Mizoram	100.72	105.12	116.29	99.04	99.14
Pondicherry	116.33	117.61	125.39	106.32	102.98
All India	**92.85**	**93.23**	**96.69**	**88.30**	**82.12**

Source : Annual Report 1994-95, Ministry of Health and Family Welfare, pp. 33-34.

TABLE 17.14 : Coverage of Children (0-3 years) under Prophylaxis Programmes, 1991

Type of supplement	*Beneficiaries receiving supple-ment*	*Source of supplements*					
		Govt. doctor	*ANM/ LHV*	*Private practitioner*	*AWW*	*Any other*	*Not known*
(1)	(2)	(3)	(4)	(5)	(6)	(7)	(8)
Rural							
ICDS:N = 3699							
Vitamin-A	1326	137	441	69	623	10	46
	(35.85)	(10.33)	(33.26)	(5.20)	(46.98)	(0.75)	(3.47)
Iron & Folic acid tablets	1019	70	338	27	558	2	24
	(27.55)	(6.87)	(33.17)	(2.65)	(54.76)	(0.20)	(2.36)
Non-ICDS:N = 519							
Vitamin-A	118	28	71	14	3	2	0
	(22.74)	(23.73)	(60.17)	(11.86)	(2.54)	(1.69)	(0.00)
Iron & Folic acid tablets	86	25	50	7	0	0	4
	(16.57)	(29.07)	(58.14)	(8.14)	(0.00)	(0.00)	(4.65)
Tribal							
ICDS:N = 2050							
Vitamin-A	897	85	295	25	470	11	11
	(43.76)	(9.48)	(32.89)	(2.79)	(52.40)	(1.23)	(1.23)
Iron & Folic acid tablets	720	56	235	15	403	2	9
	(35.12)	(7.78)	(32.64)	(2.08)	(55.97)	(0.28)	(1.25)
Non-ICDS:N = 292							
Vitamin-A	54	13	36	3	1	0	1
	(18.49)	(24.07)	(66.67)	(5.56)	(0.11)	(0.00)	(1.85)
Iron & Folic acid tablets	43	6	34	2	0	0	1
	(14.73)	(13.95)	(79.07)	(4.65)	(0.00)	(0.00)	(2.33)
Urban							
ICDS:N = 1285							
Vitamin-A	441	72	101	36	215	3	14
	(34.32)	(16.33)	(22.90)	(8.16)	(48.75)	(0.68)	(3.17)
Iron & Folic acid tablets	369	56	66	30	212	2	3
	(28.72)	(15.18)	(17.89)	(8.13)	(57.45)	(0.54)	(0.81)
Non-ICDS:N = 183							
Vitamin-A	33	16	4	8	0	1	4
	(18.03)	(48.48)	(12.12)	(24.24)	(0.00)	(3.03)	(12.12)
Iron & Folic acid tablets	20	6	6	4	0	1	3
	(10.93)	(30.00)	(30.00)	(20.00)	(0.00)	(5.00)	(15.00)

Note : Figures in parentheses are percentage of children.

Source : National Evaluation of Integrated Child Development Services, 1992, NIPCCD, New Delhi.

TABLE 17.15 : Coverage of Children (3-6 years) under Prophylaxis Programmes, 1991

Type of supplement	*Beneficiaries receiving supple-ment*	*Source of supplements*					
		Govt. doctor	*ANM/ LHV*	*Private practitioner*	*AWW*	*Any other*	*Not known*
(1)	(2)	(3)	(4)	(5)	(6)	(7)	(8)
Rural							
ICDS:N = 3662							
Vitamin-A	1551 (42.35)	144 (9.28)	489 (31.53)	28 (1.81)	848 (54.67)	9 (0.58)	33 (2.13)
Iron & Folic acid tablets	1301 (35.53)	107 (8.22)	278 (21.37)	21 (1.61)	868 (66.72)	2 (0.15)	25 (1.92)
Non-ICDS:N = 518							
Vitamin-A	91 (17.57)	21 (23.08)	62 (68.13)	4 (4.40)	2 (2.20)	1 (1.10)	1 (1.10)
Iron & Folic acid tablets	73 (14.09)	18 (24.66)	47 (64.38)	7 (9.59)	0 (0.00)	1 (1.37)	0 (0.00)
Tribal							
ICDS:N = 2055							
Vitamin-A	1033 (50.27)	111 (10.75)	241 (23.33)	15 (1.45)	640 (61.96)	8 (0.77)	18 (1.74)
Iron & Folic acid tablets	903 (43.94)	68 (7.53)	198 (21.93)	5 (0.55)	618 (68.44)	6 (0.66)	8 (0.89)
Non-ICDS:N = 297							
Vitamin-A	51 (17.17)	10 (19.61)	31 (60.78)	3 (5.88)	2 (0.19)	2 (0.19)	3 (5.88)
Iron & Folic acid tablets	36 (12.12)	4 (11.11)	29 (80.56)	1 (2.78)	2 (5.56)	0 (0.00)	0 (0.00)
Urban							
ICDS:N = 1275							
Vitamin-A	484 (37.96)	68 (14.05)	72 (14.88)	31 (6.40)	287 (59.30)	9 (1.86)	17 (3.51)
Iron & Folic acid tablets	389 (30.51)	45 (11.57)	39 (10.03)	15 (3.86)	278 (71.47)	6 (1.54)	6 (1.54)
Non-ICDS:N = 179							
Vitamin-A	42 (23.46)	14 (33.33)	13 (30.95)	6 (14.29)	1 (2.38)	5 (11.90)	3 (7.14)
Iron & Folic acid tablets	29 (16.20)	14 (48.28)	9 (31.03)	2 (6.90)	0 (0.00)	2 (6.90)	2 (6.90)

Note : Figures in parentheses are percentage of children.

Source : National Evaluation of Integrated Child Development Services, 1992, NIPCCD, New Delhi.

TABLE 17.16 : Children (0-3 years) Availing Referral Services, 1991

Indicator	*Rural*		*Tribal*		*Urban*		*All*	
	ICDS N = 3699	*Non-ICDS* N = 519	*ICDS* N = 2050	*Non-ICDS* N = 292	*ICDS* N = 1285	*Non-ICDS* N = 183	*ICDS* N = 7034	*Non-ICDS* N = 994
(1)	(2)	(3)	(4)	(5)	(6)	(7)	(8)	(9)
No. of children referred	1205 (32.58)	120 (23.12)	503 (24.54)	55 (18.84)	456 (35.49)	61 (33.33)	2164 (30.76)	236 (23.74)
Referred by								
Health Staff								
Doctor	379 (31.45)	33 (27.50)	157 (31.21)	17 (30.91)	181 (39.69)	24 (39.34)	717 (33.13)	74 (31.36)
ANM	202 (16.76)	30 (25.00)	100 (19.88)	25 (45.45)	26 (5.70)	6 (9.84)	328 (15.16)	61 (25.85)
ICDS Staff								
AWW	243 (20.17)	—	147 (29.22)	—	96 (21.05)	—	486 (22.46)	—
Supervisor	48 (3.98)	—	29 (5.77)	—	12 (263)	—	89 (4.11)	—
CDPO	4 (0.33)	—	1 (0.20)	—	0 (0.00)	—	5 (0.23)	—
Any Other	329 (27.30)	57 (47.50)	69 (13.72)	13 (23.64)	141 (30.92)	31 (50.82)	539 (24.91)	101 (42.80)

Note : No. of AWs : Rural 387, Tribal 196, Urban 126
Non-ICDS units : Rural 54, Tribal 28, Urban 18
Figures in parentheses are percentage of children.

Source : National Evaluation of Integrated Child Development Services, 1992, NIPCCD, New Delhi.

TABLE 17.17 : Children (3-6 years) Availing Referral Services, 1991

Indicator	Rural		Tribal		Urban		All	
	ICDS *N = 3662*	*Non-ICDS* *N = 518*	*ICDS* *N = 2055*	*Non-ICDS* *N = 297*	*ICDS* *N = 1275*	*Non-ICDS* *N = 179*	*ICDS* *N = 6992*	*Non-ICDS* *N = 994*
(1)	(2)	(3)	(4)	(5)	(6)	(7)	(8)	(9)
No. of children referred	838 (22.88)	121 (23.36)	428 (20.83)	49 (16.50)	312 (24.47)	43 (24.02)	1578 (25.57)	213 (21.43)
Referred by *Health Staff*								
Doctor	207 (24.70)	32 (26.45)	167 (39.02)	22 (44.90)	100 (32.05)	13 (30.23)	474 (30.04)	67 (31.46)
ANM	123 (14.68)	31 (25.62)	56 (13.08)	13 (26.53)	20 (6.41)	11 (25.58)	199 (12.61)	55 (25.82)
ICDS Staff								
AWW	235 (28.04)	—	100 (23.36)	—	75 (24.04)	—	410 (25.98)	—
Supervisor	42 (5.01)	—	43 (10.05)	—	5 (1.60)	—	90 (5.7)	—
CDPO	3 (0.36)	—	0 (0.00)	—	1 (0.32)	—	4 (0.25)	—
All	280 (33.41)	—	143 (33.41)	—	81 (25.96)	—	504 (31.93)	—
Any Other	228 (27.21)	58 (47.93)	62 (14.49)	14 (28.57)	111 (35.58)	19 (44.19)	401 (25.41)	91 (42.72)

Notes : No. of AWs : Rural 378, Tribal 196, Urban 126
Non-ICDS units : Rural 54, Tribal 28, Urban 18
Figures in parentheses are percentage of children.

Source : National Evaluation of Integrated Child Development Services, 1992, NIPCCD, New Delhi.

TABLE 17.18 : Number of Beneficiaries for Supplementary Nutrition in Integrated Child Development Services during 1994 and 1995

Sl.No.	Item	June 94	March 95
1.	No. of projects sanctioned	3,657	3,397
2.	No. of *Anganwadis* providing supplementary nutrition	2.65 (Lakhs)	2.48 (Lakhs)
3.	No. of beneficiaries receiving supplementary nutrition	209 (Lakhs)	190 (Lakhs)

Source : Department of Women and Child Development, Ministry of Human Resource Development, Government of India, New Delhi.

TABLE 17.19 : Status Reports of the ICDS as on 31st March, 1995 (Service-Education) (Central Sector Projects)

States/Union Territories	Projects					No. of Anganwadis		Total Number of Children Attending Pre-School Education					
	Sanctioned upto 31.3.95	Target (Sanc. uptill 30.6.93)	Fully operational	Reporting	Interreputed	Reporting	Providing Pre-School Education	Boys	Average per AW	Girls	Average per AW	Total children	Average per AW
(1)	(2)	(3)	(4)	(5)	(6)	(7)	(8)	(9)	(10)	(11)	(12)	(13)	(14)
States													
Andhra Pradesh	200	183	183	162	4	20,946	18,864	351,111	18.61	344,539	18.26	695,650	36,88
Arunachal Pradesh	39	39	39	25	2	1,192	1,189	14,989	12.61	13,395	11.27	28,384	23.87
Assam	83	68	68	57	6	6,944	5,467	139,941	25,60	108,172	19.79	248,113	45.38
Bihar	323	296	296	214	35	19,498	12,644	285,908	30.52	520,396	41.16	906,304	71.68
Goa	11	11	11	11	0	1,069	1,046	6,807	6.51	8,502	8.13	15,309	14.64
Gujarat	148	122	122	109	3	16,561	10.737	186,383	17.36	212,231	19.77	398,614	37.13
Haryana	58	52	52	43	1	4,793	4,453	87,397	19.63	88,581	19.89	175,978	39.52
Himachal Pradesh	42	36	36	34	1	3,848	3,019	28,460	9.43	31,328	10.38	59,788	19.80
Jammu & Kashmir	56	45	45	38	3	3,552	2,844	34,624	12.17	35,783	12.58	70,407	24.76

(Contd.)

TABLE 17.19 (*Contd.*)

(1)	(2)	(3)	(4)	(5)	(6)	(7)	(8)	(9)	(10)	(11)	(12)	(13)	(14)
Karnataka	155	137	137	116	1	21,512	21,011	357,992	17.04	385,224	18.33	743,216	35.37
Kerala	96	75	75	66	5	7,455	6,733	92,394	13.72	105,925	15.73	198,319	29.45
Madhya Pradesh	298	266	266	218	10	24,804	20.624	313,477	15.20	319,567	15.49	633,044	30.69
Maharashtra	274	206	206	155	2	25,359	23,533	557,695	23.70	549,916	23.37	1,107,611	47.07
Manipur	29	27	27	20	2	2,088	1,343	26,522	19.75	28,486	21.21	55,008	40.96
Meghalaya	30	30	30	27	2	1,455	1,348	16,815	12.47	18,899	14.02	35,714	26,49
Mizoram	19	19	19	19	1	1,088	801	14,371	17.94	24,998	31.21	39,369	49.15
Nagaland	27	26	26	24	0	2,516	106	2,700	25.47	2,877	27.14	5,577	52.61
Orissa	229	218	218	206	11	18,279	15,843	262,801	16.59	270,869	17.10	533,670	33.68
Punjab	72	65	65	60	1	6,946	6,247	106,947	17.12	107,983	17.29	214,930	34.41
Rajasthan	177	136	136	122	0	15,046	13,947	219,032	15.70	181,664	13.03	400,696	28.73
Sikkim	5	4	4	4	0	385	310	2,850	9.19	3,671	11.84	6,521	21.04
Tamil Nadu	114	111	111	107	5	9,289	8,304	140,306	16.90	153,500	18.49	293,806	35.38
Tripura	20	19	19	18	3	1,771	1,656	27,931	16.87	29,015	17.52	56,946	34.39
Uttar Pradesh	572	425	425	290	19	27,247	22,136	545,024	24.62	485,129	21.92	1,030,153	46,54
West Bengal	277	215	215	169	12	22,132	19,153	383,904	20.04	367,952	19.21	751,856	39.26
Union Territories													
A & N Islands	5	4	4	4	0	257	255	6,552	25.69	4,011	15.73	10,563	41.42
Chandigarh	3	2	2	2	0	212	200	3,765	18.82	3,897	19.48	7,662	38.31
Dadra & Nagar Haveli	1	1	1	1	1	125	125	2,512	20.10	2,648	21.18	5,160	41.28
Daman & Diu	2	2	2	2	0	84	79	1,281	16 22	1,419	17.96	2,700	34.18
Delhi	26	26	26	25	0	3,066	2,963	60,462	20.42	58,470	19.73	118,962	40.15
Lakshadweep	1	1	1	1	0	71	59	630	10.68	611	10.36	1,241	21.03
Pondicherry	5	5	5	5	1	536	536	3,763	7.02	3,956	7.38	7,719	14.40
All India, March 95	**3,397**	**2,872**	**2,872**	**2,354**	**131**	**270,126**	**227,039**	**4,385,376**	**19.32**	**4,473,614**	**19.70**	**8,858,990**	**39.02**

Source : Department of Women and Child Development, Ministry of Human Resource Development, Govt. of India, New Delhi.

TABLE 17.20 : Statewise Number of ICDS Projects Sanctioned as on Feb. 24, 1995

Name of the States/UTs	*Number of Projects*		
	Central Sector	*State Sector*	*Total*
States			
Andhra Pradesh	198	9	207
Arunachal Pradesh	39	0	39
Assam	83	0	83
Bihar	323	0	323
Goa	11	0	11
Gujarat	146	15	161
Haryana	58	48	106
Himachal Pradesh	42	0	42
Jammu & Kashmir	55	22	77
Karnataka	155	30	185
Kerala	94	24	118
Madhya Pradesh	288	0	288
Maharashtra	272	0	272
Manipur	29	0	29
Meghalaya	30	0	30
Mizoram	19	2	21
Nagaland	26	0	26
Orissa	227	0	227
Punjab	72	0	72
Rajasthan	175	17	192
Sikkim	4	0	4
Tamil Nadu	112	276	388
Tripura	19	0	19
Uttar Pradesh	532	8	540
West Bengal	277	17	294
Union Territories			
A & N Islands	4	0	4
Chandigarh	2	0	2
Dadra & Nagar Haveli	1	0	1
Daman & Diu	2	0	2
Delhi	26	2	28
Lakshadweep	1	0	1
Pondicherry	5	0	5
All India, Feb. 95	**3,327**	**470**	**3,797**

Source : Department of Women and Child Development, Ministry of Human Resource Development, Government of India, New Delhi.

TABLE 17.21 : Percentage of Children (0-1 year) Immunized, 1991

Type of project	*No. of children*	*BCG*	*Measles*	*DPT*				*Polio*			
				1st dose	*2nd dose*	*3rd dose*	*Total*	*1st dose*	*2nd dose*	*3rd dose*	*Total*
Rural N = 371	10,577	5,590 (52.8)	3,652 (34.5)	353	92	4,733	5,178 (49.0)	265	196	3,649	4,110 (38.9)
Tribal N = 202	6,714	2,944 (43.9)	2,041 (30.4)	243	157	2,496	2,896 (43.1)	224	127	1,798	2,149 (32.0)
Urban N = 125	3,535	1,881 (53.2)	1,108 (31.3)	214	92	1,443	1,749 (49.4)	182	82	1,292	1,556 (44.0)
Total N = 698	20,826	10,415 (50.0)	6,801 (32.7)	810	341	8,672	9,823 (27.1)	671	405	6,739	7,815 (37.5)

Note : Figures in parentheses are percentage of children.

Source : National Evaluation of Integrated Child Development Services, 1992, NIPCCD, New Delhi.

TABLE 17.22 : Coverage of Children (0-3 years) under Immunization, 1991

Type of vaccine	*Rural*		*Tribal*		*Urban*		*All*	
	ICDS *N = 3,689*	*Non-ICDS* *N = 519*	*ICDS* *N = 2,050*	*Non-ICDS* *N = 292*	*ICDS* *N = 1,285*	*Non-ICDS* *N = 183*	*ICDS* *N = 7,034*	*Non-ICDS* *N = 994*
BCG	2,663 (72.0)	336 (64.7)	1,309 (63.8)	121 (41.4)	1,063 (82.7)	130 (71.4)	5,035 (71.5)	587 (59.5)
Measles	1,778 (48.1)	213 (41.0)	954 (46.5)	73 (25.0)	788 (61.3)	94 (51.3)	3,520 (50.4)	380 (38.2)
Polio	2,760 (74.6)	357 (68.8)	1,406 (68.6)	144 (49.3)	1,004 (78.1)	121 (66.1)	5,170 (73.5)	662 (62.6)
DPT	2,727 (73.7)	355 (68.4)	1,426 (69.5)	156 (53.4)	971 (75.5)	104 (56.8)	5,124 (72.8)	615 (61.8)

Note : Figures in parentheses are percentage of children.
Source : National Evaluation of Integrated Child Development Services, 1992, NIPCCD, New Delhi.

TABLE 17.23 : Percentage of Children (1-6 years) Immunized, 1991

Type of project	*1-3 years*			*3-6 years*	
	No. of children	*DPT booster*	*Polio*	*No. of children*	*DT booster & II doses*
Rural N = 371	16,509	5,748 (34.8)	6,110 (37.0)	23,124	6,532 (28.2)
Tribal N = 202	9,828	2,344 (23.8)	2,833 (28.8)	13,949	3,876 (27.7)
Urban N = 125	5,489	1,974 (36.0)	2,194 (40.0)	6,964	2,103 (30.1)
Total N = 698	31,826	10,066 (31.6)	11,137 (35.0)	44,037	12,511 (28.4)

Note : Figures in parentheses are percentage of children.

Source : National Evaluation of Integrated Child Development Services, 1992, NIPCCD, New Delhi.

TABLE 17.24 : Percentage of Children with Diarrhoea who Received either ORS or Recommended Home Solution in Major States, 1992-93

Sl. No.	*States*	*Percentage*
1.	West Bengal	75
2.	Himachal Pradesh	45
3.	Maharashtra	42
4.	Orissa	41
5.	Kerala	38
6.	Assam	35
7.	Karnataka	34
8.	Punjab	33
9.	Madhya Pradesh	33
10.	Andhra Pradesh	32
11.	Tamil Nadu	27
12.	Bihar	23
13.	Uttar Pradesh	23
14.	Rajasthan	23
15.	Gujarat	21
16.	Haryana	19
	India	**31**

Source : The progress of Indian States 1995, UNICEF India Country Office, New Delhi, p. 10.

TABLE 17.25 : Population Statistics (1991 Census)—Scheduled Castes and Scheduled Tribes

States Union-Territories	Total Rural Urban	Scheduled Castes			Scheduled Tribes			Total Scheduled Tribe population in the age group 0-6		
		Persons	Male	Female	Persons	Male	Female	Persons	Male	Female
(1)	(2)	(3)	(4)	(5)	(6)	(7)	(8)	(9)	(10)	(11)
States										
Andhra	Total	10,592,066	5,379,654	5,212,412	4,199,481	2,142,817	2,056,664	862,844	436,330	426,514
Pradesh	Rural	8,758,641	4,451,782	4,306,859	3,880,254	1,976,150	1,904,104	803,235	406,013	397,222
	Urban	1,833,425	927,872	905,553	319,227	166,667	152,560	59,609	30,317	29,292
Arunachal	Total	4,052	2,491	1,561	550,351	275,397	274,954	121.201	61,330	59,871
Pradesh	Rural	2,858	1,782	1,076	518,222	258,595	259,627	114,115	57,757	56,358
	Urban	1,194	709	485	32,129	16,802	15,327	7,086	3,573	3,513
Assam	Total	1,659,412	844,617	794,795	2,874,441	1,461,560	1,412,881	586,738	294,871	291,867
	Rural	1,430,131	743,834	686,297	2,777,308	1,409,364	1,367,944	570,802	286,724	284,078
	Urban	229,281	120,783	108,498	97,133	52,196	44,937	15,936	8,147	7,789
Bihar	Total	12,571,700	6,569,360	6,002,340	6,616,914	3,357,563	3,259,351	331,090	668,211	662,879
	Rural	11,437,136	5,958,186	5,478,950	6,153,659	3,115,824	3,037,835	249,430	626,597	622,833
	Urban	1,134,564	611,174	523,390	463,255	241,739	221,516	81,660	41,614	40,046
Goa	Total	24,364	12,389	11,975	376	199	177	87	41	46
	Rural	12,747	6,479	6,268	89	48	41	22	7	15
	Urban	11,617	5,910	5,707	287	151	136	65	34	31
Gujarat	Total	3,060,358	1,589,686	1,470,672	6,161,775	3,131,947	3,029,828	1,145,512	576,225	569,287
	Rural	1,899,394	981,381	918,013	5,663,178	2,872,954	2,790,224	1,058,570	532,194	526,376
	Urban	1,160,964	608,305	552,659	498,597	258,993	239,604	86,942	44,031	42,911

(Contd.)

TABLE 17.25 (*Contd.*)

(1)	(2)	(3)	(4)	(5)	(6)	(7)	(8)	(9)	(10)	(11)
Haryana	Total	3,250,933	1,747,821	1,503,112	—	—	—	—	—	—
	Rural	2,675,277	1,438,290	1,236,987	—	—	—	—	—	—
	Urban	575,656	309,531	266,125	—	—	—	—	—	—
Himachal Pradesh	Total	1,310,296	666,055	6444,241	218,349	110,240	108,109	38,687	19,676	19,011
	Rural	1,227.321	621,406	605,915	212,940	107,162	105,778	38,029	19,347	18,682
	Urban	82,975	44,649	38,326	5,409	3,078	2,331	658	329	329
Karnataka	Total	7,369,279	3,576,069	3,613,210	1,915,691	976,744	938,947	362,101	183,767	178,334
	Rural	5,645,186	2,869,254	2,775,932	1,629,496	829,129	800,367	313,634	158,983	154,651
	Urban	1,724,093	886,815	837,278	286,195	147,615	138,580	48,467	24,784	23,683
Kerala	Total	2,886.522	1,422,614	1,463,908	320,967	160,812	160,155	48,237	24,601	23,636
	Rural	2,351,924	1,159,484	1,192,440	309,764	154,979	154,785	46,646	23,781	22,865
	Urban	534,598	263,130	271,468	11,203	5,833	5,370	1,591	820	771
Madhya Pradesh	Total	9,626,679	5,027,806	4,598,873	15,399,034	7,758,174	7,640,860	3,329,466	1,672,751	1,656,715
	Rural	7,522,394	3,920,123	3,602,271	14,652,730	7,365,693	7,287,037	3,180,391	1,597,284	1,583,107
	Urban	2,104,285	1,107,683	996,602	746,304	392,481	353,823	149,075	75,467	73,608
Maharashtra	Total	8,757,842	4,505,375	4,252,467	7,318,281	3,717,783	3,600,498	1,465,076	739,025	726,051
	Rural	5,552.004	2,836,979	2,715.025	6,405,814	3,241,782	3,164,032	1,308,098	659,812	648,286
	Urban	3,205,838	1,668,396	1,537,442	912,467	476,001	436,466	156,978	79,213	77,765
Manipur	Total	37,105	18,806	18,299	632,173	322,720	309,453	104,598	53,155	51,443
	Rural	17,705	9,075	8,630	578,930	295,691	283,239	96,379	48.938	47,441
	Urban	19,400	9,731	9,669	53,243	27,029	26,214	8,219	4,217	4,002
Meghalaya	Total	9,072	4,981	4,091	1,517,927	760,234	757,693	349,224	175,444	173,780
	Rural	4,972	2,697	2,275	1,312,093	659,859	652,234	309,497	155,585	153,912
	Urban	4.100	2,284	1,816	205,834	100,375	105,459	39,727	19,859	19,868
Mizoram	Total	691	597	94	653,565	329,819	323,746	124,987	63,490	61,497
	Rural	456	399	57	358,113	182,212	175,901	71,781	36,376	35,405
	Urban	235	198	37	295,452	147,607	147,845	53,206	27,114	26,092

(*Contd.*)

TABLE 17.25 (*Contd.*)

(1)	(2)	(3)	(4)	(5)	(6)	(7)	(8)	(9)	(10)	(11)
Nagaland	Total	—	—	—	1,060,822	545,156	515,666	184,729	92,224	92,505
	Rural	—	—	—	933,145	478,579	454,566	159,008	79,307	79,701
	Urban	—	—	—	127,677	66,577	61,100	25,721	12,917	12,804
Orissa	Total	5,129,312	2,596,464	2,532,850	7,032,214	3,512,891	3,519,323	1,326,288	663,889	662,392
	Rural	4,578,669	2,311,384	2,267,285	6,670,506	3,325,442	3,345,064	1,260,517	630,679	629,838
	Urban	550,645	285,080	265,565	361,708	187,449	174,259	65,771	33,210	32,561
Punjab	Total	5,742,528	3,065,671	2,676,897	—	—	—	—	—	—
	Rural	4,562,442	2,435,795	2,126,647	—	—	—	—	—	—
	Urban	1,180,086	629,876	550,210	—	—	—	—	—	—
Rajasthan	Total	7,607,820	4,007,220	3,600,600	5,474,881	2,837,014	2,637,867	1,170,427	597,876	572,551
	Rural	6,102,496	3,210,044	2,892,452	5,220,549	2,696,437	2,524,112	1,119,117	571,265	547,852
	Urban	1,505,324	797,176	708,148	254,332	140,577	113,755	51,310	26,611	24,699
Sikkim	Total	24,084	12,424	11,660	90,901	47,504	43,397	16,334	8,280	8,054
	Rural	21,333	11,013	10,320	83,486	43,477	40,009	15,475	7,859	7,616
	Urban	2,751	1,411	1,340	7,415	4,027	3,388	859	421	438
Tamilnadu	Total	10,712,26	5,414,599	5,297,667	574,194	293,012	281,182	93,523	47,830	45,693
	Rural	8,428,040	4,259,370	4,168,670	505,208	257,853	247,355	82,319	42,068	40,251
	Urban	2,284,226	1,155,229	1,128,997	68,986	35,159	33,827	11,204	5,762	5,442
Tripura	Total	451,116	231,516	219,600	853,345	434,225	419,120	171,466	86,404	85,062
	Rural	379,664	195,079	184,585	839,264	426,741	412,523	169,693	85,495	84,198
	Urban	71,452	36,437	35,015	14,081	7,484	6,597	1,773	909	864
Uttar Pradesh	Total	29,276,455	15,599,178	13,677,277	287,901	105,420	137,481	58,983	29,922	29,061
	Rural	25,823,388	13,736,435	12,086,953	271,028	141,149	129,879	56,310	28,557	27,753
	Urban	3,453,067	1,862,743	1,590,324	16,873	9,271	7,602	2,673	1,365	1,308
West Bengal	Total	16,080,611	8,326,832	7,753,779	3,808,760	1,938,955	1,869,805	741,366	373,953	367,413
	Rural	13,605,405	7,018,589	6,586,816	3,612,448	1,835,559	1,776,889	708,518	357,318	351,200
	Urban	2,475,206	1,308,243	1,166,963	196,312	103,396	92,916	32,848	16,635	16,213

(*Contd.*)

TABLE 17.25 (*Contd.*)

(1)	(2)	(3)	(4)	(5)	(6)	(7)	(8)	(9)	(10)	(11)
Union Territories										
Andaman &	Total	—	—	—	26,770	13,750	13,020	4,541	2,394	2,147
Nicobar	Rural	—	—	—	26,268	13,436	12,832	4,489	2,366	2,123
Islands	Urban	—	—	—	502	314	188	52	28	24
Chandigarh	Total	105,977	58,554	47,423	—	—	—	—	—	—
	Rural	14,140	8,090	6,050	—	—	—	—	—	—
	Urban	91,837	50,464	41,373	—	—	—	—	—	—
Dadra &	Total	2,730	1,418	1,312	109,380	54,102	55,278	23,922	11,857	12,065
Nagar	Rural	2,243	1,160	1,083	105,864	52,304	53,560	23,297	11,531	11,766
Haveli	Urban	487	258	229	3,516	1,798	1,718	625	326	299
Daman and	Total	3,891	1,882	2,009	11,724	6,073	5,651	2,066	1,081	989
Diu	Rural	2,395	1,144	1,251	9,192	4,783	4,409	1,637	850	787
	Urban	1,496	738	758	2,532	1,290	1,242	429	231	198
Delhi	Total	1,794,836	978,690	816,146	—	—	—	—	—	—
	Rural	207,709	113,961	93,748	—	—	—	—	—	—
	Urban	1,587,127	864,729	722,398	—	—	—	—	—	—
Laksha-	Total	—	—	—	48,163	24,160	24,003	9,216	4,761	4,455
dweep	Rural	—	—	—	21,478	10,728	10,750	4,249	2,189	2,068
	Urban	—	—	—	26,685	13,432	13,253	4,967	2,572	2,399
Pondicherry	Total	131,278	66,191	65,087	—	—	—	—	—	—
	Rural	77,727	39,204	38,523	—	—	—	—	—	—
	Urban	53,551	26,987	26,564	—	—	—	—	—	—

Note : The 1991 census was not held in Jammu & Kashmir.
Source : Census of India 1991.

TABLE 17.26 : Implementation of Programme of Creches for Children of Working and Ailing mothers by Central Social Welfare Board in States/UT's 1993-94

States/Union Territories	*No. of Institutions*	*No. of Units*	*No. of Beneficiaries*	*Amount Sanctioned (Rs. in Lakhs)*	*Amount released (Rs. in Lakhs)*
States					
Andhra Pradesh	420	997	24,925	179.52	151.03
Arunachal Pradesh	10	30	750	5.51	5.08
Assam	86	87	2,175	16.14	7.83
Bihar	13	50	1,250	8.89	10.43
Goa	17	37	925	6.74	4.14
Gujarat	90	733	18,325	130.70	109.71
Haryana	20	140	3,500	24.88	21.81
Himachal Pradesh	40	374	9,350	66.72	63.42
Jammu & Kashmir	22	60	1,500	10.32	6.62
Karnataka	207	463	11,575	82,76	62.16
Kerala	414	568	14,200	101.02	61.92
Madhya Pradesh	405	1,018	25,450	180,87	148.29
Maharashtra	256	1,024	25,600	183.53	152.49
Manipur	209	218	5,450	38.82	31.95
Meghalaya	177	188	4,700	33.40	20.54
Mizoram	135	138	3,450	24.52	15.86
Nagaland	—	—	—	—	—
Orissa	343	384	9,600	68.43	25.85
Punjab	44	179	4,475	31.81	28.80
Rajasthan	148	402	10,050	69.41	58.82
Sikkim	35	115	2,875	20.44	12.96
Tamil Nadu	313	822	20,550	147.61	127.83
Tripura	77	139	3,475	25.12	18.84
Uttar Pradesh	353	744	18,600	132.24	129.70
West Bengal	335	498	12,450	90.73	58.91
Union Territories					
A&N Islands	51	82	2,050	14.87	9.92
Chandigarh	14	26	650	4.62	2.72
Delhi	27	132	3,300	23,46	20.24
Lakshadweep	3	3	75	0.53	0.40
Pondicherry	68	87	2,175	11.61	12.61
Total	**4,332**	**9,738**	**243,450**	**1,735.22**	**1,380.88**

Source : Annual Report, Central Social Welfare Board, 1993-94.

TABLE 17.27 : Infant Mortality Rates by Sex and Residence (1990)

Indicators	*Type of Project*											
	Rural (N = 336)			*Tribal (N = 191)*			*Urban (N = 122)*			*All (N = 649)*		
	Male	*Female*	*Persons*	*Male*	*Female*	*Persons*	*Male*	*Female*	*Persons*	*Male*	*Female*	*Persons*
(1)	(2)	(3)	(4)	(5)	(6)	(7)	(8)	(9)	(10)	(11)	(12)	(13)
Live Births	3,475	3,125	66,000	1,711	1,678	3,389	1,120	1,020	2,140	6,306	5,823	12,129
Death in less than 7 days	111	70	181	89	25	114	50	30	80	250	125	375
Death between 7 days—1 year	158	101	259	74	63	137	62	32	94	294	196	490
IMR	77.4	54.7	66.6	95.2	52.4	74.0	100	63.2	81.3	86.3	55.1	71.3

Source : National Evaluation of Integrated Child Development Services, 1992, NIPPCED, New Delhi.

TABLE 17.28 : Age Specific Death Rate upto the Age of 14 years and Residence and Sex in India 1981-1991

Year	*Age Groups (in years)*								
Rural Urban Total	*0-4*			*5-9*			*10-14*		
	Male	*Female*	*Persons*	*Male*	*Female*	*Persons*	*Male*	*Female*	*Persons*
1981 Rural	43.1	48.0	45.5	4.1	5.0	4.6	1.8	1.8	1.3
Urban	20.0	20.9	20.4	1.7	1.7	1.7	1.6	1.4	1.5
Total	39.2	43.3	41.2	3.7	4.4	4.0	1.8	1.7	1.7
1982 Rural	42.2	45.7	43.9	3.4	4.3	3.8	1.9	1.9	1.9
Urban	21.2	20.5	20.9	1.4	1.8	1.5	0.8	1.0	0.9
Total	37.9	40.5	39.1	3.0	3.7	3.3	1.6	1.7	1.7
1983 Rural	40.5	43.1	41.8	3.4	4.0	3.6	1.7	2.0	1.8
Urban	21.1	21.7	21.7	2.0	1.8	1.9	0.9	1.2	1.0
Total	36.5	38.6	37.6	3.1	3.5	3.3	1.5	1.8	1.7
1984 Rural	44.2	48.2	46.2	4.1	5.3	4.7	1.7	2.2	1.9
Urban	22.6	23.8	23.2	1.6	2.1	1.8	1.2	1.3	1.2
Total	39.5	43.0	4.12	3.6	4.6	4.1	1.6	2.0	1.8
1985 Rural	41.4	45.3	43.3	3.7	4.8	4.2	2.0	2.1	2.0
Urban	19.4	22.1	20.7	1.4	1.9	1.7	1.2	0.9	1.0
Total	36.6	40.4	38.4	3.2	4.2	3.7	1.8	1.9	1.8
1986 Rural	38.6	43.3	40.8	3.3	4.2	3.7	1.6	1.8	1.7
Urban	20.3	21.5	20.9	1.6	1.8	1.7	0.9	1.1	1.0
Total	34.7	38.6	36.6	2.9	3.7	3.3	1.5	1.6	1.6
1987 Rural	37.8	41.8	39.7	3.3	4.4	3.8	1.6	1.6	1.6
Urban	18.1	18.2	18.2	1.3	1.9	1.6	1.1	0.9	1.0
Total	33.6	36.8	35.2	2.8	3.9	3.3	1.5	1.4	1.5
1988 Rural	35.1	39.1	35.7	3.6	3.9	3.6	1.6	1.8	1.7
Urban	18.8	18.8	18.7	1.6	1.8	1.7	0.7	1.2	0.9
Total	31.8	34.9	33.3	3.0	3.4	3.2	1.4	1.7	1.5
1989 Rural	31.3	35.2	33.2	2.7	3.8	3.2	1.6	1.9	1.7
Urban	16.5	17.2	16.9	1.4	1.6	1.5	0.8	1.8	0.8
Total	28.5	31.4	29.9	2.4	3.3	2.8	1.4	1.6	1.5
1990 Rural	27.3	31.0	29.1	2.6	3.1	2.9	1.5	1.6	1.5
Urban	14.8	15.4	15.1	1.3	1.5	1.4	0.8	1.0	0.9
Total	24.8	27.9	26.3	2.3	2.8	2.5	1.4	1.4	1.4
1991 Rural	28.1	30.2	29.1	2.8	3.2	3.0	1.5	1.8	1.6
Urban	15.4	16.6	16.0	1.6	1.5	1.5	1.1	0.9	1.0
Total	25.6	27.5	26.5	2:6	2.9	2.7	1.4	1.6	1.5

Source : Sample Registration System, 1981-1991, Office of the Registrar General, India.

TABLE 17.29 : Statistics on Literates Children in India Census 1991

India States/Union Territories	*Total Rural Urban*	*Persons*	*Male*	*Female*
(1)	(2)	(3)	(4)	(5)
India	**Total**	**359,284,417**	**229,531,935**	**129,752,482**
	Rural	**226,144,087**	**151,216,579**	**74,927,508**
	Urban	**133,140,330**	**78,315,356**	**54,824,974**
States				
Andhra Pradesh	Total	24,487,559	15,532,689	8,954,870
	Rural	14,438,253	9,663,607	4,774,646
	Urban	10,049,306	5,869,082	4,180,224
Arunachal Pradesh	Total	283,610	191,841	91,769
	Rural	219,058	150,095	68,963
	Urban	64,552	41,746	22,806
Assam	Total	9,516,393	5,827,649	3,688,744
	Rural	7,818,550	4,836,187	2,982,363
	Urban	1,697,843	991,462	706,381
Bihar	Total	26,402,898	18,968,636	7,434,262
	Rural	20,045,430	14,975,742	5,069,688
	Urban	6,357,468	3,992,894	2,364,574
Goa	Total	779,596	439,034	340,562
	Rural	440,237	249,196	191,041
	Urban	339,359	189,838	149,521
Gujarat	Total	21,131,400	13,025,132	8,106,268
	Rural	11,907,294	7,680,019	4,227,275
	Urban	9,224,106	5,345,113	3,878,993
Haryana	Total	7,449,012	4,950,113	2,498,899
	Rural	4,974,926	3,474,151	1,500,775
	Urban	2,474,086	1,475,962	998,124
Himachal Pradesh	Total	2,765,409	1,648,011	1,117,398
	Rural	2,348,209	1,458,039	980,170
	Urban	327,200	189,972	137,228
Karnataka	Total	21,013,193	12,871,628	8,141,565
	Rural	12,250,620	7,841,549	4,409,071
	Urban	8,762,573	5,030,079	3,732,494
Kerala	Total	22,686,461	11,542,848	11,143,613
	Rural	16,482,908	8,400,098	8,082,810
	Urban	6,203,553	3,142,750	3,060,803
Madhya Pradesh	Total	23,465,301	16,101,285	7,364,016
	Rural	14,502,947	10,638,111	3,864,836
	Urban	8,962,354	5,463,174	3,499,180
Maharashtra	Total	42,447,139	25,943,455	16,503,684
	Rural	21,986,542	13,970,829	8,015,713
	Urban	20,460,597	11,972,626	8,487,971

(*Contd.*)

TABLE 17.29 (*Contd.*)

(1)	(2)	(3)	(4)	(5)
Manipur	Total	916,612	560,884	355,808
	Rural	615,957	383,720	232,237
	Urban	300,735	177,164	123,571
Meghalaya	Total	678,105	376,870	301,235
	Rural	454,835	253,522	201,313
	Urban	223,270	123,348	99,922
Mizoram	Total	461,930	251,551	210,379
	Rural	216,867	121,942	94,925
	Urban	245,063	129,609	115,454
Nagaland	Total	617,736	363,229	254,507
	Rural	475,566	277,210	198,356
	Urban	142,170	86,019	56,151
Orissa	Total	12,915,917	8,419,391	4,496,526
	Rural	10,324,378	6,841,189	3,483,189
	Urban	2,591,539	1,578,202	1,013,337
Punjab	Total	9,932,116	5,919,225	4,012,891
	Rural	6,298,643	3,834,626	2,464,017
	Urban	3,633,473	2,084,599	1,548,874
Rajasthan	Total	13,549,088	10,129,693	3,419,395
	Rural	—	6,684,559	1,494,134
	Urban	5,370,395	3,445,134	1,925,261
Sikkim	Total	188,920	117,306	71,614
	Rural	163,072	101,510	61,562
	Urban	25,848	15,796	10,052
Tamil Nadu	Total	30,336,235	18,050,173	12,286,062
	Rural	17,312,161	10,722,930	6,589,231
	Urban	13,024,074	7,327,243	5,696,831
Tripura	Total	1,365,980	822,402	543,578
	Rural	1,062,635	656,440	406,195
	Urban	303,345	165,962	137,383
Uttar Pradesh	Total	46,144,196	33,110,849	13,033,347
	Rural	32,404,489	24,570,015	7,834,474
	Urban	13,739,707	8,540,834	5,198,873
West Bengal	Total	32,609,397	20,091,836	12,517,561
	Rural	20,238,835	12,860,262	7,378,573
	Urban	12,370,562	7,231,574	5,138,988
Union Territories				
Andaman & Nicobar Islands	Total	171,086	103,377	67,709
	Rural	118,453	71,305	47,148
	Urban	52,633	32,072	20,561
Chandigarh	Total	425,060	252,847	172,213
	Rural	31,953	22,456	9,497
	Urban	393,107	230,391	162,716

(*Contd.*)

TABLE 17.29 (*Contd.*)

(1)	(2)	(3)	(4)	(5)
Dadra & Nagar Haveli	Total	44,834	30,463	14,371
	Rural	37,102	25,706	11,396
	Urban	7,732	4,757	2,975
Daman & Diu	Total	611,096	35,987	25,109
	Rural	27,409	17,444	9,965
	Urban	33,687	18,543	15,144
Delhi	Total	5,882,297	3,539,500	2,342,797
	Rural	502,148	330,056	172,092
	Urban	5,380,149	3,209,444	2,170,705
Laksha-dweep	Total	34,548	19,605	14,943
	Rural	14,400	8,251	6,149
	Urban	20,148	11,354	8,794
Pondicherry	Total	521,213	294,426	226,787
	Rural	161,517	95,813	65,704
	Urban	359,696	198,613	161,083

TABLE 17.30 : Distribution of Literates and Illiterates among Population Aged 7 years and above by Sex and Area, 1981-1991

(*in Millions*)

Year/Area	*Literates*			*Illiterates*		
	Persons	*Male*	*Female*	*Persons*	*Male*	*Female*
1981* All Areas	234.15 (43.6)	157.08 (56.5)	77.07 (29.8)	302.06 (56.4)	120.96 (43.5)	181.10 (70.2)
Rural Areas	146.60 (36.1)	103.51 (49.7)	43.09 (21.8)	259.59 (63.9)	104.80 (50.3)	154.79 (78.2)
Urban Areas	87.55 (67.3)	53.57 (76.8)	33.98 (56.4)	42.47 (32.7)	16.16 (23.2)	26.31 (43.6)
1991**	349.76 (52.2)	223.70 (64.2)	126.06 (39.2)	320.41 (47.8)	124.77 (35.8)	195.64 (60.8)
Rural Areas	218.32 (44.5)	146.38 (57.8)	71.94 (30.3)	271.81 (55.5)	106,69 (42.2)	165.12 (69.7)
Urban Areas	131.44 (73.1)	77.32 (81.0)	54.12 (63.9)	48.60 (26.9)	18.08 (19.0)	30.52 (36.1)

* Excludes Assam where 1981 Census was not held.

** Excludes Jammu & Kashmir where 1991 Census was not held. Literacy rates and number of illiterates for 1991 are based on estimated population aged 7 years and above.

Note : Figures in parenthesis indicate percentage to the corresponding population.

Source : Annual Report, 1994-1995, Part-1, Govt. of India, Department of Education, 1995, Ministry of Human Resource Development, New Delhi.

TABLE 17.31 : Estimates of Birth Rates and Death Rates, 1995

States/ Union Territories	Birth rate			Death rate		
	Total	Rural	Urban	Total	Rural	Urban
India*	28.3	30.0	22.7	9.0	9.8	6.6
Major States						
Andhra Pradesh	24.2	24.8	22.5	8.4	9.2	5.9
Assam	29.3	30.2	21.8	9.6	10.0	6.7
Bihar	32.1	33.1	23.8	10.5	10.9	6.9
Gujarat	26.7	27.9	24.0	7.6	8.3	6.2
Haryana	29.9	31.2	25.4	8.1	8.5	6.8
Karnataka	24.1	25.1	22.1	7.6	8.5	5.6
Kerala	18.0	18.1	17.7	6.0	6.0	6.0
Madhya Pradesh	33.2	35.1	23.9	11.2	11.9	7.8
Maharashtra	24.5	26.0	22.4	7.5	8.9	5.4
Orissa	27.8	28.5	22.0	10.8	11.2	7.5
Punjab	24.6	26.0	20.8	7.3	7.8	6.2
Rajasthan	33.3	34.8	26.6	9.1	9.6	7.2
Tamil Nadu	20.3	21.0	19.0	8.0	8.8	6.6
Uttar Pradesh	34.8	36.0	28.8	10.3	10.8	8.3
West Bengal	23.6	26.1	16.8	7.9	8.1	7.2
Smaller States						
Arunachal Pradesh	23.8	24.5	15.8	6.0	6.3	1.9
Goa	14.7	15.3	13.9	7.5	8.4	6.1
Himachal Pradesh	25.2	25.8	17.9	8.7	8.9	6.1
Manipur	20.6	21.4	18.4	6.7	7.0	6.0
Meghalaya	29.0	31.8	14.8	8.9	9.7	5.1
Nagaland	N.A.	N.A.	13.3	N.A.	N.A.	1.5
Sikkim	22.5	22.8	16.4	6.9	7.0	3.0
Tripura	18.9	19.0	18.0	7.7	7.9	6.6
Union Territories						
Andaman & Nicobar Islands	18.7	19.0	17.9	5.8	6.5	3.9
Chandigarh	19.5	22.2	19.2	5.7	5.3	5.8
Dadra & Nagar Haveli	29.7	29.4	32.2	8.2	8.6	5.0
Daman & Diu	21.8	23.4	20.5	8.0	7.7	8.3
Delhi	23.3	24.9	23.2	6.0	4.9	6.1
Lakshadweep	25.5	24.8	26.1	7.6	5.0	10.1
Pondicherry	20.1	21.6	19.1	7.6	9.2	6.6

* Excludes Jammu & Kashmir and Mizoram.

N.A. = Not available due to non-receipt of returns.

TABLE 17.32 : Estimates of Infant Mortality Rates, 1995

States	*Total*	*Rural*	*Urban*
(1)	(2)	(3)	(4)
India*	**74**	**80**	**48**
Andhra Pradesh	67	74	43
Assam	77	78	59
Bihar	73	74	57
Gujarat	62	68	47
Haryana	69	70	65
Himachal Pradesh	63	64	39
Karnataka	62	69	43
Kerala	15	16	13
Madhya Pradesh	99	104	61
Maharashtra	55	66	34
Orissa	103	107	65
Punjab	54	58	39
Rajasthan	86	90	62
Tamil Nadu	54	61	39
Uttar Pradesh	86	89	66
West Bengal	58	61	45

* Excludes Jammu & Kashmir and Mizoram.

TABLE 17.33 : Registered Births and Birth Rates during 1985 to 1993

	1985	1986	1987	1988	1989	1990	1991	1992	1993
(1)	(2)	(3)	(4)	(5)	(6)	(7)	(8)	(9)	(10)
States									
Andhra Pradesh	490,411	490,426	512,366	557,205	501,251	505,207	532,948	559,809	583,205
	8.3	8.2	8.3	8.9	7.7	7.7	8.0	8.2	8.4
Arunachal Pradesh	5,042	8,061	8,065	11,445	14,623	13,780	10,631	19,553	N.A.
	7.0	10.8	10.5	14.4	17.9	16.3	12.2	21.9	N.A.
Assam	N.A.	N.A.	N.A.	124,329	117,488	N.A.	N.A.	N.A.	N.A.
	N.A.	N.A.	N.A.	5.9	5.5	N.A.	N.A.	N.A.	N.A.
Bihar	585,278	599,405	610,041	616,917	587,162	581,592	579,856	591,497	547,017
	7.6	7.6	7.6	7.5	7.0	6.8	6.7	6.6	6.0
Goa	20,916	21,300	20,859	20,914	20,501	22,258	22,922	22,147	21,597
	19.2	19.3	18.6	18.4	17.9	19.2	19.5	18.4	17.6
Gujarat	760,435	810,068	840,963	837,550	795,844	1,020,367	1,045,212	1,091,014	1,091,981
	20.3	21.2	21.6	21.2	19.8	25.0	25.1	25.8	25.3
Haryana	314,930	314,107	333,758	325,706	344,822	340,200	333,886	342,617	326,954
	21.9	21.3	22.1	21.1	21.8	21.0	20.1	20.2	18.9
Himachal Pradesh	81,101	72,739	72,961	84,899	84,151	77,020	68,526	77,508	74,330
	17.4	15.3	15.0	17.2	16.7	15.1	13.2	14.6	13.8
Jammu & Kashmir	104,205	104,394	106,474	100,540	107,415	117,458	N.A.	N.A.	N.A.
	15.6	15.3	15.2	14.0	14.5	15.5	N.A.	N.A.	N.A.
Karnataka	484,334	564,500	564,015	641,846	693,287	780,496	792,291	827,188	860,421
	11.9	13.6	13.3	14.9	15.8	17.5	17.5	18.0	18.4

(Contd.)

TABLE 17.33 (*Contd.*)

(1)	(2)	(3)	(4)	(5)	(6)	(7)	(8)	(9)	(10)
Kerala	587,966	567,210	570,283	574,312	564,066	568,981	557.697	523,455	N.A.
	21.7	20.6	20.5	20.4	19.8	19.7	19.1	17.7	N.A.
Madhya Pradesh	1,014,406	1,067,690	1,102,266	1,125,300	1,134,146	1,133,002	1,150,980	1,170,044	1,179,278
	17.6	18.1	18.2	18.2	17.9	17.4	17.3	17.2	17.0
Maharashtra	1,348,569	1,481,605	1,524,272	1,584,961	1,576,568	1,640,390	1,607,159	1,593,276	1,591,299
	19.5	20.9	21.1	21.4	20.8	21.1	20.2	19.7	19.3
Manipur	3,410	5,252	5,345	7,425	7,997	5,462	3,416	6,848	7,434
	2.1	3.2	3.2	4.3	4.5	3.0	1.8	3.6	3.8
Meghalaya	N.A.	N.A.	N.A.	N.A.	N.A.	N.A.	N.A.	N.A.	N.A.
	N.A.	N.A.	N.A.	N.A.	N.A.	N.A.	N.A.	N.A.	N.A.
Mizoram	4,104	13,422	13,060	15,297	15,046	15,125	15,245	14,269	14,260
	N.A.	N.A.	N.A.	23.8	22.7	22.3	21.9	19.8	19.2
Nagaland	14,494	15,016	16,218	18,081	18,350	17,965	19,146	20,981	21,942
	15.5	15.3	15.8	16.9	16.4	15.3	15.7	16.6	16.9
Orissa	436,072	499,578	547,107	615,618	616,278	600,620	601,167	631,294	N.A.
	15.3	17.2	18.5	20.5	20.1	19.2	18.9	19.5	N.A.
Punjab	394,820	413,529	439,611	444,487	451,317	462,022	476,286	485,395	487,761
	21.5	22.1	23.1	22.9	22.9	23.0	23.4	23.4	23.2
Rajasthan	242,529	233,768	263,877	273,273	283,526	317,471	311,051	319,086	343,131
	6.3	5.9	6.5	6.6	6.7	7.3	7.0	7.0	7.4
Sikkim	N.A.	N.A.	N.A.	3,117	N.A.	1,104	1,607	2,175	2,346
	N.A.	N.A.	N.A.	7.9	N.A.	2.7	3.9	5.1	5.4
Tamil Nadu	890,901	915,157	925,072	890.209	979,378	1,005,844	1,025,124	1,023,419	1,016,916
	17.3	17.5	17.4	16.5	17.9	18.2	18.3	18.1	17.8

(*Contd.*)

TABLE 17.33 (*Contd.*)

(1)	(2)	(3)	(4)	(5)	(6)	(7)	(8)	(9)	(10)
Tripura	26,509	31,931	35,657	40,201	46,813	56,065	53,798	45,576	48,844
	11.4	13.4	14.5	15.8	17.9	20.8	19.4	16.0	16.8
Uttar Pradesh	634,309	1,036,203	1,106,875	1,254,203	1,301,057	1,262,225	1,443,284	1,667,589	1,820,425
	5.2	8.3	8.6	9.5	9.7	9.2	10.3	11.7	12.5
West Bengal	N.A.	249,042	373,768	429,535	504,783	725,071	813,950	842,397	794,110
	N.A.	4.1	6.0	6.7	7.7	10.8	11.9	12.1	11.2
Union Territo									
Andaman & Nicobar	4,690	5,320	N.A.	N.A.	5,399	5,882	N.A.	N.A.	6,945
Islands	20.6	22.5	N.A.	N.A.	20.4	21.4	N.A.	N.A.	22.8
Chandigarh	14,737	15,341	16,551	17,266	17,747	17,496	17,835	17,440	17,711
	27.2	27.4	28.6	28.9	28.9	27.7	27.4	25.6	24.9
Dadra & Nagar	2,112	2,977	3,032	3,362	3,413	3,628	3,578	3,915	4,000
Haveli	17.7	24.2	24.0	25.9	25.6	26.6	25.6	27.3	27.1
Daman & Diu	2,343	2,424	N.A.	N.A.	N.A.	N.A.	N.A.	3,647	N.A.
	28.2	27.5	N.A.	N.A.	N.A.	N.A.	N.A.	34.9	N.A.
Delhi	208,440	207,027	227,617	242,990	245,949	266,001	272,020	273,978	270,249
	27.9	26.6	28.1	28.7	27.9	29.0	28.5	27.8	26.4
Lakshadweep	1,466	1,500	N.A.	N.A.	N.A.	1,538	1,420	N.A.	N.A.
	32.7	32.7	N.A.	N.A.	N.A.	30.6	27.3	N.A.	N.A.
Pondicherry	27,572	28,053	29,204	30,377	31,737	33,320	33,843	32,108	30,454
	40.5	40.0	40.5	40.9	41.4	42.1	41.6	38.7	36.0
India	**8,706,192**	**9,777,045**	**10,269,317**	**10,891,365**	**11,070,114**	**11,597,590**	**11,794,878**	**12,208,225**	**10,302,189**
	13.0	**13.1**	**13.5**	**13.6**	**13.6**	**14.3**	**14.4**	**14.6**	**13.9**

N.A. = Not avilable.

TABLE 17.34 : Residential Birth and Death Rates, Natural Growth Rate, Total Delivery Rate and Child Death Rate in India, 1990-1995

Residence	*Year*	*Birth rate*	*Death rate*	*Natural growth rate*	*Total Delivery rate*	*Child death rate*
Total	1990	30.2	9.7	20.5	3.8	80
	1991#	29.5	9.8	19.7	3.6	80
	1992#	29.2	10.1	19.1	3.6	79
	1993#	28.7	9.3	19.4	3.5	74
	1994#	28.7	9.3	19.4	N.A.	74
	1995#*	28.3	9.0	19.3	N.A.	74
Rural	1990	31.7	10.5	21.2	4.1	86
	1991#	30.9	10.6	20.3	3.9	87
	1992#	30.9	10.9	20.0	3.9	85
	1993#	30.4	10.6	19.8	3.8	82
	1994#	30.5	10.1	20.4	N.A.	80
	1995#*	30.0	9.7	20.3	N.A.	80
Urban	1990	24.7	6.8	17.9	2.8	50
	1991#	24.3	7.1	17.2	2.7	53
	1992#	23.1	7.0	16.1	2.6	53
	1993#	23.7	5.8	17.9	2.8	45
	1994#	23.1	6.7	16.4	N.A.	52
	1995#*	22.6	6.5	16.1	N.A.	49

Note : * Last.
# Estimate of J&K not available.
N.A. = Not available.

TABLE 17.35 : Residential Three Years Birth and Death Rates and Child Death Rate in India 1990-92 to 1993-95

('000)

Residence	*Year*	*Birth %*	*Death %*	*Child death %*
Total	1990-92#	29.6	9.9	80
	1991-93#	29.1	9.7	78
	1992-94#	28.8	9.5	76
	1993-95#*	28.5	9.2	74
Rural	1990-92#	31.2	10.7	86
	1991-93#	30.7	10.7	85
	1992-94#	30.6	10.5	82
	1993-95#*	30.3	10.1	80
Urban	1990-92#	24.0	7.0	52
	1991-93#	23.7	6.6	50
	1992-94#	23.3	6.5	50
	1993-95#*	23.1	6.3	48

Note : * Last.
# Estimate of J&K not included.
N.A. = Not available.

TABLE 17.36 : Number of Juvenile Homes/Observation Homes/Special Homes/after Care Institutions, 1992-93

State/Union Territories	*Observation Homes*	*Juvenile Homes*	*Special Homes*	*Aftercare Institutions*	*Total*
States					
Andhra Pradesh	9	5	2	1	17
Arunachal Pradesh	1	1	—	—	2
Assam	7	25	1	1	34
Bihar	10	8	5	2	25
Goa	2	2	2	—	6
Gujarat	25	5	2	11	46
Haryana	3	3	1	1	8
Himachal Pradesh	—	1	1	—	2
Karnataka	22	19	—	1	52
Kerala	12	5	2	—	19
Madhya Pradesh	22	2	3	1	28
Maharashtra	45	101	3	3	152
Manipur	1	2	1	—	4
Meghalaya	1	—	—	—	1
Mizoram	3	3	—	—	6
Nagaland	—	1	1	—	2
Orissa	12	2	—	—	14
Punjab	7	2	1	2	12
Rajasthan	11	4	1	—	16
Sikkim	1	—	—	—	1
Tamil Nadu	14	17	3	3	37
Tripura	1	1	—	—	2
Uttar Pradesh	59	10	1	—	70
West Bengal	7	19	4	6	36
Union Territories					
Andaman & Nicobar Islands	—	—	—	—	
Chandigarh	1	1	1	—	3
Dadra & Nagar Haveli	—	—	—	—	—
Daman & Diu	—	—	—	—	—
Delhi	3	11	—	—	14
Lakshadweep	—	—	—	—	—
Pondicherry	1	1	1	1	4
Total	**280**	**251**	**36**	**46**	**613**

Source : Annual Report, Ministry of Welfare, 1994-95.

TABLE 17.37 : Juveniles Apprehended in India by Age Group and Sex during 1993

Sl. No.	*Crime Head*	*7-12 years*		*12-16 years*		*16-18 years*	*Overall age group*		*Total (Boys + Girls)*
		Boys	*Girls*	*Boys*	*Girls*	*Girls only*	*Boys*	*Girls*	
(1)	(2)	(3)	(4)	(5)	(6)	(7)	(8)	(9)	(10)
A.	**IPC Crimes**								
1.	Murder	25	6	302	18	50	327	74	401
2.	Attempt to Commit Murder	19	2	200	34	34	219	70	289
3.	C.H. Not Amounting to Murder	0	0	15	0	3	15	3	18
4.	Rape	22	0	140	2	15	162	17	179
5.	Kidnapping & Abduction	7	2	113	13	48	120	63	183
	(i) Of Women & Girls	6	2	77	10	40	83	52	135
	(ii) Of others	1	0	36	3	8	37	11	48
6.	Dacoity	6	0	105	1	1	111	2	113
7.	Preparation & Assembly for Dacoity	0	0	29	0	0	29	0	29
8.	Robbery	2	1	122	0	0	124	1	125
9.	Burglary	232	9	1,279	33	35	1,511	77	1,588
10.	Theft	413	62	2,310	146	122	2,723	330	3,053
11.	Riots	45	12	1,425	31	179	1,470	222	1,692
12.	Criminal Breach of Trust	0	0	11	0	2	11	2	13
13.	Cheating	4	1	43	4	12	47	17	64
14.	Counterfeiting	0	0	1	0	0	1	0	1
15.	Other IPC Crimes	428	66	3,331	319	761	3,759	1,146	4,905
16.	Total Cognizable Crimes under IPC	1,203	161	9,426	601	1,262	10,629	2,024	2,653

(*Contd.*)

TABLE 17.37 (*Contd.*)

(1)	(2)	(3)	(4)	(5)	(6)	(7)	(8)	(9)	(10)
B.	**L&SL Crimes :**								
1.	Arms Act	0	0	94	1	7	94	8	102
2.	Narcotic Drugs & PSY. Subs. Act	3	0	7	1	4	10	5	15
3.	Gambling Act	41	0	561	10	5	602	15	617
4.	Excise Act	13	6	99	5	29	112	40	152
5.	Prohibition Act	20	8	442	22	931	462	961	423
6.	Explosives & Exp. Substances Act	1	0	0	0	1	1	1	2
7.	Immoral Traffic (Prevention) Act	0	1	6	25	146	6	172	178
8.	Indian Railways Act	1	4	7	11	0	8	15	23
9.	Registration of Foreigners Act	0	1	5	0	1	5	2	7
10.	Protection of Civil Rights Act	0	0	5	0	1	5	1	6
11.	Indian Passport Act	2	1	3	0	0	5	1	6
12.	Essential Commodities Act	0	0	1	0	0	1	0	1
13.	Terrorist & Distrupt. Activities Act	0	0	0	0	0	0	0	0
14.	Antiquity & Art Treasure Act	0	0	0	0	0	0	0	0
15.	Dowry Prohibition Act	0	0	12	2	8	12	10	22
16.	Other L&SL Crimes	2,424	39	2,015	76	306	4,439	421	4,860
17.	Total Cognizable Crime under L&SL	2,505	60	3,257	153	1,439	5,762	1,652	7,414
C.	**Grand Total (A+B)**	**3,708**	**221**	**12,683**	**754**	**2,701**	**16,391**	**3,676**	**20,067**

Note : 7-12 years means 7 years and above but below 12 years of age etc.
Source : Crime in India, 1993.

TABLE 17.38 : Juveniles Apprehended by Sex for Committing Crime under IPC and Local and Special Laws during 1993

States/ Union Territories	*Crimes Under Local and Special Laws*		*Total (Boys & Girls)*	*Crimes Under IPC*		*Total (Boys & Girls)*
	Boys	*Girls*		*Boys*	*Girls*	
(1)	(2)	(3)	(4)	(5)	(6)	(7)
States						
Andhra Pradesh	268	73	341	736	167	903
Arunachal Pradesh	0	0	0	23	1	24
Assam	10	1	11	241	16	257
Bihar	174	27	201	2,360	346	2,706
Goa	3	4	7	30	16	46
Gujarat	353	943	1,296	976	398	1,374
Haryana	38	2	40	154	28	182
Himachal Pradesh	1	2	3	37	27	64
Jammu & Kashmir	0	0	0	0	0	0
Karnataka	38	86	124	256	100	356
Kerala	0	0	0	82	4	86
Madhya Pradesh	468	47	515	2,026	226	2,252
Maharashtra	592	161	753	1,988	437	2,425
Manipur	0	5	5	7	6	13
Meghalaya	0	0	0	103	2	105
Mizoram	3	9	12	25	2	27
Nagaland	0	0	0	32	0	32
Orissa	7	2	9	123	7	130
Punjab	0	0	0	1	0	1
Rajasthan	31	19	50	550	126	676
Sikkim	4	0	4	10	0	10
Tamil Nadu	3,683	241	3,924	563	39	602
Tripura	0	0	0	10	1	11
Uttar Pradesh	73	15	88	46	20	66
West Bengal	1	1	2	31	1	32
Total (States)	5,747	1,638	7,385	10,410	1,970	12,380
Union Territories						
A & N Islands	1	0	1	2	1	3
Chandigarh	0	0	0	10	0	10
Dadra & Nagar Haveli	0	0	0	1	1	2
Daman & Diu	0	0	0	1	5	6
Delhi	14	14	28	194	43	237
Lakshadweep	0	0	0	0	0	0
Pondicherry	0	0	—	11	4	15
Total (UTs)	15	14	29	219	54	273
Total (All-India)	**5,762**	**1,652**	**7,414**	**10,629**	**2,024**	**12,653**

Source : Crime in India, 1993.

BIBLIOGRAPHY

A Brief about the Institute: NIPPCD.

Activity Report of General Secretariat: 1973-75.

Alfred D'Souza, Children in India.

An Analysis of the Situation of Children in India: UNICEF.

Annual Report—NIPPCD 1985-86; 5, Siri Institutional Area, Hauz Khas, New Delhi.

Child Welfare and Development: *Paul Chaudhary*.

Child Welfare in India: *Ika Paul Pont*.

Children Youth in National Planning and Development in India.

Facts about UNICEF: 1984.

Health Action, Vol. 2(2), February, 1989.

I.C.D.S.: UNICEF, Regional Office South Central Asia—New Delhi.

ICCW News Bulletin—November 1988.

ICCW News Bulletins—Adoption and Labour.

Indian Council for Child Welfare: Annual Reports.

Indian Muslim Customs and Festivals: Dr. *Mazda Asad*, Translated by *M.R. Sharma*.

International Child Welfare Review: Nos. 42, 59, 60.

International Union for Child Welfare: 50 Years.

National Children's Board: *Proceedings* of the inaugural meeting, September 15, 1975. (Government of India, Department of Social Welfare, Ministry of Education and Social Welfare, New Delhi).

National Plan of Action for I.Y.C., 1979: Government of India, Ministry of Education and Social Welfare, Department of Social Welfare, New Delhi.

National Policy for Children: Government of India, Ministry of Education and Social Welfare, New Delhi, January, 1975.

National Seminar on Child and the Law: NIPPCD.

Perspective Plan on Child Development (1980-2000): *NIPPCED*.

Planning Commission: A Descriptive Account by *H.K. Paranjpe:* Planning Commission Library.

Profile of the Child: *UNICEF*.

Sixth and Seventh Five Year Plans: Planning Commission Library.

Social Welfare in India: Issued on behalf of the Planning Commission, Govt. of India, New Delhi, 1955.

UNICEF Report: 1979.

UNICEF—Facts and Figures 1990.

United Nations in India.

Universal Children's Day: Department of Social Welfare, Government. of India, New Delhi.

What has been accomplished during I.Y.C.: Assignment of Children No. 47/48, Autumn 1979 UNICEF—Geneva.

Write up regarding children from Vedas, *Dr. Gopal Karandikar*, Pune.

Annual Reports—1988-89

1. Ministry of Health and Family Welfare.
2. Ministry of Human Resources and Development—Part-I (Department of Education).
3. Ministry of Human Resources and Development—Part-IV (Department of Women and Child Development).
4. Ministry of Welfare.

INDEX